Contesting the Last Frontier

Contesting the Last Frontier

Race, Gender, Ethnicity, and Political Representation of Asian Americans

PEI-TE LIEN AND NICOLE FILLER

OXFORD
UNIVERSITY PRESS

Oxford University Press is a department of the University of Oxford. It furthers
the University's objective of excellence in research, scholarship, and education
by publishing worldwide. Oxford is a registered trade mark of Oxford University
Press in the UK and certain other countries.

Published in the United States of America by Oxford University Press
198 Madison Avenue, New York, NY 10016, United States of America.

© Oxford University Press 2022

All rights reserved. No part of this publication may be reproduced, stored in
a retrieval system, or transmitted, in any form or by any means, without the
prior permission in writing of Oxford University Press, or as expressly permitted
by law, by license, or under terms agreed with the appropriate reproduction
rights organization. Inquiries concerning reproduction outside the scope of the
above should be sent to the Rights Department, Oxford University Press, at the
address above.

You must not circulate this work in any other form
and you must impose this same condition on any acquirer.

Library of Congress Control Number: 2022903770

ISBN 978–0–19–007768–6 (pbk.)
ISBN 978–0–19–007767–9 (hbk.)

DOI: 10.1093/oso/9780190077679.001.0001

1 3 5 7 9 8 6 4 2

Paperback printed by Marquis, Canada
Hardback printed by Bridgeport National Bindery, Inc., United States of America

Contents

List of Illustrations	vii
Preface	ix
Acknowledgments	xiii

1.	Introduction	1
2.	Gendered History of Immigration and Political Socialization in the Election of Asians	29
3.	Evolution of the Electoral Landscape: Expanding the Gender, Ethnic, and Geographic Horizons in Political Representation and Local Incorporation	66
4.	Getting Connected and Elected with Political Parties	110
5.	Advancing Justice through Transformative Leadership and Substantive and Symbolic Representation	149
6.	Conclusion	189

Appendix A: A Note on Terminology Used to Describe Our Research Subjects	217
Appendix B: Methods of Constructing the APAEO Database	221
Appendix C: How We Identify Social Justice Leaders and Study Issue Priorities	225
Notes	229
References	235
Index	257

Illustrations

Figures

3.1. Percentage Women and Growth Trends among National APAEO Population, 1980–2020	74
3.2. Shifting Geographic Makeup of APAEOs, 1980–2020	86
3.3. Geographic Distribution by Ethnicity in Key States, 2020	89
4.1. APAEO Partisanship by Gender, 2014–20	125
4.2. APAEO Partisanship by Ethnicity, 2020	127

Tables

3.1. National APAEO Population and Shares by Level/Type of Office, 1980–2020	76
3.2. Percentage Female by Level/Type of Office, 1980–2020	77
3.3. National APAEO Population by Major Ethnic Origin, 1980–2020	78
3.4. APAEO Ethnic Parity Ratios by Gender, 2020	79
3.5. APAEO Gender Parity Ratios by Ethnicity, 2020	81
3.6. APAEOs Serving in 2020 by Ethnicity, Nativity, and Gender (%)	82
3.7. APAEOs by Nativity, Gender, and Level/Type of Office, 2020	84
3.8. Summary Statistics of California Cities That Elected Asians to City Councils, 1980–2020	92
3.9. Top Californian Cities with Council Seats Held by Asians, 1980–2020	94
3.10. Demographic Change in Selected California Cities with Top Asian Council Seats, 1980–2010	96
3.11. Comparing Demographic and Electoral Context of Asians on City Councils in California by Gender in 2020	104

viii   ILLUSTRATIONS

4.1. APAEO Partisanship by Gender and Level of Office, 2020   126

4.2. APAEO Partisanship by Nativity Status, Ethnicity, and Gender, 2020   128

5.1. Priority Issue Concerns of APAEOS in 2020 by Gender (%)   158

5.2. Asian Pacific Americans in the 116th Congress (Voting Members)   178

Preface

We have debated numerous ways to assign the main title to a book-length manuscript that can reflect both its substantive contributions and our personal learning and growth in its making. When we first conceived the idea of a project on Asian Americans in elective office, the purpose was to help readers better appreciate Asian women and men in US elective office and understand factors behind the seemingly perpetual phenomenon of their marginalization and underrepresentation. As statistics in the book *Contested Transformation* (Hardy-Fanta et al. 2016) demonstrate, compared to other major US racial and ethnic groups, the numbers of elected officials identified as Asian are small, both in raw numbers and as compared to the nonwhite group's share in the general population. The constant sense of frustration over the need to present and confront the perceptions of Asians as outliers in American electoral politics—even among elected officials of color—led to the conception of a book that could put Asian Americans at the front and center of discussion and presentation. The impetus to write this book emerged years before the publication of *Contested Transformation*. However, we did not imagine that we could contest Asian Americans' overall image of marginalization and underrepresentation, especially women, at the beginning. We were more interested in discovering and uncovering the profound internal diversity in ethnic or national origins and geography of Asian (and, to some extent, Pacific Islander) Americans (APAs) elected in recent years to local, state, and national offices and analyzing their personal and political histories through a gendered and intersectional lens. We were keen on assembling a database that contains a complete roster of elected officials in the second decade of the 21st century, in 2014 to be exact. With frequent elections and many occurring on unexpected dates and localities, the nature of the beast made it necessary for us to constantly update and expand our database and collection of individual stories.

Meanwhile, soon after we started to describe and analyze the statistical patterns of elective officeholding by APAs and tried to make sense of the relative skeletal patterns, we realized a need to go behind the numbers and dig deeper and further back into history to identify pioneers and other

X PREFACE

significant figures in the electoral history of each major Asian ethnic community. We were especially intrigued by the stories of those who had challenged multiple and intersecting forms of structural disadvantages or oppressions that shaped the very meaning and boundaries of race, ethnicity, gender, and other aspects of social identity. We were eager to read any account of their trajectories available online (and could be accessed even in a lockdown due to the Covid-19 pandemic). Sheer coding and counting data points could no longer satisfy our curiosity and desire to learn about the rich origins and developments of the electoral landscape—one that has proven to be much less barren than we assumed. We strove to improve our understanding of the intricacies of campaign experiences by interviewing those who generously agreed to talk with our research team. In addition to consulting journalistic reports and peer-reviewed publications in political science, ethnic studies, feminist studies, and sociology, we diligently studied websites of candidates, political parties, and other campaign organizations to enable analysis at the institutional and contextual level. This unexpectedly long and winding journey of learning and discovery is how this book becomes a longitudinal, mixed-method, multiethnic, and multioffice investigation of the relatively unknown.

In a sense, the journey for Asian immigrants and their descendants to move into the mainstream by contesting their exclusion and marginalization and holding elective offices fits the legend of the American Dream. It is the last dimension in Golden's (1964) model of immigrant integration. We certainly agree with Alba and Foner (2009) that "electoral successes by immigrant minorities should still be regarded as the gold standard against which other forms of political participation should be measured" (282). However, we fear the term "frontier" may invoke an uncritical acceptance of the settler-colonial mentality (Glenn 2015), which privileges white males and marginalizes people at the intersection of race, gender, nativity, and indigeneity. Hence, we adopt the concept of contestation to challenge the status quo and treat it as an ongoing process that often involves pathbreaking and uphill battles. *Contesting the Last Frontier* is a book title we finally felt comfortable using. We appreciate the precious advice from one of the press's reviewers who urged us to consider using a more thematic and appealing main title. We hope we do not disappoint.

As the project evolved in scope and depth, we identified four main goals that we strove to fulfill for this book. The first is to capture through elective officeholding key patterns and highlights of the difficult but inevitable rise of Asian Americans in American democratic governance throughout the group's migration history. A second goal is to illustrate through ethnic representation parity ratios that, whereas Asians continue to suffer from underrepresentation in the electoral landscape as a whole, there are significant and nuanced differences by gender, ethnicity, nativity, and office level and locality in political representation and incorporation. A third goal is to assess the gatekeeping function of political parties and the bridge-building role of organizations in the election of APA women and men in historical and contemporary times. Last but not least, we assess the nature and significance of political representation by Asian Americans in elective office. Toward that goal, we employ the womanist leadership praxis framework, derived from our interpretation of the legacy of the Asian American movement and the Asian American women's movement in the late 1960s and 1970s, to help account for the substantive concept of representation and transformative leadership style embodied by selective elected officials in our database and case studies. This framework allows us to decide on individual cases to highlight the relationship among political socialization, office trajectories, leadership style, and quality of representation.

Acknowledgments

Because this book has been long in the making and involved many moving parts, we know it would be difficult to fully express our gratitude to all the parties who have helped us along the way. We apologize in advance to those whose names or efforts we inadvertently neglected to acknowledge. In this humble attempt, we would like to begin by thanking the late Professor Don T. Nakanishi and his former student and current professor James Lai, as well as the University of California Los Angeles Asian American Studies Center (UCLA-AASC) for assembling and publishing the nation's first and only rosters of elected (and appointed) Asian Americans and Pacific Islanders (AAPI) officials. We also want to thank the Asian Pacific American Institute for Congressional Studies (APAICS) and its former and current executive directors, Floyd Mori and Madalene Mielke, who helped launch and maintain an extensive online directory of AAPI elected officials. These pioneering community-serving organizations and their visionary leaders have provided the blueprint for creating our own database of Asian Pacific American Elected Officials (APAEOs).

Yet, because of the ongoing need for data collection, verification, and updates, we could not fulfill our primary project goals without the capable assistance of a fantastic group of undergraduate students at the University of California, Santa Barbara (UCSB). They not only helped verify individuals identified in the UCLA-AASC and APAICS directories but identified numerous more who would have been omitted or misidentified in our database. They also helped collect information from each candidate's and elected official's website as well as any relevant websites that contain information such as gender, ethnic or national origin, birthplace, education, partisanship, and issue positions. Some made additional, indispensable contributions by conducting personal interviews, compiling jurisdictional demographic information, or collecting and coding legislative records concerning bill sponsorship, among other tasks. Several doctoral students at UCSB deserve special mention for their extraordinarily efficient and reliable research assistance in creating annotated bibliographies, collecting biographical data of pioneering figures and present-day leaders, and supervising undergraduate

xiv   ACKNOWLEDGMENTS

students in database creation and management. They are the Hall of Famers for this project.

We want to express our sincere appreciation for the timely and invaluable research assistance provided by a team of graduate, undergraduate, and former students at UCSB over the years. Presented in reverse chronological order among graduate research assistants are Jeff Feng, Amanda Brush, and Rhoanne Esteban. Among undergraduate research assistants are Francesca Gonzales, Ajar Kerey, Vicki Wu, Anisha Ahuja, Kathryn Lew, Alexander Shinkawa, Ali Elhawary, Aileen Arellano, Stephanie Javidnia, Emily Koo, Alan Tam, Amanda Manalo, Tim J. Cioffi-Dinkel, and Melissa N. Immel. A special thanks goes to Anisha Ahuja and Amanda Brush for their research assistance in helping conduct interviews and compile numerous biographies and life stories of elected officials profiled in this project.

Equally important, we owe a million thanks to those individuals who made time to chat and offer advice for our project. They include elected officials serving at state and local levels, state legislative staff, political party and community-based organizational leaders, and political science and ethnic studies scholars in Honolulu, Los Angeles County, Orange County, Santa Clara County, San Francisco, and Alameda County of California, and in Washington, DC. Kudos to community organization leaders Charlie Woo and Aki Leung of the Center for Asian American United for Self-Empowerment, Michael Chang of the Asian Pacific American Leadership Institute, Steve Kang of the Korean American Coalition in Los Angeles, Floyd Mori of APAICS, Christine Chen of APIAVote, Cathy Dang of the Committee Against Anti-Asian Violence, Diane Wong of 18 Million Rising, Kendall Kosai and Kham Moua of the Organization of Chinese Americans, and Clark Lee of the Los Angeles County Democratic Party and California Democratic Party Asian Pacific Islander Caucus. Among community activists and scholars, we are especially indebted to the precious advice from Professor Jonathan Okamura, Professor Colin Moore, and Professor Hoku Aikau of the University of Hawai'i at Mānoa, Professor Linda Vo of the University of California, Irvine, Gene Kim, Elena Ong, and Kevin Chan. And we cannot find enough words to express our gratitude to current and former elected officials who spared their precious time to speak with us: Lily Lee Chen, Lillian Sing, Eric Mar, Wilma Chan, Polly Low, Steven Choi, Lisa Bartlett, Henry Lo, Mike Fong, Diedre Nguyen, Andrew Do, Christopher Phan, Terrance Terauchi, Warren Kusumoto, Steve Hwangbo, Gary Yamaguichi, Kaniela Ing, Joey Manahan, Gilbert

Keith-Agaran, Glenn Wakai, Clarence Nishihara, Will Espero, and Dennis Arakaki.

We cannot overstate our profound appreciation to the anonymous reviewers and readers of the Oxford University Press. Our book could not be as sophisticated and solid without the sage advice and specific instructions from them. Our editor, Angela Chnapko, deserves a special shout-out for her patience and steadfast support from the get-go. We owe our senior and very esteemed colleague Ron Schmidt special recognition for making time to read every word of our preliminary chapter drafts and for his incisive comments and insistence on improvements. We cannot say thank you enough to our dearest colleagues and long-term allies at the Asian Pacific American Caucus and the Race, Ethnicity, and Politics Section of the American Political Science Association (APSA). We are better scholars and persons because of your generous offers of critical opinions and feedback and unqualified support in the miniconference on Asian American politics at the Western Political Science Association and in the annual meetings of the APSA and Association for Asian American Studies. Here is a partial list of these allies: Andrew Aoki, Oki Takeda, Paul Watanabe, Jane Junn, Janelle Wong, James Lai, Kim Geron, Loan Le, Natalie Masuoka, Kira Sanbomatsu, Danielle Lemi, Christian Phillips, Sara D. Sadhwani, Ngoc Phan, Chinbo Chong, Fan Lu, Tanika Raychaudhuri, Vivien Leung, Chris Collet, Sangay Mishra, S. Karthick Ramakrishnan, Taeku Lee, Neil Visalvanich, Maneesh Arora, Nathan Chan, Linda Hasunuma, Tony Affigne, Valerie Martinez-Ebers, Rodney Hero, Michael Jones-Correa, Ricardo Ramirez, Christopher Stout, Nadia Brown, Sarah Roberts Allen Gershon, Benjamin Nyblade, and Laura Elizabeth Elder.

We hasten to add that Pei-te has been a multiyear grantee and beneficiary of the UCSB Academic Senate Council on Faculty Research and Instructional Resources and UCSB Undergraduate Education Faculty Research Assistance Program. They provided the necessary funding and credit-earning opportunities to support our team of researchers. She appreciates the patience and support from her colleagues and friends at UCSB in the Departments of Political Science, Asian American Studies, Feminist Studies, Black Studies, East Asian Center, and Feminist Futures Initiative. She also wants to acknowledge her former coauthors Christian Sierra, Carol Hardy-Fanta, and Dianne Pinderhughes. It was an honor and privilege to collaborate with these pioneering and political science women who provided the initial motivation and road maps for this project.

xvi ACKNOWLEDGMENTS

In closing, Nikki wants to express her deep gratitude to current and former colleagues at Highline College and UCSB for their encouragement and guidance at various stages of this project. This includes former professors and advisers at UCSB who first introduced her to the study of race, ethnicity, gender, and politics and a community called Asian America. She also wants to recognize and thank all of her students, who have been sources of inspiration and constant reminders of why these stories and perspectives are indispensable. Last but not least, Nikki is grateful for the unqualified support and advice from Maurea Brown, Jennifer Jones, Tanya Powers, and Tommy Kim in improving her teaching practice, as well as the friendship and insights of Diego Luna, Erich Elwin, Aaron Modica, Samora Covington, Aleya Dhanji, Darryl Brice, Yay-Hyung Cho, Nestor Tupufia Enguerra, Jr., Kathy Nguyen, and many others whom she has been able to learn from and collaborate with toward common goals.

1

Introduction

Candidate Kamala Harris was keenly aware of her trail-blazing place in American history, becoming the first woman, first Black, first Asian American, and first woman of color vice president-elect of the United States on November 7, 2020. She took center stage to proudly and confidently pronounce: "While I may be the first woman in this office, I won't be the last. Because every little girl watching tonight sees that this is a country of possibilities." This statement was preceded by her fond memory of her late mother, Shyamala Gopalan Harris. The latter chased the American Dream by arriving from India at the young age of 19 in 1958 to pursue a doctoral degree at the University of California, Berkeley. For tens of thousands of women college graduates in Asia who came to America to pursue a graduate degree in the next half-century, Shyamala Gopalan was a trailblazer. Then this Asian immigrant woman broke new ground by defying social norms and marrying an African American immigrant from Jamaica in 1963, years before state laws banning interracial marriage were struck down by the US Supreme Court in *Loving v. Virginia* (1967).

For some, the rise of Harris, daughter of a Black-Asian union, is meteoric, from a local district attorney (of San Francisco, elected in 2003) to the state attorney general (of California, elected in 2010) and a US senator (from California, elected in 2016) before reaching the vice presidency. For others, the wait has been too long for a woman and person of color to occupy the second-highest executive office in the United States. Also, several leading Asian Pacific American (APA) organizations and groups expressed disappointment in the lack of inclusiveness of more ethnic diversity in the proposed new presidential cabinet soon after the inauguration of the Biden-Harris administration (Pham 2021; Zhou 2021). However, by the end of the first 100 days, the new administration was praised for nominating a record number of APAs to serve in high positions (APIAVote 2021). The mixed reactions to Harris's trajectory and the shifting attitudes to the appointment of APAs by the Biden-Harris administration illustrate the complexities faced by the nonwhite minority community—in all its diversity—to find

Contesting the Last Frontier. Pei-te Lien and Nicole Filler, Oxford University Press. © Oxford University Press 2022.
DOI: 10.1093/oso/9780190077679.003.0001

an exquisite path to navigate mainstream American politics. At the dawn of the third decade of the 21st century, Asian Americans seem to have finally arrived at the center of American politics. How did they get there, and how long will they stay in the limelight? What does their arrival mean in terms of political representation and empowerment for the community? And how do they impact the contours and content of American political leadership?

The storming of the US Capitol by armed Trump supporters on January 6, 2021, represented a last-ditch effort to stop the certification of the Electoral College win by the Biden-Harris ticket. This unrest symbolizes the perilous context that gave rise to the election of Donald Trump in 2016, which became more evident by the rage of the Covid-19 pandemic in 2020. These developments were emblematic of a deeply polarized and divided state of the American democracy by party, ideology, class, race, ethnicity, and gender. Whereas American history has turned a new page into the Biden administration, the stream of pandemic-triggered rising anti-Asian violence since March 2020 not only did not show any sign of letting it down, but the Atlanta spa shooting rampage in March 2021 symbolized its growing gravity. The saturated news coverage of the tragedy might have silenced any complaint about the lack of visibility of Asian Americans. Only history will reveal how much these developments will impact the political fate of the community. However, this was not the first time Asian Americans have been under attack by the confluence of US racism, nativism, and sexism. The first anti-Asian act in Congress was passed in 1875, effectively banning the immigration of single Chinese, Japanese, and other Asian women. Despite constant challenges throughout history, the community has miraculously managed to survive and thrive. We are a community of survivors and champions. This book is a tribute to those individuals who encountered and overcame barriers to win elections and serve in public office. The electoral breakthroughs they made are building blocks for Asian America, past, present, and future.

A Quest to Demystify and Disentangle but Also to Identify

In the world of US minority politics, Asian Americans have been considered the privileged people whose socioeconomic achievements have earned them the label of the "model minority." Among US elected officials of color, Asian men and women are found to obtain the highest levels of education and family income as a whole, even if they also register the highest rates of the foreign born (Hardy-Fanta et al. 2016). Whereas the US nation has a pathetic record of women's descriptive representation in elective offices, recent research shows that women of color, including APA women, have experienced higher growth rates and better gender ratios than white women in recent decades. In the 2020 presidential election cycle, three of the Democratic presidential hopefuls were APAs. One of them, Kamala Harris, halted her campaign and became, months later, the running mate of Democratic Party presidential candidate Joe Biden.

And yet, despite these remarkable electoral successes, Asian Americans continue to suffer from a most severe case of underrepresentation when compared to other major US racial and ethnic groups. According to Sedique, Bhojwani, and Lee (2020), of the 7,383 state legislative positions in 2020, only 2% were occupied by Asians, as compared to 4% by Latinos, 10% by Blacks, and 82% by whites. Similarly, our analysis of data released by the Reflective Democracy Campaign shows that among the 1,180 elected city officials in the largest 100 US cities in 2020, only 36, or 3%, were Asian, while 316, or 27%, were Black, 171, or 14%, were Latino, and 630, or 53%, were white. Further, when dividing the ethnic share of these officials by the ethnic share of the population in these cities, we find Asians to receive the lowest parity ratio of representation at .375, compared to 1.35 for Blacks, .54 for Latinos, and 1.23 for whites. These statistics are somber reminders of the prolonged struggles for Asians to seek political incorporation in America and the continuing challenges and barriers they face in becoming candidates and elected officials.

It is also worth noting that the recent growth of APA presence in US mainstream politics took place in the tumultuous context of surging white nationalism, heightened anti-Black racism, rising xenophobia, and open hostility against immigrants, religious minorities, women, and transgender people. These were the phenomena that led to the election of Donald Trump and persisted during and after his presidency. These developments have created a severe need for research to study the election of individuals from the nation's fastest-growing population due to international migration and analyze the significance of their leadership and representation in a time of unprecedented national and global crisis in governance. The advent and onslaught of Covid-19 (dubbed the "Wuhan virus" by President Trump) beginning in early 2020, as well as President Biden's memorandum to condemn and combat racial discrimination and xenophobia against Asian Americans and

4   CONTESTING THE LAST FRONTIER

Pacific Islanders within days of his inauguration in January 2021, only added to the weight of our call.

Given the paucity of research on Asian Americans in US politics that takes a longitudinal, multiethnic, and mixed-method approach to help tease out the intricacies and contradictions showcased in the preceding paragraphs, we saw an opportunity to launch a quest that could help demystify and disentangle the curious and paradoxical nature of politics associated with being Asian (and, to some extent, Pacific Islander) in American politics. In the process, we also saw a need to identify and unearth the invisible or mostly forgotten candidates and elected officials of Asian descent who have been missing pieces in Asian American and American history and politics. In what follows, we present some foundational questions addressed in this book: Who are APA women (and men) pioneers and other trailblazers in elective office for each major ethnic community? What obstacles do they need to overcome before getting elected to their first office? How has their political socialization measured up to the gilded racial group image, and how has the perception of "being privileged, but of a foreign kind" influenced their politicization, ethnic identity, and concept of political representation? What explains the historical emergence and accelerated growth of APAs in elective offices in recent years? How might their motivation to run and their campaigning and governing experiences be impacted by the intersection of race, gender, ethnicity, and nativity in personal background and partisan political context? And, for those vowed to pursue social justice, how did they advocate for the interests of the intersectionally disadvantaged?

Our Approach to Piece Together a Missing Picture

The urgency and merits of the project are evident, but the paths to answer the posed questions are elusive. The complexity of the challenges and the degrees of time commitment required in this major undertaking are daunting. A primary source of the challenges lies in our socialization and background, which inform the very focus of our research, the questions we pose, and our relationship to the research subjects. Being progressive-leaning Asian American women ourselves, we know it is difficult, if not impossible, to maintain a neutral position as we strive to account for all the diversities and variations in the births and growths, triumphs and setbacks, and political orientations and policy interests of a relatively young and invisible community in mainstream American politics. The meaning and boundaries of the "APA" community are socially constructed and therefore contested, contingent, and mutable. The fluid and variable nature of the identity boundaries of the community is partly reflected in our personal backgrounds and experiences structured by a multitude of dimensions, including but not limited to ethnic origins or ancestry, immigration generation, motherhood, and time and place of entry to the American sociopolitical scene and the profession.

Despite our differences derived from the variously intersecting dimensions of social identity and educational trajectories to American politics and gender, racial, and ethnic studies, we were driven by the same passion and sense of mission to advance the study of Asian American politics. Being among only a handful of political science women who specialize in Asian American studies, we sought to contribute to a more nuanced understanding of the formation and impacts of the APA political community through the lens of identity politics and how it functions in the electoral arena. We approached this goal by adopting an intersectional lens that can help unveil the multiple, intersecting dimensions of identities and hierarchies behind the rise of APA women and men in mainstream American politics over time.

All social scientific understanding is interpretive in nature (Schmidt 2021); our research endeavor is no exception. However, we believe our own experiences and values enhance, rather than limit, the scope of our interpretation of community history and meanings of individual trajectories. Our reading of the long but mostly hidden community his- and herstories of elective office-seeking and exercising of leadership and representation by APA elected officials (APAEOs) shows that they embrace a particular type of voice and standing, which serves as the backbone of community-based grassroots activism and political participation. This book explores the possibility of advancing a concept of leadership praxis for social justice based on examining the personal background, campaigning strategies, governing experiences, and community-connectedness of a select group of APAEOs. These individuals made a commitment to advancing social justice through public service that spans over six decades, from the mid-1950s to 2020. In the following sections of this introductory chapter, we shall enunciate the collective history and politics rooted in social justice that informs their leadership style associated with transformation of extant social orders and the broader US political system.

There is also a practical reason for us to adopt the social justice approach. Given our reading of the progressive history of the nonwhite community and our understanding of the legacy of advancing justice by APAEOs, it provides a useful and, we contend, the only theoretical framework that is reasonable and robust enough to guide us through the seemingly endless processes of data collection, analysis, and interpretation. In the search for APAs holding elective office, from each ethnic community's first taste of electoral victory in history to the dawn of the third decade of the 21st century, we have amassed a vast amount of data. We need a string to tie together bits and pieces of information and to project a narrative that is as coherent, logical, and truthful as possible. Our data collection process was like putting together a giant jigsaw puzzle with numerous broken or missing pieces. We tried our best to be inclusive of political orientations. Our narratives covered scores of GOP elected officials whose trajectories are of significance to the development of the electoral landscape of the APA community. Still, their presence pales in comparison to that of their Democratic counterparts. Also, we were at the mercy of individuals to grant us an interview. And we relied on journalistic accounts and in-depth interviews conducted by others and made them available online (often behind paywalls) to help fill the missing pieces. The periodic changes practiced by the US Census Bureau in defining the boundaries of "Asian" and "Asian/Pacific Islander" (Brown 2020) created difficulties for us in combing through materials gathered from different periods and various sources to assemble our database. Whereas our efforts benefited tremendously from the extant rosters of elected officials, these data sources suffered from the lack of clarity and consistency in methods of data collection across time. Moreover, the nature of frequent US elections, with local elections and special elections taking place on schedules different from the biennial November elections, created additional challenges to providing an accurate and inclusive snapshot of the APA electoral landscape in any given timepoint. (We elaborate on the difficulties in defining ethnic boundaries and collecting data based on often ambiguous ascriptive attributes in Appendixes A and B.)

The following sections lay out the central ideas behind our guiding analytical framework and introduce several ideological streams that can serve as the theoretical roots of the leadership praxis for those who seek to represent the APA community and other marginalized communities substantively.

The Central Ideas

Our study is on the making of APA leaders and the content and significance of their leadership and representation among those who held elective positions at various levels (but mostly the local level) of government and served in different periods and localities. Although highly diverse as a group, these individuals defied the "model (as silent) minority" expectation and complacent group culture and took the risk of losing face, if not anything else, by running for elected office. Whether recruited to run or endorsed by a major political party, they chose to make a difference through public service. Most ran for office to seek some changes to the unsatisfying status quo. Those whose public service has engaged in institutional or social structural changes are governing leaders for social justice in the extant order that is multiplicative, intersectional, and hierarchical. Their leadership style can be referred to as social justice leadership (SJL), a form of leadership different from the white-male-dominant norm that perpetuates the marginalization of women and men of color (for a critical review, see Hardy-Fanta et al. 2016, chap. 6).

The concept of SJL and its practice have been examined extensively by other disciplines, especially in educational administration (Larson and Murtadha 2002). Within this literature, the meaning of social justice may refer to an ideal and a deliberative process of what is right and good among the people, as well as the equitable distribution of goods, the elimination of conditions that oppress certain groups while privileging others, and the full participation of all groups (Turhan 2010; Furman 2012). Typically studied among school principals, social justice leadership entails a moral/ethical stance or commitment and action to advance social justice in schools and the broader society (Wang 2018). We are extending the application of this leadership concept to US elected officials of APA descent who are of various ethnic origins and have served in multiple levels of governmental offices since as early as the 1920s.[1]

Because we are interested in the emergence of nonwhite elected officials and the consequences of their leadership and representation, we find the need to consider the structural positions of the nonwhite communities they represent at the intersection of race, ethnicity, gender, and class. We are eager to explore how these individuals navigated and challenged multiple, intersecting valences of power. Our conceptualization is inspired by several streams of ideological framework involving the birth of the Asian American movement,

8   CONTESTING THE LAST FRONTIER

the rise of Asian American feminism (AAF), and a branch of feminism for women of color (and their male allies) called womanism. Our usage of womanism is anchored in the womanist leadership praxis developed by Abdullah and Freer (2008), but we also see a connection to the concept of bridge feminism (Curwood 2015; Wu 2020), which we shall elaborate on later in this chapter. These are considered central theoretical components that inform the nature and contours of the leadership praxis for APAEOs interrogated in our study. Given the growing presence of women and immigrants and the trend of ethnic diversification of the APAEOs over time, we also strive to pay attention to the differences gender, ethnicity, nativity, and their intersections may make in the election and representation of elected officials in our study.

Before moving on, we have several clarifications to make about our central ideas. First, despite our locating part of its ideological origins in radical-left politics of the 1960s and 1970s, we do not study only the legacies of those elected officials directly involved in social movement protests and grassroots activism during that era. Second, because of the shifting nature of politics and contexts over time, we believe the APA community's pursuits for social and political change can be achieved through either grassroots organizing or elective officeholding, or both. Not only do we not see an inherent conflict between the two empowerment strategies, but we notice many elected officials for social justice were former grassroots organizers. We further notice that those individuals with community-organizing backgrounds often practice the politics of transformation once in the elective office. Third, whereas we identify our subjects for inclusion by their race, gender, and ethnicity in this study,[2] we do not believe the significance of their officeholding can be confined by narrowly construed and inflexible ideas of identity politics and descriptive representation. Instead, we subscribe to Lisa Lowe's (1996) idea of Asian American identity as heterogeneous, hybrid, and "multiply determined by the contradictions of capitalism, patriarchy, and race relations" (67). Fourth, despite Asian Americans' overall image of success in socioeconomic achievement and their expanding presence in governing positions, they have experienced sustained and prolonged marginalization and minoritized treatment in US society and politics. As a result, we maintain that the leadership praxis for social justice is necessary and central to the mission and goal of political representation for APAEOs today. Last but not least, among the body of female and male APAEOs in our study, not all fall into the definition of social justice leaders. In fact, our analysis of issue concerns (in Chapter 5) finds an estimated minority of no more than one

INTRODUCTION 9

in five do. There are also gradations of differences in issue concern, level of engagement with the community, and leadership practice among those who do. Nonetheless, we contend that these elected officials for social justice have helped define and distinguish the legacy and significance of political representation by APAEOs.

Tracing Roots: The Launching of the Asian American Movement

One can argue that the concept of this progressive and local ethnic community-centered leadership was seeded in the first wave of the Asian American movement (AAM), complete with its legacy of panethnic/racial formation and the fight for self-determination and collective empowerment sometime between 1968 and 1975. It was the era of post-civil rights protest politics for US minorities who sought empowerment of the oppressed peoples in the Black, Brown, Red, and Yellow communities. A sense of common fate and consciousness of group deprivation among Japanese, Chinese, Filipino, and Korean student leaders in the San Francisco Bay Area in 1968 led to the creation of a panethnic identity called "Asian American." In the launching phase of the AAM, radical-left ideology was the dominant discourse, and antiwar sentiment gained steam in correspondence to news of rising death tolls both of US soldiers and innocent civilians in Southeast Asia. There was a heightened degree of mistrust in US government and officials among ethnic and racial minority Americans. Meanwhile, grievances in urban ethnic enclaves were rampant and continued to be neglected by white-controlled power.

A key struggle that contributed to the rise of the early AAM was efforts to end the American war in Vietnam. Like Black, American Indian, and Latino/a activists, Asian American activists critiqued the racism and imperialism of the war. They drew connections between the racist discourses used to justify US military intervention in Vietnam and those used to justify state-sponsored violence against people of color within the United States. Asian American women (and gender-conscious men) in the AAM also highlighted the sexist nature of racist portrayals of Vietnamese women as hypersexual and subhuman. Asian American women activists were particularly inspired by their sisters in Asia who strongly condemned US imperialism and participated in anticolonial struggles in their Asian homelands and worldwide.

10   CONTESTING THE LAST FRONTIER

Another key struggle of the early AAM was efforts to transform the structure and purpose of school-based education, specifically through lobbying to create ethnic studies. Asian American college student organizations were cofounding members of the Third World Liberation Front, a multiracial alliance aligned with decolonial movements in Africa, Latin America, and Asia. Together, they lobbied for an opportunity for racial minority students to learn about their group history in courses taught by faculty members who shared their ethnic background instead of the whitewashed and color-blind version of American history taught by white instructors. Nearly all of the Asian American student groups were ethnic-specific in their founding. Still, students learned to work collaboratively to address community issues neglected by the government at the grassroots level. This kind of cross-ethnic organizing led to panethnic identity and consciousness formation as members of a new people called Asian Americans (Espiritu 1992; Wei 1993; Liu, Geron, and Lai 2008; Lee 2014; Okamoto 2014).

Campus activism fueled struggles in the streets, particularly in the multi-ethnic urban enclaves home to immigrant and low-income Asian Americans and other people of color. In New York, San Francisco, Los Angeles, Seattle, Boston, Philadelphia, and Honolulu, Asian American activists battled threats of evictions and fought to improve living and working conditions. While urban enclaves were the primary site of struggle for the early AAM, these activists also contributed to struggles in rural areas like Delano, where Filipino and Chicano farmworkers were protesting against economic exploitation, and in the Kalama Valley and Ota Camp, where local farmers were being displaced by the construction of hotels, luxury apartments, and subdivisions (Maeda 2012; Ishizuka 2016). Meanwhile, local Asian ethnic youth contributed to struggles over landownership, which was a central issue for the Hawaiian sovereignty movement that grew in strength by the early 1970s (Maeda 2012).

These "serve the people" programs sought not only to provide essential resources for survival, such as healthcare, child care, and cultural centers, but also to promote a sense of collective belonging and solidarity across the boundaries of race, gender, ethnicity, class, age, and nativity as organizing tools for institutional change (Ishizuka 2016). The prolonged campaign to save the I-Hotel in San Francisco's Chinatown is emblematic of "serve the people" approach of early AAM (Wei 1993; Habal 2007). Moreover, several organizations that played vital roles in these and other campaigns identified themselves as the "Third World" people or expressed international solidarities with national liberation movements abroad (Maeda 2012; Ishizuka 2016).

Tracing Roots: Asian American Women's Movement and Feminism for Women of Color

We also trace the practice of social justice leadership by APAEOs to the Asian American women's movement (AAWM) and the emergence of the Asian American feminist consciousness that grew out of discontent in the AAM and a rejection of mainstream (i.e., white middle class) feminism in the late 1960s and 1970s. The AAWM's most active contributors were American-born women of Japanese, Chinese, and Filipino descent who sought to name and eradicate the oppressive conditions facing Asian women in America and Asia. Few Asian American women self-identified as "feminists," and it was not uncommon for them to outrightly reject the term due to its perceived racism and separatism (Chow 1987; Ling 1989; Pulido 2006). However, participants in the AAWM can be viewed as Asian American and women of color feminists who explicitly incorporated critiques of sexism and patriarchy into their movement-building activities as Asian Americans and part of the "Third World" people. In other words, Asian American feminists did not seek "women's liberation" apart from the empowerment of Asians and other racially oppressed peoples in the United States. They also encouraged an international view of liberation that connected the multiple oppressions facing Asian and other Third World peoples in the global restructuring of the political and economic order (Wu 2018; Hong 2018). In particular, women in anticolonial Asia were featured as role models and heroes in a fashion characterized by Wu as "radical orientalism." This characterization inverts and subverts traditional orientalism's racialized and gendered hierarchies while reinforcing a strict dichotomy between the East and the West.

The Los Angeles–based movement publication *Gidra*, which featured several essays by Asian American women activists and devoted a special issue on women's liberation, exemplifies many of the stances and concerns during the late 1960s and 1970s. In the first issue in 1969, Dinora Gil, cofounder of the publication, links the idealization of white middle-class femininity and the desire for subservient women to the internalization of racist and sexist stereotypes (Gil 1969). Several other issues feature essays, poetry, and images of and/or by Asian women that connect racialized and sexualized depictions

12   CONTESTING THE LAST FRONTIER

of Asian women to US imperialism. In addition to Evelyn Yoshimura's 1971 essay in *Gidra* on how the US military dehumanizes Asian women (and men) to justify the war in Vietnam, Carolyn Saka highlights in the same issue the abuse, material hardship, and isolation of Asian war brides of US servicemen. She traced these women's experiences to the racist and sexist views of Asian women as docile and subservient and as wartime "souvenirs" (Saka 1971). Besides publishing social critiques, Asian American women engaged in grassroots organizing that addressed the sources and consequences of racism, sexism, and economic exploitation in the lives of Asian and other women of color within and beyond the US border.

AAWM activists were outspoken about the problem of "male chauvinism" and gender inequality within the AAM, and they adopted different approaches for eliminating it. Women expressed frustration in being restricted to traditionally feminine roles of cooking, cleaning, answering phones, and filing and picketing (Ling 1989). Some men, too, rejected the view that revolutionary women should play supportive, secondary roles to men (Yamamoto 1971). As Pulido (2006) demonstrates in her study of the Third World Left in Los Angeles, approaches to combating patriarchy varied across movement organizations depending on the group's racial/class position and political ideology, and gender relations evolved over time. In an interview published in the 1971 *Asian Women*, Carmen Chow of a leftist AAM organization, I Wor Kuen (IWK), explains how her approach evolved. It was from the more confrontational one of "smashing chauvinism" to working to "organize women together" to "become a strong revolutionary force . . . a force which organizes other women" (Takemoto and Umemoto 1971, 127).

The New York–based IWK, similar to East Wind on the West Coast, in comparison to their Black and Chicano counterparts in movement organizing was noteworthy for placing women in central leadership roles (Pulido 2006). Other women formed independent groups to share their stories, forge a sense of sisterhood, develop analyses of "triple oppression," and change the marginalized conditions facing women within their ethnic communities. Asian Sisters, for example, was formed in 1971 by college-age, third-generation Japanese American women in Los Angeles. They aimed to address drug abuse and suicide among young women by providing a supportive space for Asian women of Chinese, Korean, and Filipino descent and developing their political analysis (Ling 1989; Fu 2008). The San Francisco–based I-Hotel Women's Collective is another example of how women formed sisterhood as a means for addressing issues facing their ethnic communities (Maeda 2012). These radical leftist organizations resemble nonhierarchical collectives and addressed multiple issues by centering the experiences of Asian women, particularly those who did not appear to fit the "model minority as middle class" stereotype.

Transitions from Movement Politics to Mainstream Politics

The stream that fueled the launching of the AAM was cut off by the fall of Saigon and the end of the Vietnam War in 1975. The radical-left movement faced challenges in sustaining its base due to the shifts in the international order and a changing population comprised mainly of middle-class immigrants and refugees fleeing war, violence, and political persecution associated with Communist invasion in different parts of Asia. Unlike previous waves of Asian immigration, those who arrived in the post-1965 era were more balanced in gender ratio as a whole and came from far more varied national origins and socioeconomic backgrounds. These post-1965 immigrants include highly educated science, medicine, and engineering professionals and the less affluent who continued to provide low-wage labor as cooks, seamstresses, and taxi cab drivers. Over time, the urban ethnic enclaves were no longer the places where the "new" post-1965 Asian immigrants settled. Instead, "new" Asian Americans settled in suburban areas in Southern California and New Jersey that were majority white in neighborhood makeup (Lee 2014).

Simultaneously, as Omatsu (1994) observes, there had been a significant shift in the US domestic political order, with rising neoliberalism and neoconservative backlash against leftists and others on the progressive side of politics. As a result, funding for community-based organizations established under the banner of the antipoverty Great Society program of the 1960s was drastically curtailed. Along with it were threats to the livelihoods of service professionals employed by these organizations and the community members they served. In addition to external changes and threats, the demise of the initial phase of the AAM (and AAWM) can be attributed to internal problems. Ling (1989) attributes the decline of the activism by Asian American feminists in Los Angeles by the mid-1970s to many of the issues that plagued the early AAM.

14   CONTESTING THE LAST FRONTIER

Organizations that sought to "serve the people" became more focused on social service provisions that relied on increasingly scarce government funds. In contrast, radical leftist organizations struggled to respond to shifts in the international political order and the changing composition of the Asian American community. There were also generational and class shifts within the movement and tensions over the limited scope of their activism beyond their mostly East Asian ethnic communities. Furthermore, some women struggled to maintain a life of grassroots activism and principled commitment to revolutionary change as they became mothers and professionals.

To cope, some AAM activists turned to Marxism for comfort. At the same time, most either retreated from movement politics or adopted a more pragmatic and integrationist mode of participation as party activists, election campaign volunteers, and voters; a few eventually became candidates for public office themselves (Wei 1993; Liu, Geron, and Lai 2008). According to Wei, Jimmy Carter's presidential campaign in 1976 first stimulated significant Asian American interest in electoral politics by directly appealing to Asian Americans and the community's role in developing the nation (248). Jesse Jackson, however, "was the first presidential candidate to take Asian American concerns seriously" (252) in both the 1984 and 1988 campaigns. The momentum of the Asian American community to forge a collective, panethnic force for social justice was reinvigorated by the Justice for Vincent Chin campaign, following the senseless killing by, and unfair sentencing of, the convicted white father-son pair in Detroit who mistook Chin for Japanese and blamed him for their own and the city's economic plight. Vincent's mother, Lily Chin, an immigrant from China, continuously spoke out in broken English against the injustice. Both she and Helen Zia, president of American Citizens for Justice, played central roles in the multiracial grassroots campaign that prompted Congressman Norman Mineta to write a letter to the Republican US attorney general to urge his office to act on the case (Lien 2001a; Zia 2009). This and other incidents of anti-Asian hate violence that occurred throughout the decade and afterward, along with increasing economic disparities among the Asian American population, serve as important reasons to justify the continuing need and significance of the AAM mission for social justice. It also highlights the possibility and the need for movement politics and electoral politics to coalesce and march forward for the advancement of a more inclusive and equitable society.

Bridging Radical and Liberal Feminism
by Legislative Women

As the previous discussion suggests, early AAF grew out of a social movement of Asian American women and their male allies who viewed male chauvinism and a broader system of male domination as barriers to revolutionary change. Their views and practices of "feminism" more closely resemble those of other US women of color than the mainstream, middle-class, white-centered feminism that gained popularity in the 1960s and 1970s. Wu (2018) identifies this form of AAF as radical, which is separate from the liberal form that "advocated for gender liberation but did so by seeking greater access and equality within the existing US political system" (54). Wu views Congresswoman Patsy Mink as emblematic of liberal AAF and traces her politics to "her life experiences and understanding of intersectional oppression as well as the tensions and limits of a liberal politics of inclusion" (55). As a legislator, Mink's working-class background and the historical labor exploitation of nonwhites in Hawaii explained her advocacy of labor interests. The racialized sexism she faced within the Democratic Party and in the professional workplace motivated her to champion legislation that sought to create equal opportunities for women in education and the workplace, including legislation that would provide for federally funded, high-quality child care. Mink accomplished these efforts by building coalitions with white liberal feminists, working-class women, and other women of color. In this sense, the key difference between radical and liberal AAF, as Wu defines it, is the extent to which these feminists work within the system or outside/against the system to transform it.

Nonetheless, in a subsequent publication and reinterpretation, Wu (2020) argues that Mink's legislative activism encompasses radical and liberal forms of feminism. As in the case of fellow congresswoman of color Shirley Chisholm, Mink is thought to have "bridged so-called liberal forms of feminism, with her focus on legislative change and equal opportunity, with women-of-color feminisms that developed priorities based on the oppression of women of color" (305). As a third-generation Japanese American girl growing up in a stratified plantation society in Hawaii, Mink's childhood socialization profoundly shaped her political consciousness. Her experience of racial and gender discrimination, in both the political and professional realms early on in the 1940s and 1950s, fueled her conviction to advancing women's rights and interests once in Congress. Wu notes that "to lobby for

16   CONTESTING THE LAST FRONTIER

federal legislation for childcare and for women's equal rights to education, Mink worked closely with various organizations, including mainstream feminist organizations at the national level like the National Organization for Women as well as those locally-based and involving working-class women and women of color" (308). The collaboration between Mink and feminist advocates illuminates a similar "Capitol Hill" feminist partnership between movement organizations and congressional leaders (310). Yet Mink's recognition of the intersection of racial, gender, and class oppression for women of color and her legislative attempts to bridge multiple feminist political strategies (electoral and grassroots as well as liberal and radical) exemplify the practice of "bridge feminism" (Curwood 2015).

The possibility for a legislator to serve as a bridge connecting local grassroots community concerns with the insider politics of the nation-state was a primary reason for Congresswoman Pramila Jayapal to get into the electoral arena. In her autobiography, Jayapal (2020) describes her path from a college-bound immigrant from India to a grassroots organizer, state senator, and US House representative. It was not a natural path for a longtime social movement activist and leading organizer for immigrant and Muslim rights who had become "quite cynical about elected officials" (59) regarding their will to exercise leadership on "controversial" issues. She had no trust in the system or interest in running for office. Besides, nobody in the Democratic Party machine asked her to run (63). However, after seeing a wide slate of candidates talking about why they wanted to run for an open seat in the state senate, Jayapal started to realize that she had been thinking about elected office all wrong. Instead of viewing grassroots and electoral strategies as on opposite sides of politics, she began to "think about running for office as a way to organize more people, to connect people to the government, to bring organizing from the outside to the inside, to have the proverbial seat at the table but use it to lead not just to follow" (64). This realization of the possibility to advocate for and advance a progressive policy agenda as an organizer from the inside became her new theory of change. Jayapal quickly launched her first electoral campaign for the Washington State Senate seat, leveraging her extensive organizational network of volunteers to engage new people to get involved in politics by urging them to join and support a movement built for them. The rest is history. To overcome conventional barriers for newcomers in the party system, candidate Jayapal helped sign up new party members in local Democratic district organizations, who then turned out for her endorsement vote. This strategy has since become a new playbook for other newcomers (73).

Connecting Feminism to Womanism and Womanist Leadership Praxis

Womanism is rooted in the history of struggle and resistance led by Black women and other women of color positioned at the intersections of systems of oppression. Alice Walker (1983) first offered the concept in the early 1980s as an intervention in mainstream feminist discourse and social movement that theorized and practiced empowerment from the perspective of white, middle-class women. According to Walker, womanists share a common agenda with Black feminists in their commitment to Black women's self-definition and self-determination. However, the meanings of and relationship between womanism(s) and Black feminism(s) are ongoing debates that provide "a model of community building via heterogeneity and not sameness" (Collins 1996, 16). Collins is skeptical of womanism's reliance on cultural pluralist/nationalist frameworks to construct racial solidarity among Blacks. And she questions the theory's ability to incorporate the diversity of Black women's experiences, including fights against sexism and homophobia within the Black community. However, Collins believes the function of womanism as an alternative theory to Black feminism is to reconcile "'feminist' issues within African American communities" (10). Taking up the debate again, Alexander-Floyd and Simien (2006) suggest that there is more common ground between womanism and Black feminism, while also distinguishing these from Africana womanism. According to Alexander-Floyd and Simien, "The theme of alliances, which focuses on family and community centeredness, working with Black men against oppression, and Black female sisterhood, is addressed by Black feminists" (76).

To our understanding, both womanism and Black feminism emerged from a sentiment of discontent with feminism in the 1970s and 1980s. They were expressed by Black and other women of color who faced marginalization within male-dominated ethnoracial power movements and the white, middle-class-dominated feminist movement. Both theoretical terms reflected and incorporated historical and contemporaneous grassroots activism of Black and other women of color whose community work addressed multiple, overlapping systems of oppression. Womanism/Black feminism,

18   CONTESTING THE LAST FRONTIER

in other words, is not just a theoretical or scholarly project aiming at understanding the multidimensionality of oppression. Instead, according to Abdullah and Freer (2008), it is a movement or praxis that requires active engagement by leaders upon reflection toward eradicating oppression in all forms.

Political science scholars have extended the concept of womanist leadership praxis to examine elected officials of color (Abdullah and Freer 2008; Hardy-Fanta et al. 2016). In their study of Black political representation and incorporation, Abdullah and Freer define womanist leaders as elected officials who adopt collective leadership, value coalition politics, exhibit delegate style of representation, and aim to transform conventional politics. Womanist leaders view their formal/electoral positions as extensions of grassroots movements, and they pursue political transformation, rather than incorporation, through insider and outsider strategies. Their research offers examples of womanist leadership by Black elected officials (both women and men) in California whose personal styles of leadership fall along a continuum of traditional to womanist types. For Black womanist leaders, the pathway to elective office begins with deep connections to their communities. Unlike traditionalists, they are not motivated to run by personal ambition. Community-based organizations and grassroots activism are central to their campaign strategies, and they remain active in grassroots efforts and connected to community-based organizations when in office.

As Abdullah and Freer (2008) demonstrate, womanism is not exclusive to women of color. Still, the standpoints of women of color and other groups located at the intersections of various oppressions are central to a womanist leadership style. Hardy-Fanta and her coauthors (2016) are another team of political science women who employed the womanist leadership praxis to study elected officials of color. They dutifully used the scheme construed by Abdullah and Freer to analyze the intersection of race and gender in the trajectories, leadership, and representation of a national sample of Black, Latino, and Asian American elected officials. Not surprisingly, they found the model best describes the experiences of Black elected officials.

For us, extending the womanist leadership praxis framework based on studying Black elected officials to help interpret the manners and significance of the election and representation of APAEOs presents both challenges and opportunities. On the side of challenges, first, the racialization of Asian Americans as both model minorities and perpetual foreigners has put them in a triangulated racial third place different from their Black and white counterparts (Kim 1999). Second, unlike the predominantly US-born Black community, the heterogeneity, hybridity, and multiplicity that characterize the Asian American community also jeopardize the construction of a panethnic identity among APAEOs, where race-based solidarity may not be assumed. Third, regardless of their racial identity and political orientation, APAEOs are often immigrants themselves or children of immigrants who have ventured to the unchartered political territory as pioneers. This process usually involves a strong sense of anxiety of not being "American" enough ("civic ostracism," in Kim's words) and a strong desire to want to become "assimilated" into the system. Yet, as noted by Abdullah and Freer, there is a fundamental dilemma between political incorporation and political transformation. To represent numerically small and nonwhite immigrant-majority minorities such as Asian Americans, elected officials in our study often needed to figure out on their own how to become candidates and run campaigns, and, once in office, to retain their seats or attain a higher office. The lack of role models and reliable support in the political infrastructure made it complicated, even if not impossible, to be the agents of change and political transformation in a white-centered, majoritarian, winner-takes-all, single-member district-based electoral system.

Nonetheless, we also see opportunities to improve understanding of APAEO experiences through the womanist leadership framework. We agree with Abdullah and Freer (2008) that, "for women of color, a womanist framework offers a foundation through which intersectional identities of race, class, gender, and other positions of oppression can be addressed simultaneously without the requirements that one be given primacy over the other or that identities be falsely separated out and examined individually" (97). For a historically excluded, contemporarily ostracized, and internally heterogeneous immigrant community of color, such as Asian Americans, the womanist framework offers a necessary and valuable tool to help us deconstruct the multiple meanings of oppression (and privilege). Through the prism of the womanist leadership praxis, we can better study and understand how racially descriptive representatives can act for the substantive interests of the community, however defined, in advancing justice for the intersectionally disadvantaged. The story of Pramila Jayapal, but also that of Patsy Mink and numerous others profiled in this book, provides illuminating evidence for the efficacy of the womanist leadership praxis in studying elected officials beyond Blacks and California.

20 CONTESTING THE LAST FRONTIER

Defining and Assessing Minority Political Incorporation and Representation

What is political incorporation? How do we know if a previously excluded community has become incorporated? What indicators do we need to gauge the extent of incorporation for a majority-immigrant and nonwhite community? Whereas political incorporation can mean many things to different scholars, we conceive it as a process where newcomers and outsiders become insiders and participants as citizens, voters, candidates, and elected or appointed officials in a political system. Browning, Marshall, and Tabb (1986) enunciate a theory of political incorporation where they perceive a sequential relationship between the mobilization of minority interests among voters, the election of minority candidates to city councils, and the city government's responsiveness to minority interests. They identify the theory after studying the patterns of the elections of Blacks and Latinos to the governing boards or councils in 10 Northern California cities. They conclude that "the key to the higher levels of responsiveness was not representation but coalition: minority inclusion in a coalition that was able to dominate a city council produced a much more positive governmental response than the election of minority councilmembers who were not part of the dominant coalition" (576). Over two decades later, in their seminal work on the prospects of achieving equality and inclusion in the US democracy for all of its major ethnoracial groups in early 21st-century America, Schmidt et al. (2010) enlist four similar benchmarks or dimensions of how political outsiders may gain incorporation into the governing system: "1. full access to political participation, 2. representation in governmental decision-making offices, 3. substantial power/influence on governmental decisions, leading to 4. adoption of ethnoracially egalitarian public policies" (125). The multiracial team of authors is concerned about historically entrenched and institutionalized racial inequality in the US system. Still, they remain hopeful of the potency of individuals and the capability of minority groups in shepherding the passage of public policies promoting socioeconomic and other areas in need of equity for ethnoracially disadvantaged minorities.

Whereas our project has a much narrower focus on the election of and representation by public officials of Asian (and, to a lesser extent Pacific Islander) descent, we benefit from the inspiration by the theory and benchmarks set by Browning, Marshall, and Tabb (1984, 1986) and Schmidt et al. (2010). They include measures to assess the quantity and the quality and effect of political representation for minority empowerment. This definition helps address our concern about the need to study elected officials who "look like" Asians and those who can help articulate the interests and needs of the minority community and collectively contribute to developing a more just and inclusive democracy in the United States. In Pitkin's (1967) language, the former concept is called descriptive representation and the latter concept is called substantive representation. Namely, for a minority group to become incorporated, it cannot be just about having those minority members occupy elective positions in a government. In addition, we benefit from the inspiration of Elena Ong (2003), who argues that the "true empowerment" of APA women "should not be measured by political firsts but by a legacy of political succession" (337). Hence, to adequately assess the extent to which APAs have become incorporated into the US political system, we believe in the necessity to go beyond simply taking stock of individuals of Asian descent elected to various levels and types of offices. Of course, this is in and of itself a huge and ongoing endeavor. However, for a community relatively new to the electoral arena, and before assessing the elected officials' substantive contribution to public policymaking, we think it is necessary to consider the temporal component regarding the issue of sustainability in representation—specifically, whether the seat can be retained by the same or another Asian over a length of time. In addition, following the guidance set by Browning, Marshall, and Tabb (1984), we believe it is helpful to gauge the degree of equity in representation and if the share of Asians in the elected office is proportional to the share of Asians in the population.

In the end, we argue for the need to distinguish four interrelated phases of representation in the process of becoming incorporated politically for a relatively new, majority-immigrant, and rapidly growing ethnoracial minority group: (1) descriptive representation (having one or more Asian in an elective office), (2) sustainable representation (being able to retain seats over at least one election cycle and/or replace seats held by other Asians), (3) proportional representation (reaching parity in political representation proportionate to the share of the Asian population), and (4) substantive representation (having substantive influence on making policies aiming to advance the interests of Asian and other disadvantaged minorities). To Browning, Marshall, and Tabb (1986), the key concept in phase 4 is for racial minorities to become part of the (white) dominant governing coalition. In our study, the closer the number of Asian Americans who serve in a governing body comes to majority status or beyond, the more likely it is for them to occupy a position of dominance. To assess the policy responsiveness of APA legislators, we study those serving mainly in Congress regarding their ability to advance social justice for minority communities.

We caution that having achieved phase 1 does not necessarily lead to a transition to phase 2, and having achieved phase 2 does not guarantee the arrival of phase 3. Certainly, there is no guarantee of attaining phase 4 from any or every one of the previous phases. Neither do we believe it is necessary to have achieved phase 2 or 3 before a group can access phase 4. These phases can happen simultaneously and independently. There is no guarantee that there will not be backlash or regress following progress in securing more ethnic representation and community empowerment. However, we remain hopeful that this set of phases in political representation and incorporation can help us better assess the trajectories to inclusion and empowerment for separate APA communities defined by ethnicity and locality in various stages of incorporation. With the possible exception of Japanese Americans in Hawaii and only after the mid-1950s, APAs have remained essentially political outsiders in the American political scene. By considering the internal diversity along ethnic, gender, and nativity lines and geographic and ideological differences, our project is long overdue in systematically assessing the APA community's various achievements and challenges in becoming part of the American political fabric in the mainstream electoral arena. We feature stories of individual trajectories to elective offices from diverse communities since the early 20th century and analyze patterns at the individual and aggregate levels—not only for those holding an elective office in 2020 nationwide but also for those in municipal-level offices in California between 1980 and 2020. We anticipate the outcome of this unprecedented effort will help shed light on the manners and the extent to which APAs have achieved incorporation and contribute to the betterment of a more inclusive US democracy in the third decade of the 21st century.

Doing Intersectionality

Over the past several decades, intersectionality has grown in popularity among scholars and activists alike. The origins and development of the concept are often attributed to pioneering works by Kimberlé Crenshaw and Patricia Hill Collins and other Black, Latina, Native American, and Asian American feminist scholars. They understood race and racism to be deeply embedded, persistent features of American society and politics that intersected with and/or were mutually constitutive of other dimensions of social identity and structural inequality. They centered the experiences and perspectives of women whose social identities are marginalized across one or more axes of inequality, including race, indigeneity, gender, class, and sexual orientation, and they advanced multiple, fluid power-laden boundaries in their conceptualizations and empirical operations of the framework and approach in pursuit of social justice. According to Hancock (2016), the dual intellectual projects of "remedy[ing] specific instances of intersectional stigma or invisibility" (21) and "reshaping the ontological relationships between categories of difference" (34) continue to be central to intersectionality discourse. However, tensions could arise from the uneven attention to race and disparate commitments to a normative social justice outcome.

Scholars of intersectionality who study electoral politics have maintained the importance of examining the meanings of and linkages between so-called categories of difference, especially race and gender. This type of scholarship includes works that acknowledge the persistent underrepresentation of nonwhite women and men at all levels of popularly elected office (Smooth 2010b; Hardy-Fanta et al. 2016) and the uneven presence and growth of women of color in state legislatures (Scola 2006, 2007; Bejarano 2013). It also includes those investigating patterns of symbolic and substantive representation among ethnoracial minority women (Smooth 2006; Fraga et al. 2008; Brown 2014; Reingold, Widner, and Harmon 2020). The aforementioned works also interrogate disparities and commonalities between racial/ethnic women and men regarding the motivation to run, barriers to entry, and the resources needed to win.

With regard to research on APA politics, APA women scholars have led the struggle against the erasure of women of color by adding the intersecting layers of ethnicity (and nativity) to discussions of race and gender in American politics. Judy Chu's (1989) benchmark study of APAEOs in the 1984 cohort provides one of the earliest (and still uncommon today) glimpses into the racialized and gendered nature of attaining and sustaining elective office for APA women. Chu argues that these women of color pioneers encountered multiple barriers related to race, ethnicity, gender, nativity, and class in their paths to office. Their experiences were not all the same, and their identities were not always a burden on their successful election and reelections. Lien (2001a) elaborates on these issues in the last chapter of her book on the emergence of Asian Americans in the American political arena.

24   CONTESTING THE LAST FRONTIER

Following a review of the history of disenfranchisement of APA women in relation to white women and other women of color, Ong (2003) provides concrete suggestions on empowerment strategies for APA women, including leveraging district-based systems, building an electoral infrastructure that will support APA women and all candidates who advance issues important to APA women, and ensuring the political mentorship of APA women. Over the last four decades, given the seismic change in the overall picture of APAs in elective offices, it is logical to question whether and to what extent the factors identified by Chu and other scholars as structuring the election and representation of APA women remain relevant today.

A unique aspect of our research is the attention paid to the individual and group experiences structured by the intersectionality of race, ethnicity, nativity, and gender. We follow the footsteps of pioneering women of color political scientists and feminist scholars who challenged the dominance of white, middle-class US-born women (and men) in examinations of gender in American politics. These scholars also questioned the absence of a gender analysis in research on race and ethnicity. Rather than treating unequal structures and relations of power based on race, ethnicity, gender, and other socially constructed categories of difference as static and independent, they advocated for intersectional analyses that treat systems of domination as interdependent and mutually constituted (e.g., Cohen 1999; Hancock 2004; Smooth 2006; Hardy-Fanta et al. 2006; Junn and Brown 2008; Brown and Gershon 2016; Hardy-Fanta et al. 2016; Phillips 2021). Our project extends this line of research by focusing on APAs in contemporary electoral politics and by bringing the experiences of women to the fore of analysis.

Data

Our data combine both a proprietary database of elected officials to enable quantitative analysis and in-depth interviews and case studies for qualitative analysis. Employing a mixed-method approach, we shall tease out the motivation, career paths, and organized group-based resources and roadblocks on the campaign trail, as well as the various definitions and consequences of political representation by women and men for a majority-immigrant community of color. We are interested in uncovering the lived experiences of APA women and men on the campaign trail and in office and during their childhood/adolescent years. We highlight those experiences influenced by the intersections of multiple, mutually constituted forms of oppression like racism, nativism, sexism, homophobia, and classism. Prior research shows that the preponderance of US women and men of color public officials serve at the local level. Our project brings attention to a much-overlooked but essential population of elected officials whose service on school boards and city/county councils is often considered a springboard to state- and federal-level offices.

We have collected both primary and secondary data of qualitative and quantitative nature to conduct our analysis. Examples of the primary qualitative data we gathered include in-depth interviews with selective elected officials, community organization leaders, and local experts. We transcribed each interview and identified the most salient themes that emerged within and across the interviews. We also consulted peer-reviewed academic publications, reports by US governmental agencies and interest organizations, and news articles in US mainstream and ethnic media, along with campaign statements of candidates and representatives from their official websites as aids in developing narrative profiles and analysis of thematic connections.

A central piece of our quantitative data is a proprietary database of the population of APA elected officials serving in 1980–84 and 2014–20. We constructed this database using rosters of APA elected officials published by the UCLA Asian American Studies Center and the online political database maintained by the Asian Pacific American Institute of Congressional Studies. These data were tediously verified for accuracy and supplemented with a systematic collection of individualized information available online of each elected official's background, trajectories to current office, and history of community and partisan organizational involvement. To better understand the influence of electoral and demographic context on the success of APA candidates, we also gathered contextual data for all California cities where Asians served on city councils between 1980 and 2020. We collected selected demographic information such as the size and share of the Asian population in states and municipalities represented by Asians from the decennial US Census for 1980, 1990, 2000, and 2010 to construct the jurisdictional context. Last but not least, we gathered relevant campaign information in the 2020 election cycle for APA candidates who ran for US congressional and selected subnational offices. We integrated stories of their electoral fates into our main storyline to bring our analysis up to date. (See more of how we constructed our database of elected officials in Appendix B.)

26 CONTESTING THE LAST FRONTIER

Chapter Overview

This book aims to provide a longitudinal, multiethnic, and gendered view of the emergence and impact of Asian Americans in popularly elected offices at the national, state, and local levels. We present stories of their trajectories to elective office and the consequences of their leadership and representation to advance social and political rights for Asian Americans and other minority Americans. In this introductory chapter, we begin by laying out the complexity and inherent contradictions in studying the political experiences of the APA community. We justify the need for employing intersectionality as a framework for our analysis and womanist leadership praxis as a model of social justice-focused political representation rooted in the AAM and other social movements and the grassroots activism of Black and other women of color. We also argue for the need to identify an Asian American version of the womanist leadership praxis for advancing social justice and use it as a filter to screen elected officials for inclusion and focused interpretation in our narration. In addition, we define our notion of political incorporation for APAs and discuss how their political representation needs to be assessed both quantitatively and qualitatively with different indicators and over time.

Chapter 2 opens with a brief review of the gendered history of immigration and settlement patterns of the Asian population by major ethnic or national origins. This historical account helps contextualize the significance of international migration in the political socialization of pioneering women and men in elective offices and other trailblazers in each Asian ethnic community. We organize our narration in chronological order by the year of winning the first office, segmented by geographic state, ethnicity, and gender. We present information salvaged from scarce and scattered accounts of these pioneers regarding their family background, political socialization, and motivation to run for the first office. Then we interpret the impacts of immigration generation, traumatic political events, ethnic and gender identities, and family class background on the socialization and politicization of those individuals who were elected to office after the political "firsts" and who played a significant role in the development of political incorporation in each major Asian ethnic community to the present day.

In Chapter 3, we move beyond the individual trajectories to provide an aggregate-level view of the evolution of the electoral landscape that began in the territory and state of Hawaii. We analyze the growth and transformation of the population structure of the APA community since 1965 to help contextualize continuities and changes in the contours and makeup of the APAEO population between 1980 and 2020. We appraise the various gaps in descriptive representation by gender, ethnicity, and nativity among APAEOs across levels of offices nationwide and between Hawaii and California, the top two states in the number of APAs elected to offices. Then, focusing on Asian city council members in California and using data collected over eight time points, we appraise sustainability issues in their political incorporation and the relationship between demography and representation over time. Finally, based on data of the entire body of Asian state legislators in California serving in or before 2020, we examine the significance of local officeholding in their political ascension and how much electoral reform such as term limits could help or hurt their political fortune.

In Chapter 4, we return to the stories of those individual pioneers and other pathbreaking elected officials whose trajectories to officeholding we started to tell in Chapter 2. Here, we continue the narrative but focus on the roles of political parties in their campaigns for the first office and, for some, higher offices. After presenting a statistical profile of the partisan orientations of APAEOs in 2020, we explore the personal formation of partisan ties (or lack thereof) to either the GOP or the Democratic Party, by plan or by chance, in broadly chronological order and by the partisan label. Whereas the literature suggests that newcomers and minorities cannot count on political parties to support their candidacy and initial campaign, our analysis finds a more complex picture with nuanced differences and some significant deviations from the main narrative of party neglect. To help us comprehend better the evolving role of the party in the incorporation of APAs, we study Democratic Party history in Hawaii and California and the unique place of local party clubs in California. We illustrate ethnic-specific and gendered partisan patterns with selected individual campaigns and close the chapter by describing how some survived party marginalization and neglect.

Chapter 5 reviews past research on the multiple, interrelated dimensions of political representation and their distinct manifestations among Asian Americans. After providing a snapshot of the scope of issue priorities and the relative importance of social justice concerns among APAEOs serving in 2020, we return to follow the paths to the legislative halls of those pioneering and other significant figures in the electoral history of the respective APA community featured in preceding chapters. In broadly chronological order, we present separate accounts of legislative achievements for advancing justice for different communities and causes, in both historical and contemporary times, including responses to Covid-19 by the APA delegation in the 116th Congress. We interpret these legislative actions taken mainly at the federal level through ideas of bridge feminism. We link it to legislative activism at the subnational level through the lens of a womanist leadership praxis that connects legislative action with local, grassroots, organizational-based activism. Our analysis highlights the racialized and gendered processes through which legislators at the federal, state, and local levels enact their roles as social justice advocates. We underscore the need for a womanist conception of transformative leadership to address persistent and growing inequities impacting the intersectionally disadvantaged in the community.

In Chapter 6, we offer some summary observations of the political trajectories of APAEOs through the stories of two pioneering male California state legislators, one Democrat and one Republican, who entered the state assembly in the 1960s. Their encounters of racism are compared to what happened to a group of mostly female APAEOs serving in various offices and localities during the Covid-19 era. We then contrast the assimilationist with the proactive, transformative reactions of APAEOs to anti-Asian hate. We highlight specific approaches and methods of advancing justice by APAEOs serving at national, state, and local levels of office in 2020–21. Through case studies of Hmong Americans, we showcase a new generation of APAEOs who achieved political incorporation at the state and local levels by engaging local nonethnic, ethnic, women-centered, and/or partisan organizations and groups. This account is followed by a systematic analysis of the growing roles of nonpartisan ethnic and nonethnic but women-centered and mostly partisan organizations in building the political infrastructure for APA incorporation and empowerment. In the closing section, we remind readers of the heritage of advancing justice by APAEOs. We reiterate that those who could subscribe to and practice the womanist leadership praxis are the elected officials and social justice leaders who can more effectively represent and serve the racial minority community and beyond.

2

Gendered History of Immigration and Political Socialization in the Election of Asians

America is a nation built by immigrants, but until 1965, persons of white European descent dominated US immigration, and (electoral) politics was considered the last frontier in becoming assimilated or integrated (Gordon 1964). According to the pluralist idea of democracy (Dahl 1961), getting elected to public offices is an entirely predictable path toward political incorporation for US immigrants, even if some groups may take longer than others, depending on the resources they possess. This basic pluralist assumption of unproblematic, straight-line assimilation for US immigrants from all origins has been subsequently challenged by empirical research. Nonetheless, the basic tenet has been largely sustained after taking into account variations in group conditions of entry and settlement, especially for those who entered after 1965 and mostly from Asia and Latin America, and, equally important, after acknowledging contributions these newcomers can make to redefine the fabric of the American mainstream (Portes and Zhou 1993; Alba and Nee 2003).

Countering ideas of assimilation as a linear process and a function of time spent in the place of settlement, historical research on US immigrant political incorporation between 1881 and 1930 from eastern, central, and southern Europe suggests assimilation as a site of "struggle, selective incorporation, and ambiguity" (Gerstle and Mollenkopf 2001, 26). Among foreign-born white ethnics, "The thorough incorporation of first-generation immigrants into local and national political processes has been the relatively rare exception, not the rule, in the United States" (Gerstle and Mollenkopf 2001, 26). However, Gerstle and Mollenkopf expect US-born, post-1965 immigrants' children, or the second generation,[1] to "have a greater impact on American politics than their parents, just as the children of the migrants from 1880 to 1920 provided the social base for the New Deal in the 1930s" (26). Alba

---

Contesting the Last Frontier. Pei-te Lien and Nicole Filler, Oxford University Press. © Oxford University Press 2022.
DOI: 10.1093/oso/9780190077679.003.0002

30 CONTESTING THE LAST FRONTIER

(2009) argues that many ethnic and religious outsiders such as Irish, Italian, and Jewish Americans have achieved full acceptance as members of the mainstream in the second half of the 20th century due to the rapid expansion of education and labor opportunities. He predicts that due to changing demography in the United States, where many fewer whites will be coming of age than Mexican Americans and other nonwhite groups in coming decades, an assimilation opportunity is opening for members of previously disadvantaged racial and ethnic groups—as long as they can gain access to good education and jobs.

As for Asian Americans, Alba (2009) maintains that, despite past racial discrimination and continuing visibility and incidents of biased treatments, the group has broken free from a position of racial disadvantage and achieved "widespread acceptability among white Americans" (7). His research on US residential and intermarriage patterns shows that unlike Blacks and Latinos, Asians are increasingly integrated into white social milieus and families. In hindsight, the book, written right after the historic election of the first nonwhite president into the White House, paints a rather rosy picture of the possibility of blurring major US ethnoracial boundaries toward full integration for a racially visible (but socioeconomically successful) group like Asian Americans. The political climate drastically turned antagonistic with the election of Donald Trump in 2016, whose campaign rhetoric was filled with racism, sexism, and nativism against immigrants, Muslims, women, and other social minorities. And yet, a historic high of three Asian Pacific Americans (among the original 23 other candidates) contended for the Democratic Party nomination of the 2020 US presidential election. Although all three eventually withdrew from the contest, the majority-immigrant community reached a new high of participation in high-profile, mainstream politics with the election of Kamala Harris, daughter of immigrants from India and Jamaica, to the vice presidency. This result is quite a journey for a community paradoxically and simultaneously characterized as the Yellow Peril, the Perpetual Foreigner, and the Model Minority.

Our project focuses on the political incorporation of Asia-born immigrants and their US-born descendants from the early history of their gaining access to popularly elected offices to the third decade of the 21st century. We explore the extent to which the (pluralist) model of political incorporation derived from the experiences of white European immigrants fits the experiences of those from Asia. We submit that, unlike their white counterparts, for Asian Americans, issues regarding their political incorporation and the individual stories of their trajectories to public office are complicated by a web of laws prohibiting and delaying their immigration and naturalization as "aliens ineligible for citizenship." These same rules also limited their freedom to marry outside of the race, own property and business, choose places to live, open businesses, attend schools, or enter a specific profession and occupation. Nonetheless, even within the first generation as foreign-born immigrants, many ventured into the electoral arena. Some even went on to serve in Capitol Hill. This trajectory makes us curious about the meanings of being Asia-born for political incorporation in the US electoral system. Specifically, we are interested in finding out how their experiences differ from the US-born in the same ethnic community, whether these are unique for each ethnic group, if the experiences are gendered (and raced), and to what extent the relationships between nativity and political incorporation change across space and time.

This chapter begins with a brief review of migration history and introduces the political pioneers in each major (as in population size) Asian ethnic group. Then, through the lens of selective public figures in each of the major ethnic communities, we unpack and interpret the multiple meanings and evolution of being foreign-born compared to the US-born (either in the second or later generation) among Asian Pacific American elected officials (APAEOs) over time. Our narrative strives to underscore the intersecting roles of gender, nativity, and immigration generation in structuring the political socialization of pathbreaking APAEOs in major ethnic groups since the first electoral victories that we could find. We are aware that, given the practical difficulties of fully enumerating the population of APAs in (nonjudicial) elective offices in any period, our narratives of their stories of socialization and politicization may be incomplete. Our identification of the "firsts" in each community may also be subject to reinterpretation. However, we aim to highlight the pioneering and milestone developments in political incorporation for distinct Asian ethnic communities through the socialization experiences of individual trailblazers in electoral politics from early group history to the first few decades of the 21st century.

A Brief Review of Asian Immigration History

How does international migration impact the political socialization of APAEOs across immigration generations and in various ethnicities and

32   CONTESTING THE LAST FRONTIER

contexts? As told elsewhere, the history of migration and settlement of Americans of Asian descent can be traced back to a period earlier than the founding of the US nation. Unlike white European settlers, the incorporation of Asians has been obstructed by waves of legal, social, and political discrimination. In addition to obstacles created by US immigration policies, state laws, and local ordinances, decisions made by the US Supreme Court, US labor market needs and practices, and developments in the Asian homelands related to wars, famine, and other natural disasters also influenced the size and shape of the US Asian population and its opportunities for legal immigration and citizenship acquisition.[2]

Most early Chinese immigrants who entered the United States between 1848 and 1882 were male laborers recruited from the southern Chinese province of Guangdong and arrived in San Francisco, California, to work in mines or railroads in the American West. The influx of the "heathen Chinese" generated an immediate backlash from white settlers, who lobbied the California legislature to pass the Foreign Miner's License Tax in 1852. Several other local ordinances were passed to impose a system of segregation and prevent economic mobility of these immigrants. Starting in California in the 1870s with assistance from organized white workers, a nationwide movement was formed to bar entry of Chinese labor and prohibit the naturalization of those who already entered. Women of Chinese and other East Asian descents became the first victims; they were banned from immigration through the Page Act of 1875, which criminalized the entire group for their suspected connection to prostitution on the basis of race, ethnicity, gender, and class status. It was followed by the passage of the 1882 Chinese Exclusion Act (CEA), which ubiquitously targeted male laborers of Chinese descent but permitted entry of Chinese students and merchants under the exempt class status. Some Chinese laborers managed to circumvent the discriminatory law by claiming to be merchants; others did it by claiming to be the sons of Chinese American citizens (American-born Chinese were guaranteed citizenship under the Fourteenth Amendment). This "paper son" method was especially popular after the Great San Francisco Earthquake of 1906, which destroyed most immigration records. It allowed many Chinese to claim relatives and attempt to bring them into the United States by providing family details to those willing to pay a fee to obtain the information. This practice thus brought about the term "paper sons" (or "paper daughters") but also the humiliating detention and interrogation of paper holders regarding the validity of their documents in the port of entry. Until 1923, when Canada passed its Chinese exclusion act, some Chinese managed to enter the United States via Canada despite a hefty head tax that rose from $50 to $500 between 1885 and 1903.

Hawaii was another destination in the second half of the 19th century and early 20th century for Chinese, Japanese, Korean, and Filipino workers because of the active recruitment by American sugar companies for laborers to work on sugar plantations. Laborers would sign contracts to work on island plantations for several years in return for free passage and some pay, essentially a system of indentured servitude. Hawaii briefly became the only destination for US-bound Chinese laborers after the passage of the CEA in 1882 and before the implementation of the Hawaiian Organic Act (HOA) in 1900. The HOA extended Chinese exclusion to the islands but also granted US citizenship to residents of the Hawaii Republic on or before August 12, 1898, and nullified any contract made on or after that date. Compared to their counterparts on the mainland, it was more common for Chinese male workers to bring their wives to the plantation and enabled the opportunity to take root and produce the US-born generations.

Japanese workers started to arrive in Hawaii after the Japanese government lifted emigration restrictions in 1885. Plantation owners liked to import Japanese (and, to a lesser degree, Korean) workers, for they believed that interethnic competition could prevent strikes and the formation of unions among Chinese workers. As a result, by 1900, the Japanese population reached 40%, while the Chinese were 17% of the Hawaii population. Japanese laborers became even more attractive after the HOA blocked the Chinese from entry. Meanwhile, the HOA created opportunities for Japanese workers to resettle in California as farmers. Unfortunately, cries for Japanese exclusion promptly arose upon their arrival, and California became the first of several states in the West, Pacific Northwest, and Mountain West to bar Japanese immigrants from owning land through the 1913 Alien Land Law. To preclude the Japanese from immigration exclusion, a Gentlemen's Agreement was made between the US and Japanese governments in 1907–8. Japan agreed not to issue any passports to Japanese laborers in exchange for the allowance of laborers already in the United States to bring their wives, parents, and children from Japan. In 1922, through a US Supreme Court decision in the *Ozawa* case, the naturalization of Japanese immigrants was denied by their nonwhite alien status. Then, the women-centered immigration from Japan was unplugged by the 1924 National Origins Act (NOA). However, the entry of "picture brides"

34 CONTESTING THE LAST FRONTIER

or women from Japan, as well as Okinawa and Korea (Chai 1988), who only met their future husbands in the United States through the exchange of photos, was critical to the establishment of families and the continuous growth of the ethnic community over generations. At the same time, pressure to maintain an idealized nuclear family resulted in the disciplining of Japanese women, especially those who asserted their individual freedom by fleeing and divorce.

With the annexation of the Philippines in 1898 and after Chinese and Japanese laborers were excluded from entry, the Hawaiian sugar industry actively recruited Filipino workers (both men and women) to work on sugar plantations, especially in and after 1909. Called Sakadas, these workers mainly came under three-year contracts and stayed in Hawaii after the expiration of their contracts. Because the Philippines was an unincorporated US territory between 1898 and 1946, Filipinos were considered US nationals, not citizens. After the passage of the NOA in 1924, when all foreigners from Asia were blocked from entry, Filipinos were actively recruited to the West Coast states to fill the labor market need for agricultural and domestic labor. The passage of the Tydings-McDuffie Act of 1934 promised independence to the Philippines. It also reclassified Filipinos as aliens and effectively halted Filipino immigration and naturalization until the Luce-Celler Act 1946. Even if only 100 immigrants from the Philippines were allowed to enter per year, this act permitted the naturalization of Filipino immigrants already in the United States.

Koreans are another Asian immigrant population that settled first in Hawaii. Between 1903 and 1905, during the Russo-Japanese War, over 7,000 Koreans entered to work on sugar plantations. Koreans were subject to the same laws guarding against Japanese immigration after their homeland was first occupied and then annexed by Japan in 1910. According to Kim (1971), 951 Korean women entered Hawaii as picture brides and about 151 on the mainland between 1910 and 1924. In the 1950s, the Korean War triggered the entry of women and orphans covered under the War Brides Act of 1947, which allowed Asian wives of American servicemen and veterans to immigrate. However, more than three in four of the Korean-born population today did not enter until after the abolition of the 1924 national origins quota system in the 1965 Immigration Act. Overnight, quotas for Asian nations jumped from approximately 100 to 20,000 immigrants per year. For the first time in US history, large numbers of Asian immigrants were able to arrive as families, many for the sake of securing better educational opportunities for their children. The growth of Korean immigration appears to have peaked in the 1980s, and it has since been deterred by racial tensions related to the 1992 Los Angeles uprisings, in which Korean-owned stores were targeted for looting and burning.

The preponderance of today's Asian Indian Americans also did not enter until after 1965. However, the first significant Asian Indian immigration occurred as early as 1904. As in other Asian American communities, most early immigrants came as male laborers and farmers, but some came as students, political refugees, and business elites. Those of the Sikh faith were overrepresented in the early Indian immigrant population. The creation of the "Asiatic Barred Zone" through the 1917 Immigration Act blocked their immigration. The naturalization of those immigrants from India already settled in the United States was halted and even reversed in the early 1920s through racist US Supreme Court decisions. As with Filipinos, it was not until 1946 that an annual national quota of 100 Indians was allowed to immigrate, and those already in the United States were allowed to become naturalized citizens. The last groups of Asian immigrants to become eligible for naturalization were those born in Japan or Korea. It was made possible by the 1952 (McCarran-Walter) Immigration Act, which nullified the racist Naturalization Act of 1790 and all federal anti-Asian exclusion laws. The act also established a preference system inherited by lawmakers of the 1965 Immigration Act in favor of well-educated and skilled laborers, family members of citizens, and refugees.

Foreign-born Asians of Vietnamese, Laotian, Cambodian, and Hmong descent began to enter en masse as political refugees after the fall of Saigon, which ended the US war in Vietnam (1955–75). Many among the first wave that arrived in 1975 from South Vietnam were professionals or social and political elites with ties to the US military. Those who arrived between 1978 and 1994 were of much more modest background. They were often called the "Boat People" because, instead of being airlifted out of a fallen homeland as in the first wave, they were forced to flee by boat (and/or by foot) to escape ethnic persecution in Vietnam, civil wars in Cambodia and Laos, border wars between Vietnam and China, and natural disasters. After the late 1990s, instead of entering as refugees, an overwhelming majority of Vietnamese and other Southeast Asian immigrants were sponsored by family or immediate relatives of US citizens (Southeast Asian 2020).

36 CONTESTING THE LAST FRONTIER

Disentangling the Meanings of Being Foreign- versus US-Born among Pioneering APAEOs

As shown, given the relentless history of immigration and citizenship restrictions against Asian Americans, it seems miraculous to envision the election of Asians into any major public office, especially for those belonging to the foreign-born generation and in the early part of their respective group history. The predominance of early waves of Asian immigrants entered as contract laborers. In addition, federal laws and court decisions expressly prohibited groups of Asia-born immigrants from becoming naturalized. The naturalization ban took place between 1882 and 1943 for those born in China, between 1898 and 1946 for those born in the Philippines, between 1923 and 1946 for those born in India, and between 1922 and 1952 for those born in Japan and Korea. However, the most egregious violations of civil rights and liberties occurred during World War II. Nearly all Japanese immigrants and their US-born descents residing on the West Coast were ordered to evacuate and then detained behind barbed wire in US concentration camps between 1942 and 1945. As a result, it seems natural for the Asian community not to flex its political muscles until the first US-born generation reached the voting age of 21 (or 18, after the passage of the 26th Amendment in 1971) and when the society became more receptive to having non-Anglo leaders.

Yet the Asian experience also seems to be "blessed" by a concentrated settlement pattern in the US territory turned state of Hawaii (whose white Republican oligarchy was broken in 1954 by the "Democratic Revolution"). Moreover, the sustained ties to the richness of Asian cultural heritage put a strong emphasis on education, hard work, and giving back to the host country and local community. In addition, despite huge ethnic and gender gaps, idiosyncrasies in US immigration laws such as the exempt categories in the CEA (i.e., merchants, teachers, students, and tourists) or the preference categories in the 1952 and 1965 immigration acts (i.e., educated and skilled workers and their family members) contributed to the creation of a relatively advantaged sociodemographic profile for the overall population. Meanwhile, ostensibly bad things such as the Great San Francisco Quake of 1906 had silver linings to some who entered the United States during the Chinese exclusion era under false pretense as "paper sons" or children of US citizens. And the forced removal and incarceration of Japanese Americans during World War II provided a just cause for visionary community members to study law, seek public office, and help secure redress through legal and political processes.

More recently, well-connected foreign-born candidates have been able to tap into the reservoir of campaign funds and/or votes in the ethnic diaspora through forces of globalization and transnational ties. However, these candidates may also become vulnerable to the whims of contentious US foreign relations with countries in Asia accused of practicing communism or dictatorship. Also, lingering tenuous ties between Japan and other Asian homelands that originated from Japan's Imperial Army atrocities in World War II may continue to contaminate interethnic relations on US soil. These factors point to the complexity and difficulty of clearly distinguishing the political advantages from the disadvantages of being foreign-born versus US-born in the political incorporation of Asian Americans.

In what follows, mainly in chronological order by the first year of election into office, we take stock of pioneering elected officials of Asian descent in each major ethnic group by nativity and gender and separate those elected in Hawaii from those elected in mainland states. We find the very first Chinese, Japanese, and Filipino Americans elected to an office all won in Hawaii. They were all male, and all except one were from the second generation. The first Japanese woman, a Sansei, or third generation, did not get elected until more than two decades after the first elections of her male counterparts. For Korean Americans, entry to electoral politics arrived much later, and with the first elected being a third-generation woman. Possible reasons for their belated entry include a history of homeland occupation/colonization, forced identification as Japanese in the US migration process, relatively small group size, and a strong homeland independence movement.

The First Elected in Hawaii

In 1926, Hawaii-born **Yew Char**, a photographer, and son of immigrant Chinese sugar plantation workers, was one of the first two full-blooded Chinese elected to public office. Char was elected to the Territorial House of Representatives as a Democrat. Also elected in 1926 was Dr. Dai Yen Chang, a Honolulu-born dentist who was elected to the Honolulu Board of Supervisors (today's City Council). The first Japanese elected in Hawaii occurred in 1930, and they were all Nisei, or the second generation. **Norobu Miyake**, a World War I veteran, member of the American Legion, businessman, and a Republican, was elected to Kauai County Board of Supervisors during the primary. In the general election of 1930, two Nisei—one Republican (Tasuku

38 CONTESTING THE LAST FRONTIER

Oka) and one Democrat (Andy Yamashiro)—were elected to the Territorial House of Representatives.

The first Filipino elected in the United States was **Peter Aduja**. He immigrated in 1927 at the age of seven to Hilo, Hawaii, where his father worked on a sugarcane plantation as a Sakada. His father attended one year of school in the Philippines, and his mother was illiterate. In those days, Filipino men seldom attended schools beyond the eighth grade. However, his parents were different and took pride in their son's achievements (Boylan 1991). Aduja was a student body president at Hilo High, where students were predominantly Japanese Americans. He joined the US Army in 1944 and served in the segregated First Filipino Infantry Regiment. Using the GI Bill, he attended Boston University and received a law degree in 1951. He became one of the first two Filipino lawyers in Hawaii in 1953 (Ohira 2007). In 1954, Aduja was elected to the Territorial House of Representatives as a Republican in a year of the "Democratic Revolution" and left the office after serving one term. He returned to politics running as a Democrat in 1966 and served as a state representative until 1974 (Ohira 2007). His last elected office was on the City of Honolulu's Kaneohe Neighborhood Board from 1986 to 1994.

Elected to the Hawaii territorial house in 1938, **Hiram Fong** (born Yau Leong Fong) was not the first Chinese elected to that legislative body, but he was the first US senator of Asian descent elected in 1959 upon Hawaii's statehood. Born in 1907 in Hawaii to immigrant parents from Guangdong, China, he was the seventh birth of 12 children. His father worked at the local fertilizer plant, while his mother worked as a housekeeper. He grew up poor in Kalihi, Hawaii, Territory, attended local public schools, and "helped the family by selling fish and crabs he caught by hand" while in grammar school (Nakaso 2004). Unable to afford college, he worked in a navy shipyard for three years while attending the University of Hawaii and joined ROTC to receive the 30 cents a day payment for senior cadets. He started using the first name of "Hiram" while editing the student newspaper and formally changed the name in 1942 when signing up for military service in the Army Air Corps as a judge advocate.

Fong had a taste of political life while in college, working for the successful campaign of a candidate for Honolulu mayor. After receiving a law degree from Harvard, he returned to Honolulu to work as a deputy city attorney. In 1938, Fong ran for his first office in the hope of gaining public attention to kick-start a private law practice. By campaigning mainly on a theme of "local boy makes good," he easily won the 1938 Republican primary (Chou

1980). He served in the Hawaii Territorial House of Representatives until 1954,[3] when Democrats took control of Hawaii politics, and this speaker of the house lost the election by 31 votes. In 1959, Fong came out of self-imposed retirement and leveraged his coalition-building capacity (especially support from union workers) to win one of the two new US Senate seats. In 1964, Senator Fong became the first Asian American to run for his party's nomination for president of the United States. He received the votes of the Hawaii and Alaska delegations. He received the Horatio Alger Award in 1970 for outstanding accomplishments to achieve the American Dream through "honesty, hard work, self-reliance, and perseverance over adversity."[4]

Elected in 1956, **Patsy Takemoto Mink** was the first Japanese and Asian American woman to serve in Hawaii's territorial house. Mink was born in 1927 in Maui to Nisei, or second-generation, Japanese American parents. Her father was a civil engineer, and her mother was a homemaker. Her maternal grandparent arrived in Hawaii in the late 19th century to work on sugar plantations. After being passed over for promotion several times, her father established his own land survey company in Honolulu. Mink was initially not interested in party politics (Arinaga and Ojiri 1992). She turned to study law because none of the medical schools she applied to would admit women in 1948. Her father helped her open an office in the early 1950s after Mink was unable, being female, married with a daughter, and Asian American, to find a law firm in Hawaii willing to hire the first licensed Asian woman attorney (Arinaga and Ojiri 1992). Determined to seek social change, Mink became the first woman of color elected to the US Congress in 1964 and the first Asian American Democrat to enter a presidential primary race in 1972 (as an antiwar candidate in the Oregon primary). Mink's experience with racial and gender discrimination early on, both in the political and professional realms, fueled her conviction to advance women's rights and minority interests in Congress.

Jean Sadako King was born in 1925 to a white Canadian father and a Nisei mother whose family owned a coffee farm in Kona. She thought her mother "did a very courageous thing" marrying her dad in the 1930s (Nakanishi and Wu 2002). She felt that, perhaps because of this family history, having a mother who transcended racial lines in a deeply racist society, growing up she was never given the feeling that there were things that she could not do as a girl (Chu 1989). She was valedictorian and editor of the yearbook in high school. She was active in political organizing as a student, joining Hawaii Youth for Democracy and becoming an active canvasser for the labor union

40　CONTESTING THE LAST FRONTIER

movement. As the only female candidate, her first campaign was to be a delegate to Hawaii's territorial constitutional convention in 1950 (Robinson 2018). She ran on equal rights for women and minorities and an unsegregated school system. She served in the Hawaii State House (1972–74) and Senate (1974–78) before being elected lieutenant governor in 1978, making her the first Asian American woman to be elected lieutenant governor of a US state.

Ben Cayetano was the first Filipino lieutenant governor, serving between 1986 and 1994, and the first Filipino governor, in office from 1994 to 2002. He was born in 1939 in Oahu and raised by a divorced immigrant father from the Philippines. After barely graduating from a public high school, he worked various odd jobs. He decided to move his family to Los Angeles in 1963 and pursue a legal education after being frustrated by what he felt were racially motivated and politically unfair hiring practices (Wilcox 2014). Cayetano attended UCLA and Loyola University Law School and worked his way through graduation in 1971. Within a few years of his return to Hawaii, he won seats first in the state house, then state senate, from districts that were not predominantly Filipino, before winning statewide elections as lieutenant governor and governor of Hawaii. In a sense, his political rise from the ranks, representing the underdog in the fights against discrimination, has a Horatio Alger quality. However, he was also criticized for mistreating Native Hawaiians when he was the governor (Saranillio 2013).

The first Korean woman to hold a major US elective office is **Jackie Eurn Hai Young**. Born in Honolulu in 1934, Young is a third-generation whose grandparents arrived in Hawaii in 1904 to work on sugar plantations. Young's grandfather, Cho Pyung Yo, was dedicated to the independence movement in Korea during the Japanese occupation and was an active member of the Korean community in Hawaii. Having been socialized in a political family, Young recalls a childhood rich with passionate discussions about politics and community participation, all in the pursuit of equality of life for Koreans and Korea's independence (Lien and Esteban 2018). When asked why she entered politics, Young remembers her grandfather saying: "If you care for your family, you have to care about politics" (Osborn, n.d.). She says her community involvement began as a student at Punahou, where she participated in many extracurricular activities off-campus (Osborn, n.d.). Young did not start her legislative career until 1990, after years in leadership positions in state and national organizations that championed women's causes. In 1992,

The Firsts Elected in the Mainland States

On the US mainland, among those who entered electoral politics before 1980, the first elected Chinese, Japanese, and Filipina/o Americans would come decades after their counterparts in Hawaii. Not all of the pioneers were male, but except for Filipino Americans, the elections of the first women typically occurred at least a decade later than the elections of the first men from the same ethnic origin. Also, not all were elected in California or US-born. However, just like the situation in Hawaii, only the foreign-born elected officials attained a law degree before their first election, and they also attained a higher office level as state legislators than most other US-born pioneers.

Born in Guangdong, China, in 1905, **Wing Foon Ong** entered the United States at age 14. Impacted by the Chinese Exclusion Act, he was detained on Angel Island for three months for his documented claim to have a US-born father. He only entered the first grade in 1920 after moving to Phoenix to live with his uncle's family but graduated from high school six years later. He received his first taste of politics working as a houseboy for the state governor while in high school. With financial assistance from the governor's family, Ong was able to attend law school. He graduated in 1943 and opened his law office next to the family's grocery store. In 1946, Ong became the first Chinese and Asian American state legislator elected on the US mainland. He was elected to the Arizona State Legislature as a Democrat, overturning a narrow defeat of 17 votes in his first attempt in 1944.

Elected in 1956 as the first woman, first Chinese and Asian American, and first nonwhite to the Alameda County Board of Education, **March Fong Eu** was born in 1922 in Oakdale, California, to a US-born Chinese father and a Chinese immigrant mother from Guangdong. She grew up in the back of a family-run hand-wash laundry shop, and identified her low socioeconomic class background as what motivated her to improve her circumstances through education (Van Ingen 2017, 167). This pioneering woman had a bachelor's degree in dental hygiene from UC Berkeley, a master's degree in public health education from Mills College, and a doctoral degree in dental health education from Stanford. Fong Eu initially intended to teach high school but was dissuaded by a college counselor who believed it would be

42   CONTESTING THE LAST FRONTIER

very difficult for her to find a job because she was Chinese (Morris 1978). She shifted her studies to chemistry, but in another experience of racism, she was told that with her expertise in the sciences, she "could go back and help your people in China" (9). Before becoming an elected official, Fong Eu served as president of the American Dental Hygiene Association (1956–57), where she advocated for the status and rights of dental hygienists, who, she believed, are professionally undervalued and deserve the same respect and medical autonomy as nurses (Morris 1978).

The first Nisei elected to an office on the mainland, **Teruo "Bruce" Kaji,** was elected city treasurer of Gardena, California, in 1960. He was born in downtown Los Angeles in 1927 to parents who immigrated from Fukuoka prefecture in Japan. In California, his father worked as a repairman for Southern Pacific Railroad, and his mother stayed at home raising kids. When he was still in high school, he was incarcerated with his family in a US concentration camp during World War II and was drafted into the US Army from there. Trained as a Japanese-language interpreter, Kaji was stationed in Japan and the Philippines for the War Crimes Tribunal after the war. Having tasted both discrimination and patriotism early on, he returned to Los Angeles to earn a BA in accounting. He was very active in the local Japanese American community and established himself as a successful businessman and owner of a community bank before pursuing public service. He was instrumental in founding the Japanese American National Museum and became its first president (Vankin 2017).

Helen Kawagoe was the first Japanese American woman elected to an office on the mainland as Carson, California, city clerk in 1974. A Nisei by nativity, Kawagoe was born in 1928 and raised in Pasadena. Along with her parents and 13 siblings, she was also sent to concentration camps during World War II, but the family returned to their home in Pasadena after the war. Before being elected to city hall, she worked as public relations/marketing vice president of an area savings and loan association. This pioneering woman felt the pressure to conform to traditional roles in the early 1970s, for "there were few other Asians. In the local Asian community, the males said it was arrogant for a woman to run" (Chu 1989, 412). She served for more than 37 years and was known as the "mom" of Carson City Hall (Yamamoto 2013).

During the same year of 1974, and 20 years after the election of the first Filipino state legislator in Hawaii, **Thelma G. Buchholdt** was elected to the Alaska House of Representatives as a Democrat, becoming the first Filipina state legislator and the second Filipino American elected on the mainland.

Buchholdt was born in the Philippines in 1934 and came to Los Angeles, with sponsorship from her maternal uncle, to pursue a college education in 1951. She taught elementary school until the family moved to Anchorage in 1965. Buchholdt was active in the local community and ran a surprisingly close campaign for the Anchorage school board before scoring success in her campaign for the state legislature. She did not pursue and earn a law degree until after her legislative service.

The first Filipino American elected in the US mainland was **Leonard T. Velasco**, who was elected to the Delano City Council in 1972. Born in the Philippines in 1931, Velasco moved to the United States after college in 1953, settling primarily in Delano, the epicenter of the farm workers' five-year strike against grape growers in Central Valley. He was part of the Manong/Manang generation of Filipino/a immigrant workers who took part in the labor movement. He later joined the Filipino American Political Association (FAPA), which encouraged Filipinas/os to get involved in politics and helped elect Velasco and others to local electoral offices (Mabalon 2013; Rodis 2014). Velasco was a member of the Delano City Council for 24 years, including three terms as mayor. Meanwhile, up north in the Bay area, **Larry Asera** of Vallejo became the first US-born Filipino elected, at the young age of 24, to the city council in 1973. He is the grandson of one of the Filipino immigrants who first settled in Hawaii in 1906 and received graduate degrees in engineering and business administration. In 1976, he made history again by becoming the first Filipino elected to a county position as a member of the Solano County Board of Supervisors.

Other Firsts Elected in the Mainland States

For other major Asian American communities whose members arrived in the United States predominantly—if not entirely—after 1965, their community's first electoral victory was typically delivered in California, mostly by Asia-born men and women who were not trained in law. However, the two Korean American pioneers were exceptions in their nativity status. Again, when men were elected first, the first women elected from the same ethnic origin would not come until years, if not decades, afterward. However, both the first Taiwanese and Hmong American elected officials were women born in Asia.

For Asian Indians, it was **Dr. Dalip Singh Saund,** who blazed the trail to US mainstream politics. Saund was born in Punjab, India, in 1899. His

44 CONTESTING THE LAST FRONTIER

father worked as a construction contractor for the government and died when Saund was young. Neither of his parents attended school, but they highly valued education, and he was encouraged to seek the highest degree. He arrived in America through Ellis Island in 1920 during the heyday of anti-Asian sentiment. He wrote in his memoir that it was only with the support from the Sikh American community in California that he was able to complete a PhD in mathematics from UC Berkeley in 1924 (Saund 1960). Instead of returning to a colonized homeland where his family was concerned about backlash from his anti-British comments made in the United States, he moved south to California's Imperial Valley to work on a ranch run by friends from India. Although he later operated several farming businesses and owned the equipment, the contracts had to be put under a friend's name because of California's alien land law.[5]

Saund helped create the India Association of America in the 1940s to fight legalized discrimination against naturalization and landownership by Asian immigrants. He was first elected to a judgeship in Westmoreland, California, in 1950. However, the outcome was overturned because his naturalization was less than 12 months old.[6] When he ran again in 1952, he faced a barrage of discrimination and won by 13 votes. When the sitting Republican congressman decided to retire, Saund quickly announced his intention to run for the open seat as a Democrat and became the first Asian American elected to Congress in 1956 after winning 52% of the votes.

It would take almost four decades for the Asian Indian American community to see the election of the first woman from India. Born in 1951, **Swati Dandekar** moved to the United States with her husband in 1973, after graduation with a BS in chemistry and biology from Nagpur University and a postgraduate diploma from Bombay University. After the family settled down in Iowa, she became active in local community affairs and was elected to the Linn-Mar Community School District Board of Education in 1996 and served until 2002 when she won a race to the Iowa State House. In 2003, she became the first Asian Indian woman state legislator in the United States. After serving three terms as a state representative, she ran for the upper chamber and served as a senator between 2009 and 2011.

For Korean Americans, their electoral history begins with the election of **Alfred Hoyun Song** to Monterey Park City Council in 1960. Born in 1919 in Hawaii to sugar plantation workers from occupied Korea, his nativity reflected the group's early migration history to Hawaii. Song's mother emigrated as a "picture bride" at age 16 to be wed in an arranged marriage that eventually ended in divorce. Song was attending college in Southern California when the Pacific War broke out. He initially attempted to enlist in the navy but was turned away because he was not white. Song was able to join the Army Air Corps, which was directed by the US Department of War to treat Song as "any other friendly enemy alien" (Los Angeles County 2014). After the war, Song finished college and earned a law degree. He continued to suffer from racism after becoming the first Korean American admitted to the California Bar Association. After being prohibited from buying a house in Los Angeles due to racially restrictive housing covenants, he moved his family to Monterey Park, where he became the first Asian on the city council and later the first Asian elected to the state assembly.

Born in Sacramento, California, **Eleanor Kim Chow** was the first Korean American woman to hold an elective office in the United States. She served on the school board of Montebello, California, between 1971 and 1994. As the daughter of a single-parent Korean immigrant woman, Chow remembers, "My mother didn't speak English; we taught her to read and write. I had to translate for the family and to deal with my four brothers' problems at school" (Chu 1989, 414). The mother of three was active in community organizations, including Girl Scouts, PTA, the Montebello Chamber of Commerce, the Asian Pacific Family Center, and Republican Party groups. She had been recruited to run by the Asian community but waited until her children were older to avoid perceived conflicts of interest. She said the main thing that motivated her to enter politics was to make sure all children would have an equal chance (Los Angeles Times 1993).

The first Taiwanese, Hmong, and Vietnamese Americans did not get elected to office until after 1980. All had a refugee background and served only at the local level of office. **Lily Lee Chen** was born Lee Wanruo in northern China and fled with family at age 12 to Taiwan during the Chinese civil war. After finishing a college degree in Taiwan, she came to the United States in the late 1950s to pursue graduate studies in social work. She arrived at a time when the nation was struggling to deliver the promise of equal rights and opportunities for Black Americans and other disadvantaged minorities with whom she empathized as an immigrant woman of color (Arax 1985). Chen became the first Taiwanese American in US elective office following her 1982 election to the city council of Monterey Park, nicknamed "Little Taipei." Prior to that, Chen worked in human services for the County of Los Angeles and rose from a medical caseworker to a chief administer for families and children's services. She was also actively engaged in community

46   CONTESTING THE LAST FRONTIER

organizing and made frequent visits to the city hall to lobby for better city services such as traffic lights, parks, and the school auditorium.

Choua Lee fled from Laos at seven with her family and arrived in the United States in 1976. In 1991 she became the first Hmong American elected to public office in the United States, joining the board of education of Saint Paul Public Schools—as a 23-year-old college student. She set a precedent for young Hmong women to turn to community-based activism for public service (Lee 2019). Hmong—the word means "free"—people were forced to leave Laos because they aided the United States during the war in Southeast Asia and feared reprisals from the victorious communists. About half the nation's Hmong population lives in the Midwest, with the highest concentration in St. Paul, which has become a hub of Hmong American community over the years. In 2010, it was estimated that 45% of the Hmong population in Minnesota was under the age of 18, with the median age being 19.7 and 43% being foreign-born (Pfeifer et al. 2012). So Lee's nativity and youth were characteristic of the Hmong population. Although the refugee community faced severe resource challenges, the same report shows Hmong people in Minnesota had achieved a significantly higher citizenship rate (64%) among the foreign-born than the US average (43%) or state average (41%). As shown in later pages, Hmong Americans running for office would put this political capital into good use.

The first person of Vietnamese descent elected to a US public office, **Tony Lam,** entered the city council of Westminster in 1992. Born in 1936 in North Vietnam, Lam had the first taste of being a wartime refugee at age 10 when his family was forced to flee to the countryside (Lam 2002). Being separated from his family, he quickly learned to rely on his intelligence and instincts to survive. When the Vietminh won the battle of Dien Bien Phu in 1954 against the French, Lam and his family left North Vietnam for the South and became refugees a second time. However, he was able to reestablish himself by working as a local liaison for the US government and became a successful businessman. When Saigon fell to the communists on April 30, 1975, he evacuated with his family first to Guam and then to Camp Pendleton, California, where he worked as a community liaison. He owned a restaurant and actively participated in local ethnic community and Republican Party politics before being recruited by the party to run for an open seat that he narrowly won.

Democrat **Madison Nguyen** was the first Vietnamese American woman to hold an elective office when she won an election to a school board in

2001. Born in 1975, she and her family escaped Vietnam on a small fishing boat when she was four years old. Her father worked as a janitor, receiving a stipend of only $500 a month to support his wife and nine children. Madison worked in the fields alongside her parents as a teenager picking fruits in the Central Valley, an experience that helped her become a labor and civil rights activist. In 2001, hoping to encourage Vietnamese Americans to get more involved in local politics, she ran for a position on the Franklin-McKinley School District Board of Education and won (Valverde 2012). She seized an opportunity to enter the San Jose city hall in 2005 by defeating another Vietnamese woman candidate by a large margin and served on the city council until 2014, with the last three years of her service being vice mayor.

Patterns of Immigration Generation and Political Socialization after the "Firsts"

The preceding account of these political pioneers' family or personal immigration background and political socialization stories suggests that being foreign-born is not necessarily a liability in making a breakthrough in electoral politics. To the contrary, at least for Asian Americans, being foreign-born might be an asset for candidates in majority-immigrant communities that began to emerge in selected suburban localities on the US mainland after the 1970s. For both early settlers in Hawaii of Chinese, Japanese, and Korean descent and those of Chinese and Japanese descent who settled in mainland states before 1965, their political incorporation generally did not start to take shape until the arrival of the first US-born generation. This pattern is similar to European immigrants who entered between the 1880s and 1920s. However, rather than treating it as a function of time, the delay in Asians' entry to politics was influenced by racially discriminatory legal restrictions against Chinese and Japanese immigrants around the same time. US-born Asian women's entry faced further delay due to additional barriers linked to the intersection of race, ethnicity, gender, and class in their identity and group status.

For both Asia-born and US-born males, serving in the US military appears to be a critical stepping stone for incorporation. The first Filipino elected in Hawaii, Peter Aduja, entered at a young age as a US national with parents who worked on sugar plantations during Asian exclusion. His immigrant

48   CONTESTING THE LAST FRONTIER

success story could be attributed in part to his military service during World War II and the GI Bill, which paid for his law education. Born in Hawaii to Korean sugar plantation workers, Alfred H. Song enlisted in the army and finished his college and law education with the GI Bill. Bruce Kaji was born in Los Angeles to immigrant parents and also served in the US Army during World War II after living for three years in a US concentration camp. As told later in the chapter, military service played a critical role in incorporating Japanese American males in postwar Hawaii.

For the first Chinese elected on the mainland, Wing Ong, the immigrant success story would not be possible without his first gaining admission during Chinese exclusion through his father's alleged US citizenship, financial support from his uncle who helped him open a grocery store, and tuition support from his white boss and state governor, who helped him pursue a law degree. Leonard Valesco, the first Filipino elected on the mainland, completed his college degree in the Philippines. This farmer laborer turned business owner entered city hall through the organizing effort of the FAPA. The first Filipina elected on the mainland lived in Alaska, the 49th state admitted to the Union (just months before Hawaii's statehood). Thelma Buchholdt entered as a student sponsored by her uncle to attend college. Like Wing Ong, she did not score success in her first trial. Lily Lee Chen, the first Taiwanese American elected in America, also entered the United States to pursue higher education after college graduation in Taiwan; she lost her first campaign for the city council in the first majority-Asian city in America. Decades earlier, Dalip Singh Saund, the first elected Asian Indian American, also entered with a student visa (through Ellis Island) to pursue advanced higher education. His education and employment were sponsored by the Sikh community in Stockton, California. For the first woman and man elected from the Southeast Asian American communities, being foreign-born and of refugee background are common characteristics.

This quick analysis of the elections of the "firsts" underscores the necessity to consider the intersecting relationship of nativity (country of birth) and immigration status to other factors such as gender, ethnicity, locality, and political context. Given the dotted history of anti-Asian discrimination before 1965, Asian Americans of Japanese and, to a lesser extent, Chinese descent were about the only Asian ethnicities with a significant and continuous presence as settled communities in the new homeland across the Pacific. Yet for the Japanese in Hawaii, it was not their length of stay, but the rise of the second generation (Nisei) male war heroes in the early 1950s that provided the turning point in their political incorporation. For mainland Asian Americans of Chinese and Japanese descent, their incorporation was obstructed and delayed by exclusionary immigration acts and wartime incarceration. Chinese and Japanese American women suffered from additional, gender-based discrimination, which delayed their first elections. For Filipinos in Hawaii and on the mainland, their incorporation into mainstream politics was made difficult by their colonial history, class status as migrant workers, and political status as US nationals. Labor organizing became the predominant form of political participation for farm laborers, but breakthroughs in electoral politics were made possible by both the foreign-born and the US-born.

With the belated removal of racist restrictions against Asian immigration, a supermajority of today's Asian American population did not arrive until after 1965. They mostly settled on both the West and East Coasts and selected localities in between. For these newcomers from Asia (and their US-born ancestors who arrived before 1965), the lifting of citizenship restrictions and the arrival of voting rights for racial and language minorities in the post-1965 era have presented unprecedented opportunities for their incorporation. Yet the impacts of immigration on political socialization and incorporation can be complicated by the significant variations across communities in basic sociodemography, reasons for entry, contexts of exit, and existing family or community resources to help the process of adaptation and settlement.

To further illustrate and unpack the complex relationship between international migration and political incorporation, we present for the rest of the chapter the divergent socialization stories of a selected group of elected officials crucial to the development of political incorporation in each major Asian ethnic community. Our focus is on the various characteristics of political socialization related to family/group immigration history and treatment received in the host society. The discussion is segmented by nativity/immigration generation in Hawaii and mainland states and in loosely chronological order by the year of the first election of individuals serving between the mid-1950s to the first decades of the 21st century. In the order of presentation, it includes topics on the legacies of restrictive immigration legislation, wartime US military and internment experiences, children of working-class immigrant parents, pre- and early-adult migrants for education, and the 1.5 generation with a refugee background.

50   CONTESTING THE LAST FRONTIER

Nisei Wartime Heroes in Hawaii

US Senator **Daniel K. Inouye** was born in 1924 to Japanese immigrant parents in Honolulu. His grandfather was forced to migrate to Hawaii to pay off a family debt. His mother was an orphan adopted by native Hawaiians. She named Inouye after her adoptive father and expected her son to repay the debt to the Hawaiian people (Inouye and Elliott 1967). Upon turning 18, Inouye applied to enlist in the military but was denied entry because of his race as an enemy alien after Pearl Harbor. After petitioning the government to reverse its decision, Inouye volunteered again in 1943 and joined the army as a private, entering the fabled 442nd Regimental Combat Team. His unit famously rescued the "Lost Battalion" of Texans behind enemy lines in France. Inouye later lost his right arm in a return sweep through Italy, crushing his dream of becoming a surgeon (Inouye and Elliott 1967).

After experiencing the horrors of war and sacrifice to prove their loyalty, many Nisei veterans returned to the Hawaiian Islands with a new perspective and desire to change their second-class status in society. With assistance from the GI Bill, Inouye finished college and received a law degree from George Washington University. He practiced law in Hawaii before entering territorial politics in 1954 as part of the "Democratic Revolution." The desire for political, social, and economic change led many veterans in Hawaii to support the Democratic Party and align themselves with other prominent Nisei war heroes in 1954 when Democrats swept statewide positions and took control of the legislature long held by Republicans.

US Senator **"Spark" Masayuki Matsunaga** was born in 1916 to immigrant sugar plantation workers from Japan and grew up in a large family with four siblings from his mother's prior marriage. He participated in Reserve Officers' Training Corps (ROTC) while attending the University of Hawaii in Honolulu and joined the Hawaii National Guard after graduation before entering the US Army in 1941. He served as an original member of the separate all-Nisei 100th Infantry Battalion and later with the First Battalion of the 442nd Regimental Combat Team. Matsunaga fought in North Africa and Europe and was wounded in battle twice before being transferred to the Military Intelligence Service. Using the GI Bill, Matsunaga pursued a law degree at Harvard and graduated in 1951.

Matsunaga's interest in political office ignited early. While attending Kauai High School, he complained to his haole (white) social studies teacher about discrimination against Asians (Hall 1986). The teacher replied, "Run for office and fix it," Matsunaga recalled (Hall 1986). In 1954, along with Daniel Inouye and George Ariyoshi, he was elected to the Hawaii Territorial Legislature as part of the Democratic Revolution.

Governor **George Ariyoshi** was born in 1926 to Japanese immigrant parents in Honolulu. His father arrived from Japan in 1919 as a crewman on a Japanese ship. After graduating from segregated McKinley "Tokyo" High School, he was drafted into the US Army and served as an interpreter in Japan in 1944. He attended the University of Hawaii, also under the GI Bill, transferred to Michigan State University, and graduated from the University of Michigan law school. Encouraged by his teacher, Ariyoshi had embraced law as his goal since the eighth grade, and his father supported the idea early on. As a Nisei World War II veteran, Ariyoshi's political career began in 1954. He became the first Asian American lieutenant governor of Hawaii in 1970. When Governor Burns fell ill in October 1973, Ariyoshi assumed his constitutional role as acting governor and won the governor's race in 1974.

Ariyoshi comments on the formative role of ethnicity in his concept of leadership and representation. "As the first governor of Japanese ancestry," he wrote in an autobiography, "I felt a special obligation, and sometimes a special burden. From my background, I think you can see how the concept of haji came in. In Japanese terms, it was my job to avoid failure, to not bring shame on the family or on our heritage. I had to do well not only for my own sake, but for the sake of many others" (Ariyoshi 1997, 87).

Survivors of Wartime Internment

Born in 1931 to immigrant parents who were not allowed to become naturalized due to the 1924 National Origin Quota or "Asian Exclusion" Act, US Representative **Norman Mineta** grew up in segregated Japantown in San Jose. He was incarcerated with his family at Heart Mountain, Wyoming, during World War II. His father was a community leader who encouraged all to participate in community activities. His mother was equally active in San Jose's social life, serving in the parent-teacher association, volunteering with the church, and raising money for the American Red Cross. He served as the student body president in the last year of high school. After graduating from UC Berkeley, he served for three years as an army intelligence officer during the Korean War. He began his community involvement through the Japanese Methodist Church. He worked with San Jose's human relations commission

52 CONTESTING THE LAST FRONTIER

to assist displaced community members during highway construction, which led to his city council appointment in 1967 (Inouye 2013). He was elected to the San Jose City Council in 1969 and became its first Asian mayor in 1971 before being elected in 1975 to the US House of Representatives, where he served for 22 years. The highlight of his legislative accomplishments was the Civil Liberties Act of 1988, which offered monetary compensation and presidential apologies to surviving internees.

US Representative **Michael "Mike" Honda** was born in June 1941 in Walnut Grove, California to parents born in California. His grandparents migrated from Japan in the early 1990s. Honda and his family were incarcerated in Colorado, which Honda cited as pivotal to his political career, stating that "it taught me that if governments make mistakes, they should apologize" (Onishi 2007). Honda remained imprisoned even after his father joined the Military Intelligence Service. After being released from the Amache camp, his parents became strawberry sharecroppers. They eventually found more stable employment; his father worked for the Postal Service and his mother as a housecleaner (Onishi 2007). Honda attended San Jose State but left school to volunteer with the Peace Corps in El Salvador. He eventually earned a master's degree in education and went on to have a long teaching career.

Reflecting on how he decided to get involved in politics, Honda said that when he returned from the Peace Corp, he sought out a niche for himself and identified himself as an Asian American who spoke Spanish, which was a rare thing at that time. He joined the Chicano movement on his campus and followed the slogan of the Black Panthers: "If you're not part of the solution you're going to be part of the problem." In a radio interview in 2009, Honda recounted his resolve for public service: "I just decided that I'm going to be part of the solution. And I found out that politics is not a spectator sport. It's a participatory sport and that's what the founding fathers expected, and that's what the constitution required" (NPR 2009).

Honda got his first taste of electoral politics after being appointed to the San Jose Planning Commission by Mayor Mineta in 1971. In 1981, he ran for and won a seat on the San Jose School Board. In 1990, Honda became the first Asian American to serve on the Santa Clara Board of Supervisors. He was elected to the California State Assembly in 1996 to replace a termed-out white male. In 2000, he seized an open-seat opportunity to win back Mineta's congressional seat. Until January 2017, he represented a district with the highest concentration of Asian residents anywhere in mainland America, with high-tech manufacturing and computer science dominating the local economy.

California assemblyman **George Nakano** was born in 1935 to Nisei parents in a working-class neighborhood in East Los Angeles. Nakano and his family spent four years in two concentration camps during World War II. After serving in the California National Air Guard for six years, Nakano attained a master's degree in education and served as an administrator and vice principal in the Inglewood Unified School District from 1977 until his retirement in 1991. Nakano entered the Torrance City Council in 1980 as the first Japanese American to hold such office, serving until 1994. Soon after being elected to the state assembly in 1998 to replace a termed-out white female, he became the first Asian American to chair the Assembly Democratic Caucus. In 2000, Assemblyman Nakano authored the California Civil Liberties Public Education Act (A.B. 1914) of 2000, "which extended a grant program that teaches the experience of Japanese Americans before, during and immediately after WWII" (South Bay JACL 2005).

Born in San Pedro and raised in Gardena, **Warren Furutani** is a fourth-generation Japanese American (Yonsei) whose parents and grandparents were incarcerated during World War II. Beginning as a civil rights activist in the 1960s, he realized that the internment experience was always a reference point—the place to start a conversation when meeting another Nikkei for the first time. Furutani worked tirelessly to establish admissions programs for students of color at colleges and universities throughout the United States. In 1987, he became the first Asian American elected to the Los Angeles Unified School District Board of Education—the largest school district in California. While a board member, Furutani led the effort to grant honorary high school diplomas to Japanese Americans who were unable to finish high school because they were forced into concentration camps during World War II. Once elected to the California Assembly, he authored A.B. 37 (2008), which granted honorary college degrees to Japanese Americans whose education was disrupted due to their wrongful incarceration during World War II. He also spearheaded legislation (A.B. 1775 in 2010) to make January 30 an official day for honoring Fred Korematsu, who fought Executive Order 9066 in the US Supreme Court and whose conviction was not overturned until four decades after.

Descendants of Those Spared by the Chinese Exclusion

CA Assemblyman **Tom Hom** was the first Asian and nonwhite elected to the San Diego City Council in 1963. His grandfather arrived in San Francisco

54   CONTESTING THE LAST FRONTIER

in 1884 and was detained for three months under intense interrogation and cross-examination to prove that he was not a laborer but a merchant who belonged to the exempt class (Hom 2014). Hom's father entered as a teenage son of a merchant in 1909. Hom was born 18 years later in 1927 in San Diego Chinatown and did not speak English when he entered kindergarten. He remembered when his parents wanted to buy a house outside of Chinatown in 1947, they were barred by racist covenants from making the purchase (Chu 1982). Accompanied by a white agent, his stepmother won the white neighbors over by going door to door to introduce herself in very limited English. These early experiences help explain some of his progressive legislative actions as a member of the Republican Party, such as authoring the compensatory education bill (A.B. 938 of 1969), which funded programs to teach English to children of working-class immigrants. It was later renamed the English as a-second-language (ESL) program.

Paul Fong was three years old when his family moved from Macau to the Bay Area in 1955. However, his grandfather claimed to be the son of a US-born Chinese whose records were lost in the 1906 San Francisco earthquake (Knoll 2009). Chan Share was detained on Angel Island for two months in 1939 before being permitted to enter a country where Chinese could not vote, own property, live, work, get educated, or marry freely. This family history motivated Fong to fight for ethnic and racial justice. Fong called himself a "Silicon Valley homey" who met Mike Honda during high school when the latter taught science there and he was a football star (McLaughlin 2008). He attended De Anza College and received a BA and an MBA from San Jose State University. Fong later taught political science and Asian American studies at Evergreen Community College, utilizing grassroots Asian American organizing as his primary ideology. While the movement in the 1980s and 1990s focused on access to higher education for minorities, he extended that focus to include public sectors and create political institutions representative of minority concerns. Fong was first elected to the local community college board in 1993 and served until 2008, when the legislative term limit created an open-seat opportunity for him to get elected to the California Assembly.

Elected to the King County Council in 1973, **Ruby Chow** became the first Chinese American woman to serve on a city council. She was born on a fishing dock in Seattle's first Chinatown in 1920 to immigrant parents from Guangdong. Her father was one of the pioneers who built America's railroads in the West and later managed a fishing and canning company. Dodging Chinese exclusion, her mother entered from the Canadian border. Chow's father died when she was 12, leaving her mother to care for ten children at the bottom of the Great Depression. Her mother sold lottery tickets, the boys scavenged restaurant leftovers, and Ruby, the eldest daughter, dropped out of high school to work and help make ends meet. Chow later became a successful restaurant owner and entered public service to give back to the community. Chow's daughter said that the family would not have survived without the local Chinese community (Chesley 2008).

Elected first to the Washington State House in 1983, **Gov. Gary Locke** was born in Seattle in 1950 to a father born in Taishan, Guangdong, and an immigrant mother born in Hong Kong. In his early years, he lived in a public housing project. His grandfather left China in the 1890s for Washington, initially finding employment as a servant, washing dishes and mopping floors in exchange for English lessons, and brought his children and relatives over to America one by one. His father arrived at age 12 or 13 and operated a grocery store where Locke worked while receiving his education in Seattle's public schools. Locke said his father worked every day of the year and taught him respect for family, education, and hard work. Locke received a law degree from Boston University. Because his grandfather worked as a houseboy for a family in the Washington State Capitol, Locke jokingly threw in a line in his 1997 inauguration speech that it took his family a hundred years to travel one mile (Locke 1997).

Edwin M. Lee was born in 1952 in Seattle to immigrant parents from Taishan, Guangdong, China, who entered in the 1930s under the paper-son system.[7] Lee's father fought in the Korean War, worked as a cook, and managed a restaurant in Seattle before passing away in 1967. His mother was a seamstress and waitress. After receiving a law degree from UC Berkeley in 1978, he worked as managing attorney for the San Francisco Asian Law Caucus, where he helped advocate for affordable housing and the rights of immigrants and renters (Shih 2011). Before his appointment in January 2011 as mayor of San Francisco, he was the city administer under Mayor Gavin Newsom, who ran for and won the lieutenant governor race in 2010. Lee was considered a reluctant politician whose vow to not seek election if appointed was a main reason for his appointment. He broke the promise after being persuaded by a public campaign organized by civic leaders in Chinatown to run later that year, and he was elected (Alexander and Allday 2017).

56 CONTESTING THE LAST FRONTIER

Children of Working-Class Immigrant Parents

Whether born in the United States to Asia-born parents or born in Asia but arriving young with parents from Asia, the socialization background of many electoral pioneers was defined by their being the children of working-class immigrants. They include trailblazers we covered earlier, such as Yew Char, Peter Aduja, Hiram Fong, Ben Cayetano, March Fong Eu, and Alfred Song. This socialization background is well represented among the APAEOs who ran for office, including the five women and two men, three of them born in Asia, featured in what follows.

Patricia (Pat) Fukuda Saiki was born in 1930 in Hilo to Japanese immigrants. Her father was a tennis coach at Hilo High School, and her mother was a seamstress. She worked as a stewardess in college to help finance her education and taught history classes in middle and high schools after college. Her path to politics began in the mid-1960s when dissatisfaction with teachers' relative lack of autonomy in Hawaii led her to organize the first state teachers' chapter of the Hawaii Government Employees Association (Saiki 2018). Saiki recalled that the lack of women's representation was a reason for her to enter the first race: "When I ran for the House back in 1968, there were only two women in office. So I had to run on the campaign slogan of, 'This district needs a woman in the House'" (Flanagan 2002). In 1986, she became the first GOP congressional representative from the Aloha State.

Mazie Hirono was born in Japan in 1947 and had an abusive and alcoholic father. When she arrived in Hawaii with her mother and a brother at the age of eight, Hirono spoke only Japanese and had to work after school to help buy food and pay for rent. Her childhood ambition was to become either a social worker or a counselor, an interest she linked to witnessing the difficulties her youngest brother experienced after being separated for three years from his mother and siblings (Hirono 2021). The turning point for Hirono came in the summer of 1968 when she lived and worked with a group of college students and antiwar activists who volunteered for work with poor and at-risk kids. She began to identify as a feminist at that time (Totenberg 2018) when the mainstreaming of the feminist movement and the separate organizing of feminists of color took place. She started to get involved in politics, worked at the state legislature, and campaigned for others in the next few years. She served as a Hawaii state legislator and lieutenant governor between 1981 and 2002. In 2007, she became the first Asia-born woman in Congress and, by 2013, the first Asian American woman US senator.

Like March Fong Eu, **Judy Chu** has a mixed generation background. She was born in Los Angeles in 1953 to a Chinese immigrant mother who entered under the War Brides Act to marry her father, who was a second-generation Chinese American and World War II veteran (Merl 2009). Her father was an electrical technician for Pacific Bell, and her mother worked in a cannery and was a member of the Teamsters. Her paternal grandfather ran a Chinese restaurant in Watts, where Chu grew up in a predominantly African American neighborhood in South Los Angeles. This diverse childhood socialization influenced her desire and ability to build strong ties to labor and racial and immigrant minorities in her campaigns and governance. Chu attended UC Santa Barbara as a math major but became interested in politics when she enrolled in an Asian American studies class and was inspired by the activism of Pat Sumi, who spoke to the class. According to Chu, "It was the very first time it occurred to me that an Asian American woman could be a leader" (Merl 2009). Chu transferred to UCLA, earning a bachelor's degree in math and a doctorate in clinical psychology. Before entering the political arena, she was a college professor and a community organizer, initially to oppose an "English-only" anti-immigrant movement in Monterey Park in the 1980s. She became the first Asian American elected to the Garvey School Board in 1985. Before being elected as the first Chinese American woman to US Congress in 2008, she held elective offices at municipal, statewide executive, and state legislative levels.

Decades after Judy Chu set the path for launching her career by serving on the local school board, **Henry Lo**, a fellow Chinese American active in local Democratic Party politics, ran for the same board and secured a seat in 2003. Born in Los Angeles's Chinatown in the mid-1970s, Lo is the son of working-class immigrants from China. His mother was a seamstress in the garment district, and his father worked at a restaurant and simultaneously attended night school to earn a certificate to become a machinist. He mentioned during his campaign that it was through the hard work of both parents that he could study and go to college. He was recruited to attend Colby College in Maine and graduated with a BA in government. He also attended a state college part time and earned a master's in public administration. According to an interview for our project,[8] it was a belief in the social power of education that inspired him to run for the school board. Lo remained in the same office for the next 17 years until 2020, when he won a newly created district seat on the Monterey Park City Council.

58   CONTESTING THE LAST FRONTIER

Wilma Chan was born in 1949 in Boston to parents from China. She felt marginalized growing up, being often the only Asian girl in class and with immigrant parents. These early familial and educational experiences left a deep impression on her career and policy work, which featured women and children's health and welfare. She became involved in civil rights and antiwar activism in Boston Chinatown, attending movement study groups with other activists, mainly of Chinese descent. After earning her BA from Wellesley College in 1971, Chan moved to San Francisco and cofounded the Chinese Progressive Association in San Francisco, writing the first by-laws at age 22 advocating for the working class in Chinese and other minority communities. A commitment to community-based change motivated Chan to run for office, and it also facilitated her movement through the pipeline. Chan ran for a seat on the Oakland Board of Education and served there between 1990 and 1994, while pursuing an MA in administration and policy analysis at Stanford University. She then moved to serve on the Alameda County Board of Supervisors before getting elected to the California Assembly. Chan served as majority whip from 2000 to 2002, making her the first woman and Asian American to hold a majority leadership position in the state's legislature. She returned to serve on the Alameda County Board in 2011.

New York City councilwoman **Margaret Chin** was born in Hong Kong and immigrated to New York City in 1963 at age nine. Growing up in Manhattan's Chinatown and seeing her father "scratching out a living as a waiter in the Bronx" (Silverleib 2009) also left an indelible impression on Chin. Another significant early influence was an Asian American studies course taught by Professor Betty Lee Sung. Chin recalls: "Her class was the first opportunity for me to really learn about the history of Chinese Americans, and understand that our ancestors went through so much discrimination and struggles. It shaped the way that I want to contribute (to our community). It really was a turning point in my life" (Hong 2017). To pursue Sung's call for advancing equal opportunities for the city's Chinese workers, Chin helped found Asian Americans for Equality at age 20 in 1974. The primary purpose was to organize protests against the anti-Asian hiring policy of the construction company in charge of building Confucius Plaza, a government-funded housing project, in Chinatown. She was reputed to be a fierce advocate for the equal rights and protection of the city's immigrant Chinese workers long before her multiple campaigns and ultimate election to the city council in 2010.

Born in Quezon City in the Philippines in 1972, California attorney general **Rob Bonta** immigrated to California when he was two. Bonta's parents were heavily involved with United Farm Workers (UFW) movement, and Bonta grew up in a trailer near the UFW's headquarters. Bonta's childhood experiences were foundational to his political career: "I grew up going to rallies and demonstrations and with my parents strongly articulating their views about justice and how to be more fair and equitable" (Burnson 2013). Rather than becoming an activist, Bonta set his sights on becoming an attorney and being "the one who fights for the underdog" (Burnson 2013). He believed legal training was one of the most powerful ways to effect positive and profound change in the lives of those who needed it most. After being an attorney for the city and county of San Francisco, Bonta ran for and won a seat on the Alameda City Council in 2010. He became California's first Filipino state legislator in 2012 and its first Asian attorney general in 2021. Assembly member Bonta's reputation as an outspoken proponent for Filipino American rights and his excellent track record of "authoring bold, groundbreaking legislation and building strong coalitions" was cited by many in nominating him to be the state's chief law enforcement officer (Oriel 2121).

First-Generation Migrants for Secondary and Higher Education

As noted earlier, more than a handful of Asia-born individuals who entered the United States by themselves to pursue education made a name in becoming trailblazers in electoral politics within the first generation. Their successes defied the odds for political incorporation within the first generation predicted by the model for European immigrants who entered in the late 19th and early 20th centuries. The "honor roll" includes four of the pioneering "firsts"—Wing F. Ong, Dalip Singh Saund, Thelma Buchholdt, and Lily Lee Chen. Following in their footsteps and carving other pathways are individuals who entered the United States in pre-adult or early adult years and made their way to the electoral arena by leveraging the knowledge and skills learned in postgraduate education in the United States. Examples include six education migrants; five are women, profiled in what follows.

Elected in 1979 to the San Francisco Community College Board, **Judge Lilian Sing** was born in Shanghai, China, in 1942 and moved to the United States at age 15 to attend a Catholic school before a public high school in Beverly Hills. She credits her mother, a devout Catholic who sought to serve those most in need, as "a great influence" in her life, as well as her Catholic

60   CONTESTING THE LAST FRONTIER

schoolteachers, "who would go abroad and give up their whole lives to serve and to educate young girls." Sing obtained degrees in psychology and social work and worked in San Francisco public schools before graduating law school at Berkeley in the mid-1970s. Though encouraged by community members to pursue an appointed position on the San Francisco Municipal Court, Sing revealed that she confronted and fought racist and sexist stereotypes throughout her career. "They say, 'You're a judge? You don't look like a judge.' And I say, 'what does a judge look like?' . . . [Asian American women] face stereotypes, and we always have to overcome the issue of the glass ceiling. We always have to work harder than other colleagues who are not Asian, not female. . . . We don't get the equal rights. We have to strive for our rights. We have to struggle for what we achieve."[9]

In 1969, she cofounded Chinese for Affirmative Action. In addition to specializing in immigration law, Sing also had experiential knowledge of the lack of resources for newly immigrated Chinese Americans through her work at the Chinese Newcomers Service Center. This organization helps new immigrants with services that are essential for their transition and survival in the United States. In 1980, she became its first assistant director. From her living room, she cofounded, with Judge Julie Tang the Wah Mei School in 1974, the first and longest-lasting Chinese immersion school for preschoolers in San Francisco. Sing served for over 32 year on every division of the San Francisco Superior Court and was known as a "trailblazer, devoted community leader and mentor." In the same August 2015 press release announcing her retirement from the bench, Judge Cynthia Ming-mei Lee commented that Sing "set the example of compassion, dignity, collegiality and openness to new ways of achieving justice."

Elected in 1981 to the San Francisco Community College Board, **Judge Julie Tang** was born and raised in Hong Kong before coming to San Francisco in 1968 at age 18 to attend the University of San Francisco. Noting that it was the first time she experienced discrimination, she became very active on campus in Asian American studies and Asian American organizations (Chu 1989, 415). But even within these progressive community-led spaces, including campaigns for the first Asian American on the San Francisco Board of Supervisors, this immigrant woman was overlooked and made to feel ashamed of her accent—something she said she hopes to never lose "so that other Asian women who have accents will see that it is not an impediment to running" (Chu 1989, 413). Like Sing, Tang earned degrees in psychology and counseling education before earning a law degree at an elite university and was active in various grassroots community-based organizations, including ones that have brought international awareness to atrocities committed by Japan across the Asian Pacific region, including the racialized sexual abuse and exploitation of women and girls during World War II.

Born and raised in Hong Kong, **Michael Chang** moved to the Bay area after graduating from the Diocesan Boys' School in 1975. In an interview for our project, Chang mentioned that, once he arrived at the San Francisco State University campus, which was a major site for student movement, he immediately became sympathetic to the calls for empowerment and self-determination of the Asian American movement and saw its relevancy to the growing immigrant population.[10] Chang earned an MA in political science and East Asian studies and a doctoral degree in education policy from Stanford, awarded in 1989. He has been teaching at De Anza College since graduation and was invited to join an organization called Asian Americans for Community Involvement soon after his arrival on the campus. He was elected to the Cupertino School Board in 1991, then Cupertino City Council in 1995, and finally the county board of education in 2010.

Polly Low immigrated from Hong Kong in the late 1970s. She received her BS in math and computer science from UCLA and an MS from Loyola Marymount University. She has worked in the aerospace industry for over 30 years. She was active with the parent-teacher association, helping out with fundraising and other activities at the Chinese school her kids attended.[11] When someone was needed at city hall to express concern about constructing a Wal-Mart supercenter in the neighborhood, she was urged by her husband and friends to run for the Rosemead City Council. She thought her science background helped her think more clearly; her ability to articulate ideas made her a better candidate than some men in science. As a write-in candidate, she did not win in her first trial for office. She ran again in 2007 and won. She has been serving on the city council since that year.

Born in 1973 in Pune, India, **Kshama Sawant** grew up in a middle-class family and witnessed immense poverty resulting from the caste system. This consciousness led to the development of her radical-left political views and alignment with socialism. She graduated with a BS in computer science from the University of Mumbai and moved to the States with her first husband. Her interest in class disparity issues led her to pursue and earn a PhD in economics. Before running for office, she taught college classes and was an active organizer in the Occupy movement, locally resisting home evictions and foreclosures. Sawant is a member of Socialist Alternative, the national

62 CONTESTING THE LAST FRONTIER

organization that organized her campaign for Seattle City Council, on which she has been serving since 2014. Before getting elected, she ran unsuccessfully for a seat in the Washington State House of Representatives.

Born in India and raised in Indonesia and Singapore, Congresswoman **Pramila Jayapal** moved to the United States at age 16 to study at Georgetown. She earned her MBA at Northwestern and worked in various private and nonprofit sectors, mainly on economic development issues (Walsh 2017). According to her autobiography, growing up as a child immigrant in Muslim-majority and other cultures and being a US woman of color profoundly influenced her political development (Japayal 2020). However, her US community-based advocacy did not begin until after witnessing the widespread discrimination and violence against Muslim, Arab, and South Asian communities following the 9/11 attacks in 2001. In November 2014, after capturing 71% of the votes, she became the first South Asian American elected to the Washington State Legislature and the only woman of color in the state senate. She handily won an open seat race to the US House of Representatives two years later, becoming the first South Asian American woman in Congress.

1.5 Generation and Political Refugees

The term "1.5 generation" is often used to refer to foreign-born individuals who arrived in the United States before or during their early teens. It is used to acknowledge the lack of birthright citizenship of these child immigrants and suggests their greater ability, compared to than adult immigrants, to become acculturated into the US mainstream because of their youth. Political firsts such as Peter Aduja, Choua Lee, and Madison Nguyen belong to this class. Because Tony Lam entered the United States as a refugee in adulthood, his (re)socialization experience is somewhat different from other Southeast Asian American elected officials. In what follows we feature the stories of three child refugee immigrants of Southeast Asian descent who arrived in the United States between 1975 and 1983.

Ánh (Joseph) Cao was born in 1967 in Saigon (now Ho Chi Minh City), Vietnam. His father served as an officer in the South Vietnamese Army and was detained by North Vietnamese officials during the Vietnam War. At age eight, Cao immigrated to the United States with two siblings. He lived for the first several years in Indiana before relocating to Texas, where he earned a BS in physics from Baylor University in Waco in 1990. Cao's Catholic faith profoundly influenced his political socialization and later shaped his views on social policy (US House of Representatives 2018a). After college, he entered a seminary affiliated with the Society of Jesus, better known as the Jesuit order. He was sent to the Jesuit-founded Loyola University in New Orleans to study law and worked as an immigration lawyer and personal injury lawyer after graduation. Meanwhile, between 1996 and 2002, he served as in-house counsel for an organization seeking to aid the social and cultural assimilation of Vietnamese and other poor immigrants. As a community advocate for the Vietnamese community devastated by Hurricane Katrina, Cao's initial experience with politics came at the local level. In 2008, Cao was persuaded to join the Republican Party and run for Congress as a challenger to a nine-term Black Democrat indicted by the Justice Department for corruption. He pulled off an improbable election victory to serve in the House of Representatives for one term in the 111th Congress (2009–10).

Born in Laos in 1969 to a father who was a medic in the Vietnam War, **Mee Moua** and her family fled to Thailand when she was five and moved to the United States in 1978. She said in a recent interview that, as a child refugee, she "experienced firsthand the language, cultural and compassion barriers that hinder and deny vulnerable people's access to available public resources" (APAICS 2020). This experience prompted her to change her college major from premed to public policy. Moua obtained an undergraduate degree from Brown University, a master's degree in public policy from the University of Texas, and a juris doctor from the University of Minnesota Law School. She is the nation's first Hmong American elected to a state legislature and served from 2002 to 2011. Moua's victory broke barriers for Hmong women living within a patriarchal culture. It also signaled a change in mentality about their political participation. She later helped build a pan-Asian American coalition by working as the executive director of Asian Americans Advancing Justice, the nation's leading advocacy organization for promoting the civil and human rights of Asian Americans.

St. Paul city councilman **Dai Thao** was born in Laos in 1975 and experienced wartime atrocities firsthand when two of his sisters and a brother did not survive. When he was five, his family fled to Thailand, where he lived in a refugee camp until moving to the United States in 1983. Thao was raised by a single mother and grew up in extreme poverty in northern Minneapolis. He had to drop out of college to help his family deal with the housing crisis and later faced eviction for failing to make mortgage payments. These experiences had a lasting impact on Thao and shaped the reasons why he ran for office. When asked why he ran the first time, Thao said, "For too long, unjust structures have divided people by difference and driven development through the community, while routing opportunity and prosperity around it" (Jurewitsch 2013). When he ran for mayor in 2017, poverty was a top priority. "I was a kid growing up poor in public housing, fighting off the roaches and the mice so that I could have a meal, too, and we still have too many families that struggle like that. We just can't have that anymore" (MPR, KARE 2017). As early as elementary school, he spotted inequalities. He challenged his English as a Second Language teacher: Why weren't they learning what other students learned? Why were the expectations lower (Walsh 2017)? Before running for an open seat in the St. Paul City Council in 2013, he worked as a community organizer for Minnesota's Hmong population and for a faith-based social justice organization.

Conclusion

In this chapter, we strive to appreciate how the experiences of Asia-born APAEOs are qualitatively different from those of their US-born counterparts within the same ethnic community and the extent to which their experiences are gendered and racialized. By telling the socialization stories of pioneering elected officials, we convey the political significance of being foreign-born, children of immigrants who entered as refugees and students, or the 1.5 generation when running for and winning an office in the host society. These trajectories are complicated by traumatic events experienced both before and after migration, discriminatory immigration and other legislation, and issues surrounding societal biases related to race, gender, ethnicity, and class. Prior to 1965, Asian immigrants entered a settler-colonial political system rooted in white supremacy, male dominance, and capitalist exploitation inscribed in US law and civil society and that all but blocked the political incorporation of Asian Americans until (at least) decades after the arrival of each majority-male ethnic group. However, as settlers themselves whose arrival and community formations were structured by US white settler colonialism, they also benefited from the system that put indigenous peoples at a further disadvantage.

However, our study shows that being an Asian female, foreign-born, impoverished, and/or incarcerated did not create insurmountable barriers to individual political incorporation. Indeed, the meaning and significance of these socially and politically defined constructs and statuses are neither fixed nor uniform. Among Chinese and Japanese Americans in Hawaii and mainland states, second- and third-generation women pioneers were discouraged or prevented from running for office, lacked the opportunity to prove their citizenship via military combat, and were therefore not elected until at least a decade after their male counterparts. For children of working-class immigrants who came of political age after 1965, the liberalization of citizenship rights and burgeoning Asian American and feminist movements ushered in a new sense of pride in the struggles of their ancestors and passion for equality and justice that aided the entry of both women and men. Because of the many layers of adversity to overcome, there were many "Horatio Alger" stories for pioneering figures in the early history of each major ethnic community. The ability of these Asian American pioneers to overcome racism (and sexism and nativism in some instances) through hard work, education, and family values has provided some empirical backing for the "model minority" trope. Yet their electoral successes do not mean they were shielded from the negative impacts of these hostile forces during the campaigns and once in office.

In the next chapter, to facilitate a more systematic understanding of how international migration (and other factors) impacted the election and incorporation of Asians in the US electoral landscape, we employ a longitudinal, multiethnic, and multioffice database to present a statistical outlook on the APAEO population across selective timeframes and geographic contexts. By analyzing the distribution of the APAEO population by ethnicity, gender, nativity, and office level, we provide evidence at the aggregate level to answer questions regarding the extent of descriptive, sustainable, proportional, and substantive representation reached by APAs in national and selective local offices over time and in 2020. Focusing on Asians elected to California city councils, we also analyze the changing relationship between ethnic demography and ethnic representation at the municipal level between 1980 and 2020 and in 2020 alone.

3

Evolution of the Electoral Landscape

Expanding the Gender, Ethnic, and Geographic Horizons in Political Representation and Local Incorporation

To help interpret the significance of individual pioneers and their success stories in the context of the gradual opening and continuous expansion of the political landscape for APAs in the United States, we provide in this chapter a longitudinal perspective on their political rising. We do this by identifying continuities and changes in the contours and makeup of the earlier and more recent cohorts of elected officials of Asian Pacific Islander (API) descent since 1980. Particularly noteworthy in the trends is the significant rise of women, non–East Asians, and those in states other than Hawaii and California in both size and share among the APAEO population over the 40 years. These may reflect the continuous improvements in efforts by members of the APA community and our team in tracing and documenting the presence of APAEO women (and men) across the 50 states. It may also reflect the more aggressive actions in candidate recruitment and targeted campaign training for women by both parties and political organizations in recent years—a point we cover in the next chapter. Fundamentally, we believe this trend of diversification and expansion has largely shadowed the growth of the APA population during the period.

Employing a longitudinal, multioffice, and multilevel national database of APAEOs (described more extensively in Appendix B), we provide unprecedentedly detailed answers to the following questions raised for this chapter. To what extent and in which geographic direction has the APA electoral landscape evolved in the last four decades? What is unique about APAs elected in Hawaii as compared to those in California? How wide are the gaps in gender, ethnicity, and nativity across levels of office and selected geography among those currently serving? To gauge the degree of proportional representation, we calculate parity ratios by comparing the size of the gaps among elected officials to those found in the populations they represent.

Contesting the Last Frontier. Pei-te Lien and Nicole Filler, Oxford University Press. © Oxford University Press 2022.
DOI: 10.1093/oso/9780190077679.003.0003

Then, focusing on Asian city council members in California, we address how sustainable their political incorporation has been over the years. What is the relationship between demography and representation at the municipal level? Finally, for Asian state legislators serving in 2020 and earlier in California, how significant is local officeholding in their political ascension? And how much have electoral reforms such as term limits and district elections helped or hurt the electoral fate of Asians in California? We employ both individual and aggregate levels of data to help assess how factors such as race, ethnicity, and gender continue to structure the political representation of APAs into the third decade of the 21st century. We also provide new understandings of the extent of local political incorporation of Asian women and men in California.

From Protest to Politics

The number of Asian Americans elected to political offices has grown exponentially in the past four decades, since the first comprehensive national roster of Asian American elected officials became available in 1980.[1] This chapter begins by comparing and contrasting APA women and men holding elective offices between 1980 and 2020. The community's population experienced exponential growth due to the influx of migration from Asia after the liberalization of immigration policy in 1965. It was also a period when this nonwhite community's main form of political activism endured a significant change from protest to politics (Lien 2001a; Liu, Geron, and Lai 2008; Lai 2011). This transition to the politics of incorporation was influenced by structural and contextual changes happening both within and outside of the ethnic community after the fall of Saigon in 1975 and when neoliberalism in economic policy and neoconservatism in ideology took center stage of politics in the post-civil rights era. Lai (2011) breaks down the history of Asian American political participation from the second half of the 19th century to the present day into four stages, with electoral politics being the primary form from the 1970s to the present. Similar waves of political transformation occurred in African American and Latino communities as well.

Lai (2011) points out that presently Asian Americans are in the fourth stage of development. It started in the 1980s with the emergence of new sites of political incorporation in *ethnoburbs*, or small- to medium-sized cities whose population and economic growth were fueled by new immigrants

68   CONTESTING THE LAST FRONTIER

from Asia, who made up the majority or a plurality of the population (54). The suburbanization of Asian American politics," declares Lai, "represents a new dimension that is both unprecedented and uniquely different from African Americans and Latinos," whose anchor of local politics has been in urbanized areas (19). Focusing on California, Lai and Geron (2006) find that Asian candidates in these ethnoburbs were more successful than in larger urban areas because of the presence of common issue saliency and the development of key community political loci based on campaign organizations, community-based organizations, and the ethnic media. But Asian candidates' success in ethnoburbs was not just a California phenomenon. Half of the cities examined by Lai in states like Maryland, Massachusetts, Texas, Washington, and Wisconsin saw similar results. Data reported later in the chapter provide a more systematic and comprehensive examination and update of the phenomenon and thesis advanced by Lai and Geron.

Earlier, a study of the electoral history of Asian Americans notes that, with notable exceptions, mainland Asian Americans did not begin to run for public office with any regularity or success until the 1970s (Lien 2002, 78). Compared to their colleagues in Hawaii, mainland Asian Americans' entry to mainstream politics was about 20 years behind the visible entry of Japanese (and Chinese) Americans into electoral politics in the territory. This observation is verified in our account of the pioneering stories in Chapter 2 from the pre-1980 era, when electoral victories of Asian Americans were much more common in Hawaii than in the US mainland, and mainland victories were often found on the West Coast, especially in California. In fact, the nation's first systemic effort by Don Nakanishi in 1978 to enumerate the population of APA elected officials listed 76 individuals holding federal, state, and local offices in California and 60 federal and state officials in Hawaii.[2] Over 70% were of Japanese descent. These early statistics lend credence to Hawaii's continuing and lopsided influence as a place and Japanese as the ethnicity of dominance in APA electoral politics by 1980.

What explains the rise and sustained dominance of Japanese (and other Asian) Americans in Hawaii politics? What changes have occurred to the contours of Asian American politics between 1980 and 2020? We answer these questions in the following sections by briefly reviewing APAs in Hawaii's electoral history. Then we compare the 1980–84 cohort to the 2014-16-20 cohort in terms of size, office level/type, geography, and gender. Focusing on women's representation, we analyze the relationships between gender and level/type of office in the nation and the states of California and

Hawaii across the two time periods. We also pay attention to gender and ethnic differences within the foreign-born generation and how they compare to the US-born.

Rise of Asian Americans in Hawaii Politics

Hawaii is rarely discussed in the study of mainstream American politics, nor are the experiences of Asian American elected officials and voters. However, Hawaii provides a valuable case study for the potential of a functioning Western democracy to achieve multiethnic diversity and better gender parity in political representation. Hawaii is the only majority-Asian state in the nation, and it was majority Asian before the territory joined the union in 1959. With the sequential immigration of Asian workers between the 1880s and the 1930s, when a blockade of one ethnic group opened up the opportunity to enter for another, it seems logical to expect the eventual dominance of Asians in Hawaii politics after the coming of age of US-born generations. However, as briefly covered in the immigration history in Chapter 2, the fact of Asians being nonwhite and of various ethnicities in a white settlement territory/state where divide and conquer was the rule for plantation workers has not made it easy for the various ethnic communities to transition from demographic strengths to electoral gains. Some non-Japanese groups, such as Filipinos, have had a hard time getting equitable representation to the present day.

In the early 20th century, when the indigenous Hawaiian population was still a numerical majority but in decline, they remained proportionately represented in government and held the majority of appointed and elected positions (Fuchs 1961). Second-generation Japanese and Chinese Americans slowly increased their electoral presence two decades after Hawaii's unlawful annexation and the extension of birthright citizenship to Asians born in the new US territory. The dominant GOP recruited Nisei to become party members in 1917, the same year Democrat William Heen was appointed to a circuit court judgeship (Hosokawa 1969). Heen, who was part Hawaiian, would win Honolulu's city/county attorney seat in 1919, while other Chinese Americans also started to get elected to territorial and county positions throughout the 1920s and 1930s, including future US senator Hiram Fong. Whereas the Japanese population was much larger than the Chinese in the 1920s, none of the Nisei men, who all ran for office under the GOP banner,

70   CONTESTING THE LAST FRONTIER

were successful. Over the next decade, the Japanese community more than doubled its share of the electorate (to 31%) and secured 15.6% of the seats in the territorial legislature by 1940 (Haas 1992). In comparison, Filipinos/as were at an even greater disadvantage due to their colonized homeland, smaller numbers, and more recent recruitment to the bottom of Hawaii's plantation economy (Lien 2002). The racialization of the 1941 attack on Pearl Harbor led to the absolute denial of civil liberties and civil rights for Americans of Japanese ancestry (AJAs) and the immediate, albeit temporary, loss of what political power they had achieved. Zero AJAs served in the legislature during World War II; however, their numbers recovered such that they held 13.3% of the seats in the legislature following the first postwar election (Haas 1992).

During the postwar years, ethnicity rather than race or partisanship became the primary organizing principle of Hawaii politics (Okamura 2014). This transformation followed the International Longshoreman's and Warehouseman's Union's successful labor union activism, including the 1946 strike that brought together workers from different ethnic groups, mostly Filipino and Japanese, and achieved victories such as wage increases and bans on racial discrimination (85). These victories also resulted in the harassment and arrest of union leaders and an opportunity to leverage the momentum to revive the Democratic Party. Democratic Party boss Jack Burns recruited several Nisei veterans to join the party and run for office. At the same time, Nisei labor union leader Jack Kawano provided campaign resources in the form of campaigners and votes. In the historic election of 1954, seventeen Japanese American men (16 D and 1 R) were newcomers elected to the territorial legislature; they joined five AJA incumbents to make up nearly half of all legislative seats (Coffman 2003, 152).

While Japanese and, to a lesser extent, Chinese in Hawaii gained political power and enjoyed relative prestige in the second half of the 20th century, Filipinos/as, Native Hawaiians, and other Pacific Islanders continued to suffer from racial discrimination, economic inequality, and political underrepresentation in the Aloha State. Indeed, the ascension of AJAs provides a powerful antithesis to the model minority/perpetual foreigner trope and demonstrates the uneven access and power that can persist among Asian and Pacific Islander Americans (Lien 2001a, 2002). Although AJAs in general and AJA men in particular continue to be overrepresented in Hawaii politics, their dominance may be waning due to the rise of antiestablishment factions within both parties led by a new generation of non-Japanese API political leaders.

Growth and Transformation of the Population Structure of Asian (Pacific) America

As discussed in the brief migration history in Chapter 2, large numbers of male Asian (Chinese) migrant workers started to arrive in California around the mid-19th century. When Chinese exclusion laws closed the door of their immigration opportunity, another door opened for limited and selected numbers of Japanese (and Korean) immigrants to enter until 1924. When California blocked Chinese laborers from entry, they (and other Asian workers) entered the United States through Hawaii. Although the bans on Asian immigration started to lift during World War II, immigration of all Asian-origin groups was subjected to the highly restrictive and discriminatory National Origins Quota Act until 1965. Hence, the Asian population enumerated in the 1960 census was tiny in total size (less than 1% of the US population) but diverse in ethnicity, gender, nativity, and geographic distribution. According to the census statistics found in Lien (2001a, chap. 2), the Japanese were the largest group, comprising over half of the Asian population, and roughly evenly located in Hawaii and California. Over three-quarters of the Japanese population was born in the United States, and the gender ratio was roughly balanced. The Chinese population was less than half that of the Japanese and concentrated in California. Three in five were US-born, and the gender ratio was majority male. The gender ratio was even more imbalanced among Filipinos, who constituted about 20% of the total Asian population, had the highest share of foreign-born, and were the most geographically dispersed.

Over 50 years later, the Asian population as a whole has grown exponentially and transformed in ways that may have seemed unimaginable for a community barred from entering and banned from becoming citizens for the majority of the first half of the 20th century. As of 2017, Asians comprised nearly 7% of the total US population, and no Asian ethnic group had a majority presence in the Asian community. Nationwide and among Asians (alone or in combination with other races), the Chinese (excluding Taiwanese) population was the largest, but it made up less than a quarter of all Asians. It was followed in size by Asian Indians and Filipinos at slightly less than 20% each. Vietnamese and Koreans each made up about 10%. Meanwhile, the Japanese were only 7% of the Asian population. Groups at least 100,000 in population comprised about 10%; they included people who originated in South Asia other than India and those from Southeast Asia and

72 CONTESTING THE LAST FRONTIER

Taiwan. Between 2000 and 2010, the number of multiracial Asians increased from 1.6 to 2.6 million (or from 14% to 15% of the total Asian population). The population structure had also flipped when it came to gender and nativity. Females were the majority, and nearly two in five were foreign-born. Only among the two larger South Asian groups (i.e., Indian and Pakistani) did males comprise a majority of the population, and only among Japanese and Hmong were the US-born in the majority.

In terms of geographic concentrations, California and Hawaii were no longer the places where most Asian population lived. In 2010, Filipinos had the highest proportion (43%) that lived in California, followed by Vietnamese (37%), Chinese (36%), Japanese (33%), and Korean (30%). Fewer than one in five (18.5%) Asian Indians lived in California, even if the state also housed the highest share of the US Asian Indian population. In the same report of the Asian population in the 2010 census (Hoeffel et al. 2012), New York was the state with the second-largest proportion of Chinese (15%), Asian Indians (12%), and Koreans (9%) nationwide. Hawaii was the state with the second-largest proportion of Japanese (24%) and Filipinos (10%), while Texas was home to the second-largest proportion of the Vietnamese population (13%).

The Pacific Islander population in the United States is more difficult to enumerate because the US government first created the Hawaiian and Part Hawaiian categories in 1960, and only in 1980 did it include separate categories for Samoans and Guamanians (and an "Other" grouping). Coalitional impulses may have supported the fusing of Asian and Pacific Islanders into one racial category after the late 1960s when organized pan-APA / APIA (Asian and Pacific Islander American) /AAPI efforts surged. However, protests led by Native Hawaiian and other Pacific Islander organizations and activists led to creating a separate "Native Hawaiian and Other Pacific Islander" (NHOPI) racial category in 2000. According to the 2011–17 American Community Survey (ACS), an estimated 0.4% of the US population described themselves as NHOPI (alone or in combination with one or more other races). The three largest groups specified in that survey were Hawaiian (42%), Samoan (15%), and Guamanian or Chamorro (11%). These groups have roughly balanced gender ratios and are mostly US-born due to their homeland's status as a US territory or state. Nearly a quarter of Pacific Islanders identified themselves in the Other category, either because they did not specify an ethnic or ancestral group or did not report their write-in group.

Pacific Islanders are located predominantly in Hawaii and California, but ethnic and geographic diversity is again to be taken into account. Hawaii had the highest proportion of Native Hawaiians (55%) and Marshallese (33%) and the second-highest proportion of Samoans (20%). California was home to the leading proportion of Fijians (75%), Tongans (40%), Samoans (33%), and Guamanians or Chamorros (30%). Like Asian Americans, between 2010 and 2020, the growth rate of Pacific Islanders was the greatest in the South, followed by the Midwest (and the West) (Hixson, Hepler, and Kim 2012).

A Substantial but Uneven Rise in the APAEO Population, 1980–2020

According to the US census, the Asian population in 1980 was just over 3.5 million, and it surpassed 17.3 million by 2010, or growth of nearly five times in 30 years.[3] The Asian (alone and in combination) population was estimated to be 22.6 million in 2018, making it the fastest-growing population among major US racial and ethnic groups. A primary reason for the phenomenal growth was the continuous inflow of international migration from Asia. Whereas it may seem unrealistic to expect a comparable growth rate among elected officials from a majority-immigrant population, our research shows evidence of a substantial but uneven increase in the total number of elected officials during the same period. According to rosters of Asian and Pacific Islander American elected officials between 1980 and 2020, the national population of APAEOs defined in our study grew by 3.3 times. Marked by six yearly periods when reliable data are available, the total number of APAEOs has steadily grown from 178 in 1980 to 582 in 2020.

As shown in Figure 3.1, parallel to the growth of the national APAEO population, the number of APA women elected officials has grown more dramatically, from a mere 26 in 1980 to a historical high of 231 in 2020. However, despite a steady rise in women's representation, a substantial gender gap remains. Nationwide, women comprised 15% of the total APAEO population in 1980 and 21% in 1984. The share of women was 28% in 2006. It rose to 30% in 2014, 33% in 2016, and 40% in 2020. The accelerated rates of APA women elected officials in recent years might reflect impacts of the #metoo movement and other elements in the US national political scene after the 2016 election of President Trump, which motivated more women to run for office. This pattern is consistent with the higher growth rates of female elected

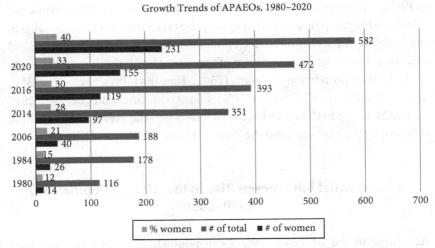

Figure 3.1 Percentage Women and Growth Trends among National APAEO Population, 1980–2020

officials of color compared to their male counterparts in the decade before the #metoo movement (Hardy-Fanta et al. 2016).

Continuing Marginalization of APA Women among Women of Color in Elective Office

How does the rise of Asian women compare to that of other women of color? Hardy-Fanta et al. (2016) trace the longitudinal growth trends of Black, Latino, and Asian elected officials in their landmark study. It reports the share of women among APAEOs to be 32% in 2012, which was lower than the 37% found among Black elected officials in 2009 (the last year with national data) or the 34% among Latino elected officials in 2012. Data from the 2019 National Directory of Latino Elected Officials show, among nonjudicial/law enforcement officials, the share of Latina women was 39%. A 2020 report on US state legislators who are first- and second-generation immigrants finds that the ratio of 36% female among APA legislators is significantly lower than the ratio of 56% female among Latina and Black legislators (Sedique, Bhojwani, and Lee 2020). To gauge the degrees of parity of officeholding by women of color as compared to their shares in the population, Hardy-Fanta et al. report parity ratios by race and gender for the 2012 cohort of US state legislators. They find that, at a .14 parity ratio, Asian women legislators are substantially underrepresented compared to Asian men and women and men legislators of Black, American Indian, and non-Hispanic white descent. Only Latina women suffer from the same level of deficit as Asian women in proportional representation at the state legislative level.

The main reason for the dismal parity ratio of Asian American women is the substantial lack of racial parity in the representation of Asian Americans in government. Data of elected officials in the top US cities in 2020 collected by the Reflective Democracy Campaign (2020) show that, out of a total of 1,180 elected officials on the record, only 3% are Asian, while 27% are Black, 14% are Latinx, and 53% are white. According to research by the New American Leaders Project, APAs account for 2%, Latinx for 4%, Blacks for 10%, and whites for 82% of the nation's state legislators in 2020 (Sedique, Bhojwani, and Lee 2020). However, among state legislators of the first and second generations, APAs account for 33%, and Latinx account for 43%. One might think the more severe gender disparity among APAs may be related to the influx of post-1965 new immigration from Asia and the vast nativity gap between Asian and other major racial and ethnic groups. Up to 67% of Asians are foreign-born, compared to 8% among Blacks and 40% among Latinos in the 2010 census. However, among the 2020 cohort of 154 APA state legislators, the share of women among Asia-born immigrants is higher than that among US-born persons of Asian descent (43% vs. 33%). We address this remarkable phenomenon in the section on the significance of being foreign-born for Asian women and men in office later in the chapter. We explore the politicization and incorporation of immigrant Asian women and men in political campaigns in the next chapter.

Variations in Growth Rates by Level/Type of Office, Gender, and Ethnicity

Although the APAEO population has experienced exponential growth since the early 1980s, the scope and direction of this evolution vary by level and type of office, and not all segments move in the same positive direction. Table 3.1 shows that, between the early 1980s and toward the third decade of the 21st century, the number of APAEOs in each level of office experienced continuous growth. The share of APAEOs holding offices at the federal and state levels has remained relatively stable, but the share of county officials has

76 CONTESTING THE LAST FRONTIER

Table 3.1 National APAEO Population and Shares by Level/Type of Office, 1980–2020

Level/Type Office	1980	1984	2014	2016	2020
	N (%)	N (%)	N (%)	N (%)	N (%)
Congress	7 (3)	7 (4)	12 (3)	13 (3)	20(3)
Statewide	4 (1)	5 (3)	6 (2)	7 (2)	7(1)
State legislature	60 (34)	51 (27)	107 (27)	126 (27)	155(27)
County	28 (15)	25 (13)	29 (7)	39 (8)	39(7)
Municipality	53 (34)	45 (24)	157 (40)	188 (40)	236(40)
School board	26 (12)	55 (29)	82 (21)	99 (21)	125(22)
Total N	178 (100)	188 (100)	393 (100)	472 (100)	582(100)

Source: Compiled by authors. See Appendix B for details.

significantly declined, while the proportion of municipal officials has significantly increased. At the school board level, despite a spike in its share of the APAEO population in the mid-1980s, school board members' share among APAEOs remains much smaller than those associated with the municipal officials. This last point on the relatively weak presence of APAEOs on local education boards, considered the entry point to elective officeholding, is a phenomenon unique to the APAEO population and different from descriptive representatives of other racial/ethnic communities observed by Hardy-Fanta and her coauthors (2016). It can be attributed to the dominance of APAs (especially Japanese Americans) in Hawaii since the mid-1950s, as well as the absence of locally elected education boards in the Aloha State. Yet, between 2014 and 2020, those serving on school boards and in Congress enjoy much higher growth than APAs serving in other office levels.

Moreover, gender ratios among APAEOs vary significantly across levels of office and time points. Looking at the percentage shares of women among APAEOs in various elective offices between 1980 and 2020 (Table 3.2), we observe that one outstanding pattern is the balanced gender ratio in 2020 compared to a complete absence of APA women in Congress in 1980. The other is the relatively high share of women in statewide offices, especially in 1980, despite the downward trend after 2014. In particular, the drop of 14 percentage points between 2016 and 2020 at the statewide level is contrary to the rising trend of women's representation in other office levels in this period. A third notable pattern is a consistent and substantial rise in women's representation among APA state legislators and county officials, especially among the latter.

EVOLUTION OF THE ELECTORAL LANDSCAPE   77

Table 3.2 Percentage Female by Level/Type of Office, 1980–2020

Level/Type Office	1980	1984	2014	2016	2020
Congress	0	0	58	46	50
Statewide	75	40	50	43	29
State legislature	15	24	29	33	36
County	4	20	24	33	43
Municipality	15	27	24	24	34
School board	23	20	40	48	53
Overall	15	21	30	33	40

Growth in women's descriptive representation at the local level is somewhat less consistent; the data show a similar surge of women's shares among municipal and school board officials in recent years. Whereas the percentage of women on school boards suffered some setbacks in the early 1980s, it steadily grew over the years and passed the 50% mark in 2020.

Reflecting the demographic and other structural changes in the APA community, we also observe a significant and continuous trend of expansion and diversification in the ethnic makeup of the APAEO population over time (Table 3.3). In the early 1980s, there was an overwhelming Japanese presence, followed distantly by Chinese and Filipinos, among APA elected officials. However, in over just four years between 1980 and 1984, we also observe a 10% drop in the Japanese share, a 4% increase in the Chinese, and a doubling of Pacific Islanders among APAEOs nationwide. Whereas those of Japanese and Chinese descent still accounted for over half of APAEOs in 2014, the Chinese took the lead in ethnic representation, even if they were no more than one-third of the APAEO population. In the 2016 cohort, Chinese continued to be at the top in terms of ethnic counts, but the combination of these two top East Asian groups no longer constituted the majority of APAEOs. The main reason for this appears to be the sharp rise of Korean American elected officials between the two time periods (see Lien and Esteban 2018), even if the numbers of APAEOs of Asian Indian, Filipino, Vietnamese, and Pacific Islander descent have also jumped. The trends of the declining dominance of Chinese and Japanese Americans, in addition to the rising presence of Asian Indian (and other South Asian), Vietnamese, and Hmong Americans, were sustained in the 2020 cohort. Meanwhile, between 2016 and 2020, APAEOs of Filipino, Korean, and Pacific Islander descent showed a slight dip in their

78   CONTESTING THE LAST FRONTIER

Table 3.3 National APAEO Population by Major Ethnic Origin, 1980–2020

Ethnicity	1980	1984	2014	2016	2020
	N (%)	N (%)	N (%)	N (%)	N (%)
Chinese[a]	26 (14.6)	36 (19.1)	127 (32.3)	136 (28.9)	176 (30.2)
Japanese	125 (70.3)	112 (59.6)	89 (22.6)	90 (19.1)	85 (14.6)
Asian Indian	n/a	n/a	43 (10.9)	53 (11.2)	75 (12.9)
Filipino	18 (10.2)	20 (10.6)	44 (11.2)	53 (11.2)	62 (10.7)
Korean	1 (0.6)	1 (0.5)	28 (7.1)	59 (12.5)	65 (11.2)
Vietnamese	n/a	n/a	19 (4.8)	26 (5.5)	38 (6.5)
Hmong/Laotian	n/a	n/a	11 (2.8)	13 (2.7)	25 (4.3)
Pacific Islander	4 (2.2)	9 (4.7)	18 (4.6)	27 (5.7)	29 (5.0)
Total	178 (100.0)	188 (100.0)	393 (100.0)	472 (100.0)	582 (100.0)

[a] Including Taiwanese.
Source: Compiled by authors. See Appendix B for details.

population shares, even if all ethnic groups (except Japanese) experienced continuous growth in the number of elected officials.

Assessing Proportional Representation by Ethnicity, Gender, and Their Intersections

To what extent does the percentage share of each major ethnic group of APAEOs approximate its share of the overall US Asian population? We use those APAEOs serving in 2020 to help illuminate the extent of proportional representation across major Asian ethnic groups at the dawn of the third decade of the 21st century. Table 3.4 presents ethnic parity ratios for APAEOs serving in 2020 and those at the intersection of ethnicity and gender. We calculate each *ethnic parity ratio* by comparing the percentage share in the APAEO population associated with each major ethnic group to the percentage share of the same ethnic group among the US Asian population using the five-year averages of the ACS (2011–15). A parity ratio of 1.0 indicates perfect representation, any score above 1.0 suggests overrepresentation, and any score below 1.0 signals underrepresentation. Nationally, Chinese Americans are 30.2% of the APAEO and 24.0% of the US Asian population, leading to an ethnic parity ratio of 1.3, a case of overrepresentation. When the Chinese count does not include Taiwanese, they comprise 22.5%

EVOLUTION OF THE ELECTORAL LANDSCAPE 79

Table 3.4 APAEO Ethnic Parity Ratios by Gender, 2020

Ethnicity	# Elected Officials	% Ethnic[a]	% US Asian Pop.[b]	Ethnic Parity	Women Ethnic Parity	Men Ethnic Parity
Chinese_1[c]	176	30.2	24.0	1.3	1.0	1.5
Chinese_2[d]	131	22.5	23.1	1.0	0.7	1.2
Japanese	85	14.6	7.2	2.0	1.3	2.6
Asian Indian	75	12.9	18.7	0.7	0.5	0.8
Filipino	62	10.7	19.0	0.6	0.4	0.7
Korean	65	11.2	9.4	1.2	0.9	1.5
Vietnamese	38	6.5	10.1	0.6	0.4	0.9
Taiwanese	45	7.7	0.9	8.6	7.8	9.5
Hmong	21	3.6	1.5	2.4	2.7	2.4

[a] The percentage share of each ethnic group of officials among the total of 582 serving in 2020.

[b] The percentage share of the total Asian population for each ethnic group based on the five-year average of the 2011–15 ACS data.

[c] Including Taiwanese.

[d] Excluding Taiwanese.

of the APAEO and 23.1% of the US Asian population, which leads to a parity ratio of 1.0, a case of equitable political representation. When Taiwanese are counted separately down the table, they have an ethnic parity ratio of 8.6, meaning the proportion of those in elected office is more than eight times their share in the population. The disparity in the methods of counting Taiwanese as elected officials in our APAEO database and the write-in option used by the US census has resulted, in part, in the superhigh ethnic parity ratios of Taiwanese Americans.[4] Homeland political tensions between China and Taiwan and anticommunist sentiment against candidates associated with Communist China but not those originating from Taiwan may be another factor to explain the significantly better ethnic representation of the Taiwanese. The group with the second-highest ethnic parity ratio, 2.4, is Hmong Americans, followed by Japanese and Korean Americans, which are other examples of overrepresentation relative to the share of each ethnic group in the Asian population. (In the last chapter, we explore the significance of community organizing and professional networking in Hmong Americans' success in the Midwest and Northern California.) Meanwhile, the ethnic parity ratios below 1.0 associated with Asian Indian, Filipino, and Vietnamese Americans show that their presence among APAEOs has

80 CONTESTING THE LAST FRONTIER

not reached proportional representation relative to their share in the Asian population.

Whereas the degree of proportional representation among Asian women across ethnic groups displays a similar order of ethnic disparity in accessing elective office, more groups of Asian women are underrepresented when we compare the share of women in each ethnic group of APAEOs to that of the general Asian population. The range of women's disparity ratios is also wider. Scoring at the bottom are Filipinas and Vietnamese American women at 0.4 each, followed in descending order of disparity by Asian Indian, Chinese (excluding Taiwanese), and Korean American women. Only four ethnic groups of women have reached parity in ethnic representation, and they are, in ascending order, Chinese, Japanese, Hmong, and Taiwanese Americans. In contrast, only three ethnic groups of Asian men do not reach parity in representation, and they are Filipino, Asian Indian, and Vietnamese Americans. Still, their parity scores are higher than their female counterparts. Among men, groups that have higher parity scores are Taiwanese, followed by Japanese and Hmong. Both Chinese and Korean American men have a parity score of 1.5.

Part of the reasons for the gendered differences in the degrees of proportional representation by Asian ethnicity lies in the varied degrees of shares of women in each ethnic group among the APAEO and the general population. In Table 3.5, we see women's percentage in each ethnic group of elected officials ranges from a high of 52% among Hmong to a low of 26% among Other South Asians, with an average of 40% across all groups. In comparison, the range of women's percentage for each Asian ethnic group in the general population is narrower, from a low of 47.9% among Other South Asians to a high of 59.2% among Chinese (except Taiwanese), and with an average of 52.2% female across all groups. How well do coethnics in elective office descriptively represent women in each ethnic group as of 2020? To investigate this question, we also calculated *gender parity ratios by ethnicity* in Table 3.5 by dividing the share of women (or men) among elected officials by the share of women (or men) in the population among each ethnic group. A gender parity ratio of 1.0 indicates a perfect representation of women (or men) in each Asian ethnic community; a ratio above 1.0 means overrepresentation, and a ratio below 1.0 signals underrepresentation of women (or men) in each Asian ethnic community in 2020.[5] By this scale, Hmong and Taiwanese have achieved gender parity among women, followed closely by Other Southeast Asians (except Vietnamese). With a women parity ratio of 0.53 and 0.54,

EVOLUTION OF THE ELECTORAL LANDSCAPE 81

Table 3.5 APAEO Gender Parity Ratios by Ethnicity, 2020

Ethnicity	# Elected Officials	# Elected Officials Women	% Elected Officials Women	% Female Pop.[a]	Women Parity	Men Parity
Chinese_1[b]	176	76	43	58.9	0.7	1.4
Chinese_2[c]	131	53	40	59.2	0.7	1.5
Japanese	85	25	29	54.3	0.5	1.6
Asian Indian	75	29	39	48.3	0.8	1.2
Filipino	62	26	42	54.5	0.8	1.3
Korean	65	28	43	54.4	0.8	1.3
Vietnamese	38	13	34	51.6	0.7	1.4
Taiwanese	45	23	51	52.9	1.0	1.0
Hmong	21	11	52	49.4	1.0	0.9
Other SE Asian	12	6	50	54.0	0.9	1.1
Other South Asian	19	5	26	47.9	0.5	1.4
Pacific Islanders	29	12	41	50.5	0.8	1.2
Total #/%	582	231	40	52.2	0.8	1.3

[a] Percentage female population in each Asian ethnic group and the Pacific Islander population based on the 5-year average of the 2011–15 ACS data for each of the top 12 Asian ethnic groups and the total NHOPI population. The percentage for "Other SE Asian" is the average of Cambodian, Thai, and Laotian population figures combined. The percentage for "Other South Asian" is from the Pakistani population.

[b] Including Taiwanese.

[c] Excluding Taiwanese.

respectively, women of Japanese and Other South Asian descent suffer the most from underrepresentation. Two other groups of Asian women who suffer from below-average representation are Chinese and Vietnamese. Finally, the degree of representation parity for Asian men is generally higher than women in the same ethnic group; and each group of men has an overall level of overrepresentation compared to their population share. The exception is Taiwanese Americans, where both men and women achieved parity, and Hmong Americans, where men are slightly underrepresented. Together, the picture of gender (dis)parity among all APAEOs displays distinct ways gender and ethnicity intersect to shape opportunities and barriers for political representation at the aggregate level.

Significance of Being Foreign-Born for Asian Women and Men in Office

To answer a question posed in Chapter 2 about the share of foreign-born immigrants among APAs holding popularly elected offices, we report in Table 3.6 a bird's-eye view of the APAEOs serving in 2020 segmented by nativity, ethnicity, and gender. Among the 527 (of the 582 in total) APAEOs in our database whose country of birth was identifiable, precisely 40% were born outside the United States and nearly all in Asia.[6] This figure continues the remarkable trend of similarly high shares of the Asia-born found among APAEOs serving in 2014 and 2016 and the figure reported by Asian respondents in the Gender and Multicultural Leadership (GMCL) survey of 2006–7. Yet, when we compare the foreign-born rate of 59% (or 73% among adults) of the Asian population in 2015, we see the 40% among those holding an elective office in 2020 as a case of severe underrepresentation of the foreign-born population. Moreover, reflecting the substantial differences in immigration history across Asian ethnic groups, the shares of the Asia-born are found to vary significantly by ethnicity. In 2020, the

Table 3.6 APAEOs Serving in 2020 by Ethnicity, Nativity, and Gender (%)

	# Asia-Born	% Asia-Born	% Women among Asia-Born	% Asia-Born in Pop.	Nativity Parity Ratio
Chinese (excluding Taiwanese)	24	22	38	60.5	0.4
Japanese	4	5	25	24.6	0.2
Indian	39	59	46	68.3	0.9
Filipino	16	29	56	50.6	0.6
Korean	33	57	46	60.4	0.9
Vietnamese	22	65	41	62.5	1.0
Taiwanese	38	84	50	63.9	1.3
Hmong	12	63	50	38.4	1.6
Other SE Asian	8	67	50	52.3	1.3
Other South Asian	15	94	20	63.1	1.5
Pacific Islander	1	0	0	0	0
Total # or %	212	40	44	58.7	.7

Note: Calculated among 527 individuals whose nativity status was verified. We were unable to verify the nativity status of 55, or 9.5%, of the 582 APAEOs serving in 2020.

EVOLUTION OF THE ELECTORAL LANDSCAPE   83

highest Asia-born rate of 94% belonged to South Asians other than Indians (e.g., Pakistani, Bangladeshi, Sikh, Sri Lankan, and Nepali), followed by that among Taiwanese (84%). Five other Asian ethnic groups in Table 3.6 have between 57% and 67% of elected officials being Asia-born. They include those born in Southeast Asia, India, and Korea. Elected officials from groups that have the longest history of US settlement also report the lowest foreign-born rates: Japanese (5%), Chinese (22%), and Filipinos (28%).

The third column in Table 3.5 shows that the shares of women among foreign-born APAEOs in each ethnic group vary significantly, but the range is not as wide as in the entire APAEO population. Among Asia-born APAEOs, Filipinos have the highest share of women, followed by an even gender ratio among APAEOs of Taiwanese, Hmong, and other Southeast Asian (i.e., Cambodian, Lao, Thai, and Burmese) descent. In contrast, immigrant women of Chinese and Japanese descent, but especially those of South Asian descent other than Indian, have the lowest rates of ethnic representation. In 2020, among foreign-born officials, women were 38% among Chinese, 25% among Japanese, and 20% among South Asians other than Indians.

The last two columns of Table 3.6 report the percentage share of the Asia-born in each ethnic population and the respective nativity ratio. We take the ethnic population count from the five-year average of the population estimates in the ACS for 2011–15. The *ethnic nativity parity ratio* is calculated by dividing the share of the Asia-born among elected officials in each ethnic origin by the share of the Asia-born in the same ethnic population. An ethnic nativity parity ratio of 1.0 indicates a perfect representation of the Asia-born population in each Asian ethnic community; a ratio above 1.0 means overrepresentation; and a ratio below 1.0 signals underrepresentation in 2020. Using this scale, the Vietnam-born are considered adequately represented. Those born in Asia of Taiwanese, Hmong, other Southeast Asian, and South Asian other than Indian descent are overrepresented. Meanwhile, those Asia-born of Japanese, Chinese, Filipino, Indian, and Korean descent are variously underrepresented by non-US-born elected officials in each ethnic community. The average ethnic nativity parity ratio is 0.68, suggesting an overall picture of underrepresentation of the Asia-born in elective officeholding in 2020. However, relative to the size of the Asia-born in each ethnic group, refugee migrants from Southeast Asia and those from Taiwan are doing exceptionally well in terms of their ability to win and hold elective offices.

How do Asia-born women and men and their US-born counterparts differ in the level/type of offices held? Table 3.7 shows that, among the Asia-born, a much higher percentage of men (54%) than women (37%) serve in elective offices at the municipal level, and only 35% of the Asia-born are women. Conversely, a higher percentage of women (32%) than men (19%) hold school board-level offices. Both Asia-born women and men share the same percentage as state legislators at 22%. Among the US-born, percentages of local officeholding are generally lower when compared to the Asia-born. In comparison, the percentages of those holding higher levels of office at the county, state, and federal offices are higher among the US-born than the Asia-born. This pattern seems to provide evidence of greater incorporation in the second or later immigration generations. Differences between US-born women and men in their levels of officeholding are generally more minor than their Asia-born counterparts. The exception is at the state legislative level, where a higher share is found among US-born men than women. Statewide offices appear to be the most inaccessible, while municipal offices appear to be the most accessible regardless of the nativity or gender of elected officials.

Finally, reflecting the centrality of immigrant women in the process of APA political incorporation and in terms of elective officeholding in 2020, the last two columns in Table 3.7 show that the share of women among immigrant APAEOs is higher than that found among US-born APAEOs (44% vs. 37%, respectively). Women born in Asia outnumber their male counterparts at the congressional, county, and school board levels, with the highest being 67% women among Asia-born members of Congress. In contrast, the office level with the highest share of women among US-born APAEOs is 48%

Table 3.7 APAEOs by Nativity, Gender, and Level/Type of Office, 2020

Level/Type Office	Asia-Born		US-Born		% F	
2020	Women N (%)	Men N (%)	Women N (%)	Men N (%)	Asia-Born	US-Born
Congress	4 (4)	2 (2)	6 (5)	8 (4)	67	43
Statewide	0 (0)	0 (0)	2 (2)	5 (2)	0	29
State legislature	20 (22)	26 (22)	36 (31)	72 (36)	44	33
County	5 (4)	4 (3)	10 (9)	16 (8)	56	38
Municipal	34 (37)	64 (54)	41 (35)	75 (38)	35	35
School board	30 (32)	23 (19)	21 (18)	23 (12)	57	48
Total N	93 (100)	119 (100)	116 (100)	199 (100)	44	37

among school board members. Why do immigrant Asian women fare better than men when it comes to ethnic political representation? We suspect one reason is the gendered division of labor in the immigrant community, where men strive for economic security while women may seek political influence after their primary caretaking responsibilities for the family are reduced. The other reason is gendered political party recruitment strategies targeting Asian (immigrant) women, which reflect gendered images of Asian American women as less threatening than their male counterparts for their success in incorporation. We explore the role of parties in detail in Chapter 4.

Evolution at the Subnational Level: Comparing APAEOs in Hawaii and California, 1980–2020

Because of the historically lopsided concentration of the APA population in the two Western states of Hawaii and California, we find it crucial to tease out the national data by adding geography as a factor that impacts the political representation of APAs in elective office. Hawaii had a total API population of 590,659 in 1980 and 916,390 in 2010, or a growth rate of 1.5 times.[7] Japanese comprised 40% of the state total of the API population in 1980, followed by 23% Filipino, 9.5% Chinese, and 3% Korean.[8] By 2010, Filipinos, Chinese, and Koreans increased their shares to 34%, 22%, and 5%, respectively, while the Japanese share declined to 34%.[9] California had a total API population of 1.3 million in 1980 and 4.9 million of the Asian-alone, or 5.6 million of the Asian-alone-or-in-combination, in 2010. When comparing the growth rates across ethnic groups, the declining share of Japanese in California is even more apparent than in Hawaii. Japanese comprised slightly over 20% of the total API population in California in 1980, compared to just over 7% of Asians (alone or in combination) in 2010. The vast disparity between Hawaii and California in the growth rates of the Asian population, especially between the Japanese and non-Japanese population, has been mirrored in the growth trends of the APAEO population in both states.

The growth patterns identified in Figure 3.2 demonstrate a seismic shift beyond Hawaii and California in the APAEO political map between 1980 and 2020. In 1980, a total of 91 APAs served in Hawaii, and they accounted for 51% of all APAEOs. In that year, 68 APAs served in California, accounting for 38% of all APAEOs, with the remaining 19 or 11% of officials elected in 10 other states. By 1984, 84 APAs in Hawaii accounted for 45% of all APAEOs and roughly the same number (86 or 46%) served in California, with the balance of the 188 officials serving in 9 other states. The sharp increase in the identification of APAs elected to school boards in California (from 25 in 1980 to 53 in 1984) appears to be the main reason for the reversal in the growth trend. Over three decades later, the 194 APAs serving in California accounted for 42%, while those 94 serving in Hawaii accounted for 20% of all APAEOs nationwide in 2016. In 2020, a historic high of 48% APAEOs served in California and those in Hawaii comprised a new low of 15%. In total, the 2020 cohort of APAEOs served in 38 states, with the largest group serving in California (277), followed by those serving in Hawaii (85), NJ (48), WA (28), and MA (19).

Geographic Representation of Asian Americans by State and Region in 2020

Where does the Asian population tend to congregate? How much has the population's geographic distribution structured the pattern of representation among the 2020 cohort of APAEOs? In the section, we present statistics to demonstrate that the places where APAs held elective offices in 2020 did not

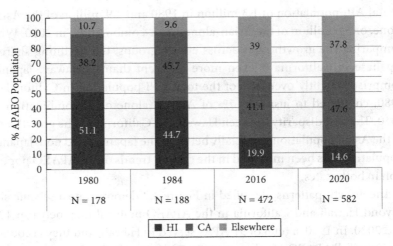

Figure 3.2 Shifting Geographic Makeup of APAEOs, 1980–2020

mirror the geographic diversity of the places where Asian Americans resided across the 50 states. To wit, about three in four APAs serving in an elective office in 2020 were from four states and all in the West region.[10] And yet, in the 2010 Census, the combined Asian population in these four states constituted less than half of the national Asian population (44.7%). Also, there are ethnic differences in the patterns of geographic distribution. However, no matter which way one looks, California's dominance in the general Asian population and the APAEO population seems invincible at the beginning of the third decade of the 21st century.

According to the census of 2010, close to half (46%) of the national Asian (alone or in-combination) population was located in the West. Moreover, nearly three-fourths of the US Asian population of 17.3 million resided in 10 US states: 5.6 million (32.1%) in California, 1.6 million (9.1%) in New York, 1.1 million (6.4%) in Texas, 0.8 million (4.6%) in New Jersey, 0.8 million (4.5%) in Hawaii, and 0.6 million (3.5%) in Washington. In comparison, among those serving in 2020, California leads the pack in accounting for 48%, or 277 of 582 officeholders nationwide. Hawaii is a distant second with a total number of 85, or 15%. It is followed by a distant third and fourth of 8%, or 48, in New Jersey and 5%, or 28, in Washington. Because the state's share of the APAEO population exceeds its share of the Asian population in each of these four states, we have a case of APA overrepresentation in elective officeholding in these states. Meanwhile, because just 1.5% of APAEOs, or nine each, are serving in New York and Texas, states that ranked second and third in size of the Asian population, this is evidence of a severe case of underrepresentation. The highly skewed and uneven geographic distribution of the Asian population and elected officials can be considered unique assets and challenges in the full and equal incorporation of APAs into US electoral politics.

Between 2000 and 2010, the South was the US region with the fastest growth rate of the Asian (alone or in any combination) population.[11] At a growth rate of 69%, it was twice as large as the West's growth rate, whose 36% growth rate was the lowest of the regions. Nonetheless, the West region continued to be home to the largest proportion of the Asian population. In 2010, at least two-thirds of Japanese (71%) and Filipinos (66%) lived in the West. Close to half of Chinese (49%), Vietnamese (49%), and Koreans (44%) lived in the West, as did 25% of Asian Indians in the United States. Moreover, six of the 10 places with the largest Asian populations—Los Angeles, San Jose, San Francisco, San Diego, Fremont, and Honolulu—were located in the West, and

88   CONTESTING THE LAST FRONTIER

five in California alone. Furthermore, among the places with populations of 100,000 or more, those with the highest proportions of the Asian population were Honolulu (68%), followed by four cities in California: Daly City (58%), Fremont, (55%); Sunnyvale (44%), and Irvine (43%).

At a rate of 57% Asian among the state's population, Hawaii had the nation's highest share of Asians (alone or in any combination) in any US state in 2010. It was home to the nation's second-largest proportion of Japanese (24%) and Filipinos (10%) in a state. Whereas California only accounted for 15% of the national Asian population, this state was home to the highest proportion of major Asian groups. Leading the ethnic pack are Filipinos, who had the highest proportion of 43%, followed by 37% among Vietnamese, 36% among Chinese, 33% among Japanese, and 30% among the Korean population that lived in California. Fewer than one in five (18.5%) of Asian Indians resided in California, even if the state housed the highest share of the US Asian Indian population. Only 8% of New York state's population was Asian, but it was home to the nation's second-largest proportions of Chinese (15%), Asian Indians (12%), and Koreans (9%). Meanwhile, whereas just over 4% of Texas's population was Asian, it was home to the second-largest proportion of the Vietnamese (13%) nationwide. Finally, Washington had 9% Asians in the state population. It was home to the nation's third largest proportion of Japanese (5.2%) and Vietnamese (4.4%).

Figure 3.3 shows the geographic distribution by ethnicity in the top four states of the APAEO population. Over half of the APAEO population in 2020 served in California or Hawaii, driven mainly by elected officials of Chinese, Taiwanese, Filipino, and Vietnamese descent who overwhelmingly served in California and by Japanese and Pacific Islanders who mostly held elective office in Hawaii. A plurality of officials of Indian and Other South Asian descent serve in California. Still, significant shares of South Asian American elected officials also can be found in New Jersey, and they are in equal proportions to the percentages of the US South Asian population residing in this state. New Jersey is also the state where Koreans are most likely to hold elective office despite the state having a much smaller share of the overall US Korean population. Although California and Washington were the states with the second and third largest Pacific Islanders population outside of Hawaii, respectively, Utah had the largest number of Pacific Islanders serving in a US mainland elective office. This pattern may be attributable to the history of Polynesian migration to Utah due to religious missions by the Church of Latter-Day Saints throughout Polynesia.

EVOLUTION OF THE ELECTORAL LANDSCAPE 89

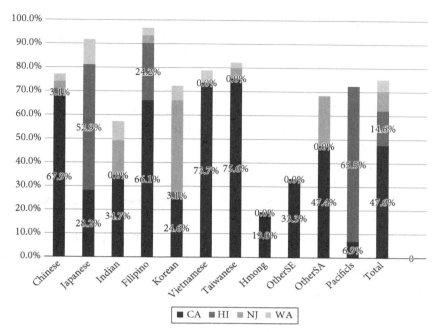

Figure 3.3 Geographic Distribution by Ethnicity in Key States, 2020

However, the difference was small (Utah led California by one officeholder in 2020) and may be more immediately traced to the post-2016 elections of two Pacific Islanders of Hawaiian, Tongan, Samoan descent to Utah city councils and distinctive barriers to Pacific Islander political representation in Washington (and California).

Within each of the top four states in Asian representation, the nativity gap among APAEOs varies widely and does not necessarily reflect the nativity gap in the overall Asian population. The nativity ratio is most skewed in Hawaii, where 91% of the APAEOs are US-born. However, three-quarters of Asians (alone or in any combination) in Hawaii are US-born.[12] In contrast, about two-thirds (63%) of APAEOs in New Jersey are foreign-born, and this figure is similar to the share for Asians (67%) living in New Jersey. Nativity is about even among the APAEOs in Washington (52% foreign-born vs. 48% US-born), which even more closely mirrors the nativity gap among the state's Asian population (54% foreign-born vs. 46% US-born). In California, a slim majority of APAEOs are US-born (57%). However, the overall Asian population is 58% foreign-born and 42% US-born. Together, these figures suggest

90   CONTESTING THE LAST FRONTIER

that, compared to US-born Asians, Asian immigrant candidates might have better chances of winning outside California or in states where Asian Americans in public office are still relatively few and rare.

Exploring Local Political Incorporation of Asian Women and Men in California Cities, 1980–2020

This part of the chapter focuses on developments at the local level and in the largest US state in Asian population. Our research examines the extent to which Asians have reached the goal of equitable representation and incorporation at the city council level between 1980 and 2020. We advance four interrelated ideas of political representation mentioned in Chapter 1 to measure local political incorporation. We investigate the empirical relationships between demography and measures of ethnic political representation both longitudinally and for those in service in 2020, especially along the gender line. Then, by tracing the trajectories of Asian state legislators, we assess the role of local service as a stepping stone to gain political influence. The chapter ends with an attempt to determine the impacts of structural reforms such as district elections and legislative term limits on electing Asians in California.

The primary data set used in this section was compiled from directories of APAEOs collected by Don Nakanishi (between 1980 and 2014) and James Lai (who joined from 1995) and published by the UCLA Asian American Studies Center. Our research team has extended the effort to compile the roster for the 2016 and 2020 cohorts. Limited in part by the availability of the directories as well as that of the decennial US census data, the APAEO data are segmented by eight time points of 1980, 1984, 1995, 2000, 2007, 2011, 2016, and 2020. The resultant data set represents APAEOs who served on the city council in California during the eight time points between 1980 and 2020. It does not reflect the entire population of APAEOs holding an elective office during the 40 years. However, we strove to be as inclusive as possible in our roster, which minimally enlists the name of officials, gender, ethnicity, the year starting and ending service, and the city where each was elected. We also collected demographic data associated with the municipality that elected Asians to the city council from the decennial US census for 1980, 1990, 2000, and 2010. In addition, we collected bios and other accounts of the political trajectories of the entire body of Asian American state legislators in Californian history until before the November election of 2020.

Summary View of Descriptive Representation by Asians on City Councils

In US politics, where underrepresentation is for racial and gender minorities a constant concern, a basic concept of advancing local political incorporation is to gain descriptive representation by winning local elections and having some presence on the city council. Taking a longitudinal and cumulative view, our research shows that in the 40 years between 1980 and 2020, roughly two-fifths of California cities, or 198 out of 482, had elected at least one Asian American to the city council. With few exceptions, especially before 2000, these cities often only had a single Asian (mostly male) on the council. By our rough count, of the total number of 555 seats (as of late August 2020) held by Asian Americans on city councils during this period, 149, or 27%, were held by women.

Table 3.8 shows the aggregate statistics of the number of California cities and their Asian demographics over time. In 1980, there were a total of 27 Asians serving on city councils representing 21 cities, which is a mere 4% of the cities in the state. Three of them were pioneering women councilmembers: Eunice Sato of Long Beach, Carol Kawanami of Villa Park, and Sue Hoff-Tsuda[13] of Fullerton. They accounted for 11% of Asian councilmembers back then. In 2020, the number of Asian councilwomen reached 48, which was more than a third of Asian councilmembers in California. The total number of Asians on city councils has grown by five times in 40 years, but the number of Asian women on city councils has grown even more during the same period, by 16 times! Meanwhile, the total number of Californian cities with Asians on the city council in 2020 reached 80 or four times the size in 1980. And the average percentage of Asians in these Asian empowerment cities has grown from 13% in the early 1980s to 31% in 2020.

These summary statistics show that there is an overall trend of sustained growth of ethnic representation over the years despite some ebbs and flows across time points. This trend is displayed by the continuing expansion of the total number of cities that elected Asians to the city council at each time point and of the number/share of seats held by Asians and Asian women. They provide evidence at the aggregate level of sustainable representation or the ability for a nonwhite, majority immigrant community to maintain some level of presence on the city council over a sustained period. Note that entries in the columns showing the percentage Asian, the city's population,

92 CONTESTING THE LAST FRONTIER

Table 3.8 Summary Statistics of California Cities That Elected Asians to City Councils, 1980–2020

California	Total Cities w/ Asian on City Council	Avg. % Asian in Cities	Avg. Pop. in Cities w/ Asian on Council	Avg. Asian Pop.	Total Asians on Council	Total Asian Women on Council	% Asian Females on Council
1980	21	13.39	91,479	6,544	27	3	11.11
1984	19	13.31	84,523	8,492	26	6	23.00
1995	29	24.86	107269	25,730	35	7	20.00
2000	25	31.24	178,177	45,903	36	7	19.44
2007	57	26.72	94,399	26,459	71	20	28.17
2011	75	28.93	98,092	29,398	111	34	32.43
2016	69	32.18	163,683	40,083	111	24	21.62
2020	80	30.94	146,457	36,847	138	48	35.00

Source: Compiled by authors. US decennial data of 1980 are used for the city populations for 1980 and 1984; those from 1990 are used for the city data of 1995; those from 2000 are used for the city data of 2000 and 2007; and those from 2010 are used for the city data of 2011, 2016, and 2020. See Appendix B for details on identifying elected officials of Asian descent.

and the Asian population in Table 3.8 are averages and do not tell us much about patterns of Asian incorporation given the significant variability across municipalities. However, we know it does not require a majority-Asian population to send Asians to city hall at any time, including in the early 1980s. In fact, in 1980, Asians could be elected as councilmembers in cities where they were as little as 1.45% of the overall population. This was the case for Eddie Nomura, who served on the city council of Sebastopol in Sonoma County, California, with a population of just over 5,595. The city has not been able to elect another Asian over the years. On the other hand, during the same time in Santa Barbara County, another Japanese American male, John Fukusawa, served on the city council of Carpinteria, where Asians were 1.57% of the city's 10,835 population. In 2020, the share of Asians in Carpinteria was still tiny, at only 3.34%, but two of the five seats on the city council were occupied by US-born Asian males of Japanese and Chinese descent: Wade T. Nomura and Roy Lee. In a later section we discuss the changing relationship between ethnic demography and ethnic representation by gender and nativity in these Asian empowerment cities over time.

Locating Sustainable Representation from Top California Cities That Elected Asians

In addition to examining whether there is sustained growth in the aggregate across time in each cohort of Asians elected to city councils, another way to measure political sustainability is by the ability for an ethnic community to retain at least one seat on the same city council over consecutive periods after the first, regardless of whether the same candidate(s) or a coethnic wins the seat. Toward that end, we examine the patterns of Asian representation in 30 California cities selected by their relatively high incidences of electing Asians to city councils in or after 1980, which coincides with the taking off of Asians elected in small and medium-size cities observed by Lai (2010). Table 3.9 shows the number of city council seats held by Asians in eight time points between 1980 and 2020 in top Californian cities of Asian incorporation at the municipal level. Entries in Table 3.10 display corresponding demographic changes between 1980 and 2010 in the same list of cities in terms of the growing shares of Asians in each city's population in each decennial census between 1980 and 2010, the size of each corresponding city's total population in 1980 and 2010, and the percentage change (mainly growth) in the size of the city's population between 1980 and 2010.

In the group of nine cities in California that elected Asians to the city council in 1980 and 1984, four cities (Monterey Park, Gardena, Union City, and Hercules) have consistently elected Asians in all eight time points over the next four decades. They are the cities where Asians received early local incorporation, and their empowerment at the municipal level has been sustained over time. Between 18% and 37% of the population in each of these four cities was Asian in 1980, which was generally higher than that in other early empowerment cities such as Fremont and Oakland, whose share of Asians in the city was less than 8%, respectively. Interestingly, over time, this group of early empowerment cities contains some of the lowest and highest rates in terms of the city's percentage Asian and its growth in population size between 1980 and 2010. For example, Monterey Park had the highest share of Asians in 2010 (68.5%), and the city doubled its share of Asians in the three studied decades, but the city's population growth rate was only 11% during the time frame. Gardena's share of Asian remained no more than one-third of the city's population over the years. There is only a 10-percentage-point increase in the city's share of Asians, even if the city's population grew by 30% in 30 years. In contrast, Hercules experienced a growth of 300% in the city's

Table 3.9 Top Californian Cities with Council Seats Held by Asians, 1980–2020

	1980	1984	1995	2000	2007	2011	2016	2020	Total Seats[a]	F/All[b]	%F[c]
Monterey Park	1	2[d]	1	1	2	3	4	4	18	4/11	36
Gardena	2	2	2	2	2	2	2	1	15	0/5	0
Fremont	1	1	0	0	2[d]	3	3	4	14	4/9	44
Union City	1	2	1	1	2	2[d]	2	2	13	1/5	20
Hercules	1	1	1	1	2	2[d]	2	1	11	1/7	14
Oakland	2	1	1	1	2[d]	1	0	2	10	3/6	50
Delano	2	2[d]	2	2	0	0	0	0	8	2/5	40
Cerritos		1	1[d]	1	2	4	4	4	17	3/10	33
La Palma		1[d]	1	0	1	2	2	2	9	2/6	33
San Francisco		2[d]	4	1	4	4	3	18		5/13	38
Cupertino			1	2	2[d]	3	4	2	14	3/7	43
Westminster			1	1	2	3	3[d]	4	14	1/7	14
Garden Grove			1	2	1[d]	2	3	3	12	3/7	43
San Jose			1	1	3[d]	3	2	1	11	1/7	14
Daly City			1	1	1	2	3[d]	3	11	1/4	25
Vallejo			1	0	1	2	4[d]	3	11	1/5	20
Carson			3[d]	3	1	1	1	0	9	1/4	25
Milpitas			1	2	1		1[d]	3	8	1/5	20
South San Francisco			1	1[d]		1	2	3	8	2/5	40
South Pasadena			1	1	1	1	1	1	6	0/3	0
Walnut				1	3[d]	2	3	3	12	1/5	20
San Marino				1	1	3	3	1	9	0/5	0
Diamond Bar				1	2	2[d]	2	2	9	2/5	40
Alameda				1	1[d]	2	2	2	8	2/5	40
West Sacramento				2	1	1	1	1	6	0/2	0
Alhambra					2	2	2	2[d]	8	1/4	25
Irvine					2	2	1	2	7	0/4	0
Colma					1[d]	2	2	2	7	2/2	100
Kerman					1	2	2	2	7	0/3	0
Temple City					1[d]	1	2	2	6	1/3	33

[a] Total seats held by Asians across time.

[b] Total number of women and all Asians elected to city council across time.

[c] Percentage of women among all Asian councilmembers.

[d] First Asian woman elected.

Note: Arranged in descending order by year of first Asian elected and total seats held by Asians.

population over the same years. The share of Asians grew from just over one-third in 1980 to about half of the city's population in 2010, even if the city's share of Asians only increased by 13 percentage points in 30 years. Delano also experienced exponential growth of 222% in the city's population, but the city's share of Asians returned to the same level of 14% between 1980 and 2010. But then, in both Cerritos and La Palma, the city's share of Asians grew by at least three times and reached majority status over the years. Still, both cities experienced no or even negative growth in the city's population. Hence, a preliminary examination of patterns in these early Asian-empowerment cities over a 40-year time frame shows no linear or clear-cut pattern in the relationship between changes in the city's population and its share of Asians over time.

Asian women's incorporation at the local level varies widely over time among the nine cities that had Asian representation on the council in the early 1980s. Oakland has the highest rates in percentage female among city elected officials of Asian descent at 50%, followed by the 44% female of Asian descent elected in Fremont and the 40% in Delano. In contrast, Gardena, a suburban city whose APA community has historically been dominated in terms of both number of, and elective officeholding by, US-born Japanese, stands out as the only city of early Asian incorporation with no Asian woman on the city council in the 40 years of our investigation. Even if Union City had Asian representation on the council early on, it did not have its first Asian councilwoman (Philippines-born Pat Gacoscos) until 2010. The first Asian women elected to city councils in California in early Asian empowerment cities include China-born Lily Lee Chen of Monterey Park, US-born Norma Nomura-Seidel of La Palma, and US-born June Fukawa of Delano. The first Asian woman elected to a city council in other early empowerment cities did not come until at least one decade later. Cerritos did not elect the first Asian councilwoman until China-born Grace Hu made the debut in 1992. The first Asian councilwoman in Fremont (Anu Natarajan, 2004–14) and Oakland (Jean Quan, 2003–11) did not make it to our database until the 2007 cohort. Hercules did not see the first Asian councilwoman until Philippines-born Myrna de Vera's election in 2010. Of these women pioneers, only Jean Quan held an elective office (on Oakland school board, 1991–2003) before her election to the city council.

Of the 11 cities that elected the first Asians to the city council by the mid-1990s, two were large cities with district elections (San Francisco and San Jose). Among these 11 cities, the highest share of Asians in the

96 CONTESTING THE LAST FRONTIER

Table 3.10 Demographic Change in Selected California Cities with Top Asian Council Seats, 1980–2010

	% Asian 1980	% Asian 1990	% Asian 2000	% Asian 2010	City Pop. 1980	City Pop. 2010	% Change in City Pop. 1980–2010
Monterey Park	33.70	57.46	63.62	68.50	54338	60269	11
Gardena	27.66	33.23	28.78	28.22	45165	58829	30
Fremont	7.20	18.90	39.81	54.54	131945	214089	62
Union City	17.75	32.30	46.91	55.28	39406	69516	76
Hercules	36.63	43.31	45.40	49.11	5963	24060	303
Oakland	7.76	14.76	16.62	18.88	339337	390724	15
Delano	14.66	21.54	17.64	14.13	16491	53041	222
Cerritos	22.07	44.80	60.72	64.62	53020	49041	−8
La Palma	12.75	31.11	46.75	50.72	15399	15568	1
San Francisco	21.71	29.13	32.63	35.83	678974	805235	19
Cupertino	6.84	22.90	46.30	66.04	34015	58302	71
Westminster	8.25	22.55	39.52	49.27	71133	89701	26
Garden Grove	5.99	20.51	32.22	38.58	123307	170883	39
San Jose	8.26	19.54	28.78	34.53	629442	945942	50
Daly City	27.98	42.50	53.56	58.44	78519	101123	29
Vallejo	12.7	22.0	24.2	28.26	80303	115942	44
Carson	15.34	24.97	24.24	27.58	81221	91714	13
Milpitas	11.92	34.67	54.34	65.08	37820	66790	77
South San Francisco	13.73	24.61	31.71	39.93	49393	63632	29
South Pasadena	11.33	21.25	28.82	34.52	22681	25619	13
Walnut	10.51	37.48	57.69	66.02	12478	29172	134
San Marino	6.68	32.30	50.30	55.90	13307	13147	−1
Diamond Bar	6.08	24.80	44.80	54.87	20845	55544	166
Alameda	13.2	19.3	26.1	35.55	63852	73812	16
West Sacramento	2.77	12.57	9.57	13.57	10875	48744	348
Alhambra	12.45	38.00	48.80	54.63	64615	83089	29
Irvine	7.78	18.10	32.33	43.27	62134	212375	242

EVOLUTION OF THE ELECTORAL LANDSCAPE 97

Table 3.10 *Continued*

	% Asian 1980	% Asian 1990	% Asian 2000	% Asian 2010	City Pop. 1980	City Pop. 2010	% Change in City Pop. 1980–2010
Colma	20.0	23.3	27.12	38.6	395	1792	354
Kerman	2.95	*	9.03	9.16	4002	13544	238
Temple City	5.07	19.38	40.32	57.40	28972	35558	23

Source: US decennial census data gathered in 1990 are used for entries in the "%Asian 1995" column. Similarly, Census 2010 data are reported in the "% Asian 2010" and "City Pop. 2010" columns.
Note: Arranged in the same order as in Table 3.9.

city's population was Daly City (42%), followed by Milpitas (35%) and San Francisco (29%), according to the 1990 census. The rest of the cities were at 25% Asian or below. Four cities on this second tier of incorporation became majority or near majority Asian (Cupertino, Milpitas, Daly City, and Westminster) by 2010. Three cities in this tier (San Francisco, San Jose, and South Pasadena) reached one-third Asian by 2010. Meanwhile, several others, such as Carson and Vallejo, whose city's share of Asians remained about 20% between 1990 and 2010. Again, there does not seem to be a correlation between percentage Asian in a city and the election of Asians to the city council within this group of cities.

In terms of women's incorporation over time among the 11 cities, both Cupertino and Garden Grove can boast having the highest gender ratio of 43% female of all Asians elected to its city council, followed by the 38% found in San Francisco. Only one city (South Pasadena) in this group has not elected an Asian woman to the city council. However, only two cities were able to elect Asian woman by the mid-1990s (San Francisco and Carson), and four of the cities did not have Asian women on the city council until 2016. The first Asian city council women elected in this second tier of empowerment include Hong Kong–born Mabel Teng of San Francisco. She was first elected to San Francisco Community College Board in 1990 and joined San Francisco Board of Supervisors in 1995. US-born Lorelei S. Olaes was the first Filipina American elected in Carson, at age 25 in 1993. In South San Francisco, US-born Karyl Matsumoto debuted her numerous terms on the city council in 1997. They also include Vietnam-born Madison Nguyen of San Jose (elected in 2005, after first elected to a local school board in 2001), Vietnam-born Dina Nguyen of Garden Grove (elected in 2006), and

Taiwan-born Kris Wang of Cupertino (elected in 2007). All of these women pioneers were immigrants from Asia, even if they entered at a different age.

In the rest of the 10 cities that did not elect the first Asians to the city council until 2000 or later, they feature some of the highest Asian shares of the city's population. Two of them (Walnut and San Marino) reached majority Asian in 2000, and three others (Diamond Bar, Alhambra, and Temple City) joined the majority rank by 2010. However, several of these more recent empowerment cities (i.e., West Sacramento and Kerman) remain less than one-sixth Asian in the city's population in the 2010 census. Only one of the 10 is a medium-size city (Irvine), six being small cities with a range of 20,000 to 100,000 in population size. The smallest of all, Colma, has the best rate of electing Asian women to the city council, however. Joanne F. Del Rosario, born in New York but raised partly in Manila, has been serving on the town council since 2006. In contrast, four of the 10 cities that have consistently elected Asian men since 2000 or 2007 have not had any Asian councilwomen by 2020; and the fifth city only elected the first Asian councilwoman in 2018. The first Asian women elected to these relatively recent Asian empowerment cities include Judy Wong of Temple City (2003–10), Mary Su of Walnut (2006–), Lena Tam of Alameda (2006–), Ling-ling Chang of Diamond Bar (2009–14), and Katherine Lee of Alhambra (2018–). All of these women pioneers except Tam, who was born in Guam, were born in Taiwan.

Between Demography and Ethnic Representation on City Councils

A quick look into the top 30 cities in California with the highest incidences of political incorporation of Asian Americans between 1980 and 2020 suggests that Asians were elected mostly from small- and medium-size cities. And the geographic landscape has been trending southward and inland as smaller cities have joined the Asian empowerment map. Of the 30 cities that have a fairly good and consistent record of Asian representation on city councils, only three had a population at or over 300,000 (San Jose, San Francisco, and Oakland) in 2010, and all were in San Francisco Bay Area. Of the five cities with a population in 2010 at or over 100,000 but below 300,000 (Irvine, Fremont, Garden Grove, Vallejo, and Daly City), three were also located in San Francisco Bay Area. Of the 12 cities with a population at or above 50,000 but below 100,000 in 2010, exactly half were located in Northern

California (Milpitas, Alameda, Union City, South San Francisco, Cupertino, and Delano). The other six midsize cities were located in Southern California (Carson, Westminster, Alhambra, Monterey Park, Gardena, and Diamond Bar). Five of these were in the Los Angeles County, with Westminster, in Orange County, the exception. Meanwhile, of the five small cities with a population between 20,000 and 50,000 in 2010, three were located in Los Angeles County (Cerritos, Walnut, South Pasadena), while West Sacramento and Hercules were in the north. Last, the four small towns that had a relatively good record of electing Asians were separately located in Los Angeles County (San Marino), Orange County (La Palma), Fresno County (Kerman), and San Mateo County (Colma). Finally, Delano, the city in the Central Valley that gave birth to the Filipino farmworkers movement, was unable to sustain the election of Asians to their city councils in more recent times, when the Latino population has fueled the city's growth.

Earlier research using national data shows a significant and positive correlation between ethnic share on the city councils and ethnic share in the city's population (Alozie 1992; Hardy-Fanta et al. 2006; Lien 2015). Can we find a similar relationship between demography and ethnic representation among Asians elected to California city councils? We answer this question first by examining the relationships developed in all the top 30 Asian empowerment cities between 1980 and 2020 identified in Tables 3.9 and 3.10. Looking longitudinally, we observe that the net change in a city's share of the Asian population between 1980 and 2010 is strongly and positively associated with the city's Asian share of council seats in 2020 ($r = .540$, $p = .002$), but it has no relationship to the total number of seats occupied by Asians in each city over the years. Also, we noted earlier that if we examine patterns in early Asian empowerment cities, there does not seem to be a linear relationship between changes in the shares and population sizes of Asians. An examination of all 30 cities confirms no significant relationship between growth in a city's population and its share of the Asian population over the years. In fact, there is an inverse relationship between the growth rate of the city's population from 1980 to 2010 and the election of Asians to city councils measured by the total number of seats held by Asians between 1980 and 2020 ($r = -.380$, $p = .035$). This finding suggests conflicts and competition between Asian immigrants and established (mostly white) local residents and other newcomers (i.e., Latinos) in cities where Asians have gained some traction on the city council (or the equivalent) over the years. It seems to echo what Lai observed in his 2011 book, where he commented on Asians being on the

100 CONTESTING THE LAST FRONTIER

tipping point of politics in localities where the influx of Asian immigrants created a sense of threat in white voters. This finding suggests the need for political leadership and community organizations to ease racial tensions and build cross-cultural bridges for people from different origins and shores to live harmoniously together.

A Closer Look at the Evidence of Proportional and Substantive Representation in 2020

We further explore the relationship between demography and ethnic representation by focusing on those Asians who served on the city councils in California in 2020 in order to disentangle the relationship between numerical growth in population and proportional representation at the local level. Among the 80 cities served by all 138 Asian council members, the average percentage Asian in 2010 was 31%, ranging from 0.01% in San Joaquin to 68.5% in Monterey Park, with half of the cities having an Asian population that was about 30% in 2010. Exactly half of these cities had a single Asian on the city council, one-third of which (or about 13) had two Asian members. The council seats' number ranges from four to 15, with over three-fourths (78%) of these city councils having five members and 14% having seven members. Here, again, we observe a strong and statistically significant correlation between percentage Asian in the city's population in 2010 and percentage Asian as a portion of the total number of seats on the city council in 2020 ($r = .635$, $p = .000$) or the number of Asians sitting on the city council in 2020 ($r = .600$, $p = .001$). This provides strong evidence that, at the dawn of the third decade of the 21st century, the level of Asian representation on city councils is tied to their ethnic density in the cities they reside in. This level of proportionality in municipal representation is a relationship not found decades ago. We believe this signals that the Asian community has reached a level of political maturity at the municipal level where nonpartisan community-based organizers and leaders, as well as partisan organizations, can leverage long-term infrastructure-building and turn majority-immigrant residents into local electoral gains. (We comment on the history and significance of some of these leading infrastructure-building organizations for political incorporation and empowerment in Chapter 6.) Together with the previous observation of more Asians being elected to more city councils as time goes by, we also see this as evidence of progress made in local incorporation and the importance of creating sustainable pathways and building the infrastructure for political incorporation in the long run.

Next, we examine the degree of proportional representation by the concept of Asian parity ratio, which is assessed by dividing the share of Asians on the city council by the share of Asians in the city's population. This exercise shows that exactly half of the 78 cities[14] reached an Asian parity ratio of 1.0, which is also the median value. The lowest value of 0.26 is found in San Jose, where only one of the 11 members was Asian despite Asians making up 34.5% of the city's population in 2010. The highest value is the 11.98 score achieved in Carpinteria, where two of the five members were Asian, elected from a city with 3.3% Asian population in 2010. The average Asian parity score is 1.69, suggesting that Asians are generally well represented in cities that elected Asians.

According to Browning, Marshall, and Tabb (1984, 1986), an indicator for minorities to achieve substantive representation is when they occupy the city council's dominant position. Looking at the number of Asian as a proportion of the size of the city council in California, we see that it ranges from as low as 9% in San Jose to as high as 80% in Monterey Park, Cerritos, and Westminster, where four out of five council members are Asian. There are seven cities where 60% (three out of five) of councilmembers are Asian. Three of them are in the south (Walnut, San Gabriel, and Rosemead), and four in the north (Daly City, Elk Grove, Milpitas, and South San Francisco). Fremont has four Asians on a city council with seven members (57%). Saratoga has two Asians among four members (50%). These statistics show that, in 2020, Asians reached the dominant position on the governing boards in 12 of the 80 cities (or 15%) in California. Meanwhile, in 19 cities two of the five council members (40%) were Asian, and two cities (Garden Grove and Vallejo) had three Asian members out of seven (43%). Thus, Asians in over a quarter of the Asian-empowerment cities have the potential to exercise influence on governing decisions. Viewed as a whole, the total of 33 cities where Asians constituted either a majority or a plurality of influence on the city council in 2020 was still a fraction of all the cities in California. Nonetheless, we believe this is evidence of substantial progress made in ethnic representation and local political incorporation by Asians since the early 1980s.

In sum, our examination of patterns of Asian incorporation into California cities over four decades reveals an overall pattern of sustained growth in the total number of cities and seats held by Asians, men or women, as well as an increase in the share of women among Asian council members between 1980 and 2020. The positive and significant relationship between population share and incorporation is only a recent phenomenon, suggesting that demography cannot be destiny. It takes local community-based leaders and organizations as well as other elements in the political loci to make political gains sustainable. Overall, it seems Asian women's representation on city councils may be facilitated by the growing presence of Asian immigrants in California cities, suburbs, and towns and community-based, grassroots organizations in the political loci. With few exceptions, once Asians were elected to a city council, then they or other Asians could continue to take a seat at the table. Having some presence of Asians on the city council signals open government and an environment of ethnic empowerment that generates, in turn, more interest by other Asians in participating in local governing.

Possible Impacts of District Elections and Presence of Asian Women

California adopted its state voting rights act (CVRA) in 2002 to make it easier to challenge jurisdictions that use at-large elections, which have been the norm in local politics and are considered upholders of white-male dominance on city councils and other governing boards. The CVRA explicitly prohibits using at-large systems if racially polarized voting occurs and if it impedes the ability of members of a race or language minority group to elect its preferred candidate. It also requires the government to pay all legal and court fees for the plaintiff should the plaintiff win; this includes cases in which the government chooses to settle before a verdict is reached. Levitt and Johnson (2016) find just 29 of the state's 482 incorporated cities used district voting before the law's passage. A report by California Common Cause identifies 59 of California's 482 cities that held district elections in 2016. Close to half (28) of those cities made the switch between 2011 and 2016. While Levitt and Johnson caution that progress would be slow coming, the pace of the switch has quickened since their report, and 96 cities made or were making the switch in 2018 (Walters 2018). Notably, as intended by the law, Latino members of local governing boards have increased. Has the CVRA had any impact on the election of Asians?

First, we ran an ANOVA test among the top 30 cities of Asian incorporation over time to see whether cities that adopted district elections (including the mixed system) are statistically different from those that did not in the

EVOLUTION OF THE ELECTORAL LANDSCAPE   103

total number of Asians and percentage Asian women on the council. Ten of the 30 cities adopted district elections, but we did not find much difference between the two types of systems for the election of Asian women and men to city councils during the study time frame. Then we ran the test only among those in service in 2020, when 27, or about one-third, of the 80 Asian empowerment cities in 2020 used the district system in municipal elections. Perhaps not surprisingly, those cities with district elections have a significantly higher number of seats on the council. However, somewhat surprisingly, we find those Asian empowerment cities with district elections to have lower shares of Asians in 2010 than those without (26% vs. 34%)—suggesting not only that Asians might not benefit from the law but that it may present a potential dampening effect on Asian incorporation. There are no other significant differences regarding district elections in our data set.

To assess the possible influence of Asian women elected officials on the local incorporation of Asians in California, Table 3.11 compares the demographic and electoral context between city councils that elected Asians and those with Asian women on board to those that did not have any Asian woman councilmember in 2020. Thirty-nine out of 80 Asian empowerment cities, or 49%, had at least one Asian woman on the city council. The two types of cities are also roughly equal in the share of adopting district-based elections. They do not differ significantly in the size of the Asian population, but the average population size of those cities having Asian women on the council is only half of those cities that did not have any Asian woman councilmember. In terms of the city's share of Asians, those cities having Asian women on the council have significantly higher percentages of Asians. Moreover, a significantly higher proportion of Asian empowerment cities that elected Asian women to city councils were cities with a majority of the city's population being Asian. Whereas the two types of cities are similar in the average size of the council, those cities having Asian women on the council have a significantly higher number and share of Asians on the council. Remarkably, a higher proportion of cities having Asian women on the council also served on councils with Asian dominance (at least 50% of councilmembers being Asian) or Asian influence (between 40% and 49% of council members being Asian). However, cities that elected Asians and had Asian women on the council have, on average, a worse representation parity ratio than those cities that did not have any Asian woman councilmember.

One takeaway point from this gendered exercise is that consistent with prior research, the election of Asian women to city councils is associated with

104 CONTESTING THE LAST FRONTIER

Table 3.11 Comparing Demographic and Electoral Context of Asians on City Councils in California by Gender in 2020

	Asian Women on Council	No. Asian Women on Council	All
# city councils	39	41	80
% city councils	49	51	100
% district elections	33	34	34
Avg. Asian pop. in city	35,687	37,950	36,847
Avg. total city pop.	95,930	194,520	146,458
Avg. % Asian in city*	36.5	25.7	30.9
% in majority-Asian city*	25.6	14.6	20.0
Avg. total council seats	5.6	5.8	5.7
Avg. # Asians on council*	2.2	1.3	1.7
Avg. % Asians on council*	39.6	24.2	31.7
% Asian dominance council*	25.6	4.9	15.0
% Asian influence council*	35.9	17.1	26.2
Avg. Asian parity ratio	1.4	2.0	1.7

* $p = .05$ or smaller.

cities having a higher share of coethnics in the population and on the governing board. This phenomenon is particularly true in cities with a majority of the population being Asian and with at least 40% of city council members being Asian. Asian councilwomen also tend to serve in smaller cities and with lower representation parity ratios. However, it is also worth noting that, in 2020, about an equal number of cities that elected Asians in California had at least one Asian woman on the city council. Although more research is necessary to better interpret the nuances in these contextual findings, Asian women's incorporation at the municipal level did not seem to be influenced by the city's electoral system.

Extending Local Successes to Winning State Legislative Seats

Extant research on the political trajectories of (mostly white and congressional) candidates and elected officials has adopted the dominant assumption of the "career ladder" model of officeholding. This is when candidates attain higher levels of office by leveraging resources and skills gained from serving at lower levels of office (Canon 1990; Navarro 2008). Hardy-Fanta et al. found mixed support for the standard "lower" to "higher" linear trajectory when examining the experiences of nonwhite elected officials who are predominantly Black and Latino. Among national GMCL survey respondents, just over half of state legislators were elected directly to a state legislature without holding a lower level of office, and the percentage is higher among men of color (60%) than women of color (48%). Among state legislators who held a prior office, less than one in five state senators served at a local-level office before entering the state legislature's lower chamber. About a quarter of state senators jumped from the municipal level, and another quarter were state representatives before entering the state senate.

In this section, we examine the extent to which Asians in the California state legislature have been able to turn electoral successes at the local level into gains at a higher level of office. We focus on the political trajectories of the entire roster of Asians elected to state assembly and state senate in California's history, beginning with Alfred Song, elected in 1962 from Monterey Park, and including those who were in service in the 2019–20 session. We also wish to comment on the impacts of electoral reforms, such as adopting legislative term limit rules on the political incorporation of Asians in California.

A total of 41 Asians served in the California State Legislature in the six decades between 1962 and August 2020, and they were overwhelmingly male (73%), Democratic (68%), and elected after 1990 (88%). By ethnicity, no group comprised a majority. About a third were Chinese (excluding Taiwanese), a quarter Japanese, 15% Taiwanese, and 9% Korean, followed by 3% Vietnamese, 2% Filipino, 1% Indian, and 1% Indonesian. Close to half (46%) were Chinese, if the ethnic count includes Taiwanese. More than two-thirds of this population served either on a local education or other elective board or city/county council/board prior to entering the state capitol, and one in five held both substate offices previously. Six served in the assembly before moving up to serve in the senate. That only four, or 10%, held no prior office suggests that the trajectories of Asians to the California State Legislature do exhibit a "bottom-up" quality. Yet even those who had not held prior elected office had experience in government, working as legislative staffers or serving in appointed positions. A higher share of women than men (18% vs. 7%) had no prior experiences of holding an elective office, and more women than men served on both local education boards and city/county councils or boards (27% vs. 17%) before entering the state legislature. Meanwhile, a higher share of men (57%) than women (46%) served only on city councils or county boards before arriving at the state capitol. Also, a higher share of men (17%) than women (9%) had previously served only on local school boards.

Sixteen, or 39%, of the legislators are non-US-born. The foreign-born rate is higher among women (46%) than men (37%). Gender gaps are also seen in that four of the five Asia-born women (80%) were Republican, but only three of 11 Asia-born men (27%) were Republican. Also, whereas all US-born Republicans were male, no US-born women were Republican. Analysis by nativity reveals differences between Asia-born and US-born legislators in their political trajectories. While the US-born comprised most of those who moved from city or county council to the state legislature, Asia-born state legislators were more likely to have served both on education boards and on city/county councils/boards. At the same time, those who held no prior office or jumped from school board to state legislative office, a smaller number to begin with, were indistinguishable by nativity status.

Legislative Term Limits: A Boost or Hurdle to Electing Asians?

Of the 41 Asian state legislators in California elected between 1962 and 2018, only five were elected before 1990, and the last one finished service in 1981. How have term limit rules impacted the electoral fate of the remaining 36 legislators? First, some history. The California State Assembly has 80 members elected to two-year terms. The California State Senate has 40 members elected to four-year terms. Legislative terms have been limited by two sets of laws passed by voters. This first set of legislative term limits was established by the passage (by a 52% to 48% margin) of Proposition 140 on November 5, 1990, which set a maximum of three two-year terms for assembly members and up to two four-year terms for state senators. The governor and all other statewide officers except the insurance commissioner can serve two terms of four years, with a limit of two terms. In addition, it imposed a lifelong ban against seeking the same office once the limit was reached. In June 2012, California voters passed (by a 61% to 39% margin) Proposition 28, which relaxed term limits by allowing legislators to serve up to 12 years in either one or both state legislative chambers. Members elected for the first time to the legislature in 2012 or later are subject to the new term limit rule.

According to McGhee (2018), the impact of Proposition 28 has been significant. Particularly in the assembly, turnover has plummeted to a 30-year low—from a peak of 50% in the 2012 election to just 8% in the 2018 election cycle. Turnover in the senate also shows signs of decline. Earlier research by Cain and Kousser (2005) on the impacts of Proposition 140 finds that term limits increased female and minority representation. It was a trend that was already underway in California (except for Asians), and postreform members were more likely to come from local government and run again when termed out. However, Cain and Kousser also observe a clear reduction in committee gatekeeping and amending of poorly written bills, and a clear increase in the hijacking of assembly bills in the senate. Of the 43 legislative seats[15] held by Asians after 1990, only 37%, or 16, were not related to term limits, and this percentage is higher among seats held by women (50%) than men (32%). In other words, the majority of Asian legislators can attribute their entry to the state legislature to the term limit rules imposed in 1990. However, less than one-third of Asian women and men (33% vs. 29%) were elected to replace seats held by termed-out white men. About one in seven (14%) was elected to replace seats held by termed-out white women, and the percentage is higher among Asian men (16%) than women (8%). Only Asian men were elected to replace termed-out Asian women (Ma and Hayashi) and Asian men (Eng and Fong). In addition, Ash Karla replaced termed-out Nora Campos, a Latina, in 2016. Janet Nguyen replaced termed-out Lou Correa in 2014. And Das Williams replaced termed-out Pedro Nava, another Latino, in 2010. On balance, it seems term limit rules passed in 1990 have facilitated the election of more Asian men than women legislators and contributed to enhancing racial diversity but not necessarily gender diversity in the state capitol. The relative lack of women in the pipeline such as on city councils might help explain the male dominance among state legislators.

However, of the 20 Asian legislators (involving 24 legislative seats) who were elected between 1992 and 2010, 13 were termed out; only four were replaced by a fellow Asian. Although there's much room to improve from the overall 31% ethnic succession rate, greater successes have been achieved after 2006, when four of the six termed-out Asian legislators were replaced by fellow Asians. Theoretically, 12 of the 14 Asian legislators elected in or after 2012 and in service until November 2020 could benefit from the 2012 extension of term limits—unless one opted not to seek reelection or lost the reelection bid. Tyler Diep (R, AD-72) is one such case in the latter scenario due to his defeat in the June 2020 primary by a fellow Vietnamese American. His seat was taken by former state senator Janet Nguyen, who defeated Garden Grove city councilwoman Deidre Thu-ha Nguyen in November 2020. All three were born in Vietnam and entered as refugees. Senator Ling-ling Chang also suffered defeat in a rematch of the 2018 recall election against a white male. Meanwhile, both Kansen Chu and Todd Gloria decided to seek a different office. In November 2020, Gloria was elected San Diego mayor, where he once served as an acting mayor before arriving at the assembly four years earlier. Chu's seat, however, was assumed by a 25-year old legislative aide and openly bisexual Alex Lee, who outdid seven other Democrats in the June primary race and won the general election overwhelmingly. Another Asian newcomer to the state legislature in 2021 is Senator Dave Min, son of Korean immigrants and a nationally recognized economic policy expert and business law professor, who defeated the Republican incumbent. We provide more comments on patterns of Asian ethnic partisan campaign dynamics in Chapter 4.

Conclusion

To help assess the significance of the political rise of APA women and men in elective office in recent decades, we provide in this chapter a longitudinal perspective on the continuities and changes in the contours and makeup of the electoral landscape of APAs. We begin with a brief account of the rise and sustained presence of Japanese (and other Asian) Americans in Hawaii politics to showcase the challenges and possibilities of political incorporation for a very diverse nonwhite population since the early 20th century. Employing both individual and aggregate levels of data gathered across time and space, we document the substantial but uneven growth of APAEOs between 1980 and 2020. We find that whereas the shares of women have steadily grown, significant gender gaps remain, and gender ratios among APAEOs vary significantly across levels of office and time periods. In addition, we observe a significant and continuous trend of expansion and diversification in the ethnic makeup among APAEOs. Based on data collected in 2020, we also assess the degrees of proportional representation by gender, ethnicity, and nativity and find disparate evidence of overrepresentation, near parity, and underrepresentation among APA groups—evidence that debunks the perpetual underachiever image of Asian Americans in political representation.

Although comparative statistics at the national level show Asians at a persistent disadvantage in descriptive representation by race and gender, our research unveils a more complex and dynamic picture of their political incorporation when we tease out differences among APAEOs by states and localities across time. Our findings from a longitudinal assessment of the extent of Asian incorporation in California city councils are instructive of the dimensions of political sustainability of this rapidly growing and largely majority-immigrant population. Our discovery of a linear relationship between ethnic density and ethnic representation in 2020 signals the community's arrival to turn demographic gains into local political incorporation—an ability that reflects the growing strength of the community-based infrastructure for ethnic empowerment. To what extent and in what ways have political parties (and other groups and organizations in the political structure) played a role in the growing presence of Asian candidates and elected officials in California and elsewhere? This is one of the main questions we answer in the next chapter and the closing chapter.

4

Getting Connected and Elected
with Political Parties

Congresswoman Judy Chu was a Garvey school board member in the mid-1980s when she provided the very first glimpse into the racial and gender dynamics of attaining and maintaining elective office from the perspective and experiences of Asian American women who served predominantly at the local level. Among the informants in Chu (1989), in chronological order of the first elective office held, were women trailblazers that we feature in Chapter 2: Patsy Mink, March Fong Eu, Eleanor King Chow, Jean Sadako King, Thelma Buchholdt, Helen Kawagoe, Lilian Sing, Julie Tang, and Lily Lee Chen. Many explained that they initially did not plan to run for office, nor was their first campaign endorsed by a political party. Yet most had extensive experience in community-based organizations and groups like parent-teacher associations and local ethnic-specific Democratic clubs, where they developed critical civic skills and support networks. Some attributed their success to encouragement from their husbands and children. In addition to personal tenacity, other reasons for their campaign successes include uniqueness in the physical appearance of being nonwhite and racialized gender stereotypes of Asian women as competent and nonthreatening. Nonetheless, an analysis of their trajectories to office also reveals struggles with patriarchal gender norms within ethnic communities and perceptions of racialized inferiority and foreignness associated with being Asian women. These pioneering political women emphasized the importance of mentorship and building networks and coalitions within and beyond the APA community—factors they reported were absent or hard to come by when there were few role models during their time.

Our account in Chapter 3 of the substantial but uneven growth of APA women and men in elective offices across ethnicity, nativity, level of office, and geography since 1980 begs the question of how much or how little has changed since Chu's (1989) landmark study conducted over three decades

Contesting the Last Frontier. Pei-te Lien and Nicole Filler, Oxford University Press. © Oxford University Press 2022.
DOI: 10.1093/oso/9780190077679.003.0004

ago. Specifically, for this chapter, her research raises questions about the relative importance of identification and involvement with the major parties, compared to participation in ethnic community-based and nonethnic, nonpartisan organizations, for leadership development and candidate success on the campaign trails for APA women and men. Political parties are considered backbones of democratic governing (at least for national and state-level offices), and local political party organizations vary considerably in their influence and structure. Yet prior research has not found parties to play much of a facilitating role in the political inclusion of newcomers, women of all colors, and those seeking local offices. In fact, given the strength of the white-dominated old boys network, some argue that parties have blocked the opportunities for minorities to enter the arena. How accurately do these findings describe the experiences of APAEOs in the past and in the present day? To what extent and in which direction have APA candidates and elected officials been able to connect with the major parties as they seek their first and higher elective offices—in both historical and more recent times? As we explore answers to these questions in this chapter, we also attempt to assess the significance of the growing roles of ethnic community-based and nonethnic women-centered organizations in cultivating and electing APA candidates for public office, especially in and after 2016. We present a more formal discussion of the role of nonparty organizations in Chapter 6.

To investigate the development of and help demystify the partisan connections of APA candidates and elected officials, we open this chapter with a review of past studies on two sets of relationships. One is between gender, race, and party recruitment and other forms of support. The other is between Asian Americans and the two parties. Our discussion then focuses on the historical rise and present-day dominance of the Democratic Party in the two important states of Hawaii and California. Then we present the statistical profile of the partisan affiliation of APAEOs serving in 2020. The bulk of the remaining chapter is dedicated to exploring the formation of partisan ties among APAEOs to either the GOP or the Democratic Party, by plan or by coincidence. We close by examining examples of APA candidates served or not served by the two parties and how ethnic and nonethnic organizations could play a crucial role in the first elections of APA women and men to local offices. In the interim, we discuss the particular pattern of partisan ties developed by several Asian ethnic groups.

112 CONTESTING THE LAST FRONTIER

Gender, Race, and Party Recruitment and Support

While mainstream accounts of political parties as organizations find their influence in political campaigns to be on the decline starting in the mid-1970s, gender and politics scholars find political parties to be particularly influential in shaping who reaches the candidacy stage and wins the election, particularly in partisan elections. In their study of state legislative campaigns, Sanbonmatsu and Carroll (2013, chap. 3) find that women are more likely than men to report being encouraged to run the first time and for their current office by their party leaders. In spite of this apparent positive influence of political parties on women state legislators' decision to run, party leaders have been found to overlook potential women candidates (Fox and Lawless 2005; Baer and Hartmann 2014), discourage them from running (Nelson 1991; Werner 1993; Sanbonmatsu 2002), or encourage them to run as sacrificial lambs in difficult races (Carroll and Strimling 1983; Carroll 1994; Baer and Hartman 2014). Research on party recruitment of Black candidates similarly finds political party organizations wanting (e.g., Moncrief et al. 2001).

Other studies find that the party recruitment of women is conditional on the inclusion of women as party chairs (Niven 1998; Sanbonmatsu 2006; Cheng and Tavits 2011; Crowder-Meyer 2013). For example, Crowder-Meyer (2013) finds that recruitment positively affects women's candidacies when women serve as the party chair, but not men. In contrast, Doherty, Dowling, and Miller (2019) find in their survey experiment that female chairs do not evaluate female candidates more favorably than male candidates, and male chairs actually evaluate female candidates slightly more favorably than male candidates. Candidates with Black and Latinx names are viewed by both parties' (mostly white) chairs to be less likely to win. However, racial demographics attenuate the penalty in the Democratic Party. Still, Democratic Party chairs are more pessimistic about nonwhite candidates' chances of winning when pitted against a white (vs. nonwhite) candidate even under favorable racial demographic contexts. Doherty and colleagues do not find significant gender differences in party chair evaluations of Black and Latinx candidates.

For Black, Latino, Asian American, and American Indian women and men serving in partisan and nonpartisan offices in the early 2000s, Hardy-Fanta et al. (2016) find political parties practically nonexistent as sources of encouragement. And while women of color are also more likely than white women to experience negative party recruitment or efforts by a party leader to discourage their bid for office, nonwhite women (and men) experience differing degrees of negative recruitment. Phillips (2021) finds that Asian American male state legislators are less likely than Asian American women to report being discouraged by their political party from running. However, the share of Asian Americans who reported being discouraged is lower than other ethnoracial groups. In comparison, nearly a third of Latinas reported discouragement from their party compared to 10% among Latinos and 8% among white women and men (Phillips 2021). Together these findings suggest Asian American candidates, particularly males, have been on the political radar of the two parties less than their Latino/a and white counterparts, and their relative invisibility could be a blessing in disguise.

In addition to not being regular targets of recruitment or encouragement by political parties, women and other minorities also face the conventional challenge of campaign financing, especially getting early money. However, recent changes in party practices that aim to help elect more women to offices have provided some relief. Whereas gender and politics scholars have identified campaign financing as the Achilles heel of women candidates, they also find political parties have become a beneficial source in their campaign successes (Baer and Hartmann 2014; Dittmar 2015). At the congressional level, both major parties have political action committees to protect vulnerable incumbents and back open-seat contenders and incumbent challengers who are deemed to be running in competitive races. According to Burrell (2018), not only have women been fully integrated into the leadership structure of national party organization committees, but congressional committees provide comparable direct and indirect support to similarly situated male and female candidates. A 2016 report by the Center for Responsive Politics, Common Cause, and Representation2020 also finds no gender difference in party leadership PAC contributions to congressional candidates between 2000 and 2014. However, female open-seat contenders in both parties and Republican female challengers receive a disproportionately small amount of the funds. Unfortunately, these studies do not include any assessment of women of color's presence in or financial backing from national party organizations and leadership PACs.

The majority of all US elected officials serve in nonpartisan offices. This phenomenon is even truer for women and men of color documented in the benchmark study by Hardy-Fanta et al. (2016), where nine out of 10 served in local offices. Even though parties do endorse candidates for nonpartisan races, Carroll and Sanbonmatsu (2013) comment that parties have played

114   CONTESTING THE LAST FRONTIER

less of a role at the local and county level than in state legislative races, for most local elections are nonpartisan. Moreover, none or negative recruitment describes the experiences of most Asian and other nonwhite men and women seeking to enter the electoral arena. Still, for a nonwhite and majority-immigrant but also multiethnic and multigenerational population, limited past studies on Asian Americans show that establishing affiliations with mainstream political parties and receiving encouragement and support from partisan organizations, no matter how little or marginal, are still more desirable than not. Joining partisan organizations symbolizes political inclusion and helps connect Asians with mainstream (i.e., white and Black) voters (Lai 2011). It can also provide the institutional and organizational structure for APA candidates and elected officials to build alliances and coalitions based on shared needs, interests, and values (Lien 2001a, chap. 4; Wong 2006).

Asian Americans and the Two Parties: A Volatile Relationship

As a nonwhite and multiethnic population, the relationship between Asian Americans and the two major political parties has been volatile and, at times, ambiguous or even perilous. On the Democratic side, Executive Order 9066 of 1942 that rounded up West Coast Japanese Americans in "relocation" centers and inland concentration camps was issued by a Democratic president and supported by a Democratic-controlled Congress. But the passage of landmark civil and voting rights legislation in the mid-1960s also occurred under a unified Democratic government. In Hawaii, a decade before civil rights era reforms on the mainland, a cohort of primarily US-born Japanese, Native Hawaiian, Chinese, and Filipino Americans revitalized the Democratic Party under the platform of eradicating racial and economic inequality. Yet, in the 1990s, the DNC eagerly courted Asian American donors for their money but quickly abandoned them as toxic waste when Republicans raised questions about the sources of campaign contributions to President Clinton's re-election campaign (Kim 2007). Innuendos and assumptions of divided loyalty, as well as allegations of the channeling of foreign money from Asia to US presidential campaign by mostly immigrant Chinese American operatives associated with the Democratic Party, were sufficient evidence of guilty by association for the entire APA community (Wang 1998; Chang 2004; Toyota 2010).[1]

Meanwhile, on the Republican side, the party of Lincoln and pro-Black civil rights that elected the first Black state representatives during the Reconstruction era essentially responded to progressive reforms in the post-1965 era with a "Southern Strategy," by dividing the Democratic electoral coalition with racist appeals and attracting disaffected white voters residing in the South and elsewhere to the GOP. In recent decades, the Republican Party also conducted smear campaigns against nonwhite immigrants and refused to pass comprehensive immigration reforms. However, it also helped normalize relationships with China, supported admissions of refugees from Southeast Asia at the end of the Vietnam War, and provided unique green cards for Chinese students who sought US protection from an oppressive communist regime after the Tiananmen Square massacre in June 1989. Yet, in the late 1990s, the GOP leaders in Congress raised doubts about the loyalty and equal citizenship of Asian Americans by conducting hearings on campaign finance controversies and espionage charges of (mostly) immigrant Chinese Americans. Prior to that, the Republican National Committee received questionable foreign money from an Asian donor back in 1992 for a seat at the dinner table with President Bush.[2] After the terrorist attacks on September 11, 2001, a Republican administration and House majority shepherded the passing of the USA Patriot Act of 2001 and the Homeland Security Act of 2002 that targeted Muslim immigrants, including those from South Asia, for additional security scrutiny. During the Covid-19 pandemic, economic depression, and mass uprisings against anti-Black police brutality in 2020, President Trump and several other prominent Republican Party figures consistently referred to the coronavirus as the "Wuhan flu" and "Chinese virus." Meanwhile, APA organizations, activists, and elected officials denounced the coded nativistic racism and provided detailed reports of increased bias, discrimination, and violent attacks targeting Chinese and other Asian Americans, especially women, immigrants, and the elderly.

Checking the balance of this tally of key events and legislation by leaders in both parties helps explain why, despite often being overlooked by or, in times of crisis or scandal, being hypervisible to both parties, Asian American voters have become steadily and increasingly identified with the Democratic Party in the past few decades (Lien 2001a; Lien, Conway, and Wong 2004; Hajnal and Lee 2011; Wong et al. 2011; Masuoka et al. 2018; Mehta 2020). The election of the first nonwhite president in 2008 as a Democrat was also a key empowerment event for the APA community in part because Obama was born in Hawaii and grew up in Indonesia, and his campaign invested an

116 CONTESTING THE LAST FRONTIER

unprecedented amount of campaign resources in APA outreach. Still, just as many, if not more, Asian American voters do not identify with either major party. Their largely non-US-born-and-raised and non-Anglophone characteristics may partially explain the relatively weak identification with either of the parties, including among elected officials. The GMCL survey of nonwhite elected officials finds that up to 17% of Asians, compared to around 10% of Blacks and Latinos, identified themselves as partisan independent or not affiliated with either party. Correspondingly, Asians have a lower rate of Democratic identification (58%) than Blacks (88%) and Latinos (76%); and Asians have a higher rate of Republican identification (25%) than Blacks (1%) and Latinos (14%).

The relative weak ties to the major parties, including among elected officials, may also reflect the lack of knowledge, interest, and commitment of US political party organizations to invest systematically in the resources of educating, training, and mobilizing the participation of Asian (and Latino) immigrants in and of the US political process in the post-1965 era (Leighley 2005; Wong 2006; Andersen 2008). Instead, these studies show that local community-based partisan clubs and nonpartisan civic and political organizations have risen to fill the gaps left open by national party organizations in incorporating immigrants. Nonetheless, more recent journalistic accounts provide some evidence of renewed interest and effort by the two major parties (and their affiliated groups) to mobilize support from this rapidly growing community (Becerra 2012; Ricardi 2014; Burrell 2018; Yoshiko Kandil 2018; Hsu 2020). Our study extends limited past research on the topic. It aims to provide a more nuanced account of the seemingly detached but also entangled relationships of APA candidates and elected officials with the two major parties over space and time. Our account begins with Hawaii, both before and after statehood.

The Rise and Entrenchment of Democratic Party in Hawaii

Hawaii is rarely discussed together with other US states in research on political representation and party politics, and maybe it deserves that distinction. Hawaii is one of the nation's most Democratic-leaning states. Democratic voters outnumbered Republicans two to one in the last presidential election. Democrats currently control the governor's mansion, US Senate and

US House seats, and both chambers of the state legislature. In fact, in the last 30 years, the highest number of Republicans in the senate was five in 2002–5; there have never been more than 19 Republicans in the 51-member House since statehood, and the peak year was 2000. In 2020, there were only six Republicans (three of them women and two of them nonwhite) in the entire legislature of 76 members, all in the lower chamber except one. There was no more than a single Republican in the 25-member state senate between 2010 and 2020.

It may be hard to fathom today, but far more Asian American legislators in Hawaii were Republicans than Democrats until the mid-20th century, as the Republican Party dominated territorial politics (Fuchs 1961; Coffman 2003; Chou 2010). Even in the two elections right after World War II, when the number of Japanese American legislators sharply rose (because they were banned from running and holding office during the war), significantly more were elected as Republicans. Whereas the GOP fielded candidates of Chinese, Japanese, and Hawaiian descent during its more triumphant days, power was in firm control by Caucasians or haoles. Appeal by the Democratic Party for more inclusive governance and leadership structure was a prominent part of the "Democratic Revolution" success story in 1954. Self-identified "Americans of Japanese ancestry" (AJAs) were recruited to join the party, and AJA men won almost one-half of the legislative seats in that election. Racial (and gender) discrimination experienced by some of these individuals with law degrees (featured in Chapter 2) during their application for positions in haole firms explains the willingness of many to shift their party identification and become Democrats after the war. Visionary Nisei International Longshore and Warehouse Union labor leader Jack Kawano was key to linking issues of the union demands for racial equality and economic reform to the Democratic Party platform. And Democratic leader John (Jack) Burns was instrumental in recruiting AJAs (notably Governor George Ariyoshi) to run for office.

The 1954 election ushered in Democratic control of the state legislature and most local offices—a dominance that has grown over time. Although these Democrats were not "revolutionaries" but centrist and moderate in political ideology, they laid the groundwork for subsequent political and economic restructuring in Hawaii society (Okamura 2014, 95). Meanwhile, the Republican Party's demise in the state can be attributable to its inability to differentiate itself from the haole oligarchy that characterized its days of dominance in the pre-1954 era (Pratt 2000). Another reason is the Republican

118   CONTESTING THE LAST FRONTIER

Party's difficulty managing internal conflicts associated with the socially conservative issue stances of the Christian right faction, such as opposition to abortion and same-sex marriage, in a solidly liberal and blue state. The ultimate lack of Republican candidates in many state and local races is another contributing factor perpetuating Democratic dominance in Hawaii.

Wither the Inouye Machine and the Dodo Bird?

In recent years, the entrenched domination of the state's Democratic Party can be evidenced by the average of 79% of Democrats in legislative sessions between 1987 and 2011 (Okamura 2014, 141–42). The state's congressional delegation has also been dominated by Democrats since 1954, with the late US senator Daniel Inouye serving nine consecutive terms and holding key leadership positions as one of the chamber's most senior members until his passing in 2012. In contrast, the very marginalized and near-extinct status of the state's Republican Party has earned itself the nickname of "dodo bird" or "dinosaur." The minimal number of Republican elected officials, notes Okamura, may also contribute to candidates' choice to run as Democrats to increase their chances. However, the reverse can sometimes be true, when a Democratic candidate runs as Republican to avoid losing in the crowded Democratic primaries. A case in point was Democratic Honolulu mayor Frank Fasi's remarkable comeback as a Republican in 1988 after losing his governor's bid as a member of the GOP in 1982 (Okamura 2014, 123). More importantly, instead of unity, Democratic domination has led to "long-term and endemic factionalism" where house Democrats are split into two major factions between "loyalists" and "dissidents." In comparison, senate Democrats are divided into three or more factions, possibly due to their long tenure (Okamura 2014, 143). Furthermore, many state voters are independents who do not consistently vote for either party or the party's favorite candidates. These independent voters were part of the success story of white Republican Linda Lingle's gubernatorial campaign in 2002, when her Japanese American woman opponent, Mazie Hirono, was dogged by party disunity provoked by the bloody Democratic primary campaign. Lingle was the first woman governor in Hawaii and the first Republican governor since 1962, when John Burns took the helm.

Independent voters were behind the meteoric rise of American Samoa–born **Tulsi Gabbard,** who, at age 21, turned herself from a self-employed martial arts instructor to a state legislator in 2002. Then she became Honolulu city councilmember in 2011 and a US House representative, representing HI-2 in 2013, succeeding Mazie Hirono. The latter moved to the US Senate to occupy a seat left open by Daniel Akaka's retirement. Between her first and second elections, Gabbard enlisted in the Hawaii Army National Guard and was deployed in Iraq (2004–5) and Kuwait (2008–9). Her father, Senator Mike Gabbard, was also born in American Samoa and well known for his religious conservatism and antigay activism before his election to the Honolulu City Council in 2002 and state senate in 2006 as a Republican. He switched to the Democratic camp in 2007 to become a more effective legislator by being affiliated with the dominant party. Soon after her election to Congress, Representative Gabbard was unanimously elected as vice chair of the DNC, succeeding Mike Honda. She resigned from the DNC post in early 2016 to become the first congresswoman to endorse Bernie Sanders's presidential campaign. Because of her white mother's faith, Gabbard is also a practicing Hindu. She consulted the Indian American community about support for a Hindu in the White House before officially launching her 2020 Democratic presidential nomination campaign in early 2019 (Diokno 2019). After withdrawing from her US House re-election campaign months earlier, she suspended her presidential campaign and endorsed front-runner Biden in March 2020.

In early 2017, House minority leader Representative **Beth Fukumoto**, a Yonsei, or fourth-generation Japanese American and the nation's youngest party leader in state legislatures, was ousted from the leadership of the Republican Party after making critical comments against President Trump in a postinauguration women's march over his disparaging remarks about women and minorities during the campaign (Lee 2017). Fukumoto was married to David Chang, a Korean American and former Hawaii GOP chairman. Earlier, she was recognized by the Millennial Action Project for her ability to transcend partisan lines as a young political leader. The *Daily Beast* singled her out as the only Asian among the shortlist of GOP women and rising stars in national politics in September 2013 (Murray 2013). Being a Japanese Republican woman in Hawaii may give an Asian American candidate some advantage compared to her counterparts on the Democratic side and her non-Japanese colleagues. Still, there's a limit to how much partisan and ethnic identities matter. Fukumoto switched to the Democratic Party and ran in the First Congressional District race in 2018 but was handily defeated in a crowded primary race.

120   CONTESTING THE LAST FRONTIER

Former state legislator **Kaniela Ing,** who is of Hawaiian, Japanese, and Chinese descent, explained the difficulties of overcoming the gatekeeping system of the Hawaii Democratic Party. In an interview for our project, he said, "There's a certain infrastructure that moves with Democratic candidates, certain donors, certain gatekeepers through networks of donors. Of course, there's construction unions, there's labor, contractors, subcontractors, public unions. And they all have their buttons to push in certain order to activate. I haven't been unsuccessful, but I'm not like the most connected institutionally into that system." Ing won his 2012 bid for a seat in the Hawaii house, his third successful campaign after winning races for the neighborhood board and student body president. As in his previous campaigns when he was an underdog, Ing won the race in 2012 out of a "brutal [effort at] knocking on doors," ending his shift as a spa attendant at a local resort before canvassing door to door until sunset. Ing served two terms before entering the First Congressional District race in 2018, where he garnered the same share of votes as fellow Democratic outsider Beth Fukumoto.

As we have mentioned, the white-controlled Republican Party dominated Hawaii territorial politics until the "Democratic Revolution" in the mid-1950s. Fueled mainly by Nisei war heroes and other AJAs, the Democratic Party has maintained its dominance in Hawaii to the present day. Because Hawaii has been a one-party state and dominated by Democrats since the mid-1950s, most lawmaking happens behind closed doors within the Democrat caucus, and campaign finance violations have plagued the ruling party. Being in the supermajority does not mean unity or harmony. Factionalism within the dominant party has allowed the minority party and other independent-minded Democrats to enter the political arena. Yet, given Hawaii's distinction of being the majority-minority state since statehood, Republicans in Hawaii are considered liberal relative to Republicans in the rest of the country. Cynthia Thielen, a state legislator since 1990 and now an outspoken Republican for change, commented: "Hawaii is a very tolerant, diverse society. And when you come in with a hard right-wing social conservatism, it's just not going to be accepted by the people" (Jeffries 2017).

The Rise of Democratic Dominance in California

In 2020, the Democratic Party of California, similar to its counterpart in Hawaii, enjoyed a robust supermajority status in both chambers of the state legislature and controlled all statewide offices. This lopsided influence made some question the viability of the state GOP (Lawrence and Cummins 2020). However, the current Democratic dominance does not describe the party's history in the Golden State. In fact, between 1862, when railroad tycoon Leland Stanford took over the governorship, and 1911, when progressive Republican Hiram Johnson was elected governor and led the state's Progressive movement, the Republican Party largely held the state through the power and influence of the Southern Pacific Railroad, the statewide machine analogous to the urban political machines elsewhere in the mainland. By aiming to stem corruption from arrogant party bosses and corporate moguls, Progressive reforms stressed individualism and nonpartisanship. They weakened the state party system by instituting direct primaries, at-large elections, nonpartisan elections, professional management, and initiative measures. California was a major center of Progressive reform activities. Still, with a few prominent exceptions, the Republican Party dominated state politics between 1917 and 1974, when Ronald Reagan ended his governorship. At the presidential level, Republicans won the state in nearly every presidential election between 1952 and 1988 (Krishnakumar, Emamdjomeh, and Moore 2016).

The first Democratic governor in the 20th century did not get elected until the late 1930s, after an aggressive turnout campaign organized by the California Young Democrats (CYD), the official youth organizing arm of the California Democratic Party. In 1953, the CYD helped create the California Democratic Council (CDC) as a grassroots movement to win back control of California state governance from Republicans. It coordinated activities of Democratic clubs statewide and played an essential role in the 1958 election of Governor Edmund G. "Pat" Brown and a slate of other state Democratic candidates. In the 1960s, several CYD leaders led a reform faction that wrested control of the organization from the Democratic assembly speaker Jesse Unruh. This reform act helped move the party to the left to support Black civil rights and anti–Vietnam War protesters. The two-term governorship of Pat Brown ushered in a golden age, making California famous for having the best higher education, the longest highways, and an economy exceeding that of nations. These features attracted large and sustained migration from Latin America and Asia. The rapid growth of Latinos and Asians in the population and electorate as well as the growing resentment of voters over the Republican Party's hard-line stance on immigration, exemplified in Proposition 187 of 1994,[3] helped explain the Democratic surge in recent decades. Democratic presidential candidates have won decisively in every election since 1992. In 2008, the CYD played a pivotal role in the election of President Barack Obama by mobilizing record turnout of young voters through the unique peer-to-peer tactic that encouraged student members to recruit other students. In 2016, candidate Hillary Clinton won a higher percentage (62.3%) of votes than any candidate after the peak score (67%) earned by Franklin D. Roosevelt in 1936. A new record was set in 2020 when 63.6% of the votes were cast for the Biden-Harris ticket.

Nonetheless, because of the legacy and continuing impact of Progressive reforms, the Democratic Party in California exists in a weak party system whose power has been stripped thin and organization fractured by efforts to crush machine politics and promote direct democracy (Lawrence and Cummins 2020). It features direct primaries (allowing voters to nominate candidates), cross-filing (allowing candidates to run across party lines), nonpartisan elections (for all local and judicial offices), and, until recently, a prohibition on parties endorsing candidates or assisting local officeholders. Also, voters approved an open-primary law in 1996, enabling voters to vote across party lines. In 2010, voters approved the top-two primary, where the two candidates who receive the most votes, regardless of party, advance to the general election. For presidential elections and party offices, partisan primaries still exist. However, there are no precinct-level party organizations, only elections for county- and state-level central committees. The state party endorsement ban was lifted after the US Supreme Court ruled in *Eu v. San Francisco County Democratic Central Committee* (1989). That decision suggested that California's extensive regulation of the internal operations of political parties violated their members' First Amendment rights of free speech and association. Yet the two parties have different practices for endorsing candidates. Republicans generally do not endorse anyone when more than one Republican is in the primary; Democrats do but with a mixed record of success. Lawrence and Cummins commented that party endorsements appeared to matter more for candidates in lower-level races, possibly because local candidates had a greater need to rely on the party to lend credibility and provide campaign resources, even in nonpartisan races (2020, 119).

When Clark Lee chaired the Los Angeles County Democratic Party and California Democratic Party Asian Pacific Islander Caucus, he commented in an interview for our project that "party endorsements could be used offensively or defensively. Party organizers may actively seek candidates to run in an identified jurisdiction that meets the qualifications for this process. Or they could engage in early endorsement for an incumbent local Democratic officeholder up for election in a jurisdiction that meets the qualification for this process."[4] He also mentioned that, whereas the caucus does not issue endorsements, it has routinely encouraged potential local APA candidates to seek endorsements with their respective county parties. The caucus also organized voter contact mobilization efforts supporting APA candidates for federal, state, and local candidates all over the state. And yet, because exactly which candidates receive endorsements is very much driven by local political dynamics, networks, and common sense for a given election cycle in an election district, we suspect this process puts less connected newcomers and relatively unknown candidates at a disadvantage. At the same time, it simultaneously opens up opportunities for racial minorities who happen to situate themselves in a location or district impacted by demographic change or other factors and whose candidacies are considered critical to the success of a party in swinging a district. The combination of high population growth from international migration and concentration of the Asian populations in more than a few highly competitive swing districts and locations such as in Orange County have made Asian candidates increasingly the prime targets of recruitment and mobilization by major party organizations and related groups. We document such incidents and practices by both parties in historical and recent elections later in the chapter.

Which Party Do APAEOs Identify With?

Outside of Hawaii and for most of Asian American history, Asians have been racial and numerical minorities and political outsiders. For those who ended up in public service, this means their experiences of becoming politicized and becoming affiliated with a major political party may involve two separate processes. Especially in the 1960s and 1970s, becoming politicized meant participation in grassroots movements to challenge the establishment and for social change. Party politics was rare and odd. For those who became affiliated with a major party, their partisan identification reflected personal connections more than the outcome of a strategic move. In addition, the legacy of Asian American movement activism appears to bode well for the party that is considered more sympathetic to minority plights, and there were many instances of former progressives/leftists turned Democrat (e.g., Mabel Tang, Ed Lee, Wilma Chan, Eric Mar in San Francisco). Ideology aside, the party banner under which Asian candidates run may also depend on opportunities offered by parties (whether the candidacy is being courted or welcomed by a particular party or not) and other political concerns.

Yet, even in currently deep-blue states such as California and Hawaii, the GOP may sometimes be perceived as providing more breakthrough opportunities for specific minority candidates. To maximize its electoral fates in majority-minority states or districts where a significant portion of (new or potential) voters are immigrants from Asia, the GOP may be motivated to recruit and target Asian immigrant women (and men) candidates. Their ascriptive identity at the intersection of race and gender may be perceived as best serving the party's needs. We offer examples of such recruitment later in the chapter on the changing politics in Orange County and adjacent areas in Southern California. Nonetheless, given the GOP's embrace of conservative, antiminority stance, the Democratic Party also sensed an opportunity to win over the conservative Asian American vote. It started to invest more in the Asian community by registering Asian Americans to vote, running in-language print ads, and putting Asian American organizers on the ground in competitive congressional districts, including in Orange County (Yoshiko Kandil 2018). These developments suggest that we might expect a more robust level of partisan connections among APAEOs than before. What is the trend of partisanship breakdown among APAEOs leading to the third decade of the 21st century? In the next section, we analyze the partisan trends and present a statistical profile of the party affiliation patterns by gender, office level, ethnicity, and nativity among APAEOs in 2020.

Understanding APAEO Partisanship by the Numbers

Identifying the partisanship of elected officials serving in partisan offices is a relatively straightforward process even if, as we will detail, some APAEOs have switched parties and, in some cases, more than once. On the other hand, nonpartisan officeholders do not run on a party label. They may avoid explicit mentions of partisanship or declare their independence so as not to alienate potential voters and constituents. However, even nonpartisan officeholders have received boosts from major parties in the form of an endorsement or access to the organizations' resources and networks. In the end, we were able to identify the mainstream party affiliation for 83% of the 582 APAEOs serving

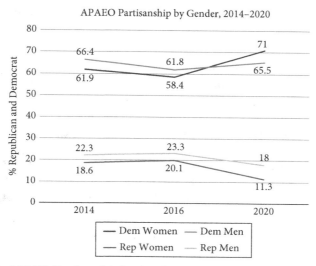

Figure 4.1 APAEO Partisanship by Gender, 2014–20

as of late August 2020. About 70% of women are identified as Democrats and 11% as Republicans. Men are slightly more likely to be identified with the two major political parties and more balanced in numbers. Still, nearly two-thirds are Democrats, and less than one-fifth are Republicans. Figure 4.1 shows that between 2014 and 2020, the share of Democratic- and Republican-affiliated women has remained consistent at each time point, while the share of men who identify with either major party has declined. It also shows a move away from the Republican Party and toward the Democratic Party after 2016, particularly among women.

When examined by level of office, as represented in Table 4.1, the partisanship breakdown among APAEO women and men holding congressional, statewide, and state legislative office in 2020 is similar, with Democrats outpacing Republicans by at least a four-to-one margin at each level office. Among the substate officeholders, the gender gap in party affiliation widens but not always in the same direction or to the same degree. For example, nearly one in five women serving at the county level is Republican, compared to one in 10 men. Likewise, there is a greater share of Democratic men compared to women serving at the county level. At the municipal level, the pattern is somewhat reversed. Women have higher degrees of partisanship compared to men and on the Democratic side. About a quarter of men serving at this level are affiliated with the GOP, but this is about the same

126 CONTESTING THE LAST FRONTIER

Table 4.1 APAEO Partisanship by Gender and Level of Office, 2020

	Women				Men				All		
	% D	% R	% NA	N	% D	% R	% NA	N	% D	% R	% NA
All	72	11	18	231	66	18	17	351	68	15	17
Congress	90	10	0	10	100	0	0	10	95	5	0
Statewide	100	0	0	2	80	20	0	5	86	14	0
State legislature	90	11	0	57	85	14	1	98	86	13	1
County	65	18	18	17	73	9	18	22	69	13	18
Municipal	77	9	15	81	53	23	24	115	61	18	21
School board	45	14	41	64	57	15	28	61	51	14	34

Note: D = Democrat, R = Republican, NA= unable to verify or missing data on partisan identity.

share as those whose partisanship is unknown or is independent. Consistent with previous literature, partisanship appears to matter, the least for women and men serving on local education boards, particularly among women, more than two in five of whom are not affiliated with either major party.

Figure 4.2 also shows wide variation in partisanship among elected officials across different Asian ethnic groups and Pacific Islanders. Democrats have the largest advantage among South Asian and Southeast Asian elected officials. The exception is among the Vietnamese, who comprise the largest share of Republicans. It is notable, however, that an even larger share of Vietnamese are Democrats. Taiwanese are the second most likely to align with the GOP, followed more distantly by Koreans. Finally, several groups of elected officials have higher than average rates of nonpartisanship, including up to a quarter of Koreans, Pacific Islanders, Filipinos, and Southeast Asians (other than Vietnamese and Hmong).

We also observe distinct patterns in party affiliation at the intersections of nativity status, ethnicity, and gender in Table 4.2. On the Democratic side, the Asia-born outnumber the US-born for all ethnic groups that are majority Asia-born. Women also make up at least a majority of the Asia-born except for Koreans and South Asians (other than Indian), where women make up 40% and 25% of the Asia-born, respectively. The share of women among the Asia-born is also substantially greater than that of the US-born for South Asians, Southeast Asians, and Filipinos/as. On the Republican side, all thirteen Taiwanese are immigrants, and over half are women. Nearly

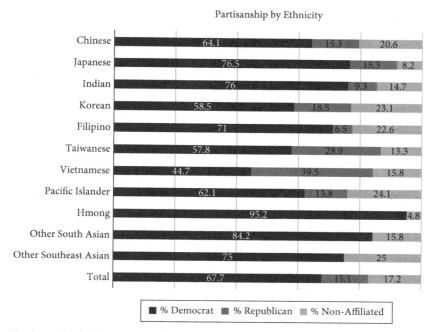

Figure 4.2 APAEO Partisanship by Ethnicity, 2020

three-quarters of GOP-affiliated Indians and Vietnamese are also Asia-born, but very few are women regardless of nativity status. Slightly more than half of Koreans are immigrants, similar to the Asia-born share on the Democrat side. However, a larger share of Korea-born Republicans are women. Finally, all or nearly all nonaffiliated South Asians, Southeast Asians, Taiwanese, and Koreans are Asia-born, and the majority are men. There are similar shares of Asia- and US-born nonaffiliated Filipinos, but Filipina women comprise a greater share of the Asia-born than the US-born. Most nonaffiliated Chinese, Japanese, and Pacific Islanders are US-born and are equally if not more likely to be women, except among the Japanese.

Becoming Partisan: Stories of Uneven and Often Tenuous Relationship

Although APAEOs have become increasingly Democratic as a collectivity, the relationship of individual elected officials to the party known for its

Table 4.2 APAEO Partisanship by Nativity Status, Ethnicity, and Gender, 2020

	Democrat				Republican			
	Total N	% Asia-Born	% Women Asia-Born	% Women US-Born	Total N	% Asia-Born	% Women Asia-Born	% Women US-Born
Chinese	78	23	39	38	17	24	25	38
Japanese	63	6	25	32	13	0	0	23
Indian	52	56	59	30	7	71	0	0
Filipino	40	23	56	35	4	25	0	33
Korean	38	53	40	44	11	55	67	40
Taiwanese	26	73	53	57	13	100	54	0
Hmong	18	61	55	57	0	0	0	0
Pacific Islander	18	0	0	29	4	0	0	50
Vietnamese	16	56	78	43	14	71	10	0
Other South Asian	13	92	25	0	0	0	0	0
Other SE Asian	9	56	60	50	0	0	0	0
Total	371	37	49	37	84	47	33	30

	Nonaffiliated			
	Total N	% Asia-Born	% Women Asia-Born	% Women US-Born
Chinese	16	13	50	50
Japanese	7	0	0	14
Indian	7	71	20	50
Filipino	11	55	67	40
Korean	9	78	43	50
Taiwanese	6	100	33	0
Hmong	1	100	0	0
Pacific Islander	6	0	0	67
Vietnamese	4	75	33	100
Other South Asian	3	100	0	0
Other SE Asian	3	100	33	0
Total	73	49	36	46

support of diversity and civil rights since the 1960s (and earlier in Hawaii) has been uneven and tenuous at best. In the following section, we examine variations in the pattern of this relationship at multiple levels of office and across time and place. While APAs elected to Congress since 2016 are among the latest successful party recruits, the strength of state and local party organizations varies widely, as does the influence of APA candidates and elected officials within them. Moreover, taking a long view and for personal and contextual reasons, the direction of partisanship of politically ambitious APAs is far from a done deal. In fact, more than a few prominent APAEOs changed their party affiliation in adulthood, especially among Japanese Americans. For example, from Democratic to GOP (S. I. Hayakawa, Tom Hom, Paul Bannai), from GOP to Democratic (Norm Mineta, Mark Takano, Will Espero, Beth Fukumoto), or back again (Yamauchi). We begin our account by featuring a number of notable Asian Republicans and their reasons for becoming affiliated with the GOP. Our analysis is arranged in loose chronological order, from federal to state and local offices, and officials elected from Hawaii to mainland states.

How and Why Some Became Republicans

Some of the early APAEOs became Republican Party members after working for a GOP official or being courted by the GOP to run for office. Some were motivated by the desire for a viable option in a one-party state dominated by Democrats. In more recent times, an elected official's identification with the conservative party can be based on religious conviction and/or the party's stance on taxation, economic development, immigration, and social policies. For Asian immigrants whose homelands in Asia were divided by the communist invasion, the party's staunch anticommunist stance can be appealing to those born in Vietnam, Korea, and Taiwan. This disposition can be especially true when the party image converges with conservative Christian faiths adopted by several Asian communities through Western imperialism and colonization. However, the party's strategic interest in winning elections seems to be critical for the GOP to recruit and support the campaigns of specific Asian candidates. Still, there often seems to be a fundamental tension between the GOP interest and that of the APAEOs who identify with the plight of racial and gender minorities.

130 CONTESTING THE LAST FRONTIER

US Senator **Hiram Fong** developed his ties to the Republican Party while in college working as a paid staff member for Honolulu mayoral candidate George F. Wright. Once elected to the Hawaii Territorial House, Fong quickly asserted himself as an independent-minded Republican who did not mind fighting the party establishment and the big sugar companies. Fong's "Wagner Act" in 1945 gave rights to agricultural workers to unionize and won him the steadfast backing of the International Longshore and Warehouse Union. His ability to forge a coalition of other independent Republicans and Democrats helped propel him to the house speakership between 1948 and 1954. The union support was also critical to his winning a US Senate seat in 1959 and subsequent campaigns. His popularity in the GOP made him the first Asian to run for US president in 1964 and 1968. He served until 1977 and left an enduring impact through his work on immigration reform and civil rights, even if he staunchly defended President Richard M. Nixon's Vietnam policies and often sided with business interests. He continued to be an elder statesman of the Hawaii Republican Party until he died in 2004 (Crass 2013).

US Representative **Patricia Saiki** started her relationship with the Republican Party in Hawaii by serving as a research assistant to Hawaii Senate Republicans and the secretary and then vice chair of the state Republican Party, before getting elected to the state house in 1968 and state senate in 1974. She became a Republican in postwar Hawaii to provide a "loyal opposition" to the growing Democratic Party. She was also encouraged by her husband, who had been active in local party politics (Flanagan 2002). Saiki did not look or act like other party members as a Japanese American woman and former union organizer. In 1982, after an unsuccessful run for lieutenant governor, she chaired the state's Republican Party. She oversaw a threefold expansion in party membership and helped President Reagan carry the state in 1984. Her revitalization of the Hawaii Republican Party helped propel her to victory as the first GOP congressional representative from Hawaii since 1959 after capturing 59% of the vote in 1986. Infighting within the Democratic Party and being an AJA helped (Okamura 2014, 150). She was a fiscal conservative who parted ways with many of her GOP colleagues on civil rights and women's equality and reproductive rights. Despite her ability to cross party lines, Saiki could not overcome the disadvantages of being a Republican and faced several defeats against Democratic Party–backed candidates.

Compared to Asian Republicans in Hawaii, those APAEOs identified with the GOP on the mainland appear to take a more hard-line stance. Born in Japan-occupied Korea, US Representative **Jay Chang Kim** moved to the

United States at age 22 as a wartime refugee and worked in restaurants and grocery stores before attending college and graduate school in Southern California. Kim believed that hard work would pay off in a free enterprise system, where lower taxes and privatizing government services are favored (US House of Representatives 2018b). In 1990, Kim entered electoral politics to "make government run more like a business" and won a seat in the Diamond Bar city council (Spiegel and Kang 1993). In 1992 local Republican officials courted Kim to run for the US House in a newly created 41st Congressional District. Riding on the tide of Korean American mobilization in the aftermath of "Sa-I-Gu," or the Los Angeles Riots, that started on April 30, 1992, Kim became the first Korean American in Congress and was known for advocating for abandoning the seniority system and cutting down committee sizes and budgets.

Louisiana governor **Bobby Jindal** was born to immigrant parents from India who came to America to pursue graduate studies. He was raised under a strong Hindu culture but learned about Christianity in high school and converted to Roman Catholicism in college. Having come of age in the Reagan-Bush era and in a southern state where the GOP was seen as the party of reform, Jindal embraced the conservative political ideology wholeheartedly. He was active as a College Republican and interned for a Republican House member before being appointed to state and federal offices overseeing health policy. Jindal entered the open-seat race for Louisiana's congressional delegation in 2004 and became the second Indian American in Congress. In addition to Jindal's fundraising ability, his status as a Christian conservative of color distanced himself from his Indian roots propelled his rise in the Republican Party (Gowen and Bridges 2015). He served two terms in the House before returning to his home state to run for governor in 2007, where he won handily with 54% of the vote in a field of 12 other candidates. Toward the end of his second term, Jindal announced his candidacy for the 2016 Republican presidential nomination in June 2015 but ended the campaign within six months.

GOP Engagement with Asian Immigrants from Vietnam, Korea, and Taiwan in Southern California

In the 1990s, Vietnamese Americans in Orange County, California, emerged as Republican candidates for city council and state legislative seats, attempting to replace term-limited Republicans and unseating Democratic incumbents. A lawyer and former staff member of several Republican elected officials, **Van Thai Tran** became the first Vietnamese American state legislator in 2004. He did it in an open-seat race only four years after his first campaign for city council, where he won with a historic number of votes. Tran's seat on the Garden Grove City Council was filled by another former Republican staff member, **Janet Nguyen**. First elected at age 28, Nguyen quickly moved to the county level in a special election in 2007, winning by a razor-thin margin of three votes over another Vietnamese American candidate. Neither was the GOP's pick, but Assemblymember Tran endorsed the latter. However, Nguyen's successful re-election to the Orange County Board of Supervisors was backed by the GOP, as was her 2014 race for an open seat in the California Senate that a Latino Democrat had vacated. Like many conservative Vietnamese American candidates, anticommunism has been a central theme for Tran and Nguyen, but there are increasingly other priorities like housing, healthcare, and immigration. In November 2020, in an intraethnic competition to replace a first-term and Vietnam-born Tyer Diep, a Republican representing the 72nd district in the California Assembly, Janet Nguyen faced competition from another Vietnam-born woman and Democrat, **Deidre Thu-ha Nguyen**. The latter was a community advocate before running for and holding a Garden Grove City Council seat representing District 3. She cited frustration at the lack of outreach to Vietnamese and Latino residents about the change from at-large to district elections, which resulted in creating one majority-Vietnamese district, District 3, as a primary motivation for her to run for public office (Vo 2016). Despite the spending of big money by the California Democratic Party to flip the seat, Janet Nguyen was able to prevail due to the GOP's edge in actively recruiting and mobilizing new immigrant voters (Staggs 2020a).

Several Korea–born immigrants based in conservative Orange County also received GOP support in their state and federal offices campaigns. However, when **Steven Seokho Choi** first started in OC politics running for the Irvine school board in 1998, he did so with the encouragement of friends and colleagues. He was not active in political parties, nor did he receive any party support. Nonetheless, he said Republican Party members predominately ran the campaign training he received from Education Alliance.[5] The former Irvine city councilman and mayor has since become an active party member and represented the 71st Assembly District on the Orange County Republican Party Central Committee. In the 2016 race to replace a white male Republican in the California Assembly, both Choi and India-born Harry Sidhu received endorsements from local GOP organizations. Choi squeezed in a victory in the primary by 0.1% and won the general election by a landslide.

Congresswoman and Orange County Board supervisor **Michelle Eunjoo Park Steel** has a personal connection to the GOP. Her spouse is former California Republican Party chairman and current California committeeman for the Republican National Committee Shawn Steel. Park Steel was born in Seoul in 1955 and raised in Japan before immigrating to the United States at college age with her mother and two younger sisters. Before her first election in 2006 to the California State Board of Equalization in an open-seat election to replace a fellow Republican, Park Steel had served in appointed positions at the state, county, and local levels. She was also a commentator on Radio Seoul. According to her campaign website, her staunch fiscal conservatism derived in part from "watching my single working mother struggle to fight an unwarranted tax bill from the California State Board of Equalization." In November 2020, she helped flip one of the few congressional seats in Orange County where the number of registered Republicans still outnumbered Democrats (Lai 2020).

Congresswoman **Young Kim** was born in Incheon and moved with her family to Guam in 1975, where she finished junior high school. Through the connection of her husband, Charles Kim, a founder of the Korean American Coalition and the Korean-Black Alliance, she served for 21 years as a California senator and as US Representative Ed Royce's community liaison and director of Asian affairs. Kim was also a popular talk show host on Korean American TV and radio shows. Kim pulled off an improbable election victory in 2014 when she defeated the white female Democratic incumbent, Sharon Quirk-Silva, for the California Assembly seat in a majority-minority OC district. However, Kim lost a rematch with Quirk-Silva and also narrowly lost to a Latino Democrat, Gil Cisneros, in a 2018 race for the US House. In a rematch in November 2020, Kim won a narrow victory by receiving 50.6% of the 39th District vote. She is one of the rare Republicans willing to speak out against Trump and enjoyed a fundraising edge despite a voter registration disadvantage (Staggs 2020b). The GOP leaders identified both Kim and Steel as "Young Guns" among the 21 candidates who represented the most competitive congressional seats in the 2020 election cycle—12, or 57%, were women (Huang 2020). Both have since become the first Korean American women in US Congress, alongside newly elected

134 CONTESTING THE LAST FRONTIER

Democrat Marilyn Strickland of Washington, who is of Black and Korean heritage. All three were born in South Korea.

As seen in previous chapters, immigrant women from Taiwan have been trailblazers serving on city councils in Southern California. Following their paths but ascending beyond the local is **Ling-ling Chang**, born in Taiwan and raised in Diamond Bar, California, since the age of three. She was president of the local water board, councilmember, and mayor before arriving at the state capitol. Chang had endorsements from GOP elites and organizations but faced scrutiny over her questionable claims about her country of birth and educational background. State and local party organizations invested nearly $2 million in her 2016 bid to replace term-limited party leader Bob Huff—whose wife was from Taiwan—in the California Senate. Chang lost narrowly in a recount but took the seat back two years later from the same Democrat in a recall election. Chang's replacement in the state legislature was a second-generation Taiwanese American and Republican Philip Chen, a former Walnut City Council member. In November 2020, Chang faced a rematch with Josh Newman, a Democrat who spent more than $3.3 million on his campaign, nearly doubling Chang's spending. Whereas Chang was considered the most moderate Republican in the state senate and publicly stated that she didn't vote for Trump in 2016, her GOP tie was too much of a liability to overcome this time around (Swatt and Swatt 2020).

Former Democrats Turned Republicans

In California, stories of party switching among Asian Americans from Democrats to Republicans appear in the 1960s and 1970s when Republican leaders took the initiative to recruit Chinese and Japanese Americans to help swing districts. Others defected into the conservative camp for ideological congruence. California assemblyman **Tom Hom** had wanted to enter politics early on, not so much to break racial barriers as a minority but to do a "good job" as a man who happened to be of Chinese descent, according to his autobiography (Hom 2014). When he first started volunteering in campaigns in the late 1950s, he was helping Democrat candidates. Yet, when he indicated an interest in running for an office himself, the Democratic Party boss tried to talk him down. By contrast, the Republican Party boss saw his potential as "the new blood that is needed in order to stimulate growth for the party" (159) and encouraged him to run and helped get him connected to the

GOP elites and network of donors. His first campaign was running against an incumbent in the heavily Democratic 79th State Assembly District in 1962. Although he did not win in his first election, the party boss thought he did enormously well and suggested Hom run for an open seat on the city council in the following year, which he did. He became the first nonwhite on the San Diego City Council in 1963. After he won re-election in 1967 with a historically high winning margin of 87%, his record attracted the attention of Governor Reagan, who urged him to run again in the 79th District. In 1968, Hom beat "the Chinaman's chance" (208) by flipping the Democratic district and helped the GOP deliver a Republican majority in the assembly, a victory that enabled the party to control the reapportionment process after the 1970 census.

Paul Bannai was the first Japanese American elected to the California Assembly and served between 1973 and 1980. Born in 1920, he was interned at the Manzanar concentration camp at the onset of World War II and volunteered from the camp to join the decorated US 442nd Regimental Combat Unit. After the war, he settled in Gardena, became heavily involved in local Japanese American community affairs, and was elected to the Gardena City Council in 1972. Councilman Bannai received a phone call in 1973 from candidate Reagan requesting his assistance in getting people in the predominantly Democratic district to vote for a Republican. Reagan mentioned that he had changed from a Democrat to a Republican to run for office and knew Bannai had also switched from a Democrat to a Republican. Later, Governor Reagan persuaded him to run for the state legislative seat held by a long-term Democrat who had suddenly passed away. Bannai said he was able to narrowly win the Democratic district mainly because of Reagan's popularity and his help in raising funds ("Obituary" 2019).

US Senator **S. I. Hayakawa** was born in Vancouver, Canada, to Japanese immigrants. After his parents returned to Japan, he moved to the United States and earned a doctoral degree in English in 1935. He would not become a US citizen until 1954, after restrictions against Japanese naturalization were lifted. Hayakawa initially identified with the Democratic Party because of the New Deal coalition, which tackled the economic crisis of the 1930s and gave America its social safety net. Over time he became more conservative, partly in reaction to the counterculture of the 1960s and partly to protest the expansion of federal government social programs. Governor Reagan named him acting president of San Francisco State College in 1968 to help quell student strikes. He formally registered as a Republican in 1973, the day after he

136 CONTESTING THE LAST FRONTIER

retired as campus president. In 1976, Hayakawa won a surprise victory in the US Senate race against a Democratic incumbent by touting himself as a political outsider (or politically innocent) and the "Republican unpredictable" in the wake of the Watergate scandal. He also drew on a strong conservative backlash against the social unrest of the era and campaigned on a platform that opposed big government and deficit spending. Starting as a decided underdog within the Republican Party, he ran a low-key, populist campaign by embracing the role of the people's candidate and won by a narrow margin.

How and Why Some Became Democrats

The image of the Democratic Party as for minorities has been appealing to APAs who felt marginalized in the white-dominated US society. This sentiment certainly describes the rise of Nisei war heroes turned political leaders in Hawaii. Their desire for political, social, and economic change and encouragement from labor union organizers led many veterans to support the Democratic Party. However, the difference they sought was not considered progressive enough for **Patsy Mink**. She helped launch the "Democratic Revolution" by working behind the scenes as a grassroots organizer to recruit political outsiders (racial minorities, laborers and labor unions, and political liberals and progressives) to help transform the male-centered local party structure. Mink founded the Everyman Organization, a group that served as the hub of the Young Democrats club on Oahu to help bring young people to the party. She was soon elected chairwoman of the territory-wide Young Democrats and later vice president of the National Young Democratic Clubs of America. Despite Mink's leadership role in the local and national Democratic Party, her numerous campaigns for the territorial, state, and federal offices were often underfunded and disfavored by the state Democratic Party, mainly because she was an outspoken woman of color with an independent mindset. When she ran for Congress in 1964, she survived by relying on a grassroots network, raising campaign funds primarily in small individual donations, and a staff of unpaid volunteers (Davidson 1994).

Whereas many of the children of working-class immigrants we met in Chapter 2 became natural allies of progressive politics and Democrats by partisanship, how mainland Asians developed a relationship with the Democratic Party is more varied than is the case with their Hawaii counterparts. In what follows we expand on the political socialization stories of a selected few to illustrate the divergent paths taken to forge their partisan ties—some are closer and more ideologically driven than others. Our account follows a chronological order and from federal to state and local offices in general.

Dalip Singh Saund, the first Asian American congressman, claimed that reading Lincoln's Gettysburg Address[6] during World War I changed the entire course of his life. In his autobiography, Saund (1960) explained that he became a Democrat during the 1930s because his rural county in California received some benefits from federal New Deal programs created to help struggling farmers and people out of work. He was elected to the Imperial County Democratic Central Committee in 1950 and was elected chair in 1954. When he jumped into the race to replace a retiring Republican member of Congress in 1956, his partisan and grassroots networks built from coordinating congressional campaigns helped him prevail over a well-funded white Republican woman veteran. He won the nationally watched campaign, despite constant issues surrounding his ethnicity, religion, and citizenship.

Seattle-born **Ruby Chow** decided to give back to the community by running for an elected office after her children were grown and serving two years on the King County Board of Equalization and Appeals. In 1973, she seized an open-seat opportunity on the King County Council vacated by a Republican white male and became the first Asian American elected to the council. The district was multiethnic and included Chinatown and Japantown, and mostly liberal. However, she was initially unsure of her political affiliation but eventually decided to register Democrat. She explained, "I felt that I belonged in the Democratic Party because it is more people-oriented. I discovered I had been a Democrat all my life and hadn't realized it" (Chesley 2008).

Arriving from Macau at age three and participating in the Asian American movement of the late 1960s and early 1970s, **Paul Fong** had been a community advocate for decades before running for his first office on the Foothill–De Anza Community College District board in 1993. Fong and 11 other Asian American community advocates cofounded the Asian Americans for Community Involvement in 1973, focusing on supporting and advocating for Southeast Asian refugees. Three years after his election to the board, Fong founded the Silicon Valley Asian Pacific American Democratic Club in 1996. He became known as the godfather of APA politics in Silicon Valley, encouraging and supporting the campaigns of several Asian Americans in Northern California, including Mike Honda and Michael Chang. In turn, Honda encouraged Fong to run in 2008 for California Assembly. Fong secured

138   CONTESTING THE LAST FRONTIER

endorsements from the California Democratic Party, several partisan clubs, unions, civil rights organizations, and a host of current and former elected officials. He won the primary by a plurality in a crowded field. He served in the assembly until being termed out in 2014.

Eric Mar's political family exposed him early on to both electoral politics and Asian American movement activism in California. His parents are second- and fourth-generation Chinese Americans who worked as state employees, and his older sister was active in the Asian American Political Alliance at Berkeley. His twin brother Gordon introduced him to the Chinese Progressive Association (CPA) during his college years, where he "learned on picket lines with Chinese and Latino immigrant workers."[7] Mar became involved in electoral politics because he saw it as a means to achieve community empowerment and systemic change. In the 1990s, he was part of a progressive alliance that included the CPA, Harvey Milk LGBTQ Democratic Club, and environmental groups to change the at-large electoral system to district-based elections. He won a seat on the San Francisco County Central Committee of the Democratic Party in 1998. When Mar ran for San Francisco supervisor of the First District, his track record as a community member and advocate for social justice enabled him to draw widespread support and overcome the obstacle of being boxed as the "Asian or Chinese American candidate." Mar explained that endorsements by the Democratic Party and the Green Party also helped. The Democratic endorsement lent legitimacy and provided support from mainstream voters, while the Green endorsement recognized his leftist activist roots and willingness to challenge the Democratic mainstream.

LA Community College trustee **Mike Fong** traces his involvement in the Democratic Party back to high school, when he volunteered for the Clinton-Gore campaign. He recalled, "My mom brought me to the headquarters. I remember that distinctly—making calls to people you don't know, cold calling, thinking, 'Hey, this is actually a little bit of fun here.'"[8] Fong continued to remain active in the local party, serving on the LA County Democratic Central Committee's candidate interview committee and the API Caucus of the California Democratic Party, among other roles. He won the party's endorsement in his first race in 2015. In a county home to the largest number of Democrats in the nation, Fong emphasized the importance of party support. "If you run for any office, you always want to have their support."[9]

Growing up in Chicago, **Michelle Wu** never expected to be involved in government or politics, much less running for office. She was the eldest of four kids in an immigrant family from Taiwan whose parents instilled the values of hard work and keeping your head down, even if her mother also reminded her later on "to help people and think about government" (Allen 2019). Wu did not think of herself as a Democrat or Republican when she volunteered in Boston's Chinatown and provided legal advice to low-income small business owners and survivors of domestic violence throughout her undergraduate years. Her first venture into electoral politics was working as a fellow at the mayor's office. She made a name for herself by creating the first guide to the restaurant permitting process and launching a food truck program. She was motivated by her frustration dealing with city bureaucracy to start a small restaurant in Chicago for her immigrant mother. She volunteered part time for her law professor Elizabeth Warren's US Senate campaign in 2012, then served full-time as its constituency director. The following year Wu took even her siblings by surprise when she announced her campaign for the city council seat occupied initially by an incumbent. At age 28, she became the first Asian American woman elected to the Boston City Council.

Former Republicans Turned Democrats/Independents

While dissatisfaction with the party establishment and stacked primary races may lead APAs to the GOP, several APA Republicans switched parties due to the GOP's social conservatism and weak general election prospects (Jeffries 2017). Some also found the idea of political independence to be more appealing. In Hawaii, **Peter Aduja,** the one-term Republican in the Hawaii Territorial House between 1954 and 1956, was asked why he ran as a Republican when most of his countrymen were plantation workers and members of the Democratically inclined International Longshoremen and Warehousemen's Union. He replied: "I always believed that the person himself determines the shape of his life, not government. . . . I've always believed in laissez-faire" (Boylan 1991, 43). Aduja's decision to run as a Republican proved fatal to his political career, compounded by his decision not to seek re-election but to run for a seat in the Hawaii County Board in 1956.

140   CONTESTING THE LAST FRONTIER

Years before Beth Fukumoto's departure, **Will Espero** worked in Democrat-turned-Republican Mayor Frank Fasi's office when he first ran for the Hawaii Senate as a Republican in 1992. In that race, he lacked support from the party, unions, business, and civic organizations. After serving on a neighborhood board, he was appointed by Governor Cayetano in late 1999 to fill a vacancy in the Hawaii House. He served one term before running for the Hawaii Senate in 2002—as a Democrat. He served three terms in Hawaii Senate, rarely faced a primary challenger, and won by wide margins in the general elections. Espero explained the relative ease of maintaining office once elected: "I get union support. I get business support—realtors, social workers, nurses, your HSTA, your teachers, those type of things. *Star-Advertiser*'s our newspaper, they endorsed me. Again, it's the power of incumbency, as you know."[10]

Born and raised in San Jose, California, in the 1930s and interned with family during World War II, **Norman Mineta** had been a staunch Republican. "After all, it was the damn Democrats that stuck us in those damn camps," he once explained (US House of Representatives 2018c). But in the 1960s, Mineta grew frustrated with the GOP's approach to the vast social issues of the day and left the party. However, his advocacy for civil rights, public housing, and transportation in appointed offices and national organizations did not mean a leap into the Democratic Party. The then-mayor of San Jose commented in an interview published by the *Washington Post* about an ineffective county Democratic committee and the dangers of partisan city politics (Mineta 1971). When the incumbent Republican congressman decided to retire three years later, Mineta entered the race and won by the closest margin of his 20-plus-year career. His bipartisan popularity as mayor and national presence, coupled with the Watergate scandal, gave him enough of an advantage to secure a win in the Republican-leaning district.

Another Californian and US House member, **Mark Takano,** born in 1960 as a Sansei, was also a former Republican. "My whole family is Republican, and I was a Republican all the way through college," Takano told the reporter of the campus newspaper of his alma mater. "But my Harvard education really had an impact. It truly made me smarter. I became a Democrat," he said (Hoffman 1992). Takano said he bucked the trend of the 1980s when more and more college students adopted the Republican platform. His original plans to be a Republican-affiliated lawyer fell through when he saw the party no longer had a place for him. Takano narrowly lost his first run for

Congress by one percentage point in 1992. In his second attempt two years afterward, he had a landslide victory in the primary but lost the general election by 17 percentage points after being outed as "homosexual liberal" by a Republican state assemblyman (Goad 2012). He became the first nonwhite openly gay member of Congress in 2013.

When **Lan Diep** won a seat on the San Jose City Council in 2016, it was on his second try and without significant political support. This son of Vietnamese refugees worked as an Equal Justice Works / AmeriCorps legal fellow at the Mississippi Center for Justice to aid Vietnamese American fishers and small business owners affected by the BP oil spill of 2010. He was named a Champion of Change in 2011 by President Obama and worked as a field organizer on Obama's 2012 re-election campaign. In mid-2019, Diep quietly left the Republican Party when he switched his party registration to "decline to state." Diep switched his party affiliation to Democrat despite the nonpartisan race shortly before winning the March 2020 primary. During the general election, Diep tried to build his Democratic credentials, a move that ignited a backlash from the Santa Clara County Democratic Party, which labeled him a "fake Democrat." Diep lost the general election to the Democratic Party–backed candidate David Cohen, who, according to the Santa Clara party chair, had spent "years helping to build and strengthen the Democratic Party" (Giwargis and Wipf 2020).

Assemblyman **Tyler Diep** also had a falling-out with the Republican Party because of his progressive immigration and labor rights stance. When it was leaked that Diep might leave the party after the election, the Orange County GOP chair openly called for and supported a conservative who could "rise to the occasion" to challenge the seat (Christopher 2019). Janet Nguyen, the former state senator, answered the call the next day. She made it to the top of the ticket during the primary election, while Diep narrowly lost the second spot to another Vietnamese woman and a Democrat. He became the fifth Asian legislator in state history, all Republican (after Hom in 1970, Chang and Kim in 2016, Nguyen in 2018, and Chang in 2020) ousted from office after serving only one term. The contrast in political fate between these Asian Republicans and the four Democrats who had their seats succeeded by fellow Asians in the California State Legislature unveils the flimsy relationship between the GOP and the minority community. It is a sobering reminder of the political risks involved in relying on a socially conservative party to advance APA incorporation.

Becoming Partisan: Accidental or Reluctant Partisans

Because of the relatively weak and evolving relationship between Asian Americans and the two major parties, it should not be surprising to find some Asian candidates and elected officials form their partisan identity on the spot rather than through the traditional route of family socialization or personal politicization. The formation of partisanship through effective persuasion or recruitment seems to be particularly true with the Asia-born and children of immigrants. Shanghai-born **Mae Yih** came to New York to attend Barnard College in 1948. She recalled how college experience taught her to be politically independent and not afraid to cross the party line. She volunteered at her children's school, eventually running for the local elementary school board, started her service in 1969, and moved to serve on a local high school board in 1975. The local Democratic Party chair urged her to run for an open seat in the Oregon State House in 1976. Yih won the election, defeating the 14-year incumbent Republican (Peng 2002).

Hawaii governor **David Ige** did not have strong ties to the Democratic Party when he was appointed to the Hawaii House of Representatives in 1985, nor was he even a party member. The state party chair had him sign the party card while driving to their meeting with Governor George Ariyoshi (Markrich and Chinen 2014). The son of a World War II veteran faced little electoral opposition throughout his 29-year career in the state legislature. He made history in 2014 as the first candidate to defeat an incumbent governor and the first Okinawan American to serve as governor. His electoral success can be attributed in part to a sizable Okinawan community network institutionalized through the Hawaii United Okinawan Association and the support of major labor unions and endorsements from the two former Asian American governors.

US Representative **Joseph Cao** was born in Vietnam and entered the United States as a refugee at age eight. The local Republican Party talked him into joining the party and running for Congress in 2008 as a challenger to a nine-term Black Democrat under FBI investigation for corruption and indicted by the Justice Department. He pulled off an improbable victory to serve as the first Vietnamese American in Congress. However, he also became one of only two Republican House incumbents to lose re-election in the 2010 midterm election. A former Jesuit seminarian, Cao's willingness to cross party lines to support measures he felt best met the needs of his largely poor, minority constituency often put him at odds with his party's leaders. "I

GETTING CONNECTED WITH POLITICAL PARTIES   143

don't want to conform to any ideology, to be put into a little corner," Cao said shortly after his election in 2008 (Nossiter 2008), and he became an uncertain ally for party leaders from the start. In 2009, he became the lone Republican who voted for Democrats' healthcare reform bill. However, citing concerns over abortion, he later voted with other Republicans to reject the Affordable Care Act. His first campaign manager observed, "It's hard to categorize him as a Republican or Democrat. In his heart, Anh is a Jesuit" (Ruggeri 2009)

For Alhambra city councilman **Gary Yamauchi**, picking his political affiliation when running for a nonpartisan office is like picking a musical chair, because he did not think partisanship mattered in the city. Born to parents who were interned during World War II, he said in a 2012 interview, "In my wildest dreams, as a kid, I never had thoughts of becoming an elected official" (Stevens 2012). Yet, due to his active involvement in many local community organizations such as Rotary Club, Chamber of Commerce, YMCA, and Go For Broke, he was urged to run for an open seat on the city council in 2004. He registered himself as a Republican in a city that was almost four to one Democratic and won the race despite opposition from the Democratic Club. After he won the seat again in 2008, he thought nothing really happened to him as a Republican, so he reregistered as a Democrat until 2012. Then, after failing to see any difference when he changed his party affiliation, he decided to reregister an independent.[11]

Turning the District Blue: Congressional Candidates Invested by the Democratic Party

Whereas Asians' presence in the US House of Representatives has been historically minimal, the number of voting delegates reached a high point of 20—all Democrats—in the 116th Congress. In what follows we feature three Asian newcomers whose first elective office is at the congressional level. They became the party's lethal weapon to win over seats from the GOP in 2016 and 2018. Their rise suggests the possibility of Asians becoming competitive candidates and partners in partisan electoral politics. Their elections also triggered aggressive GOP attempts to win back the districts, which resulted in a more significant Democratic infusion of campaign funds to keep the seats.

Born in 1978 in Ho Chi Minh City, **Stephanie Murphy** and her family fled Vietnam by boat when she was six months old. She was not affiliated with either party before running for the first time and was only recruited by the

144 CONTESTING THE LAST FRONTIER

Democratic Party one day prior to the filing deadline (Lemongello 2016). In addition to her refugee success story, Murphy's background as a national defense specialist and businesswoman, her outspoken opposition to gun violence, and Trump's misogynistic and racist statements made her an ideal candidate for Florida's Seventh Congressional District. It also mattered that the district was recently redrawn to become more evenly split between the two parties. Murphy was one of 13 women (out of 51 total candidates) the Democratic Congressional Campaign Committee (DCCC) selected for its Red to Blue program, which identifies vulnerable Republican incumbents and recruits candidates who meet the party's criteria of competitiveness or electability to run as challengers (Burrell 2018). Murphy was one of an even smaller number of Red to Blue candidates in 2016 to receive financial support from the DCCC, and the party also brought in campaign workers to help seal her victory (Comas 2016; Burrell 2018). She won with 51% of the votes.

Born and raised in southern New Jersey to immigrant parents from Korea, **Andy Kim** served as a national security adviser under President Obama and was a foreign affairs officer with the Department of State. In 2018, the Democratic Party heavily invested in the first-time candidate's campaign to unseat a two-term white male Republican incumbent who vowed to repeal the Affordable Care Act of 2010. He won endorsements from President Obama and the ASPIRE PAC, which was launched in 2011 by Congresswoman Judy Chu to support the campaigns of APA candidates and those who advance APA community issues. The district was less than 4% Asian and won by President Trump in 2016. During the campaign, he was smeared by the incumbent as "Real Fishy" in Wonton font on a picture of dead fish (Duhart 2018). He won by just over 1% of the votes.

In conservative Central Valley in California, **T. J. Cox's** 2018 campaign for the US House was infused with millions of dollars from the DCCC and Democratic PACs (Appleton 2018). Cox was a candidate in another district when the Democratic Party recruited him to run in the 21st Congressional District when the presumptive nominee, a Latino male, announced he would not be running. The founder and former president of a community development bank, Cox's ability to fundraise and his support of the Affordable Care Act made him an attractive replacement. He is also the son of a Filipino immigrant mother and a half-Chinese, half-white father from China, whose racial ambiguity may be advantageous in this majority Latino district. Cox won by less than 1% of the vote, and he was not declared the winner until weeks after the election when mail-in ballots were counted, overcoming a 25-percentage-point deficit during the primary election. In 2020, Cox appeared in the top 10 of the most endangered Democrats in the FiveThirtyEight forecast (Skelley 2020). He lost the seat to the same Republican he defeated only two years ago in another razor-thin vote.

Forgotten Candidates: Surviving Party Marginalization and Neglect

The intensive attention and support received by Asian legislative candidates from the major parties is not only a relatively new phenomenon, but it is rare. For most of the community's history, Asian candidates were the outsiders forgotten or marginalized by the parties. The racial and gender discrimination experienced by Patsy Mink within the Democratic Party in Hawaii was telling about the depth of the resistance to the candidacy and representation of a third-generation Asian woman. However, a supermajority of Asian candidates ran in nonpartisan, local elections. What helped them survive and triumph? In what follows, we feature the stories of some locally elected officials and their varied paths to office despite the lack of support from the major parties in their first political campaign(s).

March Fong Eu had been involved in Democratic clubs and volunteered on local campaigns while serving on the Alameda County Board of Education. However, she did not receive endorsements from any major organization or the Democratic incumbent when she first ran for the California State Legislature in 1966. Her campaign emphasized issue politics and her prior political experience rather than ties to party elites. Once elected, Fong Eu secured her credentials as a party loyalist by supporting Representative Jesse "Big Daddy" Unruh for the speaker position. She served on various committees and authored more than 400 bills that focused on education, preserving the environment, consumer protections, and protecting the rights of women and minority citizens. During her historic 1974 bid for California secretary of state, Eu campaigned heavily on her legislative achievements rather than party ties. She also attributed this victory win to the Watergate scandal and the growing women's movement (Van Ingen 2017).

Former Cupertino city councilman **Michael Chang** thought political parties did not play much of a role in his campaigns for education boards and city council. In fact, he thought the presence of political parties had

146 CONTESTING THE LAST FRONTIER

diminished over the years, especially in local races. While political parties can and do endorse candidates, Chang explained that more important than parties or any other formal organization were the networks developed through one's involvement in grassroots community organizations.[12] These networks served as the basis of his campaigns, which focused on mobilizing immigrant voters through a multigenerational volunteer network with in-language voter education, fundraising, canvassing, and other outreach and turnout efforts.

Former Gardena city councilman and mayor **Terrence "Terry" Terauchi** sought out but did not win the endorsement of the Japanese American–dominated Gardena Valley Democratic Club when he first ran for city council in 1998. As a member of several other Asian American community organizations, he was able to build support from rank-and-file members. He also reached out to non-Asian-majority veteran groups, law enforcement, and his congregation. During his 10-year hiatus, Terauchi maintained connections with several organizations that supported his campaigns in the late 1990s and early 2000s, which "strengthened their loyalty" when he returned to run in 2014. He explained that by staying involved in these organizations beyond the campaign trail, he built trust that his involvement was not opportunistic but based on shared values and interests (Yamamoto 2017).

When Orange County supervisor **Lisa Bartlett** decided to share her knowledge and skills as a corporate executive to help govern her city in 2006, she did not receive the endorsement of the GOP. Instead, she built support for her bid for Dana Point City Council through her professional networks and volunteer experiences in civic groups like Rotary Club. She also utilized her financial resources as a successful businesswoman. After winning the municipal race, Bartlett said she started to become more involved in the county-wide GOP central committee and Asian American community organizations.[13]

Neither did Los Alamitos city councilman **Warren Kusumoto** receive the endorsement of the GOP when he ran for city council in 2010. He was able to secure early funding through contributions from individual members of the Orange Coast Optimist Club, an Asian American youth organization, along with donations from family members and resources pooled from the slate of candidates he ran with. In addition to these donations, Kusumoto credited his positive name recognition that stemmed from his involvement in non-Asian-specific local civic groups like the Scouts, the basketball league, church, and his wife's participation in the PTA.[14]

Jane Kim's successful bid to join the San Francisco Board of Supervisors in 2011 suggests that the backing of formal organizations or institutions is not necessary to secure a victory, even in Democratic-dominated and partisan races. She launched her public service in 2007 after winning a bid to the San Francisco Board of Education as a Green Party candidate during runoff elections. As a newcomer from a third party, her first campaign was supported by unions, community groups, and the liberal media network. However, Kim's victory in 2011 was considered an "upset" because labor unions and the media did not support her. In addition, Kim's own Democratic Party endorsed her opponent. The only strategy Kim had available was the "old-fashioned" one of visiting as many constituents as possible. It was called Kim's "Fifty-Nine Precinct Strategy" (Yeung 2011). She received less support from the Korean American community, who participated little in the election, than Chinese American supporters, especially senior citizens in Chinatown, and a broad base of San Francisco youth voters.

Conclusion

Political parties and other political organizations are considered linkage institutions in the US political system. They were reputed to have helped turn demographics into power by organizing the voices and votes of newcomers and facilitating the incorporation of white (male-dominated) European immigrants who arrived in the 1880s and 1920s. However, for people of color, political parties have been inactive in their incorporation in the electoral system, if not outright obstructive. In this sense, being less on the political radar of the two parties might be considered a blessing in disguise for a minority group like Asian Americans. In the post-1965 era, when parties did engage selected individuals of Asian descent for recruitment and campaign support, these individuals were often found to be situated in legislative districts where their elections were considered strategically important to the party's fate in the legislative process. Examples include Tom Hom, Paul Bannai, Young Kim, and Michelle Park Steel on the GOP side and Mae Yih, T. J. Cox, and Stephanie Murphy on the Democratic side. Whereas the nature of party politics for Asians in Hawaii is significantly different from that in California and other mainland states, our longitudinal account of individual trajectories to partisanship (or the lack of it) followed by many of

148 CONTESTING THE LAST FRONTIER

the pioneering figures (and others significant to the representation of each major Asian ethnic community) uncovers a fairly entangled, volatile, and often ethnic- and gender-specific set of relationships. And yet our statistical account of present-day APAEOs shows that, instead of being collectively detached from the two parties, APAEOs are a predominantly Democratic community of elective leaders in the early decades of the 21st century. In the next chapter, we show that a shared ideological stance on the progressive side of politics could help APAEOs bridge differences in ethnicity, gender, and nativity among them. It could also provide a more solid foundation for coalition-building in governing and facilitating social justice advocacy for the intersectionally disadvantaged members within the Asian community and beyond. Nonetheless, APAEOs are far from a monolithic block. The election of two Korea-born GOP women to Congress from immigrant-rich Southern California in 2020 signals both the strength of immigrant incorporation and the challenge that diversity poses to concepts of representation for the Asian American community.

5

Advancing Justice through Transformative Leadership and Substantive and Symbolic Representation

In the world of US minority politics, the overall socioeconomic achievements of Asian Americans have earned them the title of the "model minority." Among US elected officials of color, Asian American men and women obtain the highest levels of education and family income as a whole, but they also register the highest rates of the foreign-born (Hardy-Fanta et al. 2016). Regardless of their accomplishments, APAEOs are members of a nonwhite population whose group history and journey to equal citizenship have been punctuated by experiences of structural racism, sexism, nativism, and labor exploitation. They are expected to confront legacies of racial exclusion and settler colonialism in the present day. How do they navigate the triangulated space between the "model minority" and the "perpetual foreigner" as community leaders and representatives in mainstream electoral politics? Previous chapters show that the gilded group image of being problem-free and privileged does not reflect the political socialization and campaigning experiences of US elected officials of Asian descent. Instead, the ability to overcome individual hardships, to survive and thrive despite group-based obstacles and setbacks, describes some of the common characteristics of those who made the electoral breakthroughs by becoming the "firsts" in their community or group or locality to win an office. By accounting for the individual trajectories to office and group patterns of officeholding, we show that their elections not only have expanded and diversified the political territory but have also provided a more nuanced understanding of the extent of minority political incorporation at national and local levels.

In this chapter, we further pursue a better understanding of the significance of their political rise by answering questions such as these: How do ethnic origin and identity shape ideas of leadership and representation?

Contesting the Last Frontier. Pei-te Lien and Nicole Filler, Oxford University Press. © Oxford University Press 2022.
DOI: 10.1093/oso/9780190077679.003.0005

150   CONTESTING THE LAST FRONTIER

How do gender and nativity also structure the observed relationships? Fundamentally, to what extent and in what ways have APAEOs been able to advocate for the interests of the intersectionally disadvantaged? We argue that the personal or family-based adversity in socialization may motivate one to run for office. It may also equip one with insider knowledge and a sense of responsibility and determination to advocate for the less fortunate or the structurally disadvantaged—both within and outside the ethnic community and jurisdiction. We also maintain that an experience with or knowledge of group-based discrimination may lead to identification with and ties to the fate of the minority community, which, in turn, can serve as a stimulant for community-based activism. These two processes help explain why some APAEOs have become effective policy advocates, transformative leaders, and representatives for social justice.

The need for transformative leadership is most urgent in crises where the physical, mental, and economic well-being of members in the APA community is adversely affected by their race, ethnicity, and gender (and other social identity markers). Examples in Asian American history include Chinese exclusion, Japanese American internment, and the forced prostitution of "comfort women" during World War II. What legislative efforts have been made by APAEOs to address past wrongs done by governments? Why and how have these APAEOs taken a proactive stance on issues of injustice and inequality? In 2020, the spike of anti-Asian violence during the Covid-19 outbreak presented an unprecedented challenge and opportunity for exercising transformative leadership to advocating for justice for Asian Americans and other structurally disadvantaged minorities. How did APA representatives in Congress respond to Covid-19?

We answer questions raised in the preceding two paragraphs in the following order. First, we discuss the multiple, interrelated dimensions of political representation and their distinct manifestations among Asian Americans. Second, we interpret legislative actions taken mainly at the federal level through affirmative advocacy and bridge feminism concepts. We link these to legislative advocacy at the subnational level through the concept of womanist leadership praxis. Third, we provide a snapshot of the scope of issue priorities and the relative importance of social justice concerns among APAEOs serving in 2020. We present separate accounts of legislative achievements for advancing justice for different Asian ethnic communities and their causes in broadly chronological order in both historical and contemporary times. Our analysis highlights the racialized and gendered processes through which legislators enact their roles as representatives at federal, state, and local levels. In addition, our discussion underscores the need for a womanist conception of leadership that can bridge grassroots and legislative activism to address persistent and growing inequities structured by intersecting oppressions. By employing the intersectionality framework and womanist leadership praxis, we hope to present a more nuanced and sophisticated understanding of the significance of the political representation of APAEOs.

Minority Political Representation in an Uneven Democracy

Theorist Hanna Pitkin (1967) imagines political representation as a multifaceted concept to help us comprehend the endlessly complex and fluid phenomenon in a representative democracy such as the United States. The descriptive dimension refers to the extent to which the social characteristics of the representatives resemble the attributes of the represented. The symbolic dimension refers to the extent to which representatives are perceived as taking a stand for the values and concerns of the represented so as to earn their trust and confidence. In the substantive dimension, the representatives are expected to be "acting in the interests of the represented, in a manner responsive to them" (209). By breaking down the concept into separate but not necessarily independent dimensions, Pitkin has helped generations of normative and empirical scholars interrogate the independent meanings of each and the interrelationships among the dimensions. Yet, Pitkin's approach was considered unsatisfactory to Hardy-Fanta et al. (2016), who commented that historically marginalized groups based on their racial, ethnic, gender, and other social attributes could create a special problem for Pitkin and other mainstream theorists. It was because these scholars tended to treat representatives "as an undifferentiated body of decision-makers presumed to be male in gender, white in race, and who experience no systemic disadvantages in the seeking and exercising of power in the electoral process" (291–92).

The conventional, race-blind, and gender-neutral approach to political representation has created numerous intriguing but also fruitful opportunities for concerned scholars of identity politics to explore the best or most adequate ways to represent the interests of marginalized groups in US governing institutions. The latter includes studies on racial minorities and women by elected officials who descriptively "look like" them. Whereas an extensive amount of research explores the possible linkages between descriptive representation and its substantive impacts on public policymaking, such lines of research typically involves African Americans, Latinos, and white women (e.g., Swain 1993; Hero and Tolbert 1995; Lublin 1997; Whitby 1997; Canon 1999; Swers 2003; Tate 2003; Rocca and Sanchez 2008; Casellas 2011; Grose 2011; Minta 2011; Minta and Sinclair-Chapman 2013; Bowen and Clark 2014; Wallace 2014; Lowande, Ritchie, and Lauterbach 2019). Most research has dealt with the US Congress and adopted an either/or approach to studying the dimensions of political representation by/for women and ethnoracial minorities, even if important works have been done on women of color in state legislatures and adopt intersectionality as a central analytical framework (e.g., Takahashi 1997; Prindeville 2004; Fraga et al. 2008; Smooth 2010b; Brown 2014; Minta and Brown 2014; Hardy-Fanta et al. 2016; Reingold, Widner, and Harmon 2020). It is only recently, with important exceptions, that scholars have paid attention to political representation by locally elected officials and racial minorities other than Blacks and Latinos.

Another overlooked area of prior research on political representation by racial minorities is symbolic representation, which "may be especially important for racial minority groups as they continue to struggle for full inclusion in mainstream American society" (Whitby 2007, 207). Whitby makes this observation after comparing how members of the Congressional Black Caucus exercise all three concepts of representation. Similarly, in her study on Blacks in Congress, Tate (2003) finds Black legislators to be more likely than non-Black legislators to propose symbolic policies addressing the concerns of Black constituents. More recently, Brown, Caballero, and Sinclair-Chapman (2018) find symbolic legislation a valuable tool for Black state legislators in Maryland to voice long-standing Black grievances and fulfill their nonmaterial needs through actions such as renaming airports. Black legislators use bill sponsorship and credit claim on votes cast as mechanisms of symbolic representation to communicate their blackness to predominantly white colleagues who may feel compelled to stand with their Black colleagues because of white guilt for past wrongs. The study's narrative analysis also points to the roles of political socialization, connections to Black community organizations and individuals, and gendered identity in explaining which issue concerns are pursued and how.

Political Representation by Asian Americans

Research on the political representation of Asian Americans has been limited. It primarily focuses on the number of racially descriptive representatives and the reasons behind their below-parity status or underrepresentation in elective office (e.g., Lai et al. 2001; Lien 2001a, 2002, 2006; Lai and Geron 2006; Doherty 2007; Huang 2012; Phillips and Bhojwani 2016; Visalvanich 2017; Go 2018; Reny and Shah 2018). Studies that examine the quality of representation by and/or of Asian Americans are scarce. Takeda (2001) provides one of the earliest attempts to study symbolic representation by examining the correlates of bill cosponsorship of a resolution in the 106th Congress to condemn all forms of prejudice against Asian Americans. H. Con. Res. 124 of 1999 was sponsored by Taiwan-born representative David Wu (D-OR-1). The resolution occurred in the aftermath of the wrongful allegations of espionage for China by a Taiwan-born nuclear scientist Dr. Wen Ho Lee. Takeda finds that members of the Congressional APA Caucus (CAPAC) and those representing districts with a larger percentage of Asians are more likely to support the resolution condemning stereotypes against Asian Americans. Chaturvedi (2015) expands on Takeda's research by examining bill (co) sponsorship of 19 House resolutions and 30 domestic bills thought to represent the interests of Asian Americans as a group in the 106th to 110th Congresses from 1999 to 2009. His research confirms the positive effects of the percentage share of Asians in the district and reports partisan differences in that Democrats (co)sponsored more bills on domestic policies for Asian Americans than Republicans. Moreover, he finds that Asian legislators are more likely than non-Asian legislators to (co)sponsor both symbolic and substantive bills related to the protection or advancement of Asian American interests.

In an exploratory study of Latino and Asian American elected officials using two nationwide mail surveys, Geron and Lai (2002) find elected officials of both nonwhite groups to be older, more financially secure, and better educated than their respective general population. Also, they report that both Latino and Asian officials are more liberal in political ideology than the general population. However, the two groups of elected officials differ in the percentages of the coethnic population in their jurisdictions; racial demography is a much stronger predictor for the election of Latinos than Asian Americans. Furthermore, perhaps reflecting differences in racial demography and cohesiveness of the community, a significant number of Latinos

154   CONTESTING THE LAST FRONTIER

aim their policies to benefit the Latino community primarily. In contrast, Asians focus on broader community issues than those narrowly defined by ethnoracial identity boundaries.

Hardy-Fanta et al. (2016) provide a more systematic and comprehensive study of elected officials from all major nonwhite groups who serve in federal, state, and local levels of government and from the intersection of race and gender. Using data from a national elite telephone survey conducted in 2006–7 and supplemented with census data, they provide corroborative evidence that Asian Americans as a group of elected officials are distinctive in the nature of their political representation when compared to that of other nonwhite groups. For example, unlike their Latinos and Black counterparts, Asian municipal officials are mostly elected from non-majority-Asian cities, and only 14% believe they represent predominately Asian districts. Among state legislators, less than one-quarter of Asians believe they represent majority-Asian districts, and Asians are more likely than their Latino/a and Black counterparts to report having majority-white jurisdictions. Also, regardless of their office level, Black elected officials report the highest, and Asian elected officials the lowest, level of shared partisanship with their constituents. In terms of the perceived socioeconomic status of constituents, 15% of Asians consider their constituencies to be working class, which is significantly lower than other elected officials of color. Regarding gender differences among elected officials, Asian men are generally more advantaged in personal and professional resources than Asian women. Finally, everything else being equal, Asian American men are significantly less likely than Asian American women and other nonwhite women and men to enact ideas of substantive representation. Namely, they are least supportive of legislative proposals that protect or advance the interests of racial and gender minorities.

Hardy-Fanta et al. (2016) also explore the empirical relationship between the two notions of enacting substantive representation. In general, those representatives who subscribe to the Madisonian or delegate view of representation see themselves as acting on instructions from their constituency via expressed preferences. Those representatives who follow the Burkien or trustee view see themselves as free agents acting on their understanding of the best interests of the constituency and the moral directives of their conscience. They analyze the GMCL survey data to explore the perceived role of representation by race and gender among elected officials of color. Up to three-fourths (72%) of Asian American men and women respondents identify themselves as trustees of constituent needs, which is a significantly higher percentage than reported by all other elected officials of color. All groups of nonwhite women and men officials consider themselves more trustees than delegates. However, nonwhite officials whose view of representation is closer to the delegate role are "more likely to perceive a correspondence between their own respective racial, partisan, and ideological identities as well as what they perceive as the most important issue stance and that of their constituents" (295).

Do the above findings suggest that Asian American elected officials, especially men, would be less likely to perceive the need for social justice actions to advocate for their constituents? We believe this question requires a large-scale quantitative data set to answer. Almost two decades ago, in the absence of such, Lien (2002) adopted a case study approach to assess the nature of representation regarding Asian American members in the US Congress throughout history. She finds that, with prominent exceptions, they generally contribute to the construction of a pan-Asian community and identity by adopting a representative role that is not bound by geographic or ethnic lines. It is the concept of surrogate representation where an elected official represents a group of people residing outside of his or her geographic jurisdiction (Mansbridge 1999, 2003). It seems to be related more to the trustee than the delegate view of representation, but it does not necessarily mean a deficiency of ethnic representation. However, Lien's study was done at the turn of the 21st century when Asian faces were few on Capitol Hill. Few Asian Americans residing outside of Hawaii had representatives who were descriptively Asian. In our study, APAEOs serving in Congress and at the subnational levels are not only fast-growing in number, but they are also highly diverse along ethnic, gender, generational, geographic, and other fault lines. Close to one-fourth of APAEOs serving in 2020 won their seats in or after 2016. This trend of continuous expansion in demographic and political terrains since 1980 and the accelerated growth rate in the last few years create an earnest need to re-examine the nature and impact of their political representation and leadership in the third decade of the 21st century.

Employing Intersectionality and Womanist Leadership Praxis in Studying APA Substantive Representation

Perversely, the pandemic created an opportunity to increase the visibility of APA legislators to contest racial formations of Asian Americans as the silent

156 CONTESTING THE LAST FRONTIER

(model) minority through bill sponsorship and other gestures or protests and resistance against discrimination and mistreatment. Our research of the APA congressional members' response to Covid-19 provides strong evidence of the substantive meanings of descriptive representation, even if their APA-targeted legislation was mainly symbolic in nature. Those legislators who sponsor legislation that aims to address racism, economic hardship, disparities in accessing healthcare, and other issues caused by Covid-19 appear to be practicing affirmative advocacy. Strolovitch (2007) refers to this concept in her study of representational politics involving interest groups where social justice leaders advocate and fight for the intersectionally disadvantaged members despite a predominant bias for the advantaged members. Her seminal research showcases the necessity of employing the intersectionality framework to improve understanding of the interplay of power and powerlessness for individuals and groups situated at the intersection of race, gender, sexuality, class, and other dimensions of identity politics.

We believe APA women in Congress, like their Black and other women of color colleagues, occupy an "outsider within" (Collins 1986) vantage point that is at once a source of oppression and resistance. Their legislative responses to the Covid-19 crisis could fall into the reign of bridge feminism practiced by Patsy Mink and Shirley Chisholm, the first Asian and Black women in Congress. Curwood (2015) interprets Chisholm's writing and speeches and describes her leadership style as practicing bridge feminism. She finds the Black congresswoman not only managed to connect grassroots and local activism with the insider politics of the nation-state, but was also able to bridge the ongoing Black freedom struggles with those of women's movements. Wu (2020) studies tensions between the radical and liberal forms of feminism among Asian American activists through Mink's lobbying for federal legislation to protect women's equal rights to education and child care. She argues that Mink also practiced bridge feminism by connecting her concern over women of color's oppression with her conviction in promoting structural change and equal opportunity for women through the legislative process. For us, Mink also practiced transformative leadership by bringing grassroots movements' goals to the mainstream electoral arena and straddling between organizations that serve mainstream feminist concerns and local community-based ones that serve the needs of working-class women and women of color.

For the predominance of APA elected officials who serve below a national-level office, we believe the concept of bridge feminism is similar to the idea of womanist leadership praxis advocated by Abdullah and Freer (2008) and introduced in Chapter 1. To recap, in their study of Black political representation and incorporation in California, Abdullah and Freer define womanist leaders as elected officials who adopt collective leadership, value coalition politics, exhibit a delegate style of representation, and aim to transform conventional politics. Womanist leaders view their formal/electoral positions as extensions of grassroots movements for social justice, maintaining connections to the community through their involvement in grassroots, community-based organizations. They pursue political transformation of, rather than incorporation into, the status quo of politics dominated by white males through insider and outsider strategies. The authors believe womanism and womanist leadership praxis is not exclusive to Black women but could also be adopted by other groups of women and men located at the intersections of various structural dimensions of oppression. Because the womanist leadership praxis helps interpret how racially descriptive representatives can act for the substantive interests of the community, we believe in the necessity and merits of employing the framework to help improve understanding of the experience of APAEOs, especially those who are committed to advancing social justice. We recognize the possible limitations of the Black-based framework to interpret the separate and unique processes of racial, ethnic, gender, and other formations among APAs. However, many of the APAEOs featured in our study are transformative leaders who can help advance justice for the intersectionally disadvantaged—and not just limited to those serving at the national level offices.

Priority Issue Concerns of APAEOS in 2020: A Statistical Outlook

To what extent have APAEOs been able to perceive social justice and equality concerns as part of their issue priorities? Leveraging our large-scale database of APA elected officials, we address this question by providing a statistical outlook on the issue priorities of those APAEOs serving in 2020. (See detailed methodology on how we identify and code issue priorities in Appendix C). We examined APAEO issue priorities across 11 topical areas covering education, immigration, public health/safety, family/youth/elderly, women, business/economy, labor, environment, APIA civil rights, fiscal/budget, and government services. We also created a separate issue category called "social

158   CONTESTING THE LAST FRONTIER

justice and equality concerns." This is for elected officials seeking to eradicate social inequality or to work on issues that address injustice for individuals or groups situated at the intersection of race, gender/sexuality, and class or some combination of these social and structural dimensions of inequality. Examples include those who seek equality and justice for at least two of the disadvantaged groups in US society, such as immigrants, women, workers, APIA and other racial/ethnic minorities, LGBTQ, and other minority Americans.

Table 5.1 presents the frequency distribution of issue priorities as a whole and by gender among APAEOs serving in 2020. We find that the most common issue priority for APAEOs is education. Over four in 10 officials indicate a need to promote education, improve the educational system, and improve access to education. The second most common issue priority, which describes the preference of 30% of the APAEOs in our data, is a tie among three issue areas: the need for government reform to improve the delivery of public services, the need to improve access to healthcare, safer streets, and safer schools, and the need to support small businesses and "smart" economic growth. Between 23% and 22% of APAEOs are found to treat climate change and environmental protection, fiscal responsibility, and balancing

Table 5.1 Priority Issue Concerns of APAEOS in 2020 by Gender (%)

Issues	All	Women	Men	Rank
Education**	43	55	34	1
Government reform and public services	30	30	30	2
Health and public safety	30	33	28	2
Business and economy	29	30	29	4
Environment	23	25	22	5
Fiscal and budget	22	25	20	6
Social justice/equality concerns**	20	31	14	7
Family youth and elderly care**	15	21	11	8
APA civil rights*	12	17	9	9
Women's rights**	8	16	2	10
Labor/jobs*	6	8	4	11
Immigration**	6	9	3	11
N	564	224	340	

* Gender difference is significant at .05 ** gender difference is significant at .001.
Note: See Appendix C for methodology on studying issue priorities of APAEOs.

the budget as among their top issue concerns. About 15% of officials in our database expressed priority concerns over domestic violence and services for youth, the elderly, and working families. Issues concerning cultural rights, hate crimes, and civil rights for APAs or racial minorities, in general, are ranked 9th and by 12% of APAEOs. Issues concerning the rights of women, workers, and immigrants are at the bottom of priorities and received single-digit mentions by our elected officials.

Exactly one in five APAEOs serving in 2020 is found to treat the need to help advance social justice and equality concerns as among their issue priorities. Analyzed by gender, a significantly higher proportion of women (31%) than men (14%) indicate their concerns over social justice and equality issues. Similarly, APA women officials show significantly greater concerns than their male counterparts over education, family-youth-elderly care, women's rights, and immigration. Female officials prioritize labor and APA civil rights issues more than do male officials, even if the gender gaps are narrower. However, there are no statistically significant gender differences in health and public safety, business and economy, environment, government reform and public services, and fiscal and budget issues.

Focusing on those who prioritize social justice and equality concerns, we note that, whereas there are variations in the degree of expressed concern across ethnic origins, those differences are not statistically significant. Equally important, neither do we find foreign-born officials to express a lower level of concern over social justice issues than their US-born counterparts. However, APAEOs who are Democrats show a much higher level of priority concern over social justice and equality issues than those who are Republican in partisanship. The percentage gap is 26% among Democrats and 6% among Republicans. Also, those with unknown partisanship are twice as likely as those with no partisan identity to express social justice concerns (10% vs. 5%). Moreover, APAEOs who hold higher levels of office tend to be more likely to list social justice and equality concerns as among their top issue priorities. Namely, we find 45% among Congress members, 43% among statewide officeholders, 30% among state legislators, 16% among municipal officials, and 13% among county officials and school board members as committed to advancing social justice as defined in our study.

In sum, the preceding discussion shows that only a small but significant segment of the APAEO population serving in 2020 was committed to advancing social justice. This attitude was more common among women elected officials, Democrats, and those in higher positions of power. In what

160 CONTESTING THE LAST FRONTIER

ways have these APAEOs been able to symbolically and/or substantially advance justice? As in previous chapters, we take a longitudinal and qualitative approach to examine in both historical and contemporary times the evidence found in the political trajectories of roughly the same group of individuals featured earlier in our book. Below, we take stock of the legendary contributions of pioneering as well as former and presently serving APAEOs in their leadership efforts to help advance equal protection and rights for racial minorities, women and girls, immigrants, and to help redress past wrongs regarding Japanese American internment, Chinese exclusion, and wartime military sex slaves in Asia. Then, taking advantage of the Covid-19 outbreak in 2020, we analyze congressional members' bill sponsorship as emblems of symbolic representation. We interpret women's legislative activism through concepts of bridge feminism and womanist praxis. We end with a tribute to mostly locally elected officials linking their grassroots activism to fighting in city halls to help reduce or eradicate inequity and advance justice for the intersectionally disadvantaged.

Pioneering Advocates for Civil and Voting Rights

India-born **Dalip Singh Saund**, the first APA elected to Congress with full voting rights in 1956, was praised by his colleagues as "a classic American success story" upon his death.[1] He declared himself as "a living example of American democracy in practice" while traveling abroad in the late 1950s during the Cold War (Saund 1960). Because of the racism and nativism received before reaching Congress, he fiercely supported the 1957 Civil Rights Act.[2] The "Judge" used his own story to advocate for its passage, pointing out that, although being born in India did not prevent him from becoming a congressional member, being born Black in Mississippi would have. He was also a fierce critic of overseas spending by the US government. Saund wanted to spend less money on military aid and more on cultural exchanges and infrastructure projects in the developing world. This way, farmers and rural villagers who needed money the most could receive it rather than kings and dictators. Unfortunately, this was a position that went against the policy of the Kennedy administration and contributed, in part, to his re-election defeat.

Hiram Fong, son of an indentured laborer from China, became the first Asian elected to the US Senate in 1959. He took his role seriously as a surrogate representative for Chinese and Asian Americans and as a link between Asia and the West. "Being the first Asian there in the Senate," Senator Fong once said, "I was very, very careful. I knew that if I did anything that was in the line of dereliction of duty, why it would shame me or shame my family. It would shame those of my ethnic background and it would shame my people of Hawai'i" (Nakaso 2004). Fong believed in the merits of bipartisanship and extended that philosophy beyond diplomacy and immigration to civil rights. Fong often voted for social legislation that aligned him with Democrats and moderate Republicans. He cast votes for much of President Johnson's Great Society legislation, including the Civil Rights Act of 1964 and the establishment of Medicare in 1965. Fong was instrumental in ensuring that Asians would be allowed to immigrate in the same numbers as people from other continents in the landmark Immigration Reform Act of 1965. He also contributed substantially to the Voting Rights Act of 1965, writing an amendment providing for poll watchers to guarantee the safety and fairness of elections. In addition, Fong supported the 1970 Equal Rights Amendment. In 1971 alone, he introduced 75 private bills, mostly for immigration relief, more than any senator in that year. He retired from the Senate in 1977.

Early Champions of Women's Rights

"I didn't start off wanting to be in politics," **Patsy Mink** once told a reporter. "I wanted to be a learned professional, serving the community. But they weren't hiring women just then. Not being able to get a job from anybody changed things" (Honolulu Advertiser 2002; Stringer 2018). Mink turned to the Democratic Party to change things, and she started by organizing young people to join the party. This third-generation Japanese American became the first Asian American woman elected to Hawaii's territorial house in 1956 and the first woman of color elected to Congress in 1964. Once in office, she introduced and supported legislation to improve early childhood education, women's pay and access to education, environmental protection, open government, and equal opportunity. She authored the landmark "equal pay for equal work" law in Hawaii while chairing the territorial senate Education Committee. During her first tour in Congress and as a member of the House Education and Labor Committee, Mink coauthored the 1972 Title IX Amendment of the Higher Education Amendment, which requires equal financing for women's sports and education programs sponsored by

162   CONTESTING THE LAST FRONTIER

the federal government. Written to prohibit discrimination based on gender by educational institutions receiving federal monies, it would have its most significant impact on women's participation in collegiate sports.

Because her entry into politics predated the modern era of Black civil rights and women's movements, Mink confronted many stereotypes and faced discrimination based on the intersection of her race, ethnicity, and gender. When lobbying colleagues to pass the 1972 act, she submitted a statement based on her personal experience: "Discrimination against women in education is one of the most insidious forms of prejudice extant in our nation." Mink felt a special responsibility to advocate for women early in her House career. She said, "Because there were only eight women at the time who were Members of Congress, . . . I had a special burden to bear to speak for [all women], because they didn't have people who could express their concerns for them adequately. So, I always felt that we were serving a dual role in Congress, representing our own districts and, at the same time, having to voice the concerns of the total population of women in the country."[3]

It was no exaggeration to say that Mink saved funding for women in sports when opponents tried to pass an amendment in 1975 to exempt school athletes from Title IX. Mink had to rush to her daughter, who was in a bad car incident and missed the vote, which ended in a 212 to 211 victory for opponents. Upon learning the circumstances of her absence, her colleagues banded with her in another vote the following day to block the hostile amendment. Title IX was renamed the Patsy Takemoto Mink Equal Opportunity in Education Act after her sudden death in 2002 to honor her vital role in crafting, defending, and providing continued support for the pivotal legislation that advances equal rights for American women and girls (Craig 2012).

Also entering electoral politics in 1956, **March Fong Eu** did not view herself as a representative for women or Asian Americans; instead, she concentrated on trying to be the best in whatever job she undertook as a "citizen legislator rather than a woman's rights advocate" (Morris 1978, 5). Eu sought to transcend group identity and ideological differences by finding common ground. During her campaigns, Fong Eu said she viewed herself as "a kind of a chameleon" that would change her color to suit the context (Van Ingen 2017, 169). In 1967, she made the news headlines by blocking the assembly from adjourning early for an annual all-male golf tournament (Wildermuth

2017). In the following years, Fong Eu became very well known "for her campaign to ban pay toilets in public spaces . . . , arguing that they discriminated against women because urinals were free" (Mills College 2018). Although her male colleagues ridiculed her, and through several legislative sessions where her bills were heard but died, A.B. 1650 of 1974 was finally passed and signed by Governor Reagan, banning pay toilets in public buildings (Brekke 2017). During her time in the assembly, Fong Eu served on and often chaired various committees, amassing a record of more than 400 bills, especially on issues related to education, preserving the environment, consumer protections, and protecting the rights of women and minority citizens.

The *Leading the Way* exhibition (California State Archives 2019) cited a talk, "The Self-Sufficient Woman," given by Fong Eu in 1973 about her groundbreaking career as a Chinese American woman in politics:

> There is no argument to the opinion that this nation could benefit greatly by increased participation by women in decision-making positions. We do bring to bear unique experiences and insights, unlike our male counterparts. Let us dissolve the misperception of considering the world to be like the setting for a John Wayne western. Let us hope more men will begin to listen. Let us hope more men will respond. But more men will listen only if we speak clearly. And more men will listen if we speak intelligently. More men will listen as more women believe in themselves and the cause they are fighting for. Our society will be much better when we put our self-sufficiency in action.

The statements and legislative advocacy of Mink and Fong Eu highlight different approaches and rhetorical strategies APA women adopted to advocate for women's rights before the modern era of Black civil rights and women's movements, as well as the Asian American movement in 1968 and Asian American / woman of color feminist formations. Mink ran in majority-Asian districts and often against Japanese men and white women. In contrast, Fong Eu ran and won in a more racially diverse race and district where Asians made up a small percentage of the population, and ideological fractures within the Democratic Party were more apparent. These political and local contextual factors may help explain the different ways Mink and Fong Eu negotiated, viewed, and enacted their racial, ethnic, and gender identities to champion women's rights.

164 CONTESTING THE LAST FRONTIER

Japanese American Redress in Congress and the California State Legislature

Having personal or familial experience of trauma may impact one's socialization, self-identity, political views, and legislative action. For APAEOs, the most obvious and predictable relationship between one's ethnicity and legislative action is probably the redress movement for Japanese American removal and incarceration during World War II. The personal experience of being stripped of human and civil rights due to racism and wartime hysteria motivated Japanese American elected officials such as Mineta, Matsui, Honda, and Nakano to pursue public office and advocate for civil rights and social justice. Having grandparents or relatives who were interned served as another call for action. Being Japanese American but without direct ties to the internment experience, such as those residing outside of the West Coast states or in Hawaii during World War II, does not diminish their interest in and commitment to pursuing justice. Whereas Nikkei legislators played a leading and indispensable role, the redress success would not be possible without support from APAs other than Japanese and non-APAs who identify with the plight of Japanese Americans and the need for a collective demand for justice.

The redress efforts made by APAEOs began in the late 1960s when Senator Inouye submitted a bill to repeal the Emergency Detention Act of Title II of the Internal Security Act of 1950. That legislation gave the government broad authority to detain suspected communists and other subversives and presented the threat of arbitrary arrests in free speech and political imprisonment, especially for people whose "race" was associated with a threat to the nation. In 1971, Representative Matsunaga introduced H.R. 234, otherwise known as the No Detention Act, to completely repeal Title II of the Internal Security Act of 1950. It overwhelmingly passed the House, and the Senate passed the bill by voice vote. It was signed into law by President Nixon in 1971. In 1976, President Ford signed Proclamation 4417, which formally terminated Executive Order 9066 (issued by President Roosevelt in 1942) and admitted government wrongdoing in the evacuation and relocation of Japanese Americans during World War II. Senators Inouye and Fong and Representatives Matsunaga, Mineta, and Mink surrounded President Ford in the signing ceremony.

Senator Inouye, along with other Japanese American members of Congress, was critical to passing the Civil Liberties Act of 1988. After meeting with Japanese American Citizens League (JACL) leaders over redress in 1979, Inouye suggested the prudent idea of lobbying for a congressional study commission that would issue a report on the factors behind the incarceration of Japanese Americans rather than push for monetary compensation from the start. Inouye and Matsunaga introduced S. 1647, the Commission on Wartime Relocation and Internment of Civilians Act, in 1979. Following the commission's findings, Inouye let Matsunaga take the lead in sponsoring the Civil Liberties Act of 1988 that provided an official apology and reparations. He played another key role in the appropriation process by suggesting turning reparations into a federal entitlement program with annual funding.

Senator Matsunaga was known to be one of the hardest-working and most personable senators around. Rather than confront an issue in public, he preferred what the Japanese call *nemawashi*, which loosely translated means "tending the garden" or "thorough preparation"; he would go around to colleagues behind the scenes to explain what he wanted and to seek their support (Halloran 2002). When Matsunaga was ready, he would make public his proposal with its support already lined up. He worked with the American Civil Liberties Union to lobby each senator on the need for reparations. By securing 75 senators to cosponsor S. 1009 of 1987, the companion redress bill in the Senate, he was credited with "almost single-handedly" getting the redress bill passed in the 100th Congress despite severe personal health problems and mounting national budget deficit in an economic recession (Hatamiya 1993).

Congressman **Norman Mineta** was 10 years old when his family was relocated to Wyoming's Heart Mountain concentration camp, where they lived behind barbed wire for three years. When asked in 2006 if internment influenced his decision to go into public service, Mineta replied, "No question it did" (US House of Representatives 2018c). The experience also shaped Mineta's emphasis on the accessibility and accountability of political leaders and the need to work across racial and ethnic boundaries to ensure equality and justice. He was instrumental in drafting and passing the groundbreaking H.R. 442, being the first person to testify, which eventually became the Civil Liberties Act of 1988. He was secretary of transportation when terrorists struck on 9/11. Mineta used the Japanese American internment experience to oppose racial profiling and discrimination against Muslim and Arab Americans in the wake of the catastrophe.

166   CONTESTING THE LAST FRONTIER

Representative **Bob Matsui** was six months old when his family was incarcerated and in separate camps for three years. This adversity was formative in his commitment to advancing social equality and justice. Motivated by President Kennedy's call for public service during college, he ran a grassroots campaign to win a seat on the Sacramento City Council. He served there until elected to Congress in 1978. As a junior House member of Japanese descent, he worked with Mineta on H.R. 442, the redress bill with 166 cosponsors, but focused his efforts on reparations. He used his seat on the Ways and Means Committee and expertise on tax codes to lobby support and declared early on his denial of monetary compensation to keep detractors from accusing him of self-interest.

Two Nikkei women in the House also contributed in distinctive ways to the redress movement. Republican congresswoman **Pat Saiki** of Hawaii had relatives in California who were rounded up and incarcerated in Topaz, Utah. She broke with her party in 1987 to cosponsor the redress bill, lobbying fellow GOP members to support the bill by direct and persuasive moral appeals and voting to expedite payments after the 1988 Civil Liberties Act became law. During the 1970s, Representative Mink worked with Representative Matsunaga to educate Americans about Japanese Americans' internment. In the late 1990s, during her second tour of Congress, Mink was instrumental in helping pass legislation to compensate Japanese Latin Americans who were incarcerated in US camps but denied access to reparations authorized in the 1988 Civil Liberties Act.

In California, Assemblyman **Mike Honda**, a third-generation Japanese American, was also incarcerated as a baby with parents in a concentration camp in Colorado. The personal experience prompted Honda to author the California Civil Liberties Public Education Act of 1998 (A.B. 1915). It authorized $1 million in state funding to support the development of educational resources about World War II incarceration of Japanese Americans and the importance of protecting civil liberties, even in times of national crisis. Two years later, a fellow Sansei and World War II internee, Assemblyman **George Nakano,** authored the California Civil Liberties Public Education Act of 2000 (A.B. 1914). It eliminated the three-year funding limitations of the grant program (started by Honda's bill) that prompted teaching of Japanese Americans experiences before, during, and immediately after World War II.

Assemblyman **Warren Furutani** had both his parents and grandparents incarcerated during World War II. While a board member at Los Angeles United School District, he led the effort to grant honorary high school diplomas to Japanese Americans unable to finish high school due to their forced removal and incarceration during World War II. Once elected to California Assembly, he authored A.B. 37 of 2008, which granted honorary college degrees to Japanese Americans whose education was disrupted by their wrongful incarceration during World War II.

Growing up in the Mountain West, Assemblyman **Floyd Mori**'s family was not rounded up and incarcerated during World War II. However, he became aware of the significance of his ethnicity and being Asian American when serving a mission in Hawaii with other Japanese Americans. He was heavily involved with the redress movement after getting elected to the state legislature in 1975. To him, "Japanese American incarceration during World War II has remained at the forefront of my career as a public office holder and as a participant in the advocacy efforts for civil rights" (Medlock 2016).

Finally, one does not need to be a Japanese American to be impacted by the trauma of forced removal and mass incarceration. A case in point is Congresswoman **Judy Chu**, whose mother migrated from China to marry her father, who served in the US military during World War II. She became interested in politics after taking an Asian American studies class. The activism of Pat Sumi, a Sansei Asian American movement activist born to parents incarcerated in Heart Mountain, Wyoming, inspired her. Chu said she learned for the first time that an Asian American woman could be a social justice community leader.

Nonetheless, it would be remiss if we do not mention that not all Japanese Americans in Congress supported redress. A case in point is **S. I. Hayakawa** who served one term in the US Senate (1977–83). Reputed to be an iconoclast, he opposed in 1979 a call by the JACL for the US government to redress civil rights violations committed against Japanese Americans relocated from the West Coast during World War II. He said, "For the JACL to ask for the restitution is merely the rekindling of resentment and racism that no longer exists" (Maki, Kitano, and Berthold 1999, 81). In 1982, he opposed JACL's call for reparations, arguing that the internment was a good thing and reminded Japanese Americans of their successful integration into American society vis-à-vis other ethnic groups and their relative level of wealth and education achievement. He also warned the community that, in an era of budget constraints and widespread public concern about Japanese economic gains versus the United States, such a program would invite a "backlash." He also sought to defund affirmative action programs throughout his one-term Senate career and opposed busing and bilingualism. In 1981, he submitted a

168   CONTESTING THE LAST FRONTIER

bill to repeal the bilingual requirements of the Voting Rights Act extension of 1975. After leaving Congress, he founded the political lobbying organization US English, which was dedicated to making English the United States' official language.

Whereas Hayakawa's opposition to redress made him an outlier among APAs in Congress, Maeda (2009) argues that his assimilationist ideology and racial logic represent the dogma of a class of conservative Asian Americans. He analyzes Hayakawa's thinking through the widely popular book *Language in Action* (1941), which attributed American racism to linguistics and argued that "rational thought is a necessary and sufficient antidote to racism" (46). Maeda believes these ideas underscore Hayakawa's positioning in US Black-white conflicts as the racial middleman and nonmilitant model minority.

Redress for Chinese Exclusion

Inspired by Japanese Americans' success in receiving redress for unjust treatment during World War II, activists in the Chinese American community have wanted to receive a similar apology from the US government for depriving Chinese nationals of immigration and immigrants from naturalization between 1882 and 1943. A breakthrough was reached in 2012 after concerted lobbying from leading APA advocacy organizations and groups in the 1882 Project.[4] Representative Judy Chu, the first Chinese American woman in Congress and chair of CAPAC, was able to help sponsor and secure unanimous consent from colleagues in both chambers for Congress to express regret for passing the Chinese Exclusion Act in 1882 and other legislation that discriminated against people of Chinese origin in the United States. A Senate bill preceded this legislative success in the previous year. In October 2011, the Senate passed by unanimous consent S. Res. 201, sponsored by Senator Scott Brown (R-MA) and as initial cosponsors Dianne Feinstein (D-CA), Orrin Hatch (R-UT), and Daniel Akaka (D-HI). According to Chu's office, H. Res. 683 in the 112th Congress was only the fourth congressional expression of regret since the Civil Liberties Act of 1988. Representative Mike Honda was among the nine initial cosponsors. However, unlike the Senate bill, the House bill contained a disclaimer that "nothing in this resolution may be construed or relied on to authorize or support any claim, including but not limited to constitutionally-based claims, claims for monetary compensation or claims for equitable relief against the United States or any other party, or serve as a settlement of any claim against the United States."[5] The disclaimer created a space for continuing need for advocacy and representation in the pursuits of justice for Chinese exclusion.

Representative Chu's activism on this issue was preceded by an effort at the state level. In California, Assemblyman Paul Fong learned that his grandfather was detained at the Angel Island Immigration Station in 1939 for being Chinese. This family connection to the history of Chinese exclusion made him propose and help pass A.C.R. 42 of 2009, which demanded both recognition of Chinese American and Chinese immigrant contributions to California and the state's expression of regret for past discriminatory laws against the Chinese. This success at the state level laid the foundation for supporters to lobby Congress to demand the same at the national level. Nevertheless, to some in the Chinese American community, Assemblyman Fong was controversial for proposing and passing the shark fin law (A.B. 376 of 2011). The act banned the possession, sale, and distribution of shark fins and was perceived by the Chinese community as promoting environmental protection at the expense of ethnic community interest (Kim 2015).

Earlier in the late 1990s, Representative David Wu (D-OR-1), who was born in Taiwan, sponsored and helped pass a concurrent resolution in the aftermath of congressional hearings on contributions made by Asian donors to the 1996 Clinton-Gore re-election campaign and on espionage charges against a Taiwan-born nuclear scientist for spying for China. H. Con. Res. 124 of 1999 was viewed as a symbolic gesture for US Congress to express concern over "recent allegations of espionage and illegal campaign financing that have brought into question the loyalty and probity of Americans of Asian ancestry." Among the 75 cosponsors were Representatives Matsui, Mink, Scott, Faleomavaega, and Underwood. Takeda (2001) finds cosponsorship to be more likely among members of CAPAC and representatives elected from districts with a larger share of Asians.

In the 116th Congress, Representative Grace Meng, together with Representative Chu, introduced a resolution that recognized the Chinese railroad workers for their contributions to the construction of the Transcontinental Railroad from 1865 to 1869 and the development of the United States. It also honors the Chinese railroad workers who lost their lives working in the Sierra Nevada and acknowledges the Chinese railroad workers for all the risks they faced while enduring discrimination and unequal pay and mistreatment to complete the construction of the Transcontinental Railroad. H. Res. 165 of 2019 had 33 cosponsors in the House, including

170 CONTESTING THE LAST FRONTIER

APA representatives Ami Bera, Ro Khanna, Raja Krishnamoorthi, Ted Lieu, and Michael San Nicolas. A companion bill in the Senate, S. Res. 681, was sponsored by Senator Catherine Cortez Masto of Nevada, the first Latina in the US Senate, in August 2020. Nevada has topped the list of states with the fastest-growing Asian and Pacific Islander populations for the past several decades. As of 2015, Asians comprised 9.7% and Pacific Islanders 1.3% of the state's total population, up from just 2.9% and 0.2%, respectively, in 1990.[6]

Like the redress for Japanese removal and incarceration, it was a grassroots effort led by Chinese Americans that encouraged Representative Judy Chu and other APAEOs of Chinese descent to champion legislation that recognized the community's call for redress for past and ongoing wrongs. As Fong's story also demonstrates, having members of one's family subject to institutionalized racism can further one's drive for justice. Moreover, each of the preceding cases illustrates that APAEOs who act as extensions of grassroots community concerns for social justice forge pan-APA and cross-racial coalitions with white and nonwhite elected officials by transcending and transforming narrow boundaries of ethnic group identity and interests.

Justice for "Comfort Women"

In the early 1990s, following the emergence of a grassroots movement in Korea, Korean American immigrant women began advocating for justice so-called comfort women (McCarthy and Hasunuma 2018; Comfort Women 2018). The term "comfort women" refers to the roughly 400,000 girls and women from Korea, China, Taiwan, the Philippines, and other occupied areas in Asia who were forced into sexual servitude by the Japanese military during World War II. The Japanese government has never officially apologized for the sexual enslavement of these women, and it has tried to whitewash this part of history in textbooks. Seeing a corollary to the internment of Japanese Americans by the US government during World War II, Mike Honda played a leading role in pursuing justice for these women.

While serving in the California State Assembly, Honda led a coalition (with six non-Asian legislators) to pass a resolution (A.J.R. 27) in 1999, urging the government of Japan to "formally issu[e] a clear and unambiguous apology for the atrocious war crimes committed by the Japanese military during World War II and immediately paying reparations to the victims of those crimes." Whereas some members of the Japanese American community considered it controversial, this action helped him win "many friends among Chinese, Korean, Filipino and other Asian Americans whose ancestral countries suffered under Japanese imperialism" (Kang 2000). A.J.R. 27 also calls upon Congress to adopt a similar resolution—something Representative Honda was able to sponsor and help pass the House in 2007.

H. Res. 121 asked the government of Japan "to formally acknowledge, apologize, and accept historical responsibility in a clear and unequivocal manner for its Imperial Armed Forces' coercion of young women into sexual slavery." It demanded the Japanese government refute any wrongful claims of history and educate current and future generations about this horrible crime. Honda was vocal on educational transparency and the importance of referencing injustice against "comfort women" in history textbooks. Despite facing backlash from his own ethnic community, Honda upheld his focus on victims' constitutional rights and provided compensation and reparations for their being subjects of racialized sexual discrimination and abuse. Honda's ability to shepherd the resolution was due primarily to the grassroots activism of Asian women nationally and internationally who formed coalitions across gender, ethnic, generational, and national lines to seek redress and reparations.

In various local Asian communities in the United States, redress for comfort women took the form of erecting memorials for these women in public space. In San Francisco, Judge **Lillian Sing** retired from her position in the San Francisco Superior Court to testify in front of the San Francisco Board of Supervisors in support of a resolution to build a "comfort women" memorial statue. Around the same time, she cofounded with retired judge **Julie Tang** the Comfort Women Justice Alliance, a grassroots movement organization, to raise public awareness and coordinate efforts to build a memorial statue in the city. The *Comfort Women: Column of Strength* statue was erected in 2017 despite international opposition from the Japanese government.

This was not the first time that Judges Sing and Tang worked to bring historical awareness to atrocities wrought by Japanese imperialism through multigenerational, pan-Asian coalition-building. In 1996, they founded the Rape of Nanjing Redress Coalition to bring international awareness to the massacre and other war crimes committed by the Japanese government and its redress to Chinese victims. These two Chinese immigrant women leaders were confident that this would help the current generation of Chinese and Japanese Americans understand the possibility of cross-ethnic and pan-Asian coalitions. In the "comfort women" campaign, however, Sing saw a

172   CONTESTING THE LAST FRONTIER

broader coalition that could form around the global human rights issue of wartime treatment of women and girls and knew that it would require her to take on more of an advocacy role than permitted of a judge.[7]

Former San Francisco supervisor **Eric Mar** learned about the Nanjing massacre and the atrocities against women and girls in China by the Japanese Imperial Army from his grandmother. These lessons planted an awareness of human rights and the problem of patriarchy. Still, the grassroots campaign led by Julie Tang, Lillian Sing, and others across the United States to build public memorials connected him more directly to the issue and inspired him to become more involved. Mar embraced a delegate style of representation by forging close connections with community groups and prioritizing their issues, particularly those disadvantaged at the intersections of oppressions. He approached his role not as one of the heads of a movement but as one who respects and recognizes voices that are often ignored. In the "comfort women" struggle, he continued to practice bottom-up leadership and tried to amplify the voices of those who have often been silenced in history.

In an interview with us after he stepped down from the supervisor's office,[8] Mar described how this approach did not always work in progressive coalitions in San Francisco: "It was challenging for me because when I worked in coalitions with, for example, labor and retail workers or low-wage workers, I would always engage the coalition before making decisions. But a lot of my colleagues would make decisions without grassroots leadership input. But I feel good that I tried to be principled about that and kept strong relations with community-based groups." He cited frustration with the "co-optation of grassroots social justice movements" and "opportunism" and "backstabbing" in San Francisco City Hall as reasons for leaving public office.

To Mar, barriers to coalition-building included a masculinist environment of competition and conflict and the lack of organizational infrastructure within and beyond the APA community. He pointed out in the same interview that coalitions for social justice could perpetuate the marginalization of the intersectionally disadvantaged, including women and girls, Southeast Asians, and Pacific Islanders. As a policymaker and advocate, Mar saw the detrimental effects of ethnocentrism and nationalism within APA communities. He also mentioned a culture of elitism, gatekeeping within ethnic-specific communities, the nonprofit industrial complex, and the difficultly of framing issues to reach a broader audience while not "watering down" the problem as challenges he encountered.

ADVANCING JUSTICE THROUGH LEADERSHIP   173

As Chinese immigrant women, both Sing and Tang experienced marginalization within the mainstream electoral arena and in San Francisco APA community politics. They had long known the necessity of expansive, intersectional coalitions and insider/outsider strategies to fulfill their commitments to social justice and equality. Their racial, ethnic, gender, and immigrant identities all figured into their decades of pan-Asian, cross-racial, transnational coalition-building to address issues facing intersectionally marginalized women and families, both at the grassroots level and in the San Francisco courts. In the "comfort women" struggle, it was their and other Asian immigrant women's transformative leadership that encouraged US-born Asian men like Honda and Mar to tie their personal connections and political commitments to the struggle for justice against imperialism, racism, and the sexual exploitation of women and girls. Yet as Mar cogently explained, there are multiple, distinct challenges for APAEOs serving at the local level who seek to remain connected to and extensions of grassroots movements and community concerns for social justice, especially for a heterogeneous and politically disjointed panethnic community and in a large city like San Francisco where ethnoracial diversity and economic inequality are extreme and where, as we demonstrated in Chapter 3, there is a relatively long history of sustained descriptive representation by Asian Americans and women, in particular.

Advancing Immigration and Immigrant Rights

Judy Chu was born to an Asia-born mother and US-born father and grew up in a working-class family in a predominantly Black neighborhood in South LA. This diverse childhood socialization explained her strong ties to labor and racial and immigrant minorities. After marrying Mike Eng, Chu settled in Monterey Park when the controversy over Chinese-language storefront signs was feverish. The couple helped form a multiracial coalition called Citizens for Harmony in Monterey Park to celebrate the city's various cultures and led a petition drive to rescind a racially divisive resolution passed by the city council (Merl 2009). Some of Chu's progressive standpoints raised eyebrows among Chinese American constituents, including her support for a union at a local Chinese newspaper and a local hospital, as well as her approval for same-sex marriage (Pierson 2006). Nonetheless, Chu said she was "particularly proud of her efforts in helping workers unionize" in

174   CONTESTING THE LAST FRONTIER

places that have "a largely Chinese clientele. . . . And it would be hypocritical for her to not support same-sex marriage, considering that a century ago the Legislature was using similar rhetoric to prohibit Chinese from marrying whites" (Merl 2009).

She won a seat in the California State Assembly in 2001. She immediately earned a reputation as "a builder of alliances across ethnic, political and social lines" (Winton 2001). An example of Chu's work to support a multitude of ethnic groups was her authorship of A.B. 309, which required "businesses that negotiate with customers in any of four major Asian languages to provide contracts written in the same language" (Pierson 2004). Chu also authored A.B. 2428, or "Kenny's Law," "that required judges to routinely issue orders of protection for victims of hate crimes and their families. It was named after 17-year-old Kenneth Chiu, a Taiwanese American who was stabbed to death by a white supremacist neighbor in Laguna Hills" (Pierson 2006).

Chu became the first Chinese American woman elected to the House of Representatives in a special election in 2009 to replace Hilda Solis of CA-32, which was two-thirds Latino. In 2011, Chu became chair of CAPAC, a position that also co-led the Congressional Tri-Caucus. Because of her district's diverse and immigrant-majority population, she felt responsible for representing her constituents by working on their concern over a visa backlog in the family visa program. Chu is a staunch supporter of immigration reform and publicly broke with the Obama administration over practices at the border and has likened immigrant detention centers to Japanese internment camps (Chu 2015). She has also stood up to the Trump administration's stance on immigration and has introduced bicameral legislation that seeks to halt the Muslim ban (Coleman 2019).

Japan-born **Mazie Hirono** was Hawaii's lieutenant governor when she fell victim to the state's male-dominated party politics in 2002. She became the first Democrat to run unsuccessfully for the governorship in 40 years after being forced to re-enter the race late and without union or party support after the white male party favorite dropped out due to campaign finance violations (Boylan 2007a). Despite the loss, Hirono kept active in the Democratic Party, founding the Patsy Mink Political Action Committee, which aims to (re)elect pro-choice Democratic women in Hawaii. In 2006, she received poetic justice by becoming the first Asia-born woman in Congress. In an interview after swearing in as a representative (Boylan 2007b), Hirono acknowledges that she "stands on the shoulders" of another Second District Democratic woman, the late Patsy Mink. "I don't feel I have to live up to Patsy. I think I'm very good in the legislative arena, talking with people and building alliances, but Patsy showed us what it took to succeed—a willingness to take risks, to break out of one's comfort zone and leap into the unknown" (Boylan 2007a). And Hirono said she's not in Congress to take up space; she wanted to make a difference. Her fierce attitude is also inspired by her single mother, who worked two jobs to keep the family together and, upon securing a better job at a local newspaper, risked it all to walk the picket line supporting a union (Hirono 2021). In 2013, Hirono became the first Asian American woman US senator.

Growing up working class and without healthcare inspired her to advance affordable healthcare legislation in the House of Representatives. She was also active in promoting abortion rights and contraceptive access and reforming the environment of harassment around both issues, which she supported through signing the Access to Birth Control Act. She authored legislation to strengthen Title IX (Patsy Mink Equal Opportunity in Education Act). In the US Senate, she supported immigrants, healthcare, Deferred Action for Childhood Arrivals (DACA), legislative transparency, and racial justice. She was known to question every executive and judicial nominee, no matter the position, on whether they had been accused of sexual misconduct (North 2019), and she was one of the main cosponsors of a bipartisan amendment to initiate the removal of all Confederate symbols and monuments in the US military. Hirono also repeatedly spoke out against the Trump administration's immigration policies and affirmed mass demonstrations against the so-called zero-tolerance policy and grassroots movements for immigrant, racial, and gender justice. While Hirono rarely shared personal details, she took to the Senate floor on June 20, 2018, to tell her firsthand experience of the pain and trauma her mother and younger brother endured as a result of being forced apart for nearly three years.[9]

India-born **Pramila Jayapal** began her community-based advocacy in the wake of widespread discrimination and violence against Muslim, Arab, and South Asian communities following the 9/11 attacks. In 2001, she founded the nonprofit Hate Free Zone and grew the organization (now OneAmerica) into the most significant multiracial immigrant rights advocacy in Washington. In 2013, she led We Belong Together, a national partnership between the National Domestic Workers' Alliance and National Asian Pacific American Women's Forum to provide a gender lens to immigrant rights advocacy. Jayapal was motivated to run for office because she realized that her entire work for social justice had been influenced by "the

176   CONTESTING THE LAST FRONTIER

critical intersections between education, affordable housing, adequate family income, transportation, criminal justice and immigrant rights" (Turnbull 2014). Once she became a Washington state legislator, she secured funding for preapprenticeship programs that ensure women and people of color have access to sufficient wages and union jobs. She also succeeded in securing reproductive healthcare access for Medicaid recipients and language access for students and parents. In addition, she sponsored legislation to provide survivors the ability to track their rape kits and secure tuition-free community college for Washington residents.

Jayapal also publicly shared her personal experience in the US immigration system. She lost her status as a permanent resident because of her inability to return to the States in time due to medical complications with her son's premature birth in India. It took her three years to restore her status. She explained, "I became determined to get my citizenship as soon as I was eligible so that I would never again face the prospect of being separated from my son, who was a United States citizen by virtue of being the child of a United States citizen father" (Jayapal 2017). Even if she is a member of Congress, this personal experience helped her empathize with immigrants' fears of being denied entry and separated from their families under the Trump administration.

As the current cochair of the Democratic Progressive Caucus, Jayapal has used her formal leadership positions to advance progressive issues. She is at the forefront of the fight for a long list of ambitious left-wing priorities, from Medicare-for-all to the Green New Deal. Yet, unlike the more confrontational and grassroots approach taken by other women of color, Jayapal has adopted a cooperative approach in negotiating with Speaker Pelosi and her allies as an activist insider by taking a page from Pelosi's own deal-making playbook (Nielsen 2019). Being a member of the House LGBTQ Equality Caucus, she unexpectedly shared a tearful story about the freedom her child gained once embracing their gender-nonconforming identity during a House Judiciary Committee meeting about the Equality Act and urged protection of that freedom (Fitzsimons 2019). Jayapal also publicly shared for the first time the story of her abortion in a 2019 *New York Times* op-ed. And following a 2021 US Supreme Court ruling that upheld a Texas law banning abortion after six weeks and encouraging citizens to sue healthcare providers and anyone else involved in providing care to a person seeking the abortion, this congresswoman and grassroots organizer created an online petition and urged her supporters to sign on as a "citizen co-sponsor" of the Women's Health

Protection Act. The bill was first introduced by Representative Judy Chu in the 116th Congress and reintroduced in the 117th with 211 cosponsors, 19 of which signed on following the ruling.

Responding to the Covid-19 Crisis in the 116th Congress

The 116th Congress (2019–20) included a historic high of 17 voting members of API descent, including three senators and 14 representatives. The record-high number of nine women, or 53% of the APA congressional delegation, is the highest gender ratio in the delegation of any major US racial group. The combination of the unprecedented visibility of APA members in the 116th Congress and the Covid-19 outbreak in 2020, a pandemic that had led to a rise in anti-Asian racism,[10] provides a rare opportunity for us to systematically examine the extent and nature of APA political representation at the congressional level and to help fill a void in scholarship on legislative studies.

Who are APA voting members in the 116th Congress? Table 5.2 shows that Californians dominate the delegation; two are from Hawaii, and the rest are from six other states. The average length of tenure in the legislator's current office is 7.6 years, ranging 2 years (i.e., Cox and Kim were elected in 2018) to as high as 28 years (i.e., Scott was elected in 1992). As many as six members (35%) were born in Asia. Nevertheless, four entered the United States as a baby or at a young age. Both Senator Duckworth and Representative Jayapal did not enter the United States until their late teens, but both received their first English-based education in Asia. This cohort of legislators is fully Democratic by partisanship. They are diverse in ethnic origin, encompassing all six major Asian ethnic groups and including a high degree of subethnic diversity within those of Chinese descent. Moreover, they are racially diverse, with five of the members having multiracial backgrounds. Both Senator Harris and Representative Scott are also Black by descent, and Senator Duckworth, Representative Gabbard, and Representative Cox can trace their ancestry to European whites. All are members of the CAPAC.

In terms of jurisdictional racial makeup, the average percentage Asian (alone) is 18.4, Black is 9.1, Latino is 20.6, and white is 46.4. Only one district (Khanna, CA-17) is majority Asian (alone), and one district (Takano, CA-41) is majority Latino. Yet Hawaii as a state is majority Asian if including multiracial Asians in the count. Six of the jurisdictions are majority (non-Hispanic) white, ranging from 51% in T. J. Cox's CA-21 to 80% in Andy Kim's

Table 5.2 Asian Pacific Americans in the 116th Congress (Voting Members)

Sex	State-Dist.	Last Name	First Name	Title	Year Elected Current	Year Elected First	US-Born	Ethnicity	% Asian	% Nonwhite
F	CA	Harris	Kamala	Sen	2016	2003	Yes	Black/Indian	15.3	63.2
F	HI	Hirono	Mazie	Sen	2012	1980	No	Japanese	38.6	78.2
F	IL	Duckworth	Tammy	Sen	2016	2012	No	Thai Chinese/White	5.9	39.0
F	CA-27	Chu	Judy	Rep	2009	1985	Yes	Chinese	37.9	70.8
F	CA-6	Matsui	Doris	Rep	2005	2005	Yes	Japanese	16.1	61.1
F	FL-7	Murphy	Stephanie	Rep	2016	2016	No	Vietnamese	4.3	40.4
F	HI-2	Gabbard	Tulsi	Rep	2012	2002	Yes	Samoan/White	28.8	70.2
F	NY-6	Meng	Grace	Rep	2012	2008	Yes	Chinese/Taiwanese	40.5	66.8
F	WA-7	Jayapal	Pramila	Rep	2016	2014	No	Indian	10.5	24.0
M	CA-7	Bera	Ami	Rep	2012	2012	Yes	Indian	15.1	42.8
M	CA-21	Cox	TJ	Rep	2018	2018	Yes	Filipino/Chinese/White	11.2	49.1
M	CA-17	Khanna	Ro	Rep	2016	2016	Yes	Indian	51.0	73.2
M	CA-33	Lieu	Ted	Rep	2011	2002	No	Chinese/Taiwanese	13.5	31.5
M	CA-41	Takano	Mark	Rep	2013	1990	Yes	Japanese	5.9	73.9
M	IL-8	Krishnamoorthi	Raja	Rep	2016	2016	No	Indian	12.7	52.7
M	NJ-3	Kim	Andy	Rep	2018	2018	Yes	Korean	3.5	19.9
M	VA-6	Scott	Robert C.	Rep	1992	1978	Yes	Black/Filipino	2.6	54.9

Source: Compiled by authors from the APAEO database of 2020.

NJ-3. Finally, 11 members, or two-thirds of the APA delegation, oversee majority or near majority-minority constituencies. Because few won seats from majority-Asian districts/states, proportionally few of the bills sponsored by them target APA needs. However, demography does not dictate advocacy by those who wish to promote social change.

As discussed earlier, APA members in Congress have a track record of legislative activism, passing legislation to help redress past wrongs against APAs and other minorities. Whereas Japanese American males spearheaded redress efforts, congresswomen such as Patsy Mink and Judy Chu marshaled congressional campaigns for women's rights and redress for Chinese exclusion. In addition, there were two other legislative successes in advancing justice championed by APA women in Congress. One was a 2016 bill coauthored by Representatives Grace Meng (D-NY) and Ed Royce (R-CA) to remove racist and outdated language such as "orientals" and "negroes" from federal laws. H.R. 4238 had 76 cosponsors in Congress, including all 51 CAPAC members. After Senator Hirono helped it pass the Senate, the act became Public Law 114-157 within three months of its introduction.[11] The second one was a bipartisan resolution (S. Res. 118) introduced by Senator Kamala Harris in 2017 to condemn hate crime and any other form of racism, religious or ethnic bias, discrimination, incitement to violence, or animus against a minority in the United States. Duckworth was one of the cosponsors. APA cosponsors on the House side included Chu, Gabbard, Jayapal, Murphy, Bera, Khanna, and Krishnamoorthi.

To what extent and how have APA members in the 116th Congress responded to the Covid-19 outbreak? In a preliminary investigation, we observed various political actions taken by legislators to address challenges caused by Covid-19 and concerning racism, economic hardship, disparities in accessing healthcare, and other issues. Examples of such representative acts include sponsoring and cosponsoring bills and resolutions, calling for hearings, and organizing and submitting letters to leaders. To appraise the responsiveness of the APA congressional delegation to this pandemic, we examine APA legislative advocacy between February and mid-May 2020, or the first three months after the Trump administration declared the coronavirus a public health emergency on January 31, 2020. Racializing the coronavirus as the "Wuhan virus," "Chinese virus," or "Kung flu," the administration was quick to ban nearly all non-US travelers from China to enter the United States. Yet it did not declare Covid-19 a national emergency until March 13, 2020.

Our research documents all the bills sponsored (authored and introduced) as recorded in Congress.gov, the official website for US federal legislative information, by APA members during the first three-and-a-half-month period of the known pandemic spread in the United States. In addition, we perused press releases of each APA member to determine if they could claim credit in producing more inclusive evidence of legislative activism that recognizes the value of allyship and coalition-building across legislative chambers and congressional districts. We also believe it is an adequate approach to document affirmative advocacy (Strolovitch 2007) in Capitol Hill and can capture a more precise level of engagement than what is implied in the traditional concept of bill sponsorship. The primary focus of our analysis is to assess APA legislators' responses to Covid-19 and how they are connected with APA community needs. We analyzed the timing of the action, quantity and type of bill sponsorship, issue focus of sponsored bills, and possible linkage to each legislator's group identity at the intersection of race and gender. To categorize the bills, we developed a predetermined issue list based on prior research of legislative records and employed a research assistant to sort bills into issues. (See more details on methodology and findings in Feng and Lien 2020.)

In total, we find APA members helped sponsor 69 bills (including 19 bills they introduced together with non-APA members) during the study period. Only three of the bills explicitly targeted APAs and were related to Covid-19; all were resolutions, and APA women sponsored all of them (H. Res. 908, S. Res. 580, and H. Res. 956). Despite their symbolic nature, several bill sponsors declared the importance of introducing the bills after hearing reports about anti-Asian discrimination directly from their constituents. In addition, Representatives Chu and Meng used the organizational legitimacy of CAPAC to release statements pressuring bureaucrats and politicians and win seats in Covid-19 committees. Similarly, Senators Harris, Duckworth, and Hirono urged federal agencies such as the Department of Justice and the US Commission on Civil Rights to do more in the face of rising anti-Asian racism. On the personal and community level, APA legislators carried a knowledge of systemic oppression on their shoulders and used it to guide their decisions and actions. According to Representative Takano, whose grandparents and parents faced internment, "We as Asian-Americans know that in times like these, mass blame and mass guilt gets assigned to a group of people" (Stevens 2020, 18). While nearly all the APA-sponsored bills stalled in committees and the letters did not generate much response, these actions signal APA legislators' commitment to the APA community.

Among the 17 issue categories covered by the 69 bills, the one that received the highest sponsorship from APA members is that Covid-19 triggered anti-Asian sentiment and hate incidents. Nine of the 17 members drafted a bill or sponsored one prepared by fellow APA colleagues. In the finance or economy bill issue category, as many as eight of the 17 APA legislators sponsored or coauthored a bill introduced by fellow APA colleagues. They were also active in advocating for worker relief or protection, immigrants, students or education, and healthcare—in each issue category, bills were sponsored by seven of the 17 APA members. In addition, as of May 28, 2020, in the 116th Congress, APA members sponsored five of the seven non-Covid and APA-targeted bills.

Analyzed by gender, APA women legislators were more likely to introduce bills targeting APA constituents than their male counterparts. In addition, through sponsorship of legislation targeting women, immigrants, and the poor in addition to APAs, APA women legislators are more likely to practice legislative advocacy and help advance interests of the intersectionally disadvantaged than APA men legislators during our study period. Moreover, those women legislators who have a prior record of minority advocacy (Chu, Meng, Hirono, and Harris) are more proactive in their responses to Covid-19. Importantly, in the first months of the Covid outbreak in 2020, the legislator's gender identity of the all-Democratic APA delegation in the 116th Congress is found to be a significant predictor of bill sponsorship. In contrast, the shares of Asians or nonwhites in the jurisdiction or the legislator's nativity and length of tenure in the current office are not. Finally, because APA women sponsored nearly three-fourths (14 out of 19) of the coauthored bills in our study, they are significantly more likely than their male counterparts to form coalitions with other APA and non-APA women and men when drafting bills. The non-APA sponsors are diverse by race and gender identity and include men and women of Black, Latinx, and white descent.

In Chaturvedi's (2015) research of five congressional sessions between 1999 and 2009, he identifies (co)sponsorship of pro-APA interest legislation as a pattern of substantive representation even if they were mostly (co) sponsored by non-APA members. A reexamination of the 49 APA-targeted bills in his research over a 10-year period shows that only eight of the 32 (co)sponsors were of APA descent (including two nonvoting delegates of Pacific Islander descent), while the rest included 11 white, nine Black, and three Latino members of Congress. One-third of them were women. Asians had the best gender ratio at 50%, followed by 33% female among Blacks and

182 CONTESTING THE LAST FRONTIER

Latinos, and 27% among whites. As APAs have increased their presence in Congress, the proportion of APA-focused bills sponsored by APA members has significantly increased and overtaken the number sponsored by non-APA members by 2020. However, because there were only Democrats in the APA delegation in the 116th Congress, we could not test the significance of partisanship.

From Grassroots Organizing to Legislative Activism at the Subnational Level

Our study of bill (co)sponsorship and other legislative activities among APA voting members of the 116th Congress provides strong evidence of APA representational politics being a racialized and gendered phenomenon. In this section, focusing on those serving below the federal level, we argue that APAEOs' efforts to advance social justice and equality could be mediated by their connections and relationships with underrepresented communities and constituent groups. In addition, contextual and institutional factors associated with office type, jurisdictional makeup, and local political context are possible confounding factors. In what follows, presented in chronological order of the first elective office held, are selected cases of APAEOs who have served or are currently serving at state and local levels. Their trajectories to elective office and the quality of their representation fit the womanist leadership praxis model specified earlier. Some are familiar names whose socialization stories we featured in Chapter 2. The others are recently elected officials who represent the new generation of transformational leaders for social justice. Each of these stories links grassroots community activism with legislative advocacy. There are examples of this pattern in the stories of those who fought for justice for comfort women, immigrants, and redress for Japanese and Chinese Americans that we covered earlier in the chapter. Serving at the local level has the benefits of proximity to local community-based organizations. Yet the relatively limited scope and specific responsibilities of local offices (for those not in big cities) might have also limited their ability to advocate for justice. This inherent bias partly explains the strong presence of big cities among local elected officials in our study.

Former California assemblywoman and two-time member of the Alameda County Board of Supervisors **Wilma Chan** grew up feeling marginalized as a daughter of Chinese immigrants during rising conservatism and social movements. She became involved in community activism and cofounded the Chinese Progressive Association in San Francisco to advocate for the Chinese working class through coalitional work. For her, working the system and challenging it are not mutually exclusive, and they include coalitional efforts to appeal to shared values and interests. Commenting on the significance of the Rainbow Coalition for Asian Americans and the need for Asian American political power, Chan once wrote: "The electoral arena is not only useful in pursuing short-term reforms, but in realizing the longer range goals of organizing and drawing out the most progressive among our peoples who see the need for fundamental change and revolution" (Chan 1984). Like many womanist activists, she ran for office to seek change for the community where she had already done a lot of work. For Chan's first election, it was to ensure that all voices could be heard on issues related to education. In the late 1980s, the Oakland Board of Education opened the proposal to change the length of the school year to year-round for public comment but failed to translate the proposal into other languages than English. The majority of Chinese and Latino parents, including Chan herself, were against the proposal but effectively excluded from the debate. Chan fought to get the proposal translated and even offered to translate it into Chinese herself but was turned down in a two-to-one vote.[12]

Whereas Chan's campaigns focused on recruiting and mobilizing Asian American voters, Asian Americans have never comprised a plurality of the constituents. Most of the issues she has focused on, including education, housing, and immigration, are not exclusive to Asian Americans. She explained that she works to "find the similarities across different communities," particularly from the perspective of the most vulnerable groups.[13] Chan's self-described leadership style is low-profile but hard-hitting, stating, "I'm pretty ruthless about getting things done" and "I work the system to get things done. You won't actually see me because I'm doing it" (DelVecchio 2000). Her legislative achievements are far-reaching. She is very widely known for spearheading the fight and authoring legislation that made California the first state to ban flame retardants in textiles, a major cause of congenital disabilities, with the highest levels found among working-class pregnant women and children (Cone 2003). Additionally, Chan authored groundbreaking legislation to implement a no-lead standard in drinking water pipes and fixtures. Upon her untimely passing in November 2021, Chan was fondly remembered as "a fierce leader and devoted champion for

184 CONTESTING THE LAST FRONTIER

accessible and affordable health care, child care, housing, immigrant rights, senior services, and ensuring people's basic needs were met" (Oddie 2021).

New York City councilwoman **Margaret Chin**'s experience growing up in Manhattan's Chinatown as the daughter of working-class immigrant parents from Hong Kong also left an indelible mark on her political socialization and career plan. She cofounded Asian Americans for Equality as a college student in the mid-1970s and continues to be involved in grassroots mobilizing and advocacy after entering electoral politics. Before her election to the city council in 2010, Chin had run and lost three primary campaigns due to the lack of ethnic-based voters. She attributed her eventual success to aggressive voter education, mobilization efforts of Chinese immigrants, and bilingual ballots with an accurate Chinese translation of candidate names. However, in her interest in cultivating the ethnic vote, Chin faced intense criticisms from some community activists for purportedly not adequately representing low-income constituents (Kim 2012; Xiaoqing 2017). She also faced criticism from immigrant Chinese Americans when she called for the indictment of police officer Peter Liang, who accidentally and fatally shot Black American Akai Gurley while on duty in east Brooklyn (Fuchs 2016).

California assemblyman and former member of the San Francisco Board of Supervisors **David Chiu,** the eldest child of immigrant parents from Taiwan, grew up in Boston and received his bachelor's, master's, and law degrees from Harvard University. Chiu calls himself a hands-on leader in the local community before running for office. He was president of the Asian American Bar Association of the Greater Bay Area and the board chair of the Chinatown Community Development Center and the Youth Leadership Institute. He served as a criminal prosecutor at the San Francisco District Attorney's Office and as a civil rights attorney with the Lawyers' Committee for Civil Rights. He was elected three times to the leadership of the San Francisco Democratic Party. The desire to serve the community has been part of each career decision he has made. When he ran for his first office on the San Francisco Board of Supervisors in 2008, the goal was to address the significant challenges facing San Francisco. With a reputation as a consensus maker, Chiu was the first board president in San Francisco history elected by fellow supervisors to three consecutive terms and the first Asian American to hold the post. As supervisor, Chiu authored 110 ordinances across a wide range of policy areas, including affordable housing, job creation, public safety, healthcare, the environment, transportation, civil rights, language access, ethics, and technology.

ADVANCING JUSTICE THROUGH LEADERSHIP   185

On the challenges of representing the APA community, Chiu said in an interview in 2009: "In a community like San Francisco, part of the reason we have faced barriers to Asian American political participation is that there are a lot of Asians with disparate political interests, based on generational differences—first-generation immigrants versus second-generation Asian Americans, for example—or based on differences created by income" (Kim and Tong 2009, 3). He was keenly aware that his majority-immigrant district has different housing, education, and economic development concerns than those held by nonimmigrant, middle-class Asian Americans. Chiu also commented that immigrants from Hong Kong, mainland China, or Taiwan had brought different homeland politics to Chinatown, making it more difficult to create political consensus. He credited his 2008 campaign success to the instrumental pan-Asian support from Chinese and other Asian American communities, which provided significant volunteer, fundraising, and community support for the race. He thought fractures within Asian communities had hindered community empowerment. However, in the November 2008 election, the lack of representation motivated the Asian community in San Francisco to not engage in infighting and factionalism. The instant runoff system in the city also helped by encouraging ethnic bloc voting and helping avoid the dilution of votes when there were multiple ethnic candidates in a race.

Like many other elected officials born in Southeast Asia, St. Paul city councilman **Dai Thao** arrived in the United States at a young age after witnessing wartime atrocities in Laos and waiting in a refugee camp in Thailand for several years. Growing up in extreme poverty and being raised by a traumatized single mom shaped his commitment to help eradicate unjust structures for the multiply disadvantaged and serve the entire community that adopted him and his family. Before winning an open seat in the St. Paul City Council in 2013, he worked as a community organizer with TakeAction Minnesota's Hmong Organizing Program, which included working on the 2008 Obama campaign and organizing for the faith-based social justice organization ISAIAH. His experience as a community organizer taught him that people had linked destinies despite their differences. He told a reporter that "our destinies are linked; that the quality of life for my children depends on the quality of my neighbors['] and their children['s lives]" (Jurewitsch 2013). As a community organizer, he sought to bridge differences within the heterogeneous APA community and across ethnic, racial, gender, and sexual lines by

186 CONTESTING THE LAST FRONTIER

stressing the strength of diversity and helping people find common ground (Jurewitsch 2013).

As the first Hmong city councilmember in a major hub of Hmong Americans, Dai Thao advocated for paid sick leave, which has affected him personally as a father of a newborn baby who suffered from health complications that required constant hospital visits (Melo 2016). He also supported community-centered development projects and stressed the need to take a balanced approach to development, opposing plans that did not adequately address the need for affordable housing (Melo 2017). In addition, Thao has led efforts in police reform to improve community-police relations and expand restorative justice initiatives, including increased access to diversion and sentencing reform (Melo 2017). In 2020, he and fellow Hmong councilmember Nelsie Yang filed a lawsuit against the state for violating the Voting Rights Act after being wrongfully charged for helping a Hmong woman vote in 2017 when he was running for mayor.

Philadelphia city councilwoman **Helen Hae-liun Gym** is a big believer in both municipal offices and local organizing. She proclaimed that "a person like me comes into office when our community movements are strong" (Gym 2020). This daughter of Korean immigrants found a true political home once she started volunteering at Asian Americans United in Chinatown, Philadelphia. Her professional experience includes cofounding both Parents United for Public Education, a collective of public school parents in Philadelphia, and the Folk Arts–Cultural Treasures Charter School. She was the founder and editor of the Philadelphia Public School Notebook and taught at Lowell Elementary School. By the time she ran for office in 2015, she already had two decades of community-organizing experience running youth leadership programs and citywide campaigns for educational reform. She saw herself as "part of a movement of educators, parents, and youth who decried an inequitable and racist system of schooling and funding" and fought a 17-year state takeover of the district (Gym 2020).

Even if Gym is now on the other side of politics, she continues to identify with and stay connected to the grassroots and the pursuit of an alternative vision of education justice. In her 2019 re-election campaign, she reminded voters that she introduced and passed the most expansive "Fair Workweek" law in the nation, ensuring protections for part-time workers in the poorest major city in America. These include two-week advance notice of their schedules, protection against retaliation, and a chance to qualify for full-time hours. She also fought for housing as a human right, established the first legal defense fund for tenants facing eviction, and won a citywide initiative to end the eviction crisis. Her advice for people considering a career in politics and/or public service: "If you want more people taking office and making change, then invest in the movements that make their leadership possible" (Gym 2020). Gym is the vice chair of Local Progress, a national network and movement of local elected officials to advance racial and economic justice.

Conclusion

This chapter presents evidence of how and why representation by APA women and men matters. In particular, guided by the womanist leadership praxis framework, we look at the progressive-minded APAEOs. They are mostly Democrats in partisanship and represent all of the voting members of the 116th Congress and roughly two-thirds of APAEOs in state and local offices before fall 2020. For these popularly elected officials, ethnic origin plays a formative role in their political socialization. Those who personally encountered group-based discrimination and mistreatments often took the lead in drafting bills that could respond to collective grievances. Nonetheless, it is not the only dimension of identity that figures into their personal experiences, motivation, and strategies to advance social justice. Indeed, the legislative achievements highlighted in this chapter show how APAEOs, depending on their personal experiences and connections to specific grassroots, community-based efforts, have leveraged multiple identities that included people of color, immigrants, refugees, women, the working class, LGBTQ people, and others. They have advanced justice for all and not just on the basis of their descriptive group interests.

Yet our study of bill sponsorship by APA voting members in the 116th Congress shows that women were more likely to address the needs of the APA community and intersectionally disadvantaged groups during a time of heightened racist violence and economic devastation. This finding that APA women legislators appear to be more effective at drawing upon multiple identities and experiences with discrimination echoes findings in prior research among Black and Latina legislators (e.g., Fraga et al. 2008; Smooth 2010b; Brown 2014; Hardy-Fanta et al. 2016; Reingold, Widner, and Harmon 2020). We find that APA men who bridge grassroots community activism and legislative advocacy also possess multiple, fluid notions of identity and demonstrate an awareness of the daily and organized struggles of Asian women

188 CONTESTING THE LAST FRONTIER

and the importance of their community contributions. Finally, our efforts in expanding the analysis longitudinally and to different levels of office and localities demonstrate distinct challenges and opportunities for APAs to engage in coalitional politics while sticking close to grassroots communities situated at the intersections of identities and structural oppressions.

6

Conclusion

In an oral history interview conducted in the mid-1980s, former California senator Alfred Song (1966–78) recalled that soon after moving his family to Monterey Park in the late 1950s, he became a frequenter of the city's planning commission on behalf of the homeowners' association. His active community involvement led to his appointment to the commission. He was then persuaded by neighbors on the commission and members of the Monterey Park Democratic Club to run for the city council. His law practice was just starting at that time, and he had no intentions of entering politics. "And before I knew it, I was in politics" (Sonenshein 1986, 11). When the assemblyman in his district decided to pursue Congress, Song was urged to run for the open seat. By borrowing $3,000 from the bank and with another $3,000 from the campaign treasury, he kicked off "a poor man's campaign" with a lot of walking, making numerous appearances and speeches, shaking many hands, and having an army of mostly women volunteers from the local Democratic Club to hand-address mailers. His campaign also received a boost from endorsements by California Democratic Council and organized labor. Song became the first Asian American elected to the city's council in 1960, to the assembly in 1962, and then the state senate in 1966.

How Song blazed the trail in electoral politics was part of the long line of incredible success stories told in Chapter 2 and elsewhere in this book. Whereas some began to aspire to enter politics before or during high school, most APAEOs, both men and women, did not think of holding elective office as a career goal. Many were motivated to run for office by a sense of urgency to address grievances facing the local or ethnic community or individuals and groups marginalized by their race, gender, or other social identities. Most of these elected officials could enter the political arena because of a break in the ecosystem, such as the opportunity created by an open seat or a newly drawn district. However, many were already involved in local community organizations and neighborhood affairs before launching the first campaign for office. Some also secured appointments to city planning or other governing commissions before serving in elective position(s). Predominantly being

Contesting the Last Frontier. Pei-te Lien and Nicole Filler, Oxford University Press. © Oxford University Press 2022.
DOI: 10.1093/oso/9780190077679.003.0006

190   CONTESTING THE LAST FRONTIER

children of immigrants or Asia-born themselves, they did not have many resources but needed to work hard to raise funds and earn trust from voters, who often did not share their ethnic identity. When campaign funds were limited, they compensated by walking door to door, making appearances in coffee shops, street corners, and other places where people gather. They also built up their political capital by working for an elective official or candidate or joining local political clubs to get endorsements from major parties. Finally, the city where Song began his political career, Monterey Park, has been a political incubator of Asian Americans. The city also elected Lily Lee Chen, Judy Chu, Mike Eng, and Henry Lo—individuals whose political socialization and trajectories to office are part of the stories that make up the backbone of this book.

Interpreting the Role of Race and Racism:
A Tale of Song and Hom

Song's first campaigns for office took place before the Civil Rights Act of 1964 and the Voting Rights Act of 1965. He moved his family to Monterey Park because he could not buy a house in Los Angeles due to racist covenants against nonwhites. Whereas his district had no more than 1% to 2% Asian, Song said his ethnic background was probably a positive factor in his campaigns—by being perceived as an "acceptable minority" (Sonenshein 1986, 18). Yet at the time when anti-Asian sentiment was the norm, he was advised never to use his picture, so as to avoid backlash. Because he experienced race-based discrimination at almost every turn in life, a primary reason to pursue legislative office was to use his knowledge of the law to advance justice for all. As a liberal Democrat, his legislative achievements include creating the California Evidence Code, enhancing enforcement of child support, outlawing harassment of voters at the polls, tightening consumer protection laws, supporting press freedom, and improving available healthcare. However, his crowning achievement is the Song-Beverly Consumer Warranty Act, commonly known as the "lemon law." It was passed in 1970 and is still considered the nation's most robust protection law for automobile consumers. The lawmaker's background as the son of a single mother and Hawaii sugar plantation worker who migrated from Korea as a picture bride is a story invisible in American society and politics. As students and teachers of Asian American politics, we did not learn this story and many others until the research for this book.

CONCLUSION   191

The reason for Song's sudden fall from the political limelight is also worth telling. Given his legislative acumen and accomplishments, Song said he never received any serious challenge to his re-election bids until 1978, when he lost his senate seat. Song attributed his unexpected loss to bad publicity associated with his being under FBI investigation for corruption, which was abandoned soon after the election due to the lack of evidence. He suspected this legal trouble was orchestrated by his ex-wife—a disgruntled white woman he was briefly married to in a quick marriage that ended in a nasty divorce.[1] Song tried to make sense of the corruption charge at the end of the lengthy interview: "Let's face it, it would seem to me that as long as we remain mortals, this thing called racial prejudice will never be eliminated" (Sonenshein 1986, 207).

The context of Song's loss in 1978 is reminiscent of the defeat of another California state legislator, Tom Hom, in 1970. In his autobiography, Hom (2014) wrote that, despite his feeling of having played an indispensable role in GOP's success in the late 1960s, he sometimes felt forgotten by the party as a freshman legislator. His political career ended abruptly in 1970. With only three weeks left in the re-election campaign and polls showing him winning by a large margin, he was accused of conspiracy and bribery—along with the entire city council and the mayor—by the district attorney for an old vote to raise taxicab fares. All were exonerated weeks after the election due to the lack of evidence. Reflecting on what happened decades later, Hom was convinced that "politics were behind the indictment process, from the powers in Sacramento to the rivalry of the district attorney race" (218).

Song was sure that racism had played a role in his demise. Hom did not explicitly express the sentiment, but he certainly felt the whim of racial discrimination early on and remembered the need to wear a badge declaring "I'm Chinese" during World War II to avoid being mistaken as of Japanese descent. Then, in 1947, he recalled his stepmother had to go door to door with a white real estate broker and friend to beg white neighbors to let in a Chinese family to an uptown community in San Diego (Chu 1982). Despite being fully aware of "real and *de facto* discrimination," Hom was motivated to enter politics to prove that a person who happened to be of Chinese descent could "run as an All-American boy" and represent everyone (Hom 2014, 159–60). He became the first Asian American elected to the municipal council of a major city and the first GOP Asian American in the California Assembly. In the end, he could not hide the frustration at being exploited

192 CONTESTING THE LAST FRONTIER

and sidelined in party politics and decided to quit politics after an electoral defeat.

This tale of the two male US-born Asian American candidates and elected officials shows that race (and racism) does not discriminate by partisanship, even if people may interpret the significance differently, especially at the intersections of race and gender. Both Song and Hom were initially recruited to run by members of a (mostly white, US-born old boys network, and they mentioned the largely supportive role of Asian American women as campaign volunteers, mothers, and wives. Relatedly, numerous accounts in this book suggest that Asia-born women and nonnative English speakers are subject to greater scrutiny in their campaigns due to social stigma associated with their gender and foreign-born background. And persons of Japanese descent, regardless of immigration generation and locality, all needed to embrace the consequences of being associated with a homeland government that ordered attacks on Pearl Harbor during World War II. In the context of the Covid-19 pandemic, being (perceived) of Chinese descent to the present day could expose a candidate and elected official to the accusation of being a communist sympathizer and with links to an "enemy" homeland.

Being "Kung Flu"

Wei Ueberschaer was a former teacher and education advocate for at-risk kids and an active community volunteer with the PTA and school advisory council for over 20 years. She won election to the Santa Rosa County School Board in conservative panhandle Florida in 2018. In a meeting on May 3, 2021, as she was reading a statement as chairperson of the board to urge respect for differences in opinions on lifting the masks mandate in schools, several parents in the audience interrupted. They called her a communist, questioned her GOP partisanship, and yelled: "This is Santa Rosa County, not China" (Kornfield 2021). On her Facebook page, a nasty comment left earlier in the year: "You have blood on your hands!!" was followed by another one posted on May 8, 2021: "Wei wants America to be just like China. A tyrannical Dictatorship where everyone wears Masks and does as the Government says or goes to Jail."[2]

As we close the writing of this book, the hate speech hurled at this second-generation Chinese American woman and school board chair was the latest incident of hate attacks on Asian Americans, including those holding an elective public office. Representative Grace Meng mentioned in March 2020 that President Trump's xenophobic and anti-China talk made her feel unwelcome as a foreigner and outsider (N. Wu 2020). Representative Ted Lieu expressed in the same interview fears for his safety when leaving his home to get groceries. Asian American candidates and elected officials, especially Chinese and female, have been scapegoated for the coronavirus pandemic. But one does not need to be of Chinese descent to be a victim of intimidation and hate triggered by anti-China sentiment. On March 16, 2021, four Korea-born and two China-born women were among the eight who were murdered in a shooting rampage targeting Asian-owned spa businesses in the Atlanta area. Only days after, second-generation Vietnamese American **Hoa Nguyen** received a knock at her front door and was terrified to find a handwritten note "Kung Flu" (Benner 2021). Nguyen was a candidate for a seat on the David Douglas School Board in Portland, Oregon. She described having experienced many racial incidents on her campaign website,[3] such as finding a sticky note on her backpack saying, "Go back to your country!" Trying to move away from a racially hostile environment was the main reason for her move to Portland from New Orleans, Louisiana, during middle school.

In San Francisco Bay Area, Foster City vice mayor **Richa Awasthi** was shaken by a five-pound river rock hurled at her house that narrowly missed her husband in mid-December 2020. She told a reporter that some people were not happy to see her 2018 election to the city council, and the Asian Indian couple had experienced a lot of hatred and attacks, including angry phone calls and emails (Lee 2020). A similar horror story occurred months ago to **Amourence Lee**, whose father is of Chinese-Hawaiian heritage and her mother Jewish and the daughter of a civil rights leader in Atlanta. Elected in 2020, Lee is the first Asian American woman to sit on the San Mateo City Council after being appointed first in 2019. On June 2, 2020, a rock was thrown through a bedroom window when she and her family were inside the house. This incident followed a stream of vandalism targeting the Asian American community, and anti-Asian signs and slogans appeared across the city, including graffiti with hateful messages like "F*** China," "Chinese Disease," and "Thanks, China" (Stutman 2020).

"Is This Patriot Enough?"

How to respond to the wave of anti-Asian hate? From some APA candidates and elected officials, one option is to show more patriotism. **Lee Wong** was a 20-year army veteran born and raised in China, orphaned at age 12, who immigrated to the United States at age 18 to finish high school in 1971. Because he had experienced the suspicion of not being American enough, Wong said he "deliberately went to the army to learn about Americanism and democracy" (Rice 2021). He was elected to the three-member Board of Trustees of West Chester Township, Ohio, in metropolitan Cincinnati in 2005 and ran unsuccessfully for the state senate as a Republican in 2020.

Wong made the headline news in the first board meeting after the Atlanta spa shooting. After the end of official business, this chairperson unexpectedly removed his shirt and tie to reveal large scars on his chest that he received during combat training and asked: "Is this patriotic enough?" Wong said he once was beaten up in Chicago with injuries that required treatment in a hospital when he was a young man. He heard anti-Japanese racial slurs hurled against him during the beating and took the assailants to court, but the suspects never received any jail time (Vigdor 2021). In the *New York Times* interview, Wong said he had put up with racism and remained silent over the years for fear of facing more discrimination and abuse. He could no longer stay silent in the tidal wave of anti-Asian violence.

This reaction resembles what a first-time candidate and US presidential hopeful **Andrew Yang** wrote in an op-ed to the *Washington Post* on April 1, 2020, commenting on the rise of hostility and aggression against Asians during COVID-19. The *New York Times* called Yang's campaign "one of the most surprising developments of the 2020 presidential race" when the political outsider attracted a surprisingly high intensity of loyalty and passion among his followers (Stevens 2019). However, Yang also had his share of being the invisible and the perpetual foreigner on the campaign trail (Cole 2019; Yam 2019). It was then a disappointment to some APAs on the progressive side of politics that, after citing Japanese Americans' volunteering to serve in the US military during internment, he would suggest the following in the opinion piece. "We Asian Americans need to embrace and show our American-ness in ways we never have before. We need to step up, help our neighbors, donate gear, vote, wear red white and blue, volunteer, fund aid organizations, and do everything in our power to accelerate the end of this crisis. We should show without a shadow of a doubt that we are Americans who will do our part for our country in this time of need" (Yang 2020).

Yang's call for action to respond to anti-Asian hate received mostly critical reactions from APA observers, even if some defended his stance (Zhan 2020). Some found the call for APAs to prove their Americanness reinforced the model minority trope. Jeff Yang tweeted: "The idea that Asians can overcome racism by bending our heads and working harder—shrugging it off when it happens to us, ignoring it when it happens to others—is the main pillar of model minority myth, and it has been devastating for coalitions with Black Americans and other POC" (April 2, 2020, 10:07 a.m.). Others found it offensive when Yang only praised Japanese American service during World War II but was not critical of the racism that put Japanese Americans behind barbed wire. Moreover, Yang failed to mention that the reward for that patriotism was the stripping of citizenship and property. Some came to Yang's defense and felt that critics were misconstruing Yang's message. Melissa Chen tweeted (April 2, 2020, 9:01 p.m.): "People are mad, I think, because he doesn't immediately take a victimhood posture." Others thanked Yang for his leadership and the reminder for the community to step up and do something to help with the crisis. Yang quenched the fire the next day by twitting that he's "very proud of my heritage and know that different people will have different takes" (April 3, 2020, 6:26 a.m.).

On Capitol Hill, with anti-Asian sentiment raging following President Trump's repetitive and inflammatory remarks about the "Chinese virus" (N. Wu 2020), Representatives Chu, Meng, and Liu also found the pressure and need to play up the theme of loyalty and good citizenship. They proposed on May 8, 2020, a congressional resolution (H. Res. 956) to recognize a nationwide food drive organized by the United Chinese Americans and the contributions of Chinese Americans to the United States throughout history. But, as shown in the previous chapter, this kind of assimilationist response was an exception to the legislators themselves and the totality of historical and contemporary actions taken by other APAEOs featured in this book.

A Heritage of Advancing Social Justice

As discussed in Chapter 5, almost all of the bills sponsored by APAs in the 116th Congress in the first few months following the White House declaration of Covid-19 as a national health crisis in early 2020 could be linked to the idea of advancing justice. They advocated for the interests of Asian and other minority Americans who have been structurally disadvantaged by the intersection of their race, gender, nativity, and/or class identities. Whereas we only analyzed the Covid-related legislative behavior within the first three and a half months of the outbreak in 2020, we also studied APA-targeted bill sponsorship patterns in earlier periods among APAs in Congress and the California State Legislature. Our results indicate a strong record of advancing social justice by these predominantly Democratic lawmakers—a heritage carried on and practiced in the 117th Congress. In March 2021, Representative Grace Meng reintroduced H.R. 1843, the Covid-19 Hate Crimes Act. She introduced the same legislation in May 2020 (H.R. 6721) to provide greater federal government oversight of Covid-19 hate crimes and require the Department of Justice to provide Congress with regular updates on the status of reported bias incidents. A corresponding bill (S. 937) to facilitate the expedited review of Covid-19 hate crimes was introduced by Senator Hirono in late March 2021 and passed by the Senate by a near-unanimous vote within a month. On May 18, the birthday of Vincent Chin, the House passed the anti-Asian hate crime bill by a vote of 364 to 62, with all the nay votes from Republicans. President Biden signed it into law on May 20, 2021. (Not all in the progressive community found the cause to celebrate, however. We shall comment on the tensions between the mainstream and grassroots approaches to incorporation and empowerment at the end of the chapter.)

As noted in Chapter 5, perversely, the pandemic has increased the visibility of APA legislators to contest racial formations of Asian Americans as the silent model minority through symbolic and substantive legislation. Relative to their male counterparts in the 116th Congress, APA women legislators could be interpreted as more eager to advocate on behalf of the intersectionally disadvantaged in their attempts to redistribute resources to those who were hit hardest by Covid-19. Their legislative activism is consistent with the progressive history of Asian Americans in elective office. And the location of practicing social justice leadership is not restricted to the US national capital and that of California. It can also be found in the campaigns and governing of Asian American women and men, mostly 1.5- and second-generation immigrants and refugees, serving at the local level in Minnesota, New Jersey, and elsewhere before the outbreak of the coronavirus and anti-Asian violence.

Instead of a redoubled show of loyalty and patriotism, a long line of elected officials of API descent across the nation chose to openly condemn racism and echo the call for better data collection and tracking reported suspected hate crimes. In Michigan, State Senator **Stephanie Chang** (D-MI) called out the majority leader, Senator Mike Shirkey (R-MI), for making a racist comment about the coronavirus as the "Chinese flu" in January 2021 (Chang

2021). Chang is the first Asian American woman elected to the Michigan legislature. She worked as a community organizer in Detroit for nearly a decade before winning a seat in the state house in 2014 and the senate in 2018. Her action in this incidence showcased a style of community-based leadership for social justice.

In California, the API Legislative Caucus chair, Senator Richard Pan, and vice chair, Assemblyman Evan Low, issued a joint statement in early February 2021 condemning the surge in hate crimes targeting Asian and Pacific Islander Americans (APILC 2021). They urged Governor Gavin Newsom to sign A.B. 85, the pandemic budget bill, which he did later in the month. Members of the caucus on the budget committee (Assemblymen Phil Ting, David Chiu, and Al Muratsuchi) helped draft the bill to include $1.4 million earmarked for researchers at the Asian American Studies Center at the University of California, Los Angeles and the Stop AAPI Hate website for better tracking and documenting of anti-Asian incidents.

In Illinois, the state senate unanimously passed on May 25, 2021, the Teaching Equitable Asian American Community History Act, making the state the first in the nation to require K-12 public schools to include Asian American history in all curricula (Oceguera 2021). The legislation was introduced in January by State Representative Jennifer Gong-Gershowitz, the second Chinese American in the chamber, and cosponsored by Theresa Mah, the first Asian American elected to the Illinois General Assembly back in 2016. Ram Villivalam, the first Asian American and Indian American elected to the Senate, in 2018, introduced the senate version. The AAJC-Chicago led the grassroots effort to draft the bill language.[4]

APAEOs serving at the local level did not wait long to express their concern over rising hate crimes. Within months after the outbreak of Covid-19 in 2020, a sample of cities across California acted to pass resolutions to demand better reporting and tracking of hate crime data (Goodrich 2020). The Irvine City Council, which is majority Asian (with an Asian Indian woman mayor, a Korean councilwoman, and a Chinese councilman), unanimously adopted a resolution in May 2020. They called on law enforcement to work with state and federal law authorities to investigate and document credible Covid-19-related hate crimes and threats and commit to collecting and publicly reporting data on the virus-related bias. Similar resolutions were passed in Garden Grove, Torrance, Los Angeles, Orange County, Santa Clara County, and San Mateo County—governing bodies with at least one of the elected members of Asian descent.

198 CONTESTING THE LAST FRONTIER

In Santa Ana, **Thai Viet Phan** became the first Asian elected to the city council in a district-based system in November 2020 (Kopetman 2020). Born in Thailand to parents who fled war-torn Vietnam, this former refugee served as an appointee on the Santa Ana Planning Commission and held several leadership positions in ethnic professional, cultural, and non-APA- specific civil rights organizations. She has been an advocate for an oversight commission of local law enforcement, reforms to the community policing program, a local Vietnamese community liaison, and in-language services and resources (Pho 2021). In early March 2021, she spearheaded an emergency ordinance mandating increased pay for grocery store and pharmacy workers (Pho, Robledo, and Munson 2021). She also held a joint news conference with several Asian American elected officials in Orange County where she named and denounced the racist, misogynistic roots of anti-Asian violence. In addition, she coordinated with a local grassroots organization to publish an op-ed in the *Los Angeles Times*, denouncing the detention and deportation of Southeast Asian immigrants and refugees as anti-Asian violence and calling on the governor to pardon An Thanh Nguyen (Phan 2021).[5] Phan also helped usher the unanimous passage of a city council resolution supporting the VISION Act (A.B. 937), which would end the transfer of individuals eligible for release from local jails and state prisons to federal immigration enforcement officials.

In March 2021, as a direct response to worsening anti-Asian racism and violence across the country and a recent incident targeting a local Chinese-owned butcher shop in Sacramento, California, Hmong American councilwoman **Mai Vang** introduced a resolution to the city council condemning anti-Asian hate and laying out strategies to keep Asian American and Pacific Islander residents safe (Wong 2021). She called for the city to partner with the AAPI community for culturally appropriate data collection, acknowledge the specific experiences of AAPI residents and how systemic barriers can discourage reporting anti-Asian discrimination, and invest in community-based intervention to keep people safe. Before being elected to the Sacramento City Council in 2020, she served on the city's unified school district board of education for four years. Vang has been an active community organizer who cofounded Hmong Innovating Politics to strengthen the power of disenfranchised communities through innovative civic engagement and strategic grassroots mobilization (Yu 2019).

Meet the New Generation of APAEOs: The Incorporation of Hmong Americans

Both Thai Viet Phan and Mai Vang are part of the new generation of APAEOs from previously invisible, underprivileged, and underserved Asian American populations. In Chapter 3, we note that, at a growth rate of 127% between 2014 and 2020, the number of elected officials of Hmong descent has grown dramatically and only ranks second to those of Korean descent in growth rate. In 2020, Hmong elected officials had the second-best parity ratios in descriptive representation (after Taiwanese) by ethnicity, gender, and the intersection of the two among APAEOs. Hmong Americans have been at or near the bottom of socioeconomic status among the Asian population; Hmong elected officials were born in refugee camps or US-born but grew up in low-income families. What explains their extraordinary accomplishments in the electoral arena?

According to Wong (2017), the Hmong community has a favorable attitude toward democratic politics and believes that a career in public office is desirable for the young and is a worthy life goal that will help the community. Wong also argues that Hmong Americans consider political participation a social act embedded in one's social network. Hence, US-educated Hmong women participated actively and equally as their male counterparts in electoral politics. Our study also finds that Hmong Americans could score remarkable successes in the electoral arena by engaging local ethnic and clan networks to help educate and turn out new voters. They have achieved victories by mobilizing local community-based and/or state and local partisan organizations to help recruit and elect progressive Hmong women and men. As child refugees or children of refugees, their political incorporation has been facilitated by their identification with the local Democratic Party (Democratic Farm-Labor, or DFL), whose progressive policy stance sent welcoming signals to newcomers with limited means. However, getting endorsed by a major party was neither necessary nor sufficient for success; some could triumph despite running against party-backed candidates in the primary. In what follows, focusing on those elected to the state legislature in Minnesota (and elsewhere), we present the stories of a handful of pioneering and recently elected Hmong Americans.

Mee Moua got her first taste of running a campaign for public office when she helped her uncle, Neal Thao, get elected to the St. Paul School Board in 1994. Throughout the 1990s, at least eight other Hmong men, except for the

200   CONTESTING THE LAST FRONTIER

first, Choua Lee, were elected to school boards and city councils in Minnesota and Wisconsin. Hmong women, including Moua, who led the Hmong Bar Association and the Hmong Chamber of Commerce, broke ground in the legal and business professions. When a Minnesota Senate seat became vacant in November 2001, Moua decided to run. Despite lacking the party endorsement and Hmong clan leaders initially hesitant to endorse her, Moua was able to triumph by employing a network of young Hmong professionals who helped build a solid voter base within and beyond the Hmong community (Xiong 2018). Moua also received strong backing from Progressive Minnesota (now TakeAction Minnesota), a political group focused on community organizing, citizen education, student advocacy, and feminist issues (Vang 2015).

Months after Moua's election, **Cy Thao** became the second Hmong American state legislator. Like Moua, Thao was born in Laos and forcibly displaced after the fall of Saigon, arriving in Minnesota by way of a refugee camp in Thailand. The 2002 election was not Thao's first campaign, however. He first ran in 2000 as an Independence Party–endorsed candidate after participating in the 1998 youth-led protests against racist comments made by a local radio host and subsequently led a voter registration drive. In that race, he came in second behind the DFL candidate with 23% of the vote. When the incumbent retired, Thao entered again, secured the DFL party endorsement, and won a landslide victory. These pioneering success stories have provided a blueprint for campaigning as Hmong for later generations.

Born in a refugee camp in Thailand and raised in Minnesota since the age of one, **Fue Lee** was active in student affairs during college and got his first taste of electoral politics while volunteering for Minneapolis city councilman Blong Yang's 2013 campaign. After graduating, he worked in state government and served as a legislative staffer for several senior-ranking elected officials. He cofounded the Asian American Organizing Project with other Hmong American elected officials and party activists, including Mee Moua and Jay Xiong, to increase the participation of APAs in building a just and equitable society. In 2016, Lee entered the race for the state house seat against the party-backed, white male, 10-term incumbent "because candidates that were supposed to represent all of the city and its communities weren't doing their job" (Hutchins 2016). Lee's campaign paid off as he presented himself as a community member who understood the community's needs, particularly among working-class people of color. He became the first person of color and Asian descent to represent the district.

Born and raised in MN to refugees from Laos, **Tou Xiong** earned a law degree in St. Paul and, like fellow Hmong American legislators, worked for community organizations and state government after that. However, unlike most other Hmong candidates, he was a "DFLer," working behind the scenes on campaigns and voter outreach for six years before running for office (SHB 2015). Xiong received the party endorsement in his first campaign for a seat on the Maplewood City Council in 2014 and began serving on the district party committee the same year (SHB 2015). When he decided to move up the ladder and run for a state house seat in 2018, he was endorsed again by the party and the retiring incumbent.

Samantha Vang was also born and raised in Minnesota to refugee parents. After graduating from a local college, she worked as the coordinator for civic engagement programs at a community organization that seeks to increase the political participation and influence of Minnesota's immigrant and refugee populations. Being a recent college graduate battling student loan debt with a low-income job, Vang had every reason not to run for office but decided to out of frustration with the status quo. In order "to be part of the process of building a system that works for everyone regardless of who they are" (APAICS 2020), she entered the open-seat race for the Minnesota State Legislature the night before the filing deadline in 2018. The 24-year-old progressive woman of color narrowly defeated the party-backed candidate, another young Hmong woman with extensive political experience in the primary. Even though Vang didn't win the DFL endorsement, she edged out her opponent by engaging potential voters who don't traditionally head to the polls (Yuen 2018). "I think it's really important that we have someone who is intentional about including other communities who haven't been involved in the process," said Vang (Yuen 2018).

Kaohly Her also pursued a career working in community organizations after leaving the banking/financial sector. She cofounded a philanthropic organization to fund local community projects and served as the executive director of an organization aiming to improve the lives of Hmong women. Motivated by her triple role as the daughter of an elderly refugee woman trying to navigate the healthcare system, the mother of daughters attending underserved schools, and a community activist involved in ending violence against women, Her had thought more than once about running for office. She even attended several women's candidate training programs but doubted whether it was the right time or whether she was qualified. In 2018, with the support of women mentors and endorsements from her party, major

202 CONTESTING THE LAST FRONTIER

labor unions, and 501(c)(4) organizations like TakeAction Minnesota and Women Winning, she threw her name in for the open seat and won handily. In July 2020, she was part of the People of Color and Indigenous Caucus that authored the Minnesota Police Accountability Act, which contains substantial police accountability reforms and measures to ensure racial justice. She wrote the provision on arbitration reforms.

When **Tina Maharath** filed to run for the seat to replace a term-limited Republican white male in 2018, the 27-year-old woman of color received a cold reception from the Democratic Party. The first Laotian and Asian American woman to serve in the Ohio State Senate was not the first or even the second choice of the county party committee; they wrote her candidacy off as a lost cause after learning of her troubled past. She overcame a disadvantage of over $700,000 in campaign ads and a fundraising deficit to defeat the Latina opponent and state representative by 705 votes. Maharath's razor-thin victory might be explained by the backfiring of the GOP's smear campaign and her focus on door-to-door campaigning around the district (Pelzer 2018). Her past internships at the state house and the US Senate, her fellowship at APIAVote, and her involvement in several local partisan and panethnic cultural groups helped, too. She became the only Ohio Democrat to flip a state senate seat since 2006. When asked why she decided to run despite the brutal Republican attack ads, Maharath cited her experience as a child of refugees who came to the United States in the 1990s as something much more traumatizing and challenging than running for electoral office (Siegel 2018).

In California, **Sheng Thao** became the first Hmong American Oakland City Council member in 2018. Like many Hmong Americans of the 1.5/second generation, Thao grew up in poverty and worked low-wage jobs from a young age. She got her start in electoral politics through the 2012 Asian Pacific Islander American Public Affairs summer internship program for Councilwoman Kaplan. Thao was offered a job shortly after the internship and climbed the ranks from community liaison/scheduler to chief of staff in less than three years. Thao said that the experience working in the public office made her realize she wanted "to help people who have a lesser voice get through bureaucracies" (Hoge 2019). Thao did not get the endorsement of the mayor or the departing incumbent for her candidacy. Unions contributed significantly to her campaign late in the race, but Thao still raised less than her opponent. What ultimately made the difference was her grassroots campaign, where she walked door-to-door with the help of volunteers,

CONCLUSION   203

including fellow Hmong American elected officials. Another winning factor was the ranked-choice voting system, which aided nonwhite candidates in other cities such as Minneapolis, San Francisco, and Berkeley, California. In late December 2020, as president of the League of California Cities Asian Pacific Islander Caucus, Thao openly condemned rock-throwing attacks on two Bay area Asian American women councilmembers as "an act of terrorism that has no place in our democracy" (Lee 2020).

In January 2020, 24-year-old **Nelsie Yang** became the first Hmong woman and the youngest person ever elected to the St. Paul City Council in a seat held by a retiring white male for more than 20 years. Running for office was unimaginable for Yang, born and raised in Minnesota by low-income Hmong refugees. Her parents worked as medical assembly workers, relied on public assistance, and lost their family house to foreclosure just two days before her high school graduation. After studying abroad in Thailand, she took a trip to her mother's village in Laos and was shocked by the parallels between her family living in Laos and Minnesota. Yang was determined to channel the anger and frustration about economic disparity into action by campaigning for Councilman Dai Thao in 2015. She later became an organizer at TakeAction Minnesota, where she ran community-centered and grassroots campaigns for renters' rights, raising the minimum wage, and criminal justice reform. Yang also served as a campaign coordinator for the DFL during the 2016 presidential election, helped train hundreds in the workings of the caucus system, and was a national delegate for Senator Bernie Sanders. In an interview with Women Winning (2019), Yang mentioned that she ran for the city council "to work towards eliminating poverty, eliminating deep disparities, and building communities that do well." As a community organizer, Yang campaigned on engaging new and diverse community members to drive elected leaders to listen and make decisions that benefit the community.

Building Up the Political Infrastructure through Ethnic Community-Based and Other Organizations

Political parties and other political organizations and interest groups are linkage institutions in the US political system. They can help turn demographics into power by organizing the voices and votes of the respective constituency. Nonetheless, in candidate-centered campaigns of the present

204   CONTESTING THE LAST FRONTIER

day, the party endorsement process, especially in a weak-party state, is not considered a bridge to the system for political newcomers and prospective candidates from nonwhite and majority-immigrant communities. However, this does not mean that these candidates do not seek out party endorsements or that party endorsements are inconsequential. More than a handful of APAEOs, including those whose stories we highlighted in Chapter 4, joined existing or formed new local partisan organizations. A few served on state party committees after winning public office. Yet even for these candidates, who are much more likely to be Democrats than Republicans, they could not rely on their partisan ties alone to run a successful campaign. For historically marginalized communities that are relative newcomers to US mainstream politics, such as Asian Americans, some contend that "true empowerment" will hinge on the minority community's ability to create community-based infrastructure for leadership development and campaign training.

Rising Importance of (Nonpartisan) Ethnic Organizations

Stories of the new generation of Hmong American women and men in elective office illustrate an emerging pattern of political socialization and trajectories to office in the first decades of the 21st century. Departing from the traditional reliance on the two parties to provide a bridge to mainstream electoral politics, Asian Americans aspiring for elective office at state and local levels have turned increasingly to ethnic community-based and non-ethnic organizations for candidate training and campaign support. These nonpartisan ethnic and women-centered nonethnic organizations are the backbones of the political infrastructure for newcomers and outsiders to step into the political arena. Regardless of the role of parties in their campaigns, APAEOs have developed the knowledge, skills, and other resources necessary to enter and win through involvement in nonpartisan ethnic community-based organizations (CBOs). This section summarizes the history, mission, programs, and participants of selected nonpartisan ethnic CBOs, which are key to building up the political infrastructure for sustainable Asian American political incorporation and empowerment.

The Japanese American Citizens League (JACL), being one of the oldest and most extensively studied Asian American organizations, offers a case study in the limitations and opportunities of ethnic CBOs in developing transformational leadership and political representation among

CONCLUSION 205

nonwhite immigrant communities. The JACL was founded in 1929 by second-generation Japanese American men (who also tended to be older and more likely to have advanced degrees and established professions than the majority of Nisei) as a national umbrella organization to combat anti-Japanese sentiment (Takahashi 1997, 54–57). In addition to lobbying and using litigation to challenge discriminatory laws, the JACL published the *Pacific Citizen* to advocate voting as the most important demonstration of "good citizenship." It also denounced ethnic bloc voting as un-American, urged unquestioned loyalty to the United States, and promoted Republican ideals despite its official nonpartisan stance. Cofounder Dr. Clarence Arai was also active in local Republican Party organizations and ran for office twice in the 1930s, albeit unsuccessfully (64–65). Other Nikkei, who tended to be younger and more working class, were critical of the conservative "Old Guard." They formed new and joined existing ethnic and nonethnic Democratic youth organizations; some were involved in the Communist Party and the labor movement. They saw bridging generational and ideological divides as necessary amid the racialization of all Japanese persons as the enemy race (66–74).

After suppressing dissent in the face of anti-Asian racial oppression during World War II, the national JACL renewed its assimilationist approach in the postwar era. It lobbied for the passage of the McCarran-Walter Act, which permitted naturalization of the Japan-born, submitting amicus curiae briefs in landmark civil rights cases, and investing in the model-minority image of the "iconic Nisei soldier" (Daniels 1988; Wu 2013). While the JACL's appeal to liberal redemption contributed to the electoral success of Nisei veterans in the 1950s and 1960s, progressive Nisei and Sansei continued to offer an alternative vision and practice of citizenship on college campuses, streets, and capitol hills. Their grassroots organizing and legislative advocacy led to the JACL's support for redress during a 1978 national convention and the eventual passage of the Civil Liberties Act of 1988. Several JACL leaders covered earlier in this book also cut their teeth in electoral politics. For example, George Nakano founded the Torrance chapter of the JACL in 1983, three years after becoming the first Japanese American elected to the Torrance City Council. In 1996, former Gardena city clerk Helen Kawagoe became only the second woman to serve as president of the male-dominant national JACL after decades of involvement in the local chapter and city politics. Kawagoe, who was known as "bulldog" and "mama," encouraged younger generations to get (more) involved, including her successor, California state assemblyman Floyd Mori (Rafu 2020). Mori later served as the first executive director of the APAICS, which we discuss subsequently.

The reforms of the civil rights era, emergence of ethnoracial power and feminist movements, and the increase of Asian immigrants after 1970 contributed to the increasing number and professionalization of ethnic nonpartisan organizations with highly trained staff and programs funded through private foundations and federal and state grants. These included the Organization of Chinese Americans, the Organization of Chinese American Women, and the Korean American Coalition of Los Angeles. While these organizations were rooted in ethnic-specific communities, they created panethnic coalitions characteristic of the Asian American movement to address common issues facing different ethnic groups. New federal standards for racial classification in 1977 that merged "Asian" and "Pacific Islander" into one racial category also encouraged the adoption of the "APA" label despite the dominance of East Asians in these formations (Espiritu 1992). In addition, restrictions on political activism that accompanied these organizations' tax-exempt status necessitated a more politically neutralized focus on service provision and leadership development (Kwon 2013).[6] For example, the Asian Pacific Planning and Policy Council was formed in 1976–77 as an umbrella organization after nearly a decade of ad hoc coordination across mostly ethnic-specific CBOs to advocate for social service programs for an increasingly diverse APA community in Los Angeles County.[7] Leadership Education for Asian Pacifics was founded in 1982 as a national, nonpartisan CBO with a mission to achieve full participation and equality through leadership training for students, college faculty and staff, nonprofit organization staff, and business executives.

Throughout the 1990s, APA elected officials and professionals formed several nonpartisan panethnic CBOs to build a pipeline of APA candidates and grow a community-based infrastructure. In 1994, Secretary of State Norm Mineta and Guam delegate Robert Underwood cofounded the APAICS as the educational arm of the Congressional Asian Pacific American Caucus created that same year. APAICS seeks to promote APA participation and representation at all levels of the political process by creating and disseminating knowledge about APAs in public office and filling a pipeline of APAs across levels of office. The organization hosts national and regional leadership academies that feature discussions with incumbent elected officials and local community stakeholders, training in campaign operations, and networking opportunities. As of July 2019, its website listed the 37 national academy

CONCLUSION 207

alumni who had held congressional, state legislative, county, municipal, or education board offices across fourteen different states.[8] Men comprised the vast majority of all alumni (62%) and were most diverse in terms of ethnic background compared to that of women. Only 11 or 38% of alumni were women, and all but three were Chinese or Japanese by ancestry. Under the leadership of the first woman executive director, Madalene Xuan-Trang Mielke, APAICS launched the Women's Collective in 2019 to inspire and support the political engagement of AAPI women.

Nearly 15 years before the launch of the APAICS Women's Collective, APA women who attended the 1995 UN Conference on Women in Beijing returned to the United States with a renewed commitment to building the collective power of APA women to achieve social justice. These and other women activists formed the National Asian Pacific American Women's Forum in 1996 in Los Angeles, focusing on increasing civic engagement and advocacy for policy change on a multiplicity of issues.[9] Around the same time in 1995, Martha Lee, who was then working as the National Hispanic Leadership Institute's program director, formed the Asian Pacific American Women's Leadership Institute (APAWLI) together with several other APA women professionals. The self-described "Warrior Sisters" launched a three-week leadership program to develop an awareness of self and community among APA women and nurture their desire to change the conditions that created barriers in their own lives and communities. The APAWLI alumni include former California state senator Ling-ling Chang, Daly City vice mayor Juslyn Manalo, North Clackamas board member Kathy Wai, and Duane County supervisor Huong Nguyen. These women participated in the program before launching their first or successive bids for higher office.

Founded by De Anza Community College professor and Cupertino mayor Dr. Michael Chang in 1997, the Asian Pacific American Leadership Institute (APALI) is unique for its multiethnic and grassroots approach to leadership development. One of APALI's initial programs served as a training ground for high school students to become civic leaders by developing their awareness of identity, history, and power structures. Later, the institute expanded its programming to Latinx and Asian adult professionals to improve political engagement across diverse communities. The APALI's Alumni on the Move program reflects the organization's multiethnic, multigenerational, cross-sector, and local approach. Toward the end of 2020, about a quarter of the 31 featured alumni were Latinx, and 71% were Asian. A higher share held leadership positions in nonprofit organizations, corporations, or nonelected positions in local government than popularly elected office, especially among women. Alumni included two Democratic California Assembly members who graduated from APALI in the early 2000s before their first office bids at the local level. Seven were elected to local education boards and/or city councils in the Silicon Valley area shortly before, during, or after graduating from APALI.[10] As Chang explained, most adult participants were already civically engaged; his focus was on building a community-based network that facilitated community-based institutional change.[11]

Congressman Mike Honda, California state treasurer Matt Fong, and other APA community advocates in California sought to replicate the local and national models at the state level when they founded the Asian Pacific American Leadership Foundation in 2004. According to its website,[12] prominent alumni in the candidate training class of 2004 include California controller and treasurer Betty Yee, San Francisco assessor and California assemblyman Phil Ting, Campbell city councilman and California assemblyman Evan Low, San Francisco Board of Education and Board of Supervisors member Eric Mar, and Alameda city councilwoman Lena Tam. Those who graduated from the 2016 candidate training class include city councilmembers Malia Vella of Alameda, Jeff Maloney of Alhambra, Juslyn Manalo of Daly City, and Melissa Ramoso of Artesia. Comparing these two time points shows that the program has helped expand gender, ethnic, and geographic representation among APAEOs in California.

Before she moved on to serve in statewide and federal offices, Assemblywoman Judy Chu founded the California Asian Pacific Islander Legislative Caucus Institute (CAPILCI) in 2006 to fill the pipeline of persons of API descent in the California legislature. According to its website,[13] under the leadership of Maeley Tom and Georgette Imura, two women with decades of combined experience in senior-level administrative staff positions in both chambers of the California legislature and on state and national campaigns, the institute launched its inaugural Capitol Academy program that same year. The program aims to identify and train API local elected and appointed officials for higher office through experiential learning at the state capitol. In 2017, CAPILCI expanded its approach to pipeline development and created the API Legislative Staff Academy to support the professional development of API staffers in the legislature or administration and beyond. As of 2019, nine Capitol Academy alumni served in the California Assembly; all were male and elected from Southern and Northern California / Bay Area districts, including both Democrats and Republicans.

One of the few national nonpartisan organizations to adopt a multiethnic, immigrant-centered approach to pipeline and infrastructure building is New American Leaders (NAL). NAL was founded in 2010 by Dr. Sayu Bhojwani, an India-born woman, former undocumented immigrant, longtime South Asian community advocate, and the first commissioner of immigrant affairs for the state of New York. Bhojwani's advocacy stemmed from her frustration at the lack of representation of immigrant communities. As of May 2020, there were over 921 NAL alumni, of whom 24% were of API descent, 57% were women, and 61% who ran for office between 2016 and 2019 won ("What We Do").[14] Stephanie Chang, a former grassroots organizer in Detroit and the first Asian woman elected to the Michigan legislature, was one of the early NAL graduates. Chang cofounded the Michigan chapter of APIAVote, a national nonpartisan organization dedicated to increasing APA political participation and representation. At least nine other Asian alumni of NAL were elected for the first time in or after 2016 to school boards, city councils, and state legislatures, and often as historic "firsts." They include former San Jose city councilman Lan Diep, former Indiana representative Chris Chyung, Irvine mayor Farrah Khan, Ohio state senator Tina Maharath, Plymouth-Canton School Board members Anupam Chugh Sidhu and Tania Ganguly, Nevada assemblywoman Cecelia Gonzalez, Georgia representative Marvin Lim, and Michigan representative Ranjeev Puri. Diep explained in an interview with NAL that the 2012 training helped him develop campaign materials and a supportive network of fellow second-generation immigrant elected officials and candidates. He also noted, however, that "you can only take so many trainings. . . . Really, you've just got to put yourself out there" ("Lan Diep" 2020).[15] The 2020 election cycle showed that NAL alumni were heeding the advice. However, Diep's (and Chyung's) re-election campaigns also demonstrated the need for continued and expanded support networks within and beyond political parties, especially for first- and second-generation immigrant Asian men to sustain ethnic representation.[16]

Increasing Prominence of Women-Centered Nonethnic (Partisan) Organizations

It is not only nonpartisan ethnic organizations that have contributed to developing an Asian American pipeline and electoral infrastructure. Women-centered nonethnic mainstream organizations, some with close partisan ties,

210   CONTESTING THE LAST FRONTIER

have played an increasingly prominent role, especially after Trump's election in 2016. Although their origins can be traced to the women's suffrage movement, a plurality of organized groups sought to recruit, train, and/or fund women candidates were formed in the mid-1960s to mid-1970s during the height of the feminist movement (Kreitzer and Osborn 2018). The National Women's Political Caucus (NWPC) was formed in 1971 by a multiethnic group of women in Congress, appointed public officials, Democratic and Republican Party leaders, and community-based organizers to increase women's political participation.[17] In 1974, NWPC launched the "Win With Women" campaign to explicitly recruit, train, and support feminist women candidates who were pro-ERA and pro-choice. Following the Women's Campaign Fund and the National Organization for Women, NWPC created its first PAC in 1977. Nonetheless, despite the impulse to create a unified front, white feminists did not see NWPC cofounder Shirley Chisolm as a "realistic candidate" in the 1972 campaign Democratic presidential nomination (Curwood 2015). Today, as in the past, few women-centered campaign organizations explicitly address the diversity among women despite the distinct barriers facing different ethnic groups (Kreitzer and Osborn 2018; Sanbonmatsu 2015; Hardy-Fanta et al. 2016). Moreover, despite bipartisan roots, the vast majority of women's candidate groups use abortion stance as a key eligibility criterion that effectively makes them Democratic (or Republican) due to the two party's opposing positions (Kreitzer and Osborn 2018). Still, these organizations have become influential players on the campaign trail, incentivizing party organizations to get behind a candidate through their direct contributions and access to a donor network (Dittmar 2015). Like other nonpartisan organizations, they also engage in recruitment and candidate training activities. To what extent and how have mainstream women-centered organizations contributed to the election of APA women?

Founded in 1985 by Democratic Party activist Ellen Malcolm, EMILY's List provides pro-choice Democratic women candidates access to their extensive donor network. In 1994, the organization expanded its strategy beyond fundraising by launching its first WOMEN VOTE! Project in California. In 2009, with her victory in the special election of California's 32nd Congressional District, Representative Judy Chu became the 80th woman that EMILY's List has helped elect to the US House of Representatives. WOMEN VOTE! ran an extensive direct mail program to reach out to 24,000 voters throughout the 32nd District, helping Chu rise above a crowded primary field and cruise to a general election victory. EMILY's List had supported the campaigns of all Democratic Asian American women serving in the US House of Representatives as of November 2018. Out of the nearly 1,100 candidates for state and local offices that EMILY's List helped elect between 2001 and 2018, less than 3%, or approximately 30, were Asian American women. A plurality of these candidates currently or previously served in California or Hawaii and are of Japanese or Chinese ancestry.[18]

Democratic women-centered campaign organizations that are locally based have recruited, trained, and supported APA women other than Japanese and Chinese and beyond California and Hawaii. EMERGE America was founded in 2005 by former Democratic committee and candidate fundraiser Andrea Dew Steele as a national umbrella organization following three years of recruiting and training self-identified Democratic women to run for elected office in Northern California. In addition to recruiting women through their network and hosting candidate trainings, EMERGE supports Democratic women candidates through "strong and strategic relationships with other political groups," including Democratic Party committees and EMILY's List, national labor unions, and progressive PACs like Run for Something.[19] EMERGE has affiliate organizations in 29 states and reported in 2017 that 37% of alumni are women of color and 73% of alumni won their elections. In our APAEO database, we identified at least 20 Asian American women serving as of 2019 who graduated from EMERGE. The majority were foreign-born, South Asian or Southeast Asian by ethnicity, and served at the municipal level in three regions: Northern California, the Pacific Northwest (Washington, Oregon), and the Northeast (Massachusetts, New Jersey). Mayor Sadaf Jaffer participated in EMERGE New Jersey before running for city council as a write-in candidate. Though unsuccessful the first time, she persisted by cofounding Inspiring South Asian American Women (ISAAW) and entering the race again in 2017. ISAAW is a nonpartisan CBO that seeks to promote civic engagement and interest in public office among South Asian women. Both groups were critical to Jaffer's success in 2017: "My EMERGE sisters and my ISAAW sisters are my primary network" (Sharma 2019).

Several studies find that Republican women face more barriers to enter the electoral arena and score success than their Democratic counterparts (Lawless and Fox 2010; Sanbonmatsu and Carroll 2013; Thomsen and Swers 2017; Burrell 2018). The lack of comparable infrastructure and pipeline development for Republican and conservative women, coupled with a disproportionately white-male party base, may lead to acute disadvantages for APA women. On the other hand, women elected officials, party chairs,

212 CONTESTING THE LAST FRONTIER

and activists have formed some PACs and leadership programs to increase the number of Republican and conservative women in elected office over the past several decades. For example, the VIEW PAC was founded in 1997 by Republican women in Congress and professionals to increase Republican women in Congress. Its website lists 40 currently and formerly serving Republican women it has supported, three of which are APAs serving in the 117th Congress.[20] Founded in 2010, Maggie's List aims to elect fiscally conservative women across office levels through candidate training, get-out-the-vote programs, and financial support.[21] Out of the 119 candidacies Maggie's List has endorsed since 2001, only six were by APA women.

More recently, US Representative Elise Stefanik (NY-21) formed the Elevate PAC to increase Republican women in Congress by focusing on the primary race. It was established following the 2018 midterm elections and after her service as the first recruitment chair of the National Republican Congressional Committee. According to Elevate's website,[22] Stefanik recruited more than 100 women to run for Congress, but few could make it out of the primary. Only two new Republican women were elected to Congress in 2020, and both are immigrant women from South Korea. In an interview with the *New York Times*, Representative Young Kim commended these efforts to recruit Republican women who are more descriptively representative of the American population. "They really wanted to not just recruit us, but to provide the support we needed to get out of the primaries. . . . It says there are efforts to grow our party by including many individuals—like me, an immigrant, a mother of four, someone who speaks different languages. They see those more as assets" (Cowan 2020).

Looking Back and Looking Forward

We started writing this book to tell a story, the missing story of the political rising of Asian Americans in mainstream American politics. As we approach the end of this prolonged and multifaceted process, we realize that there are simply too many stories to uncover and tell in a single volume. Whereas we aim to provide a coherent interpretation of the individual stories through the womanist leadership praxis, we also find the need to preserve the nuances in the political trajectories of individual APAEOs and recognize differences across individuals and groups in family history and political socialization, relationship with partisan and campaign organizations, concepts of leadership and representation, and in issue concerns and jurisdictional responsibilities. The APA community is distinguished for its internal diversity. We would do a disservice by not acknowledging this fact. Our database includes elected officials who are conservative by ideology and Republican by partisanship, but they do not represent the mainstream of APAEOs, then or now. The reality of APAs being a racial minority that has suffered triangulated racial persecution throughout history may push the community to elect officials who understand and can help fight racism and other forms of oppression. The Covid-19 outbreak and the surge in anti-Asian racism and hate violence provided a vivid reminder of the underlying challenges for APAs in elective office. The issues of race and racism and the intersection of racism and sexism (for women) and nativism (for the foreign-born) are part and parcel of our group history and US society. However, we also provide evidence of why the health pandemic has provided opportunities to voice concerns and advocate for change, including institutional change. APAs on the left and right sides of politics (as well as those who fall between or outside the left-right ideological spectrum) may have different interpretations of these group-based challenges, but all are part of the community that has a heritage and legacy of advancing justice.

In May 2021, as APA congressional members were lobbying colleagues in the House of Representatives, nearly 85 Asian American groups (and LGBTQ organizations) signed a petition to oppose the Covid-19 Hate Crimes Act (Yam 2021). Leaders in this wave of grassroots organizing contested that the bill bolstered law enforcement and criminalization and could not keep the minority community safe. They also believed that it contradicted Asian solidarity with Black, Brown, undocumented, trans, low-income, sex-worker, and other marginalized communities. They were concerned that, by proposing to partner with law enforcement in data collection and sharing, the bill ignored that police violence was also anti-Asian violence. The latter disproportionately targeted Brown Asians and those with mental health concerns. Instead, the rainbow coalition of progressive organizations and groups advocated for a shift in resources from law enforcement to community-based solutions, including investing in mental health care infrastructures, neighborhood trauma centers, and community food banks, among other programs.

This tension between the mainstream and grassroots approach to advancing justice is not new to Asian American history. In the introductory chapter, we discuss the impetus of the early Asian American movement for identity, liberation, and empowerment and how movement politics transitioned to mainstream politics with the changing political context. We define social justice leadership as a form of leadership distinct from the traditional white-male dominant norm perpetuating the marginalization of women and men of color. We surmise that those APAEOs whose public service has engaged in institutional or social structural changes are transformative leaders for social justice. We find APAEOs with grassroots organizational ties are more likely to advocate for social justice after being elected to office and maintain ties to the community and organizations. They are the ones who embody the womanist leadership praxis by adopting a collective (rather than an individualistic) concept of leadership, value coalition politics, exhibit a community-based style of representation, and aim to transform conventional politics. They participated in or helped form organizations to deliver social services and construct the electoral infrastructure of the community. Because their electoral successes were often the result of multicultural coalitions, these leaders are particularly keen on promoting a sense of linked or shared fate across communities, broadly defined.

Given all the diversities and differences within the APA community and the existence of multiple layers of intersecting interests, we do not believe it ought to be a zero-sum competition between the two strategies for political incorporation and community empowerment. With the continuous expansion of APA presence in Congress (and other governing bodies) and civil society, we anticipate this type of tension to rise and more frequently. We consider it a sign of political maturity of the pluralistic community when APA grassroots organizations formed coalitions with other advocacy organizations to participate in policy debates regarding the best ways to redistribute wealth and resources into areas like healthcare, housing, and social services. As the anti-Asian violence shows no signs of subsiding, the need becomes more urgent for APAEOs and CBOs to find common ground and solutions to address the structural inequalities exacerbated by the Covid-19 pandemic. We believe those APAEOs who subscribe to and adopt womanist leadership praxis are social justice leaders who can more effectively bridge differences in ideology, goals, and approaches in representing and serving the APA community and beyond.

Finally, our research shows that those elected officials who practiced social justice leadership also see intersectional linked fate with other minoritized communities outside the APA community. It will be the focus of another project to better document and explore evidence of cross-racial coalition-building involving APAs in different types of office, context, and locations. Another fruitful avenue for future research is to apply the modified womanist leadership praxis model initially introduced by Adbullah and Freer (2008) and interrogated in its applicability for APAEOs in this project to the experiences of other groups of women and men such as Latinx, Black, American Indian, and white officials, respectively, collaboratively, and/or collectively. We also hope future studies can interrogate the origins and extent of social justice leadership and their ramifications for the womanist leadership praxis model at a micro level that pays greater attention to the intersecting influence and unique dynamics of gender, ethnicity, and immigration generations for APAEOs serving in local-level offices and localities beyond Hawaii and California. Because we have focused on APAEOs on the progressive side of politics, we also see a need for future research to explore the making of APAEOs who espouse a conservative agenda and identify with the GOP stance on social issues. In the end, we hope to have laid some groundwork for future scholars to present an even more comprehensive picture of how APAEOs arrive at, navigate to serve in their expected roles of representation, and contest (or conform to) their structural positions as (perceived) newcomers and outsiders on the last frontier.

APPENDIX A

A Note on Terminology Used to Describe Our Research Subjects

The boundaries of racial and ethnic terms have been a deeply contested area in studying identity and politics in the United States. We hope to clarify for readers in this brief note the general parameters of our usage of specific terms to describe the focused population in our study.

Who Are the Elected Officials in Our Study?

Our study is mainly on Asian American elected officials holding congressional, statewide, state legislative, county, municipal, and school board offices in the 50 US states. They include members of Congress (senators, representatives, and nonvoting delegates), statewide officeholders (governor, lieutenant governor, secretary of state, attorney general, state treasurer, or state auditor/controller), state legislators (state senators and representatives or assembly members), county officials (commissioners, board of supervisors), municipal officials (mayors, vice mayors, city/town/village councilmembers, and boards of aldermen/selectmen), and local school board members. Our study does not include judicial or law enforcement positions. Neither do we include party officials. Except for congressional delegates, the Pacific Islander American elected officials enumerated in our database are limited to those who are partly Native Hawaiian or other Pacific Islander Americans and hold elective positions outside of the unincorporated US territories of American Samoa, Guam, the Northern Mariana Islands. Whereas multiracial Native Hawaiian and other Pacific Islanders are rare in our database, we use the inclusive term "Asian Pacific American elected officials" (APAEOs) to acknowledge the very diverse origins of elected officials in our study and the populations they represent.

Why Do We Prefer "APA" over Other Terms?

The primary focus of our study is on Asian Americans, a US population that was estimated to be 22.6 million in 2018,[1] which is 16 times larger than the estimated 1.4 million Native Hawaiian and Other Pacific Islander (NHOPI) population in 2018. In addition to the difference in size, the two populations have different histories of US dispossession and settler colonialism (Morey et al. 2020). However, umbrella terms encompassing both groups, such as "Asian Pacific Americans" (APAs), "Asian Americans and Pacific Islanders" (AAPIs), and "Asian and Pacific Islander Americans" (APIAs), have been commonly used in academia, the media, and US politics and society writ large. We suspect this may be due to four main factors: (1) the US census enumeration of the Asian population in the United States, which included categories for Hawaiians and other Pacific Islanders in the years between 1960 and 2000, (2) the presence of interrelationships and offspring from

218   APPENDIX A

intermarriages between Asian and Native Hawaiians or other Pacific Islanders, (3) xeno-phobic hate violence against both Asian and Pacific Islanders, and (4) perceived benefits and need by community organizations and leaders for panethnic organizing and cross-racial coalition-building for collective empowerment.

We recognize and respect the differences between the experiences of US persons of Pacific Islander descent and those of Asian descent and will not use racial terms that contain the "P" or "PI" unless warranted by the situation. When necessary and possible to disentangle the accounting of the two groups, we discuss Asian American and Pacific Islander American experiences separately. Nonetheless, we readily admit the difficulties to consistently and discuss the experiences of Pacific Islander Americans separately from those of Asian Americans due to historical practices and societal norms in a nation where the two groups have often been treated as one under the same racial rubric. In fact, we find the need to continue using umbrella terms such as APA, AAPI, and APIA (and often interchangeably) when this is the usage in prior literature and by community-based organizations, public officials, the media, and others. For connectivity and convenience, we opt to use "Pacific Islander" in-stead of the Office of Management and Budget's 1997 term "Native Hawaiian or Other Pacific Islander" to describe the identity of a population that includes any persons, including Asians, who can trace part of their ancestry to Native Hawaiian or Other Pacific Islander origins.

Which US Population Do APAEOs Represent?

According to the Office of Management and Budget 1997 *Revisions to the Standards for the Classification of Federal Data on Race and Ethnicity* applicable to the 2000 and 2010 censuses, "Asian" refers to persons "having origins in any of the original peoples of the Far East, Southeast Asia, or the Indian subcontinent, including, for example, Cambodia, China, India, Japan, Korea, Malaysia, Pakistan, the Philippine Islands, Thailand, and Vietnam" (Hoeffel et al. 2012, 2). When responding to US census questions on race and ethnicity, a US resident who self-identifies as Asian and belongs to one of the six major ethnic groups (i.e., Asian Indian, Chinese, Filipino, Japanese, Korean, and Vietnamese) can simply check the box next to one's ethnic origin. Those Asians who belong to other Asian ethnic origins will need to check "Other Asian" and write in their specific ethnic origin. Similarly, persons who self-identify as Pacific Islanders and belong to one of the three major groups of Native Hawaiian, Guamanian or Chamorro, and Samoan can just check the box next to one's ethnic origin. Pacific Islanders who belong to other ethnic origins will need to check the "Other Pacific Islander" box and write in their specific ethnic origin. A write-in area for reporting an Asian or Pacific Islander origin not found in the response category was introduced in the 1990 census and continued in the 2000 and 2010 censuses.

Identifying and counting persons of Asian descent in the United States has been made difficult by the changing definitions used by the US census to measure race (Perez and Hirschman 2009; Brown 2020). The first racial category for Asians was introduced na-tionwide in 1870 under "Chinese." The "Japanese" category was added in 1890. By 1920, "Filipino," "Korean," and "Hindu" categories were added. In the 1950 census, "Korean" and "Hindu" were considered only as part of the foreign-born population and were not part of the Asian counting. In 1960, "Hawaiian" and "Part Hawaiian" were added to the existing Asian categories of "Chinese," "Japanese," and "Filipino." In 1970, "Korean" returned to the Asian category. By 1980, "Asian Indian" and "Vietnamese" along with "Samoan" and "Guamanian" were added to the "Asian" racial category. The 1990 census added the category of "Other Asian or Pacific Islander." Starting in 2000, Asian and Pacific Islander populations were counted separately under "Asian" or "Native Hawaiians and Other Pacific Islander" (NHOPI) categories of race.

Engaging Multiracial Asian America

Whenever possible, our conceptualization and analysis of research on persons of Asian (and Pacific Islander) descent include those whose ascribed or claimed ethnoracial identity includes groups other than Asians (or Pacific Islanders). According to Hoeffel et al. (2012), before 1960, an individual's race was determined by census takers, known as enumerators. The concept of self-identification was adopted in the 1960 census and afterward. Around this time, the census recognized race as a social construction, not an objective, biological, or genetic reality. Yet it was not until census 2000 that Americans could choose more than one race to describe themselves. This change in practice led to the creation of a separate multiracial category and the separate enumeration of monoracial and multiracial individuals. Compared to the US average (2.9% in census 2010), a significantly higher percentage of Asian Americans and Pacific Islanders describe themselves as more than one race.

In 2000, 4.2% of the 281.4 million persons residing in the United States and enumerated in the decennial census identified themselves as "Asian alone or in combination" with one or more other race(s). The comparable statistics in 2010 show that 5.6% of the 308.7 million US persons were "Asian alone or in combination." Between 2000 and 2010, the Asian alone-or-in-combination population grew by 46% from 11.9 million in 2000 to 17.3 million in 2010, making Asians the fastest-growing racial group.

In 2010, 17.3 million US residents reported being Asian alone or in combination, 14.7 million, or 85%, identified as Asian alone, and 2.6 million, or 15%, identified as multiracial Asians or Asians with another racial background. This figure increased from the 2000 census, where over 1.6 million people, or 14%, of the Asian alone-or-in-any-combination population identified as being multiracial Asian. With the percentage share of multiracial Asians among the total Asian alone-or-in-any-combination population being 0.6% in 2000 and 0.9% in 2010, the growth rate of multiracial Asians was 60% over the decade.

Among the majority of the 2.6 million multiracial Asians in 2010, 1.6 million, or 61%, identified as "Asian and white." Those who identified as "Asian and Black" were much fewer in number (186,000, or 7%), even if this number was slightly higher than those who identified as "Asian and NHOPI" (166,000, or 6%). In 2000, those who identified as "Asian and white" were 52%, those who identified as "Asian and NHOPI" were 8%, and those identified as "Asian and Black" were 6% of the multiracial Asian population. Between 2000 and 2010, those identified as "Asian and white" experienced the highest growth rate of 87%, followed by "Asian and Black" at 74%. The growth rate of those who identified as "Asian and NHOPI" was significantly lower at 19% over the decade.

APPENDIX B

Methods of Constructing
the APAEO Database

We did not start from scratch in finding US elected officials of API descent. The idea of a political directory of APAEOs was initiated by Don Nakanishi of UCLA Asian American Studies Center in 1978 and joined by his student James Lai in the mid-1990s. After UCLA ceased publication of the *National APA Political Almanac* in 2014, the APA Institute of Congressional Studies (APAICS) started an online platform where elected officials could voluntarily enter their name, office title, partisanship, and ethnicity information to help build a public national electronic directory. Based both on the 2014–15 edition of the *Political Almanac* and the political directory on the APAICS website in early 2015, we began putting together a database of our own. It included basic demographic information and information on political socialization, career pipeline, organization network, and issue positions, among other details of each case. Given the open-ended and iterative nature of finding new APAEOs (or the same individuals serving in a new level of office), we updated and cross-checked each individual's personal information in our database more than a few times between 2016 and 2020. Our ongoing database enhancement efforts involve verifying the accuracy of the extant information by searching official campaign and government websites and election returns. This process helps decide if there is a need for updates with recently elected (or previously omitted) elected officials from the same office in the same locality and government. Given our systematic research methods, we suspect some individuals might have been inadvertently omitted but not in a nonrandom fashion.

Whereas we follow the various definitions used by the US census to identify elected officials of Asian (and Pacific Islander) descent, our community-based approach in enumeration also ensures that the multiethnic and multiracial community recognizes individuals who made it to our APAEO database as representing each major ethnic group among the AAPI population. When given a list of last names of elected officials in a popularly elected office, our task of finding APAEOs is made easier when elected officials themselves are Asian alone and with a single Asian ethnic origin, which describes a supermajority of the APAEO population. However, Asians who are adopted by non-Asian parents or are the offspring of interracial marriages would be missed by the last-name (and visual or phenotypic cues) approach, as would Asian women who marry non-Asians and assume their spouse's surname. Importantly, our quest to find Asians in elective offices went far beyond surnames and visual cues. We read biographies, archived and current news articles, project reports, and research publications. In addition to gathering data from campaign and/or official government websites, we also sifted through lists of organizational affiliations and various voter guides, among other pieces of information available online.

222   APPENDIX B

Deciding the Ethnic Identity of Mixed-Ancestry APAEOs

For monoracial and multiracial Asian and Pacific Islander individuals with mixed ethnic origins, we would enter the ethnic identity of the less populous and/or newcomer group among the existing population of elected officials. This means if someone is both Chinese and Filipino, we will count this person as of Filipino descent. By the same token, if someone is both Japanese and Korean, we will count this person as Korean by ethnicity. However, the decision is also context-driven. If someone is of Chinese and Japanese descent in Hawaii, we will count this person as Chinese. However, a similarly mixed-ancestry person would be counted as Japanese in California, where there are many more Chinese than Japanese in office.

The similar rule of privileging the numerical minority among public officials applies to multiracial Asians with mixed-ethnic origins. A case in point is Congressman T. J. Cox, who is white, Chinese, and Filipino, but we put him in the Filipino American category. Whereas all multiracial Asians serving in the defined elective offices for our study are eligible to be included in our database, not all may have been recognized as part of the APA community in the past. A case in point is Senator John Ensign of Nevada. Although he claimed to be part Filipino, he was not recognized as part of the APA representatives in Congress, or a core member of the Congressional APA Caucus, or a member of the local Filipino community. Racial identification for multiracial legislators seems to be more a function of one's networks and relationships than blood ties, especially when it involves members from a political party that has not been considered friendly to the APA community for the majority part of history.

Classifying Sub-State-Office Levels

While the majority of local or substate offices can be grouped into three distinct levels (school board, city or municipal, and county), there are exceptions. San Francisco, for example, is officially recognized as both a city and a county, and it is the only such government in California. We consider the city and county of San Francisco (San Francisco Board of Supervisors) a municipal-level office when our primary interest is to account for the growth of APAEOs in California cities. When our interest is in accounting for longitudinal and nationwide changes, we include these officeholders in county-level counts to compare to the trends of officeholding in other counties in California and elsewhere, including in the state of Hawaii, where city and county councils are also combined. Education board members whose jurisdictions are county-based or state-based rather than local school-based are counted as county-level or statewide offices, respectively.

Identifying Individual Partisanship with the Two Major Parties

For elected officials holding partisan offices, locating party affiliation is a relatively straightforward process. This information is readily available on the official websites of individuals and institutions and in the election results. For nonpartisan officeholders serving at the school board, municipal, and county levels, locating partisanship is much more labor intensive. We began by searching the biographies and official websites but found nonpartisan officeholders to avoid explicit mentions of partisanship. In these cases, we looked for clues from major party endorsement lists and mentions of membership in local party clubs or participation in party-based leadership development programs. Despite our best efforts, we were unable to identify the major party affiliations of some. In 2020, only 66% of school board members, 79% of municipal officials, and 82% of county-level officials, or an overall rate of 83% of APAEOs serving in 2020, were found to identify with either of the two parties.

For a small number of elected officials who did not identify as Democrats but with a party on the progressive side of politics, we put them in the Democratic Party category in the context of two-party politics. Examples include many in Minnesota who identified as DFL or Democratic-Farmer-Labor Party and Seattle city councilwoman Kshama Sawant, who identified herself as a Socialist Alternative.

APPENDIX C

How We Identify Social Justice Leaders and Study Issue Priorities

As suggested in Chapter 1, our selection of APA social justice leaders is guided largely by the four measures of womanist leadership praxis identified by Abdullah and Freer (2008): (1) trajectory to office that includes a history of community connection and entrenchment; (2) active membership in community-based organizations; (3) motivation to run for office based on recruitment rather than personal ambition; and (4) campaign strategies that engage community-based organizations and grassroots leaders. We also share their conception of Black leadership "as falling along a continuum ranging from traditional to womanist" (109). Toward that end, we conceive of womanist leadership praxis as multidimensional, situational, and fluid in service of advancing social justice. There are gradations of differences across each dimension among those who fit into the category, and they may enter and leave this particular realm of politics in different career stages and contexts or circumstances.

The initial screening for social justice leaders in the database for those serving between 2014 and 2020 was based on their (self) reported issue priorities. For those serving in the early 1980s, it was their known legislative accomplishments. For both groups of earlier and more recent elected officials (EOs), we initially selected those who expressed commitments to or sought to advance equality and justice on the various issues. For those who were in service sometime between 2014 and 2020, we examined their issue positions across 11 issue areas covering education, immigration, public health/safety, family/youth/elderly, women, business/economy, labor, environment, APIA civil rights, fiscal/budget, and government services (see the subsequent discussion of the methodology of studying issue priorities). We wanted to select individuals who had worked on issue concerns at the intersection of race, gender, and class inequalities or at least two of them. Examples include those who sought equality and justice for at least two of the structurally disadvantaged groups in US society such as immigrants, women, workers, APIA and other racial/ethnic minorities, LGBTQ, and other minority Americans. To the extent data were available online, we used similar standards to gauge earlier generations of APAEOs. The two processes often converge for veteran EOs who have a long record of service. It is also biased for those who are/were in more prominent positions. We are aware of the limitations in methodology. Still, we do not see it as a problem, as our purpose is to identify and learn from APAEOs who have promoted social justice.

We understand that not everyone will agree with our methods and criteria for selecting and categorizing social justice leaders. We are also aware of the incremental nature of the legislative process and the slowness of policy change. Therefore, although our study features and celebrates the accomplishments of reputable APAEOS who practiced womanist ideas, our discussion also includes individuals who are new to the electoral arena and in the process of making legislative imprints, including those serving at the local level.

226 APPENDIX C

Methodology for Studying Issue Priorities

Issue priorities were identified through statements on campaign websites, third-party sites like Smart Voter where candidates upload information, and digital encyclopedias like Ballotpedia maintained by professional staff, media interviews, biographies, and membership in civic and political organizations, and personal interviews conducted by the research team. For Hawaii state legislators whose data were limited, we also identified issue priorities based on committee service. For those who had a record of legislative work, we also used information found in bill sponsorships. We performed simple online searches of the EOs to identify these sources. In many cases, candidate websites and websites maintained by EOs listed issue areas that they prioritized and provided brief descriptions of their stances. In other cases, EOs highlighted issue priorities in their past accomplishments and/or future plans more informally or generally through statements made in media interviews, newsletters, biographies. Certainly, not all were equally open or descriptive about their issue priorities. Those who happened to be running at the time of the data collection process were more likely to be analyzed. Moreover, certain offices, particularly at the lower level, may not have websites, and their candidacies or service coverage may be slimmer than those in more visible positions. Issue priorities may also vary by level of office. It was certainly the case for school board members, who are much more likely to mention education as an important issue.

After reading statements or descriptions from the above sources, we generated an initial list of issue types and coded them thematically using keywords or phrases. We also included contextual clues where available to ensure consistency in coding across different EOs and compiled these as textual data for our reference. Additional categories were added and amended throughout the data collection and coding process so as to reflect the most representative picture of issue areas common to APAEOs. This process led to the creation of 11 issue areas: Education; Immigration; Health and Safety; Family, Youth, and Elderly; Women's Rights; Business and the Economy; Labor and Jobs; Environment; APIA Civil Rights; Fiscal and Budget; and Government and Public Services.

In addition, we created a separate issue category called "social justice and equality concerns" for EOs who seek to help eradicate social inequality or worked on issue concerns that address injustice for individuals or groups situated at the intersection of race, gender, sexual orientation, and class or some combination of these social and structural dimensions of marginalization. Examples include those seeking equality and justice for at least two structurally disadvantaged groups in US society, such as immigrants, women, workers, APIA and other racial/ethnic minorities, LGBTQ, and other minority Americans. We recognize that this additive approach to group identity may not capture the concerns of intersectionally disadvantaged groups, such as low-income immigrant women of color.

Because we were interested in identifying what types of issues APAEOs prioritized rather than examining their personal issue stances or approaches, individuals included in the same issue category may have divergent political views or perspectives. In several instances, multiple issue priorities could be found within the same campaign statement. To the extent possible, we also performed random checks for the accuracy of coding.

What follows are descriptions of the 11 issue areas and examples of coding decisions.
Education: promote education, improve the educational system, improve access to education

"By working collaboratively, we are finding innovative ways to improve our educational system [*Education*], address our traffic, the growing numbers of homeless encampments, abandoned vehicles, and illegal dumping, while ensuring our community members have access to essential government services [*Government and Public Services*]" (Cedric Gates, official website, http://www.cedricgates.com/).

"Promote excellence in education and life-long learning" (Ruth Low, campaign website, https://votersedge.org/ca/en/election/2020-11-03/los-angeles-county/city-council-city-of-diamond-bar/ruth-low).

"Partner with business [*Business and the Economy*] and foundations to improve education [*Education*] for our youth [*Youth*]" (Madison Nguyen, 2014 candidate statement).

Immigration: promote or protect immigrant rights, legislative advocacy on immigration policy

"It is imperative that immigration reform is both common-sense and compassionate" (Grace Meng, official website, https://meng.house.gov/issues/housing).

"Implement effective policies to attract international talent to Kentucky, work with immigrant and refugee communities to ensure that they have access to the resources that they need, and bring an informed and experienced voice in Frankfort so that our district and our state thrive economically and culturally" (Nima Kulkarni, 2018 campaign website).

Health and Safety: accessibility and affordability of healthcare, improving healthcare, health services, public safety, safe streets, student safety, safe learning environment, expand Medicare

"I worked to trim the budget and identify key areas to increase efficiency [*Fiscal and Budget*] and consolidate work while maintaining safe streets, improving public safety [*Health and Safety*] and promoting economic development [*Business and the Economy*]" (Suzanne Lee Chan, 2012 candidate statement).

"Health care is a big expense to the state and its citizens. We need affordable solutions to improve the availability for all Texans to choose the right healthcare for themselves. ObamaCare is not the solution and will put a huge, unfair mandate on the state and the people of Texas. Encouraging the free market, both for-profit and nonprofits, to meet the needs of Texas is the solution" (Nghi Ho, 2014 campaign website in Ballotpedia).

Family, Youth, and Elderly: parental leave, family violence, services for youth and the elderly, working families

"Family and sexual violence impacts Georgians of every gender, race, age, and socio-economic status. I have worked with community organizations to support victims of domestic violence and sexual assault. I will fight for a system that protects our families, seniors, children and survivors. We will break the silence" (Bee Nguyen, official website, https://www.beeforgeorgia.com/).

Women's Rights: equal pay, reproductive justice, women's representation, domestic violence, sexual assault, women's rights, supporting working mothers, parental leave if mothers are specifically mentioned

"As President of Maryland's women's caucus, I launched the Sexual Harassment Evaluation (S.H.E.) Committee. This bipartisan group of women legislators drafted policies to address sexual harassment, many of which became law this year" (Aruna Miller, campaign website, https://ballotpedia.org/Aruna_Miller).

228 APPENDIX C

Business and Economy: promote economic growth, support small business, "smart growth," real estate, strengthen economy

"To enhance business vitality" (Emily Lo, 2010 candidate statement).

"Revitalization of the economy for the creation of jobs and business opportunities" (Rida Cabanilla Arakawa, official legislative website, http://www.capitol.hawaii.gov/memberpage.aspx?member=cabanilla).

Labor and Jobs: job creation, unemployment, support working class, working poor, increase minimum wage

"Government needs to get out of businesses' way so good paying jobs can be created for our middle class" (Niraj Antani, 2022 official website).

Environment: climate change, protect and preserve natural resources, environmental justice, environmental sustainability, environmental protection

"The impacts of climate change range from disruptive to destructive, and they grow more urgent each season. As weather patterns change due to greenhouse gas emissions, it's not enough to be resilient, to wait for the next hurricane or flood or drought and then marshal relief efforts." (Michelle Wu, official website, https://www.michelleforboston.com/issues).

APIA Civil Rights: cultural rights, hate crimes, civil rights for APAs or minorities in general, involvement in APA-specific civil rights, professional, and civic organizations

"There's a great deal of work left to accomplish to address disproportionate discipline of students of color, opportunity gaps, preparing all of our students for promising futures, and connecting with all our communities as our district continues to grow" (Betty Patu, 2017 candidate statement).

"I helped protect racial minorities throughout the state by working on a case that led to a historic settlement that prevented racial profiling" (Rob Bonta, 2012 candidate statement).

Fiscal and Budget: balancing the budget, concerns over revenue streams, fiscal accountability responsibility, government spending, cut "waste"

"Fought wasteful spending at every turn, pushed for smaller, more efficient government, and led the fight for accountability and transparency" (Nikki Haley, 2011 official website).

Government and Public Services: improving police, housing, public employees, fixing streets, public transportation, libraries, improving city infrastructure, disaster relief, and general improvements to government services

"Brokered a landmark public safety deal, breaking a Council deadlock, to fund a new police academy in 2021–2022, while also holding OPD accountable for overtime costs and pushing to diversify the police force by hiring more women of color and Oakland residents" (Sheng Thao, 2022 official website).

"Building new affordable housing and promoting housing developments near public transportation" (Evan Low, 2020 campaign website).

Notes

Chapter 1

1. In the Hawaii Territory, indigenous Hawaiians—mostly male and many of mixed Pacific Islander and European ancestry—held elective office in the territorial legislature and in US Congress as delegates without full voting rights after the first postannexation election in 1900.

2. By race, we mean the socially and politically constructed macrocategories and their meanings based on perceived phenotypic, somatic, and cultural differences and often used to maintain a social and political hierarchy. By ethnicity, we mean the socially and politically constructed differences based on perceived cultural and ancestral ties. Within political science, ethnicity is commonly associated with national and regional origins. In other disciplines like ethnic studies, ethnicity may also refer to macrocategories (i.e., panethnicity) associated with a common history, culture, and/or tradition. We understand these definitions to be non-mutually exclusive. When the concepts of race and ethnicity are intertwined, we use the term "ethnoracial." By gender, we mean the socially and politically constructed categories and meanings commonly associated with biological sex, masculinity, and femininity. We use the terms "male" and "female" interchangeably with man and woman, recognizing that notions of biological sex are inherently gendered.

Chapter 2

1. We use "first generation" to refer to individuals born outside of the United States proper or incorporated territories (excluding those born abroad of an American parent). They are also called the "foreign-born." The term "second generation" refers to US-born individuals who have at least one foreign-born parent. The term "third generation" denotes US-born individuals with two US-born parents but at least one foreign-born grandparent.

2. For fuller appreciation of the immensely rich and complicated Asian American history, see classic works by Daniels 1988, Takaki 1989, Chan 1991, and Okihiro 1994. See Lee 2014 for coverage of more recent developments in history. Also see Glenn 1986 and 2002 as well as Hune and Nomura 2003 and 2020 for women-centered narration and interpretation of group history. We use these sources and more to draw the narration of brief history in this section.

230 NOTES

3. Fong was forced to resign his territorial house seat in 1942 while on active military duty, but his wife helped him campaign in 1944, and he won back the seat.
4. https://horatioalger.org/members/member-detail/hiram-l-fong/.
5. The law was established in 1913, amended in 1920, and ruled unconstitutional by the California Supreme Court in 1952. It prevented aliens ineligible for citizenship—aka Asian immigrants—from owning property or leasing land at the time.
6. Immigrants from India were barred from naturalization by the negative decision in *United States v. Bhagat Singh Thind* (1923) until 1946, when Congress passed the Luce-Celler Act allowing naturalization for Indians (and Filipinos). In his autobiography, Saund (1960) accounted for his hard work organizing support for Congress to open citizenship to people of Indian descent living in the States. He became naturalized on Dec 16, 1949.
7. According to Knight (2011), it was rumored that Lee's father was born a Mah or a Mar, variants of the same name, and immigrated to the United States as a "paper son." However, the same report noted that Lee had said that his father was adopted by a Mah family in a neighboring village that had no sons.
8. Henry Lo, interview by Alan Tam, May 8, 2016.
9. Lilian Sing, telephone interview by Nicole Filler, May 9, 2018.
10. Michael Chang, telephone interview by Anisha Ahuja, July 18, 2016.
11. Polly Low, telephone interview by Anisha Ahuja, July 30, 2016.

Chapter 3

1. The nation's first systemic effort to create such a roster was initiated by Don Nakanishi in 1978. However, it did not include a complete record of state officials or those serving at sub-state-level offices in Hawaii until the second edition in 1980.
2. Although there was no record of other state and local elected officials in Hawaii in the 1978 roster, individuals holding these offices were identified in the roster published in 1980; it included 31 city and county officials and eight appointed state board of education members.
3. Comparison between the 1980 and 2010 census population is made difficult by the change starting in 2000 allowing multiracial individuals to check more than one racial category. Also, prior to 2000, census reporting of the Asian population includes Pacific Islanders. After 2000, Native Hawaiians and Other Pacific Islanders (NHOPI) were counted separately from Asians.
4. Whereas we count all the elected officials of ethnic Chinese descent who are either foreign-born and migrated from Taiwan or US-born but with parents from Taiwan as Taiwanese, only those individuals who identified as Taiwanese but not Chinese and wrote in "Taiwanese" as their ethnicity in the census form would count as Taiwanese in the US census data.
5. Because the US census uses mutually exclusive, binary categories for sex (male/female) and we view these categories as inherently gendered, the share of women and

NOTES 231

men in each Asian ethnic group equals 100. Likewise, we did not find any APAEOs who identify as gender nonconforming or transgender.

6. Eight (1.4%) were born in Latin America, Canada, or New Zealand and are mostly Asian Indian by ethnicity. All but one Pacific Islander American elected official was born in the United States, including its territories. Not all are US citizens at birth; people born in American Samoa are US nationals jus solis and must obtain US citizenship through the naturalization process or jus sanguinis in order to vote and run for office. In this way, those who were born in American Samoa and serving in an elective office other than the territory's congressional delegation may have more in common with Asia-born officials due to their shared status as nonwhite immigrants and naturalized citizens. By our count, there are just three American Samoa–born APAEOs who fit this description in 2020: Tulsi Gabbard (US Congress), Mike Gabbard (Hawaii State Legislature), and Elizabeth Kautz (mayor of Burnsville, Minnesota). Our data set does not include officials serving in US territorial governments.

7. Because of the lack of comparable statistics between the two time periods and given the much higher proportion of the mixed-race population in Hawaii, we calculated the 2010 API population in Hawaii by taking the sum of the Asian alone or in combination population and the NHOPI-alone population. Total API population figure for 1980 comes from Table 73 of US Census General Social and Economic Statistics for Hawaii, p. 35.

8. 1980 US Census, General Population Characteristics, Hawaii, Table 15, p. 9.

9. Detailed racial groups alone or in combination for Hawaii, 2010 US Census SF2.

10. The West census region includes Alaska, Arizona, California, Colorado, Hawaii, Idaho, Montana, Nevada, New Mexico, Oregon, Utah, Washington, and Wyoming.

11. The South census region includes Alabama, Arkansas, Delaware, the District of Columbia, Florida, Georgia, Kentucky, Louisiana, Maryland, Mississippi, North Carolina, Oklahoma, South Carolina, Tennessee, Texas, Virginia, and West Virginia.

12. All of the US population estimates in this paragraph are taken from the 2011–15 ACS and refer to the Asian alone or in combination category.

13. She's in Judy Chu's article and included as a Nikkei candidate in this news article https://pacificcitizen.org/wp-content/uploads/archives-menu/Vol.086_%2310_ Mar_17_1978.pdf. However, the article mentioned she's a Caucasian married to George Tsuda. If excluding this white woman, the percentage female in 1980 is 7%.

14. Two cities—San Joaquin and El Cerrito—were removed as outliers due to their exceedingly high parity scores as a result of the less than 1% Asian in the city's population.

15. Five of the 36 legislators who served after 1990 (Liu, Yee, Lieu, Pan, and Chang) had two elections that involved their entry into the assembly and the senate. Muratsuchi entered the assembly twice after he lost his first seat.

Chapter 4

1. John Huang, a key player in the campaign-finance controversy and a former executive of the Indonesia-based Lippo Group, was appointed in late 1995 as the vice

232 NOTES

finance chairman of the Democratic National Committee (DNC), a title created for Huang that no other DNC employee held. He pleaded guilty in 1999 to a charge of violating federal campaign finance regulations for arranging a $156,000 in illegal campaign contributions from Lippo Group employees to mostly Democratic Party political committees. Huang was sentenced to one year of probation, a $10,000 fine, and 500 hours of community service.

2. In the 1998 final report of the congressional hearings on campaign finance violations by Asian donors, Michael Kojima, a Japan-born naturalized citizen who failed to pay child support, was found to give $500,000—derived probably from foreign funds—to bring 10 Japanese nationals with him to a 1992 dinner in the White House.

3. This 1994 ballot initiative aims to prohibit undocumented immigrants from accessing nonemergency healthcare, public education, and other public services. Whereas it received support from 59% of voters, it also triggered mass protests and activated a new generation of Latino and Asian voters for the Democratic Party.

4. Clark Lee, email interview by Pei-te Lien, March 13–19, 2015.

5. Steven Choi, communication over email with Anisha Ahuja, June 6, 2016.

6. Delivered in 1863 by US president Abraham Lincoln during the Civil War (1861–1865), this famous speech reminded American people of the nation's founding principles of liberty, equality, and a government of the people, by the people, and for the people.

7. Eric Mar, telephone interview by Nicole Filler, April 17, 2018.

8. Mike Fong, in-person interview by Anisha Ahuja, May 10, 2016.

9. Fong, interview.

10. Will Espero, in-person interview by Anisha Ahuja, April 20, 2016.

11. Gary Yamauchi, telephone interview by Alan Lam, May 23, 2016.

12. Michael Chang, telephone interview by Anisha Ahuja, July 18, 2016.

13. Lisa Bartlett, telephone interview by Anisha Ahuja, June 20, 2016.

14. Warren Kusumoto, in-person interview by Anisha Ahuja, June 16, 2016.

Chapter 5

1. *Congressional Record*, House, 93rd Cong., 1st sess. (May 15, 1973): 15756.

2. This was the first US civil rights legislation after 1875, which helped established the Civil Rights Section of the Justice Department and empowered federal prosecutors to obtain court injunctions against interference with the right to vote. It also established the US Commission on Civil Rights with authority to investigate discriminatory conditions and recommend corrective measures. It had limited impact on extending the Black right to vote due to opposition from southern Democrats. https://www.eisenhowerlibrary.gov/research/online-documents/civil-rights-act-1957.

3. Patsy T. Mink, oral history interview by US Association of Former Members of Congress, March 6, March 26, June 7, 1979, Manuscript Reading Room, Library of Congress, Washington, DC: 43.

NOTES 233

4. More about the campaign to promote public awareness of the history and continuing significance of the Chinese Exclusion Act of 1882 is available at the project website https://1882foundation.org/about-2/.

5. H. Res. 683—Expressing the regret of the House of Representatives for the passage of laws that adversely affected the Chinese in the United States, including the Chinese Exclusion Act. Washington, DC: Congress, June 18. https://www.congress.gov/bill/112th-congress/house-resolution/683/text.

6. "1990 Census of Population General Population Characteristics: Nevada," US Census Bureau, Table 3. https://www2.census.gov/library/publications/decennial/1990/cp-1/cp-1-30.pdf. Figures for 2015 include Asian and Native Hawaiian and Other Pacific Islanders alone or in combination with one or more other races in Table DP05 of the 2011–15 American Community Survey 5-Year Estimates Data Profile.

7. Lilian Sing, telephone interview by Nicole Filler, May 9, 2018.

8. Eric Mar, telephone interview by Nicole Filler, April 17, 2018.

9. Hirono also related immigrant detention to the incarceration of Japanese Americans during World War II. For the full transcript of her speech, see "Forced Family Separation" in *Congressional Record*, Senate, 115th Cong., 164, 103 (June 20, 2018), S4294–S4295.

10. See http://www.asianpacificpolicyandplanningcouncil.org/stop-aapi-hate/ for a systematic effort by a coalition of AAPI community organizations and leaders to document reports of anti-Asian hate incidents related to Covid-19.

11. It amends the Department of Energy Organization Act and the Local Public Works Capital Development and Investment Act of 1976 to modernize terms relating to minorities by striking "Negroes, Spanish-speaking, Orientals, Indians, Eskimos, and Aleuts" and inserting "Asian American, Native Hawaiian, Pacific Islanders, African American, Hispanic, Native American, or Alaska Natives."

12. Wilma Chan, telephone interview by Nicole Filler, June 12, 2019.

13. Chan, interview.

Chapter 6

1. Song acknowledged in the interview that he had a "weakness" for "beautiful women" (Sonenshein 1986, 177), which possibly explained the rushed marriage.

2. https://www.facebook.com/WeiUeberschaerforSchoolBoard/.

3. https://www.hoa4pdx.com/meet.

4. https://www.advancingjustice-chicago.org/teaach/.

5. To learn more about An Nguyen's story and the VietRise #KeepAnHome campaign, see https://vietrise.org/our-programs/immigrant-justice/. For one analysis of the significance of Southeast Asian American youth-led campaigns against the school-to-prison-to-deportation pipeline, see Das Gupta 2019.

6. As tax exempt under Internal Revenue Code Section 501(c)(3), these organizations are prohibited from participating on behalf of or in opposition to any campaign for

elective public office. They are also restricted in the amount of lobbying activities they can engage in. See https://www.irs.gov/charities-non-profits/charitable-organizations/the-restriction-of-political-campaign-intervention-by-section-501c3-tax-exempt-organizations.

7. http://www.asianpacificpolicyandplanningcouncil.org/about-a3pcon/.
8. https://apaics.org/programs/national-leadership-academy/ (accessed November 1, 2020).
9. https://www.napawf.org/history.
10. https://apali.org/.
11. Michael Chang, telephone interview by Anisha Ahuja, July 18, 2016.
12. https://apalf.org/about/apalf-alumni-successes/.
13. https://www.apicaucusinstitute.org/.
14. https://newamericanleaders.org/what-we-do/ (accessed May 13, 2020)
15. https://newamericanleaders.org/videos/lan-diep/.
16. In 2018, Bhojwani founded the NALF, an affiliate 501(c)(4) organization that supports the candidates through endorsements and indirect campaign support. In October 2020, she announced she was stepping down from NAL and NALF to launch the Women's Democracy Lab (WDL). The WDL aims to support the political leadership of Black, AAPI, Latinx, Native, and/or immigrant refugee women for systems and culture change.
17. https://www.nwpc.org/history/.
18. https://www.emilyslist.org/pages/entry/women-we-helped-elect.
19. https://emergeamerica.org/about/frequently-asked-questions/.
20. The three APA women are Young Kim (CA-39), Michelle Park Steel (CA-48), and Amata Coleman Radewagen (AS-Del) https://viewpac.org/who-we-support/.
21. http://maggieslist.org/about.
22. https://elevate-pac.com/about/.

Appendix A

1. https://www.census.gov/newsroom/facts-for-features/2021/asian-american-pacific-islander.html.

References

Abdullah, Melina, and Regina Freer. 2008. "Towards a Womanist Leadership Praxis: The History and Promise of Black Grassroots/Electoral Partnerships in California." In *Racial and Ethnic Politics in California: Continuity and Change*, ed. Bruce Cain and Sandra Bass, 95–118. Berkeley, CA: Berkeley Public Policy Press.

Alba, Richard. 2009. *Blurring the Color Line: The New Chance for a More Integrated America*. Cambridge, MA: Harvard University Press.

Alba, Richard, and Nancy Foner. 2009. "Entering the Precincts of Power: Do National Differences Matter for Immigrant Minority Political Representation?" In *Bringing Outsiders In: Transatlantic Perspectives on Immigrant Political Incorporation*, ed. Jennifer L. Hochschild and John H. Mollenkopf, 277–294. Ithaca, NY: Cornell University Press.

Alba, Richard D., and Victor Nee. 2003. *Remaking the American Mainstream: Assimilation and the New Immigration*. Cambridge, MA: Harvard University Press.

Alexander, Kurtis, and Erin Allday. 2017. "Mayor Ed Lee, 1952–2017: Once a Reluctant Politician, He Came to Shape Today's San Francisco." *San Francisco Chronicle*, December 12. https://www.sfchronicle.com/politics/article/Ed-Lee-1952-2017-SF-s-first-Asian-American-12424649.php.

Alexander-Floyd, Nikol G. (Nikol Gertrude), and Evelyn M. Simien. 2006. "Revisiting 'What's in a Name?': Exploring the Contours of Africana Womanist Thought." *Frontiers* 27(1): 67–89.

Allen, Rachael. 2019. "The Next Mayor of Boston? City Councilor Michelle Wu, a Chicago Native and Harvard Law Grad, Has Emerged as One of the City's Most Effective Politicians." *The Atlantic*, April 22. https://www.theatlantic.com/politics/archive/2019/04/michelle-wu-changing-traditional-boston/587473/.

Alozie, Nicholas O. 1992. "The Election of Asians to City Councils." *Social Science Quarterly* 73(1): 90–100.

Andersen, Kristie. 2008. "Parties, Organizations, and Political Incorporation: Immigrants in Six US Cities." In *Civic Hopes and Political Realities: Immigrants, Community Organizations, and Political Engagement*, ed. Karthick Ramakrishnan and Irene Bloemraad, 77–106. New York: Russell Sage Foundation.

Antani, Niraj. 2022. Official website. https://www.nirajantani.com/issues/ (accessed March 14, 2022).

APIAVote. 2021. "APIAVote's Statement on Biden-Harris Administration's First 100 Days." April 30. https://www.apiavote.org/press/apiavote-issues-statement-biden-harris-administrations-first-100-days.

Appleton, Rory. 2018. How Did TJ Cox Erase a 25-Point Primary Loss to Become the Valley's Next Congressman?" *Fresno Bee*, December 12. https://www.fresnobee.com/new/politics-government/politics-columns-blogs/political-notebook/article222436900.html.

REFERENCES

Arax, Mark. 1985. "Lily Lee Chen: Her Roots—and Perhaps Her Political Goals—Lie beyond Monterey Park." *Los Angeles Times*, November 14. https://www.latimes.com/archives/la-xpm-1985-11-14-ga-2678-story.html.

Arinaga, Esther K., and Rene E. Ojiri. 1992. "Patsy Takemoto Mink." In *Called from Within: Early Women Lawyers of Hawaii*, ed. Mari Matsuda, 251–280. Honolulu: University of Hawaii Press.

Ariyoshi, George R. 1997. *With Obligation to All*. Honolulu: Ariyoshi Foundation, distributed by University of Hawaii Press.

Asian Pacific American Institute of Congressional Studies (APAICS). 2020. Women's Collective: Inspiring AAPI Women. https://www.apaics.org/copy-of-nadya-okamoto (accessed March 6, 2022).

Asian Pacific Islander Legislative Caucus (APILC). 2021. "California Legislature Approves $1.4 Million in State Funding to Help Address Surge of Hate and Xenophobia Directed toward Asian Americans." Press release, February 22. https://apicaucus.legislature.ca.gov/products/california-legislature-approves-14-million-state-funding-help-addr ess-surge-hate-and.

Baer, Denise L., and Heidi Hartmann. 2014. *Building Women's Political Careers: Strengthening the Pipeline to Higher Office*. Washington, DC: Institute for Women's Policy Research.

Becerra, Hector. 2012. "DNC: Asian American Leaders Tout Political Progress." *Los Angeles Times*, September 3. http://articles.latimes.com/2012/sep/03/news/la-pn-dnc-asian-americans-20120903.

Bejarano, Christina E. 2013. *The Latina Advantage: Gender, Race and Political Success*. Austin: University of Texas Press.

Benner, Mike. 2021. "Portland Woman Running for Seat on David Douglas School Board Received Hateful Note." KGW8, April 5. https://www.kgw.com/article/news/local/portland-woman-running-for-seat-on-board-received-hateful-note-david-douglas/283-d1812768-39f5-401c-9570-2926265e63a0.

Bonta, Rob. 2012. Candidate statement. http://www.smartvoter.org/2012/11/06/ca/state/vote/bonta_r/philosophy.html (accessed March 14, 2022).

Bowen, Daniel C., and Christopher J. Clark. 2014. "Revisiting Descriptive Representation in Congress: Assessing the Effect of Race on the Constituent-Legislator Relationship." *Political Research Quarterly* 67(3): 695–707.

Boylan, Dan. 1991. "Crosscurrents: Filipinos in Hawaii's Politics." In *The Filipino American Experience in Hawaii*, ed. Kiyoshi Ikeda, Michael G. Weinstein, Jonathan Y. Okamura, Amefil R. Agbayani, and Melinda Tria Kerkyllet, 39–55. Manoa: University of Hawaii at Manoa. http://www.efilarchives.org/pdf/social%20process%20vol%2033/boylan_politics.pdf.

Boylan, Dan. 2007a. "The Immigrant Congresswoman." *MidWeek*, March 2. http://archives.midweek.com/content/story/midweek_coverstory/the_immigrant_congresswo man/P1.

Boylan, Dan. 2007b. "An All-American Success Story." Career Kokua, Research and Statistics, Department of Labor & Industrial Relations, State of Hawaii, March 21. https://careerkokua.hawaii.gov/career/article/?id=193.

Brekke, Dan. 2017. "March Fong Eu, Political Trailblazer for Women and Asian-Americans, Dies at Age 95." *California Report*, December 22. https://www.kqed.org/news/11639077/march-fong-eu-political-trailblazer-for-women-andasian-americ ans-dies-at-age-95.

REFERENCES 237

Brown, Anna. 2020. "The Changing Categories the U.S. Census Has Used to Measure Race." *Pew Research Center*, February 25. https://www.pewresearch.org/fact-tank/2020/02/25/the-changing-categories-the-u-s-has-used-to-measure-race/.

Brown, Nadia E. 2014. *Sisters in the House: Black Women and Legislative Decision Making.* New York: Oxford University Press.

Brown, Nadia E., Guillermo Caballero, and Valeria Sinclair-Chapman. 2018. "Racial Identity, Symbolic Legislation and the Benefit of Black Representatives in the Statehouse." *Western Journal of Black Studies* 42(3–4): 136–146.

Brown, Nadia E., and Sarah Allen Gershon, eds. 2016. *Distinct Identities: Minority Women in U.S. Politics.* New York: Routledge.

Browning, Rufus P., Dale Rogers Marshall, and David H. Tabb. 1984. *Protest Is Not Enough: The Struggle of Blacks and Hispanics for Equality in Urban Politics.* Berkeley: University of California Press.

Browning, Rufus P., Dale Rogers Marshall, and David H. Tabb. 1986. "Protest Is Not Enough: A Theory of Political Incorporation." *PS: Political Science and Politics* 19(3): 576–581.

Burnson, Robert. 2013. "Assemblyman Rob Bonta of Alameda Flourishes Despite Detractors." *Oakland Magazine*, March 5. https://www.alamedamagazine.com/Alameda-Magazine/March-2014/Assemblyman-Rob-Bonta-of-Alameda-Flourishes-Despite-Detractors/.

Burrell, Barbara. 2018. "Political Parties and Women's Organizations: Bringing Women into the Electoral Arena." In *Gender and Elections: Shaping the Future of American Politics*, 4th ed., ed. Susan J. Carroll and Richard L. Fox, 220–249. Cambridge: Cambridge University Press.

Cain, Bruce, and Thad Kousser. 2005. *Adapting to Term Limits in California: Recent Experiences and New Directions.* Denver and Washington, DC: National Conference of State Legislatures. https://www.ncsl.org/Portals/1/documents/jptl/casestudies/Californiav2.pdf (accessed March 5, 2022).

California State Archives. 2019. "Leading the Way: March Fong Eu and a Lifetime of Service." Curation of Exhibit by Lisa C. Prince and edited by Nancy Lenoil and Tamara Martin. https://artsandculture.google.com/exhibit/LAJyVTUYInY2IQ(accessed March 6, 2022).

Canon, David. 1990. *Actors, Athletes, and Astronauts: Political Amateurs in the United States Congress.* Chicago: University of Chicago Press.

Caring Across Generations. 2018. "New York City Council Member Margaret Chin Honored as 2018 Care Campion." April 19. https://caringacross.org/new-york-city-council-member-margaret-chin-honored-as-2018-care-champion-by-national-caregiving-advocacy-group-caring-across-generations/.

Carroll, Susan J. 1994. *Women as Candidates in American Politics.* 2nd ed. Bloomington: Indiana University Press.

Carroll, Susan J., and Kira Sanbonmatsu. 2013. *More Women Can Run: Gender and Pathways to the State Legislatures.* New York: Oxford University Press.

Carroll, Susan J., and Wendy S. Strimling. 1983. *Women's Routes to Elective Office: A Comparison with Men's.* New Brunswick, NJ: Center for the American Woman and Politics, Eagleton Institute of Politics, Rutgers University.

Casellas, Jason. 2011. *Latino Representation in Congress and State Legislatures.* Cambridge: Cambridge University Press.

238 REFERENCES

Chai, Alice Yun. 1988. "Women's History in Public: "Picture Brides" of Hawaii." *Women's Studies Quarterly* 16(1/2): 51–62.

Chan, Sucheng. 1991. *Asian Americans: An Interpretive History*. Boston: Twayne.

Chan, Suzanne Lee. 2012. Candidate statement. http://www.smartvoter.org/2012/11/06/ca/alm/vote/chan_s/paper1.html (accessed March 14, 2022).

Chan, Wilma. 1984. "1984 Elections and Political Power for Asian Americans." *East Wind* 3(1): 16–17. Archive of the League of Revolutionary Struggle. https://unityarchiveproj ect.org/wp-content/uploads/East-Wind-Vol-3-No-1-Spring-Summer-1984-1.pdf.

Chang, Michael. 2004. *Racial Politics in an Era of Transnational Citizenship: The 1996 "Asian Donorgate" Controversy in Perspective*. Lanham, MD: Lexington Press.

Chang, Stephanie. 2021. "Senator Chang on Majority Leader Shirkey's Racist Remarks." Press release, January 19. https://senatedems.com/chang/news/2021/01/20/senator-chang-on-majority-leader-shirkeys-racist-remarks/.

Chaturvedi, Neilan S. 2015. "Evaluating Asian American Representation through Bill Sponsors and Cosponsors from 1999 to 2009." *Journal of Asian American Studies* 18(3): 313–346.

Cheng, Christine, and Margit Tavits. 2011. "Informal Influences in Selecting Female Political Candidates." *Political Research Quarterly* 64(2): 460–471.

Chesley, Frank. 2008. "Chow, Ruby (1920–2008)." HistoryLink.org Essay 8063. https://www.historylink.org/File/8063.

Chou, Michaelyn Pi-Hsia. 1980. "The Education of a Senator: Hiram L. Fong from 1906 to 1954." PhD dissertation, University of Hawaii.

Chou, Michaelyn P. 2010. "Ethnicity and Elections in Hawai'i: The Case of James K. Kealoha." *Chinese America: History & Perspectives*: 105–111.

Chow, Esther Ngan-Ling. 1987. "The Development of Feminist Consciousness among Asian American Women." *Gender and Society* 1(3): 284–299.

Christopher, Ben. 2019. "Fight or Switch? One Republican Legislator Ditches GOP, the Other Gets Primaried." *CalMatters*, December 8. https://calmatters.org/politics/califor nia-election-2020/2019/12/republican-moderate-legislators-gambits-chad-mayes-tyler-diep-assembly-reelection-party-label/.

Chu, Amy. 1982. "The Climb to Gold Mountain: San Diego's Chinatown." *San Diego Reader*, April 8. https://www.sandiegoreader.com/news/1982/apr/08/climb-gold-mountain-san-diegos-chinatown/#.

Chu, Judy. 1989. "Asian Pacific American Women in Mainstream Politics." In *Making Waves: An Anthology of Writings by and about Asian American Women*, ed. Asian Women United of California, 405–421. Boston: Beacon Press.

Chu, Judy. 2015. "Lessons Learned from Karnes and Dilley." *Medium*, July 2. https://med ium.com/congressional-progressive-caucus/lessons-learned-from-karnes-and-dilley-f78c2f9fca74.

Coffman, Tom. 2003. *The Island Edge of America: A Political History of Hawaii*. Honolulu: University of Hawaii Press.

Cohen, Cathy J. 1999. *The Boundaries of Blackness: AIDS and the Breakdown of Black Politics*. Chicago: University of Chicago Press.

Cole, Brendan. 2019. "Right-Wing Radio Host Says New York-Born Andrew Yang 'Should Go Back to China.'" *Newsweek*, September 6. https://www.newsweek.com/racism-and rew-yang-jesse-lee-peterson-1457984.

REFERENCES   239

Coleman, Andre. 2019. "Chu Introduces Legislation to Block Trump's Latest 'Muslim Ban.'" *Pasadena Weekly*, January 31. https://pasadenaweekly.com/chu-introduces-legislation-to-block-trumps-latest-muslim-ban/.

Collins, Patricia Hill. 1986. "Learning from the Outsider Within: The Sociological Significance of Black Feminist Thought." *Social Problems* 33(6): s14–s32.

Collins, Patricia Hill. 1996. "What's in a Name? Womanism, Black Feminism, and Beyond." *Black Scholar* 26(1): 9–17.

Comas, Martin. 2016. "Political Newcomer Murphy Pulls Stunner, Unseats Mica; Demings Defeats Lowe." *Orlando Sentinel*, November 7. https://www.orlandosentinel.com/politics/os-election-us-congress-20161107-story.html.

Cone, Marla. 2003. "Assembly Moves to Ban Toxic Flame Retardants." *Los Angeles Times*, May 28. https://www.latimes.com/archives/la-xpm-2003-may-28-me-flame28-story.html.

Comfort Women History and Issues: Teachers Resource Guide. 2018. Education for Social Justice Foundation.

Cowan, Jill. 2020. "California Today: Young Kim Discusses the California G.O.P., after Trump." *New York Times*, December 14. https://www.nytimes.com/2020/12/14/us/young-kim-california-gop.html.

Craig, Pamela Barnes. 2012. "Happy Belated Birthday, Title IX." Law Library of Congress Blog, November 12. https://blogs.loc.gov/law/2012/11/happy-belated-birthday-title-ix/.

Crass, Scott. 2013. "Hiram Fong First Asian-American Senator, an R from Hawaii." *Hawaii Free Press*, June 7. http://www.hawaiifreepress.com/ArticlesMain/tabid/56/ID/9851/Hiram-Fong-First-Asian-American-Senator-An-R-From-Hawaii.aspx.

Crowder-Meyer, Melody. 2013. "Gendered Recruitment without Trying: How Local Party Recruiters Affect Women's Representation." *Politics & Gender* 9(4): 390–413.

Curwood, Anastasia. 2015. "Black Feminism on Capitol Hill: Shirley Chisholm and Movement Politics, 1968–1984." *Meridians* 13(1): 204–232.

Dahl, Robert. 1961. *Who Governs? Democracy and Power in an American City*. New Haven, CT: Yale University Press.

Daniels, Roger. 1988. *Asian America: Chinese and Japanese in the United States since 1850*. Seattle: University of Washington Press.

Das Gupta, Monisha. 2019. "'KNOw History / KNOw Self': Khmer Youth Organizing for Justice in Long Beach." *Amerasia Journal* 45(2): 137–156. https://doi.org/10.1080/00447471.2019.167175.

Davidson, Sue. 1994. *Jeannette Rankin and Patsy Takemoto Mink: A Heart in Politics*. Seattle, WA: Seal.

DelVecchio, Rick. 2000. "Gloves Off in Assembly Race: Democrat Chan Challenges Independent Bock in East Bay." *San Francisco Chronicle*, October 17. https://www.sfgate.com/politics/article/Gloves-Off-in-Assembly-Race-Democrat-Chan-2733098.php.

Diokno, Ed. 2019. "Indian American Voters Choosing between Gabbard or Harris." Views from the Edge Blog, May 5. https://dioknoed.blogspot.com/2019/05/harris-gabbard-booker-vie-for-indian.html.

Dittmar, Kelly. 2015. "Encouragement Is Not Enough: Addressing Social and Structural Barriers to Female Recruitment." *Politics & Gender* 11(4): 759–765.

240 REFERENCES

Doherty, David, Conor M. Dowling, and Michael G. Miller. 2019. "Do Local Party Chairs Think Women and Minority Candidates Can Win? Evidence from a Conjoint Experiment." *Journal of Politics* 81(4): 1282–1297.

Doherty, Steven. 2007. "Political Behavior and Candidate Emergence in the Hmong-American Community." *Hmong Studies Journal* 8: 1–35.

Duhart, Bill. 2018. "Racist Font Used in Attack Ad against Korean American Candidate, Democrats Say." NJ.com, September 19. https://www.nj.com/camden/2018/09/gop_dismisses_claim_of_shameful_racist_attack_in_n.html.

Espiritu, Yen Le. 1992. *Asian American Panethnicity: Bridging Institutions and Identities.* Philadelphia: Temple University Press.

Feng, Jeff L., and Pei-te Lien. 2020. "How AAPIs in Congress Responded to COVID-19." *AAPI Nexus* 17(1–2): 289–330.

Feng, Jenn. 2020. "Sen. Kamala Harris Is First Black Woman and First Asian American Vice Presidential Nominee on a Major Party Ticket." *Reappropriate.co*, August 11. http://reappropriate.co/2020/08/sen-kamala-harris-is-first-black-woman-and-first-asian-american-vice-presidential-nominee-on-a-major-party-ticket/#more-29723.

Fitzsimons, Tim. 2019. "'My Child Is Free': Congresswoman Gives Tearful Speech About Nonbinary Loved One." *NBC News*, April 2. https://www.nbcnews.com/feature/nbc-out/my-child-free-congresswoman-gives-tearful-speech-about-nonbinary-loved-n990246.

Flanagan, John. 2002. "Talk Story: First There Was Pat." *Honolulu Star-Bulletin*, November 10.

Fox, Richard, and Jennifer Lawless. 2005. *It Takes A Candidate: Why Women Don't Run for Office.* Cambridge: Cambridge University Press.

Fraga, Luis Ricardo, Linda Lopez, Valerie Martinez-Ebers, and Ricardo Ramírez. 2008. "Representing Gender and Ethnicity: Strategic Intersectionality." In *Legislative Women: Getting Elected, Getting Ahead*, ed. Beth Reingold, 157–174. Boulder, CO: Lynne Rienner.

Fu, May. 2008. "'Serve the People and You Help Yourself': Japanese-American Anti-drug Organizing in Los Angeles, 1969 to 1972." *Social Justice* 35(2): 80–99. http://www.jstor.org/stable/29768489.

Fuchs, Chris. 2016. "Former NYPD Cop Peter Liang's Guilty Verdict Leaves a Community Divided." *NBC News*, February 16. https://www.nbcnews.com/news/asian-america/former-nypd-cop-peter-liang-s-guilty-verdict-leaves-community-n518056.

Fuchs, Lawrence. 1961. *Hawaii Pono: A Social History.* New York: Harcourt, Brace, and World.

Furman, Gail. 2012. "Social Justice Leadership as Praxis: Developing Capacities through Preparation Programs." *Educational Administration Quarterly* 48(2): 191–229. https://doi.org/10.1177/0013161X11427394.

Geron, Kim, and James Lai. 2002. "Beyond Symbolic Representation: A Comparison of the Electoral Pathways and Policy Priorities of Asian American and Latino Elected Officials." *Asian Law Journal* 9(1): 41–81.

Gerstle, Gary, and John Mollenkopf. 2001. "The Political Incorporation of Immigrants, Then and Now." In *E Pluribus Unum?*, ed. Gary Gerstle and John Mollenkopf, 1–30. New York: Russell Sage Foundation.

Gil, Dinora. 1969. "Yellow Prostitution." *Gidra* 1(1): 2, 4.

REFERENCES 241

Giwargis, Ramona, and Carly Wipf. 2020. "Lan Diep a Democrat? San Jose Party Officials Say Not So Fast." *San José Spotlight*, October 14. https://sanjosespotlight.com/lan-diep-a-democrat-san-jose-party-officials-say-not-so-fast/.

Glenn, Evelyn Nakano. 1986. *Issei, Nisei, War Bride: Three Generations of Japanese American Women in Domestic Service*. Philadelphia: Temple University Press.

Glenn, Evelyn Nakano. 2002. *Unequal Freedom: How Race and Gender Shaped American Citizenship and Labor*. Cambridge, MA: Harvard University Press.

Glenn, Evelyn Nakano. 2015. "Settler Colonialism as Structure: A Framework for Comparative Studies of US Race and Gender Formation." *Sociology of Race and Ethnicity* 1(1): 52–72.

Go, Min Hee. 2018. "It Depends on Who You Run Against: Interracial Context and Asian American Candidates in US Elections." *International Journal of Intercultural Relations* 65: 61–72.

Goad, Ben. 2012. "2012 Elections: Takano Sees Changed Political Landscape." *Press-Enterprise*, September 21. https://www.pe.com/2012/09/21/2012-elections-takano-sees-changed-political-landscape/.

Goodrich, Jessica. 2020. "Cities Adopt Anti-discrimination Resolutions amid Coronavirus Pandemic." *Voice of OC*, May 19. https://voiceofoc.org/2020/05/cities-adopt-anti-discrimination-resolutions-amid-coronavirus-pandemic/.

Gordon, Milton. 1964. *Assimilation in American Life: The Role of Race, Religion, and. National Origins*. New York: Oxford University Press.

Gowen, Annie, and Tyler Bridges. 2015. "From Piyush to Bobby: How Does Jindal Feel about His Family's Past?" *Washington Post*, June 23. https://www.washingtonpost.com/politics/from-piyush-to-bobby-how-does-jindal-feel-about-his-familys-past/2015/06/22/7d45a3da-18ec-11e5-ab92-c75ae6ab94b5_story.html.

Grose, Christian. 2011. *Congress in Black and White*. New York: Cambridge University Press.

Gym, Helen. 2020. "AAPI Run: Helen Gym, Philadelphia City Council Member." Interviewed by Hannah Han. *Reappropriate.co*, September 14. http://reappropriate.co/2020/09/aapi-run-helen-gym-philadelphia-city-council-member/.

Haas, Michael. 1992. *Institutional Racism: The Case of Hawaii*. Westport, CT: Praeger.

Habal, Estella. 2007. *San Francisco's International Hotel: Mobilizing the Filipino American Community in the Anti-eviction Movement*. Philadelphia: Temple University Press.

Hajnal, Zoltan L., and Taeku Lee. 2011. *Why Americans Don't Join the Party: Race, Immigration, and the Failure (of Political Parties) to Engage the Electorate*. Princeton, NJ: Princeton University Press.

Haley, Nikki. 2011. Official website. https://governor.sc.gov/About/Pages/GovernorBio.aspx (accessed March 14, 2022).

Hall, Carla. 1986. "The Senator & His Space Refrain." *Washington Post*, August 13, C1.

Halloran, Richard. 2002. *Sparky: Warrior, Peacemaker, Poet, Patriot*. Honolulu, HI: Watermark.

Hancock, Ange-Marie. 2004. *The Politics of Disgust: The Public Identity of the Welfare Queen*. New York: New York University Press.

Hancock, Ange-Marie. 2016. *Intersectionality: An Intellectual History*. New York: Oxford University Press.

Hardy-Fanta, Carol, Pei-te Lien, Dianne M. Pinderhughes, and Christine M. Sierra. 2006. "Gender, Race, and Descriptive Representation in the United States: Findings from

242 REFERENCES

the Gender and Multicultural Leadership Project." *Journal of Women, Politics & Policy* 28(3–4): 7–41.

Hardy-Fanta, Carol, Pei-te Lien, Dianne M. Pinderhughes, and Christine M. Sierra. 2016. *Contested Transformation: Race, Gender and Political Leadership in Twenty-First Century America*. New York: Cambridge University Press.

Hatamiya, Leslie T. 1993. *Righting a Wrong: Japanese Americans and the Passage of the Civil Liberties Act of 1988*. Stanford, CA: Stanford University Press.

Hero, Rodney E., and Caroline J. Tolbert. 1995. "Latinos and Substantive Representation in the U.S. House of Representatives: Direct, Indirect, or Nonexistent?" *American Journal of Political Science* 39(3): 640–652.

Hirono, Mazie K. 2021. *Heart of Fire: An Immigrant Daughter's Story*. New York: Viking Press.

Hixson, Lindsay, Bradford Hepler, and Myoung Ouk Kim. 2012. *The Native Hawaiian and Other Pacific Islander Population: 2010*. https://www.census.gov/prod/cen2010/briefs/c2010br-12.pdf (accessed March 7, 2022).

Ho, Nghi. 2014. Campaign website. https://ballotpedia.org/Nghi_T._Ho (accessed March 14, 2022).

Hoeffel, Elizabeth, Sonya Rastogi, Myung Ouk Kim, and Hasan Shahid. 2012. "The Asian Population: 2010." 2010 Census Briefs No C2010BR-11. https://www.census.gov/prod/cen2010/briefs/c2010br-11.pdf(accessed March 7, 2022).

Hoffman, Geoffrey. 1992. "Harvard Grad Turns Democrat to Win Votes." *Harvard Crimson*, October 21. https://www.thecrimson.com/article/1992/10/21/harvard-grad-turns-democrat-to-win/?print=1.

Hoge, Patrick. 2019. "Sheng Thao Breaks Through." *Oakland Magazine*, March 4. https://www.oaklandca.gov/news/2019/sheng-thao-breaks-through.

Hom, Tom. 2014. *Rabbit on a Bumpy Road*. San Diego, CA: Sunbelt.

Hong, Grace Kyungwon. 2014. "Intersectionality and Incommensurability." In *Asian American Feminisms and Women of Color Politics*, ed. Lynn Fujiwara and Shireen Roshanravan, 27–42. Seattle: University of Washington Press.

Hong, Mike. 2017. "Dragon Ladies." *Asian American Writers Workshop*, August 11. https://opencitymag.aaww.org/dragon-ladies/.

Honolulu Advertiser. 2002. "Hawai'i, Nation Lose a Powerful Voice." *Honolulu Advertiser*, September 29. http://the.honoluluadvertiser.com/article/2002/Sep/29.

Hosokawa, Bill. 1969. *Nisei: The Quiet Americans*. New York: W. Morrow.

Hsu, Hua. 2020. "Are Asian Americans the Last Undecided Voters?" *New Yorker*, October 26. https://www.newyorker.com/magazine/2020/11/02/are-asian-americans-the-last-undecided-voters.

Huang, Josie. 2020. "These Asian American GOP Women Want to Make OC Red Again." *Laist*, March 2. https://laist.com/news/young-kim-gil-cisneros-michelle-steele-harley-rouda-peggy-huang-katie-porter-asian-american-gop-republican-women-oc-orange-county-red.

Huang, Tao-Fang. 2012. "The Myth of Political Participation among Asian Americans." PhD dissertation, University of Texas, Austin.

Hune, Shirley, and Gail Nomura, eds. 2003. *Asian/Pacific Islander American Women: A Historical Anthology*. New York: New York University Press.

Hune, Shirley, and Gail Nomura, eds. 2020. *Our Voices, Our Histories: Asian American and Pacific Islander Women*. New York: New York University Press.

REFERENCES   243

Hutchins, Marcelle. 2016. "These Elected Officials Are among the Few Who Were Born outside the US." *The World*, November 10. https://www.pri.org/stories/2016-11-10/these-elected-officials-are-among-few-who-were-born-outside-us.

Inouye, Daniel, and Lawrence Elliott. 1967. *Journey to Washington*. Englewood Cliffs, NJ: Prentice Hall.

Inouye, Karen M. 2013. "Mineta, Norman." In *Asian and Pacific Islander Americans*, ed. Gary Y. Okihiro, vol. 2, 531–533. Pasadena, CA: Salem Press.

Ishizuka, Karen. 2016. *Serve the People: Making Asian America in the Long Sixties*. New York: Verso.

Jayapal, Pramila. 2017. "The Country I Love." *New York Times*, July 4. https://www.nytimes.com/2017/07/04/opinion/immigration-naturalization.html.

Jayapal, Pramila. 2020. *Use the Power You Have: A Brown Woman's Guide to Politics and Political Change*. New York: New Press.

Jeffries, Adrianne. 2017. "The Republican Party Is Dying in Hawaii." *The Outline*, March 22. https://theoutline.com/post/1270/the-republican-party-is-dying-in-hawaii-beth-fukumoto?zd=1&zi=ot7atw6d.

Junn, Jane, and Nadia Brown. 2008. "What Revolution? Incorporating Intersectionality in Women and Politics." In *Political Women and American Democracy*, ed. Christina Wolbrecht, Karen Beckwith, and Lisa Baldez, 64–78. Cambridge: Cambridge University Press.

Jurewitsch, Andreas Sao Sue. 2013. "Interview with Dai Thao, Candidate for Saint Paul City Council, Ward 1 2013." *Twin Cities Daily Planet*, October 24. https://www.tcdailyplanet.net/interview-dai-thao-candidate-saint-paul-city-council-ward-1/.

Kang, K. Connie. 2000. "Group Seeks to Boost Profile of Asian American Voters." *Los Angeles Times*, August 22. https://www.latimes.com/archives/la-xpm-2000-aug-22-me-8316-story.html.

Kim, Claire Jean. 1999. "The Racial Triangulation of Asian Americans." *Politics & Society* 27(1): 105–138.

Kim, Claire Jean. 2015. *Dangerous Crossings: Race, Species, and Nature in a Multicultural Age*. New York: Cambridge University Press.

Kim, E. Tammy. 2012. "Compromise City: A Battle over Affordable Housing." Asian American Writers Workshop, March 11. https://aaww.org/compromise-city-a-battle-over-affordable-housing-on-the-lower-east-side/.

Kim, Haeyoung, and Clarence Tong. 2009. "A New Face of Change: The Rise of Newly Elected San Francisco Board of Supervisors President and HKS Alumnus David Chiu." *Asian American Policy Review* 18: 1–5.

Kim, Thomas. 2007. *The Racial Logic of Politics: Asian Americans and Party Competition*. Philadelphia: Temple University Press.

Kim, Warren Y. 1971. *Koreans in America*. Seoul: P. Chin Chai Printing.

Knight, Heather. 2011. "Mayor Ed Lee: What's in a Name?" *San Francisco Chronicle*, August 29. https://www.sfgate.com/news/article/Mayor-Ed-Lee-What-s-in-a-name-2333369.php.

Knoll, Corina. 2009. "Legislature Apologies for Past Discrimination against Chinese." *Los Angeles Times*, July 23. https://www.latimes.com/archives/la-xpm-2009-jul-23-me-chineseapology23-story.html.

Kopetman, Roxana. 2020. "Q & A with Santa Ana Candidates for Ward 1 Council Seat." *OC Register*, October 29. https://www.ocregister.com/2020/10/24/q-a-with-santa-ana-candidates-for-ward-1-council-seat/.

244 REFERENCES

Kornfield, Meryl. 2021. "Florida Parents Heckle Asian American School Board Member over Mask Mandate: 'You're a Communist.'" *Washington Post*, May 7. https://www.washingtonpost.com/health/2021/05/07/asian-florida-school-board-member/.

Kreitzer, Rebecca J., and Tracy L. Osborn. 2018. "The Emergence and Activities of Women's Recruiting Groups in the U.S." *Politics, Groups, and Identities* 7(4): 842–852. https://doi.org/10.1080/21565503.2018.1531772.

Krishnakumar, Priya, Armand Emamdjomeh, and Maloy Moore. 2016. "After Decades of Republican Victories, Here's How California Became a Blue State Again." *Los Angeles Times*, December 2. https://www.latimes.com/projects/la-pol-ca-california-voting-history/.

Kulkarni, Nima. 2018. Campaign website. https://kydemocrats.org/media/nima-kulkarni-a-strong-informed-voice-for-kentucky/ (accessed March 14, 2022).

Kwon, Soo Ah. 2013. *Uncivil Youth: Race, Activism, and Affirmative Governmentality.* Durham, NC: Duke University Press.

Lai, James S. 2011. *Asian American Political Action: Suburban Transformations.* Boulder, CO: Lynne Rienner.

Lai, James S., Wendy K. Tam Cho, Thomas P. Kim, and Okiyoshi Takeda. 2001. "Asian Pacific- American Campaigns, Elections, and Elected Officials." *Perspectives on Politics* 34(3): 611–617.

Lai, James S., and Kim Geron. 2006. "When Asian Pacific Americans Run: The Suburban and Urban Dimensions of Asian American Candidates in California Local Politics." *California Politics & Policy* 10: 62–88.

Lai, Stephanie. 2020. "In Big Republican Victory, Harley Rouda Concedes to Michelle Steel in O.C. Congressional Race." *Los Angeles Times*, November 10. https://www.latimes.com/california/story/2020-11-10/in-big-republican-victory-harley-rouda-concedes-to-michelle-steel-in-o-c-congress-race.

Lam, Tony. 2002. "Breaking Down the Walls: My Journey from a Refugee Camp to the Westminster City Council." *UCLA Asian Pacific American Law Journal* 8(1): 156–165.

Larson, Colleen, and Khaula Murtadha. 2002. "Leadership for Social Justice." In *The Educational Leadership Challenge: Redefining Leadership for the 21st Century*, ed. J. Murphy, 134–161. Chicago: University of Chicago Press.

Lawless, Jennifer, and Richard Fox. 2010. *It Still Takes a Candidate: Why Women Don't Run for Office.* Rev. ed. New York: Cambridge University Press.

Lawrence, David G., and Jeff Cummins. 2020. *California: The Politics of Diversity.* 11th ed. Lanham, MD: Rowman & Littlefield.

Lee, Henry. 2020. "Rock Thrown through Foster City Vice Mayor's Home." December 17. https://www.ktvu.com/news/stone-hurled-into-foster-city-vice-mayors-home.

Lee, Mai Na M. 2019. "Hmong and Hmong Americans in Minnesota." MNopedia, Minnesota Historical Society. http://www.mnopedia.org/hmong-and-hmong-americans-minnesota (accessed April 22, 2021).

Lee, Shelley Sang-Hee. 2014. *A New History of Asian America.* New York: Routledge, Taylor & Francis Group.

Lee, Traci G. 2017. "Hawaii Republican Leader, Vocal in Trump Opposition, Ready to Leave GOP." February 2. http://www.nbcnews.com/news/asian-america/hawaii-republican-leader-vocaltrump-opposition-ready-leave-gop-n716071.

Leighley, Jan. 2005. "Race, Ethnicity, and Electoral Mobilization: Where's the Party?" In *The Politics of Democratic Inclusion*, ed. Rodney Hero and Christina Wolbrecht, 143–162. Philadelphia: Temple University Press.

REFERENCES   245

Lemongello, Steven. 2016. "Democrats Find a Challenger against Mica." *Orlando Sentinel,* June 23. https://www.orlandosentinel.com/politics/os-democrats-find-a-challenger-against-mica-20160622-story.html.

Lien, Pei-te. 2001a. *The Making of Asian America through Political Participation.* Philadelphia: Temple University Press.

Lien, Pei-te. 2001b. "Race, Gender, and the Comparative Status of Asian American Women in Voting Participation." In *Asian Americans and Politics: Perspectives, Experiences, and Prospects,* ed. Gordon Chang, 173–193. Stanford, CA: Stanford University Press.

Lien, Pei-te. 2002. "The Participation of Asian Americans in U.S. Elections: Comparing Elite and Mass Patterns in Hawaii and Mainland States." *UCLA Asian Pacific American Law Journal* 8(1): 55–99.

Lien, Pei-te. 2006. "The Voting Rights Act and Its Implications for Three Nonblack Minorities." In *The Voting Rights Act: Securing the Ballot,* ed. Richard Valelly, 129–144. Washington, DC: CQ Press.

Lien, Pei-te. 2015. "Reassessing Descriptive Representation by Women and Men of Color: New Evidence at the Subnational Level." *Urban Affairs Review* 51(2): 239–262.

Lien, Pei-te, M. Margaret Conway, and Janelle Wong. 2004. *The Politics of Asian Americans: Diversity and Community.* New York: Routledge.

Lien, Pei-te, and Rhoanne Esteban. 2018. "Korean American and Electoral Politics." In *A Companion to Korean American Studies,* ed. Rachael Miyung Joo and Shelley Sang-Hee Lee, 585–607. Leiden: Brill.

Ling, Susie. 1989. "The Mountain Movers: Asian American Women's Movement in Los Angeles." *Amerasia Journal* 15(1): 51–67.

Litvak, Ed. 2017. "Margaret Chin's Record Was the Main Focus of District 1 City Council Forum." *The Lo-Down,* September 8. http://www.thelodownny.com/leslog/2017/09/margaret-chins-record-was-the-main-focus-of-district-1-city-council-forum.html.

Liu, Michael, Kim Geron, and Tracy Lai. 2008. *The Snake Dance of Asian American Activism.* New York: Lexington Books.

Lo, Emily. 2010. Candidate statement. http://www.smartvoter.org/2010/11/02/ca/scl/vote/lo_e/ (accessed March 15, 2022).

Locke, Gary. 1997. "Governor Gary Locke's Remarks: Governor Gary Locke's Inaugural Address January 15, 1997." https://www.digitalarchives.wa.gov/GovernorLocke/speeches/speech-view.asp?SpeechSeq=107 (accessed March 7, 2022).

Los Angeles County. 2014. "Metro Station Named After Alfred Hoyun Song," http://ridley-thomas.lacounty.gov/communitydevelopment/metro-station-alfred-hoyun-song/ (accessed March 04, 2022).

Los Angeles Times. 1993. "Montebello: Longtime School Board Member to Be Honored." *Los Angeles Times,* September 30. https://www.latimes.com/archives/la-xpm-1993-09-30-hl-40472-story.html.

Low, Evan. 2020. Campaign website. http://evanlow.com/evanlowforassembly/meet-evan/ (accessed March 14, 2022).

Lowande, Kenneth, Melinda Ritchie, and Erinn Lauterbach. 2019. "Descriptive and Substantive Representation in Congress: Evidence from 80,000 Congressional Inquiries." *American Journal of Political Science* 63(3): 644–659.

Lowe, Lisa. 1996. *Immigrant Acts: On Asian American Cultural Politics.* Durham, NC: Duke University Press.

Lublin, David Ian. 1997. *The Paradox of Representation: Racial Gerrymandering and Minority Interests in Congress.* Princeton, NJ: Princeton University Press.

246 REFERENCES

Mabalon, Dawn B. 2013. *Little Manila Is in the Heart: The Making of the Filipina/o American Community in Stockton, California.* Durham, NC: Duke University Press.

Maeda, Daryl J. 2009. *Chains of Babylon: The Rise of Asian America.* Minneapolis: University of Minnesota Press.

Maeda, Daryl J. 2012. *Rethinking the Asian American Movement.* New York: Routledge.

Maki, Mitchell T., Harry Kitano, and S. Megan Berthold. 1999. *Achieving the Impossible Dream: How Japanese Americans Obtained Redress.* Urbana: University of Illinois Press.

Mansbridge, Jane. 1999. "Should Blacks Represent Blacks and Women Represent Women? A Contingent Yes." *Journal of Politics* 61(3): 628–657.

Mansbridge, Jane. 2003. "Rethinking Representation." *American Political Science Review* 97(4): 515–528.

Markrich, Michael, and Karleen Chinen. 2014. "The Great 2014 David vs. Goliath Match-Up." *Hawaii Herald,* July 16. https://www.thehawaiiherald.com/2014/07/16/the-great-2014-david-vs-goliath-match-up/.

Masuoka, Natalie, Hahrie Han, Vivien Leung, and Bang Quan Zheng. 2018. "Understanding the Asian American Vote in the 2016 Election." *Journal of Race, Ethnicity, and Politics* 3(1): 189–215. https://doi.org/10.1017/rep.2017.34.

McCarthy, Mary M., and Linda C. Hasunuma. 2018. "Coalition Building and Mobilization: Case Studies of the Comfort Women Memorials in the United States." *Politics, Groups, and Identities* 6(3): 411–434. https://doi.org/10.1080/21565 503.2018.1491865.

McGhee, Eric. 2018. "New Term Limits Add Stability to the State Legislature." Public Policy Institute of California Blog, November 12. https://www.ppic.org/blog/new-term-limits-add-stability-to-the-state-legislature/.

McLaughlin, Ken. 2008. "'Godfather' of Silicon Valley's Asian-American Political Community Steps into Spotlight." *Mercury News,* June 8. https://www.mercurynews.com/2008/06/08/godfather-of-silicon-valleys-asian-american-political-community-steps-into-spotlight/.

Medlock, Kimiko. 2016. "Civil Rights Advocate Recounts the Japanese American Story." *Discover Nikkei,* January 19. http://www.discovernikkei.org/en/journal/2016/1/19/civil-rights-advocate/.

Mehta, Dhrumil. 2020. "How Asian Americans Are Thinking about the 2020 Election." FiveThirtyEight.com, September 18. https://fivethirtyeight.com/features/how-asian-americans-are-thinking-about-the-2020-election/.

Melo, Frederick. 2016. "St. Paul Council Member Dai Thao Sees Paid Sick Leave in Personal Terms." *Pioneer Press,* August 19. https://www.twincities.com/2016/08/19/a-major-league-soccer-stadium-a-paid-leave-vote-and-a-new-child-council-member-dai-thao-has-had-a-busy-couple-months/.

Melo, Frederick. 2017. "Dai Thao Has Been Called Idealistic. A Constant Campaigner. And Now, St. Paul Mayor?" *Pioneer Press,* November 2. https://www.twincities.com/2017/10/25/dai-thao-st-paul-mayoral-election-hmong-refugee/.

Merl, Jean. 2009. "Judy Chu Becomes First Chinese American Woman Elected to Congress." *Los Angeles Times,* July 16. http://articles.latimes.com/2009/jul/16/local/me-judy-chu16.

Mills College. 2018. "Mills College Mourns the Loss of Mills Alumna and Former California Secretary of State March Fong Eu '47." January 9. https://www.mills.edu/news/news-stories/MillsMournsMarchFongEu.php.

REFERENCES   247

Mineta, Norman. 1971. "San Jose Mayor Finds Role of Parties Waning." *Washington Post*, December 16, A14.

Minnesota Public Radio (KARE). 2017. "Dai Thao, St. Paul Mayoral Candidate." Kare11. com, October 15. https://www.kare11.com/article/news/politics/dai-thao/483610875.

Minta, Michael D. 2011. *Oversight: Representing the Interests of Blacks and Latinos in Congress*. Princeton, NJ: Princeton University Press.

Minta, Michael D., and Valeria Sinclair-Chapman. 2013. "Diversity in Political Institutions and Congressional Responsiveness to Minority Interests." *Political Research Quarterly* 66(1): 127–140.

Moncrief, Gary F., Peverill Squire, and Malcolm E. Jewell. 2001. *Who Runs for the Legislature?* Upper Saddle River, NJ: Prentice Hall.

Morey, Brittany N. 'Alisi Tulua, Sora Park Tanjasiri, Andrew M. Subica, Joseph Keawe'aimoku Kaholokula, Corina Penaia, Karla Thomas, Richard Calvin Chang, Vananh D. Tran, Ninez A. Ponce, Paul Ong, and Elena Ong. 2020. "Structural Racism and Its Effects on Native Hawaiians and Pacific Islanders in the United States: Issues of Health Equity, Census Undercounting, and Voter Disenfranchisement." *AAPI Nexus* 17(1–2): 43–74.

Morris, Gabrielle. 1978. "March Fong Eu: High Achieving Nonconformist in Local and State Government." Interview by Gabrielle Morris. *California Women Political Leaders Project*. Berkeley, CA: University of California. https://archive.org/details/marchfonga chiev00eueurich (accessed March 7, 2022).

Murray, Patricia. 2013. "9 Women Remaking the Right." *Daily Beast*, September 3. https://www.thedailybeast.com/9-women-remaking-the-right.

Nakanishi, Don T., and Ellen D. Wu. 2002. "Jean Sadako King." In Nakanishi and Wu, *Distinguished Asian American Political and Governmental Leaders*, 81–83. Westport, CT: Greenwood Press.

Nakaso, Dan. 2004. "Hiram Fong dead at 97." *Hawaii Advertiser*, August 18. https://web.archive.org/web/20040910152724/http://the.honoluluadvertiser.com/article/004/Aug/18/br/br03p.htmlNPR2009.

Navarro, Sharon A. 2008. *Latina Legislator: Leticia Van De Putte and the Road to Leadership*. College Station: Texas A&M University Press.

Nelson, Albert J. 1991. *Emerging Influentials in State Legislatures: Women, Blacks, and Hispanics*. New York: Praeger.

Nguyen, Madison. 2014. Candidate statement. http://www.smartvoter.org/2014/06/03/ca/scl/vote/nguyen_m/statement.html (accessed March 15, 2022.)

Nielsen, Ella. 2019. "Pramila Jayapal Is Congress's Activist Insider." *Vox*, February 20. https://www.vox.com/2019/2/20/18141001/pramila-jayapal-congressional-progress ive-caucus-house-democrats.

Niven, David. 1998. *The Missing Majority: The Recruitment of Women as State Legislative Candidates*. Westport, CT: Praeger.

North, Anna. 2019. "Sen. Hirono Is Asking William Barr—and Every Other Nominee—about Sexual Misconduct." *Vox*, January 15. https://www.vox.com/2019/1/15/18184 139/senator-mazie-hirono-william-barr-attorney-general.

Nossiter, Adam. 2008. "History and Amazement in House Race Outcome." *New York Times*, December 7. https://www.nytimes.com/2008/12/08/us/politics/08cao.html.

NPR. 2009. "Asian-Americans Carve Out a Place in Politics." March 29. https://www.npr.org/templates/story/story.php?storyId=104699812.

248 REFERENCES

"Obituary: Paul Bannai, 99: Former Assemblyman, VA Administrator." 2019. *Rafu Shimpo*, October 20. https://www.rafu.com/2019/10/obituary-paul-bannai-99-for mer-assemblyman-va-administrator/.

Oceguera, Rita. 2021. "Illinois Tackles Anti-Asian Hate with the TEAACH Act." *Injustice Watch*, May 25. https://www.injusticewatch.org/news/2021/teaach-act-anti-asian-hate/.

Oddie, Sarah. 2021. "In Memory of Alameda County Supervisor Wilma Chan." Alameda County Board of Supervisors: District 3, November 10. https://district3.acgov.org/in-memory-of-alameda-county-supervisor-wilma-chan/

Ohira, Rod. 2007. "Peter Aduja, Distinguished Local Filipino." *Honolulu Advertiser*, February 22. http://the.honoluluadvertiser.com/article/2007/Feb/22/ln/FP702220 334.html.

Okamoto, Dina G. 2014. *Redefining Race: Asian American Panethnicity and Shifting Ethnic Boundaries.* New York: Russell Sage Foundation.

Okamura, Jonathan. 2014. *From Race to Ethnicity: Interpreting Japanese American Experiences in Hawaii.* Honolulu: University of Hawaii Press.

Okihiro, Gary. 1994. *Margins and Mainstream: Asians in American History and Culture.* Seattle: University of Washington Press.

Omatsu, Glenn. 1994. "The 'Four Prisons' and the Movements of Liberation: Asian American Activism from the 1960s to the 1990s." In *The State of Asian American Activism and Resistance in the 1990s*, ed. Karin Aguilar-San Juan, 19–67. Boston: South End Press.

Ong, Elena. 2003. "Transcending the Bamboo and Glass Ceilings: Defining the Trajectory to Empower Asian Pacific American Women in Politics." In *Asian American Politics: Law, Participation, and Policy*, ed. Don Nakanishi and James Lai, 331–354. Lanham, MD: Rowman & Littlefield.

Onishi, Norimitsu. 2007. "Congressman Faces Foes in Japan as He Seeks and Apology." *New York Times*, May 12. https://www.nytimes.com/2007/05/12/world/asia/12ho nda.html.

Oriel, Christina M. 2021. "Rob Bonta Makes History as California's First Filipino American Attorney General." *Asian Journal*, March 24. https://www.asianjournal.com/ usa/california/rob-bonta-makes-history-as-californias-first-filipino-american-attor ney-general/.

Osborn, Scott. n.d. "Dr. Jackie Young '52: 2014 Charles S. Judd Jr. '38 Humanitarian Awardee." Punahou Alumni. https://www.punahou.edu/awards-detail?pk=160939 (accessed February 2, 2022).

Patu, Betty. 2017. Candidate statement. https://info.kingcounty.gov/kcelections/Vote/ contests/candidates.aspx?cid=3228&candidateid=3252&lang=en-US&pamphletson= true (accessed March 14, 2022).

Pelzer, Jeremy. 2018. "Democratic Underdog Tina Maharath Wins Ohio Senate Seat." November 27. https://www.cleveland.com/politics/2018/11/democratic-underdog-tina-maharath-wins-ohio-senate-seat.html.

Peng, Tzy C. 2002. "Mae Yih." *Chinese American Forum* 17(4): 7–11.

Perez, Anthony Daniel, and Charles Hirschman. 2009. "The Changing Racial and Ethnic Composition of the US Population: Emerging American Identities." *Population and Development Review* 35(1): 1–51.

REFERENCES   249

Pfeifer, Mark E., John Sullivan, Kou Yang, and Wayne Yang. 2012. "Hmong Population and Demographic Trends in the 2010 Census and 2010 American Community Survey." *Hmong Studies Journal* 13(2): 1–31.

Pham, Loan Anh. 2021. "Biden's Cabinet Has No AAPI Secretary." January 8. https://asamnews.com/2021/01/08/no-aapis-as-secretary-aapis-nominated-for-other-positions-in-biden-administration/.

Phan, Thai Viet. 2021. "Op-ed: Vietnamese Refugees Who've Served Prison Time Unjustly Face Deportation. That Must Change." *Los Angeles Times*, April 7. https://www.latimes.com/opinion/story/2021-04-07/vietnamese-immigrant-ice-deportation.

Phillips, Christian Dyogi. 2021. *Nowhere to Run: Race, Gender and Immigration in American Elections*. New York: Oxford University Press.

Phillips, Christian Dyogi, with Sayu Bhojwani. 2016. *States of Inclusion: New American Journeys into Elected Office*. New American Leaders Project.

Pho, Brandon. 2021. "Santa Ana's Vietnamese Residents Often Find Community in Other Cities, These Leaders Want to Change That." *Voice of OC*, April 5. https://voiceofoc.org/2021/04/santa-anas-vietnamese-residents-often-find-community-in-other-cities-these-leaders-want-to-change-that/.

Pho, Brandon, Anthony Robledo, and Linley Munson. 2021. "Santa Ana and Costa Mesa Move Forward on Mandating Hazard Pay for Grocery Clerks." *Voice of OC*, March 3. https://voiceofoc.org/2021/03/santa-ana-and-costa-mesa-move-forward-on-mandating-hazard-pay-for-grocery-clerks/.

Pierson, David. 2004. "New Law Aims to Protect Asians." *Los Angeles Times*, May 3. https://www.latimes.com/archives/la-xpm-2004-may-03-me-bill3-story.html.

Pierson, David. 2006. "Political Power Couple Facing New Dynamic." *Los Angeles Times*, June 2. https://www.latimes.com/archives/la-xpm-2006-jun-02-me-chinavote2-story.html.

Pitkin, Hanna Feniche. 1967. *The Concept of Representation*. Berkeley: University of California Press.

Portes, Alejandro, and Min Zhou. 1993. "The New Second Generation: Segmented Assimilation and Its Variants." *Annals of the American Academy of Political and Social Science* 530: 74–96.

Pratt, Richard C. 2000. *Hawai'i Politics and Government*. Lincoln: University of Nebraska Press.

Prindeville, Diane-Michele. 2004. "The Role of Gender, Race/ Ethnicity, and Class in Activists' Perceptions of Environmental Justice." In *New Perspectives on Environmental Justice: Gender, Sexuality, and Activism*, ed. Rachel Stein, 93–108. New Brunswick, NJ: Rutgers University Press.

Pulido, Laura. 2006. *Black, Brown, Yellow, and Left: Radical Activism in Los Angeles*. Berkeley: University of California Press.

Rafu Staff Report. 2020. "Obituary: Helen Kawagoe, Former JACL President and Longtime City Clerk of Carson." *Rafu Shimpo*, April 15. https://rafu.com/2020/04/obituary-helen-kawagoe-former-jacl-president-and-longtime-city-clerk-of-carson/

Reingold, Beth, Kirsten Widner, and Rachel Harmon. 2020. "Legislating at the Intersections: Race, Gender, and Representation." *Political Research Quarterly* 73(4): 819–833.

Reny, Tyler, and Paru Shah. 2018. "New Americans and the Quest for Political Office." *Social Science Quarterly* 99(3): 1038–1059.

250 REFERENCES

Ricardi, Nicolas. 2014. "Is GOP Minority Recruitment Affirmative Action?" Associated Press, May 17. http://news.yahoo.com/gop-minority-recruitment-affirmative-action-131039015--election.html.

Rice, Brian. 2021. "'The Timing Was Right': West Chester Trustee Lee Wong Shares Why He Chose to Bare His Scars." *Cincinnati Enquirer*, March 25. https://www.cincinnati.com/story/news/2021/03/25/west-chester-trustee-lee-wong-shares-why-he-chose-bare-his-scars/7004839002/.

Robinson, Greg. 2018. "The Groundbreaking Political Career of Jean Sadako King." *Hapa Japan*, March 15. http://hapajapan.com/article/jean-sadako-king.

Rocca, Michael S., and Gabriel Sanchez. 2008. "The Effect of Race and Ethnicity on Bill Sponsorship and Co-sponsorship in Congress." *American Politics Research* 36(1): 130–152.

Rodis, Rodel. 2014. "The Month That Changed Filipino-American History." Inquirer.net, September 17. https://globalnation.inquirer.net/111217/the-month-that-changed-filipino-american-history.

Ruggeri, Amanda. 2009. "Republican Joseph Cao's Unlikely Journey from Seminary to Congress." *U.S. News*, March 9. https://www.usnews.com/news/articles/2009/03/04/republican-joseph-caos-unlikely-journey-from-seminary-to-congress.

Saiki, Patricia. 2018. "The Honorable Patricia Saiki Oral History Interview." Office of the Historian, U.S. House of Representatives, September 20. https://history.house.gov/Oral-History/Women/Women-Transcripts/saiki-transcript/.

Saka, Carolyn. 1971. "War Brides." *Gidra*, January: 8.

Sanbonmatsu, Kira. 2002. "Political Parties and the Recruitment of Women to State Legislatures." *Journal of Politics* 64(August): 791–809.

Sanbonmatsu, Kira. 2006. *Where Women Run: Gender and Parties in the American States*. Ann Arbor: University of Michigan Press.

Sanbonmatsu, Kira. 2015. "Electing Women of Color: The Role of Campaign Trainings." *Journal of Women, Politics & Policy* 36(2): 137–160, https://doi.org/10.1080/1554477X.2015.1019273.

Sanbonmatsu, Kira, and Susan Carroll. 2013. *More Women Can Run: Gender and Pathways to the State Legislatures*. New York: Oxford University Press.

Saranillio, Dean Itsuji. 2013. "Why Asian Settler Colonialism Matters: A Thought Piece on Critiques, Debates, and Indigenous Difference." *Settler Colonial Studies* 3(4): 280–294.

Saund, Dalip Singh. 1960. *Congressman from India*. New York: Dutton. http://www.saund.org/dalipsaund/cfi/cfi.html.

Schmidt, Ronald, Sr. 2021. *Interpreting Racial Politics in the United States*. New York: Taylor & Francis.

Schmidt, Ronald, Sr., Yvette M. Alex-Assensoh, Andrew L. Aoki, and Rodney E. Hero. 2010. *Newcomers, Outsiders, & Insiders: Immigrants and American Racial Politics in the Early Twenty-First Century*. Ann Arbor: University of Michigan Press.

Scola, Becki. 2006. "Women of Color in State Legislatures: Gender, Race, Ethnicity and Legislative Office Holding." In *Intersectionality and Politics: Recent Research on Gender, Race, and Political Representation in the United States*, ed. Carol Hardy-Fanta, 43–70. New York: Routledge.

Scola, Becki. 2007. "Women of Color in State Legislatures: Gender, Race, Ethnicity and Legislative Office Holding." *Journal of Women, Politics & Policy* 28(3–4): 43–70.

Sedique, Nuru, Sayu Bhojwani, and Jessica Lee. 2020. *State of Representation 2020: New Americans in State Legislatures*. New York: New American Leaders. https://newamer

icanleaders.org/wp-content/uploads/2017/05/State-of-Representation-2020-New-American-Leaders.pdf.

Sharma, Ahmed. 2019. "South Asian American Woman Breaks Boundaries with Historic Mayoral Election." *News 4 San Antonio*, January 30. https://news4sanantonio.com/news/nation-world/south-asian-female-breaks-boundaries-in-new-jerseys-mayoral-election.

SHB Writer Staff. 2015. "Tou Xiong Is Running for Maplewood City Council." *Suab Hmong News*, June 29. https://shrdo.com/tou-xiong-is-running-for-maplewood-city-council/.

Shih, Gerry. 2011. "Mayor Lee Leads Growing Asian-American Clout." *New York Times*, January 16. https://www.nytimes.com/2011/01/16/us/16bcmayor.html?_r=2&pagewanted=all.

Siegel, Jim. 2018. "Democrat Tina Maharath Completes Unlikely victory in Ohio Senate Race." *Columbus Dispatch*, November 28. https://www.dispatch.com/news/20181127/democrat-tina-maharath-completes-unlikely-victory-in-ohio-senate-race.

Silverleib, Alan. 2009. "Woman Poised to Be 1st Chinese-American to Represent N.Y.'s Chinatown." *CNN Politics*, October 30. http://www.cnn.com/2009/POLITICS/10/30/chinatown.candidate.chin/.

Skelley, Geoffrey. 2020. "The Most Vulnerable Incumbent in the House Is a Democrat, but Republicans Are Defending More Competitive Seats." *FiveThirtyEight*, October 19. https://fivethirtyeight.com/features/the-most-vulnerable-incumbent-in-the-house-is-a-democrat-but-republicans-are-defending-more-competitive-seats/.

Smooth, Wendy. 2006. "Intersectionality in Electoral Politics: A Mess Worth Making." *Politics & Gender* 2(3): 400–414.

Smooth, Wendy. 2010a. "African American Women and Electoral Politics: A Challenge to the Post-race Rhetoric of the Obama Moment." In *Gender and Elections: Shaping the Future of American Politics*, 2nd ed., ed. Susan J. Carroll and Richard L. Fox, 165–186. New York: Cambridge University Press.

Smooth, Wendy. 2010b. "Intersectionalities of Race and Gender and Leadership." In *Gender and Women's Leadership: A Reference Handbook*, ed. Karen O'Connor, 31–40. Thousand Oaks, CA: Sage.

Sonenshein, Raphael. 1986. "Oral History Interview with Hon. Alfred H. Song." California State Archives State Government Oral History Program, August 18–19, Sacramento, 221.

South Bay JACL. 2005. "Nakano Ends a Memorable Career in the California State Assembly." https://web.archive.org/web/20110728041950/http:/www.southbayjacl.org/newsletters/2005/spring05.pdf(accessed March 7, 2022).

"Southeast Asian American Journeys: A Snapshot of Our National Communities." 2020. Southeast Asia Resource Action Center (SEARAC) and Asian Americans Advancing Justice–Los Angeles. https://www.searac.org/wp-content/uploads/2020/02/SEARAC_NationalSnapshot_PrinterFriendly.pdf(accessed March 7, 2022).

Spiegel, Claire, and K. Connie Kang. 1993. "The Fast, Rocky Rise of Jay Kim." *Los Angeles Times*, October 27. https://www.latimes.com/archives/la-xpm-1993-10-27-mn-50196-story.html.

Staggs, Brooke. 2020a. "Republican Janet Nguyen Declares Victory over Democrat Diedre Nguyen in Race for 72nd Assembly District." *Orange County Register*, November 12. Http://www.ocregister.com/2020/11/12/republican-janet-nguyen-declares-victory-over-democrat-diedre-nguyen-in-race-for-72nd-assembly-district/.

252 REFERENCES

Staggs, Brooke. 2020b. "Republican Challenger Young Kim Unseats Democratic Rep. Gil Cisneros in 39th District." *Orange County Register*, November 13. https://www.ocregister.com/2020/11/13/republican-challenger-young-kim-unseats-democratic-rep-gil-cisneros-in-39th-district/.

Stevens, Matt. 2012. "How I Made It: Gary Yamauchi, Owner of Tri-Star Vending." *Los Angeles Times*, March 11. https://www.latimes.com/business/la-xpm-2012-mar-11-la-fi-himi-yamauchi-20120311-story.html.

Stevens, Matt. 2019. "Andrew Yang's Quest to 'Make America Think Harder.'" *New York Times*, September 6. https://www.nytimes.com/2019/09/06/us/politics/andrew-yang-2020.html.

Stevens, Matt. 2020. "How Asian-American Leaders Are Grappling with Xenophobia amid Coronavirus." *New York Times*, 10 April. https://www.nytimes.com/2020/03/29/us/politics/coronavirus-asian-americans.html.

Stringer, Kate. 2018. "No One Would Hire Her. So She Wrote Title IX and Changed History for Millions of Women. Meet Education Trailblazer Patsy Mink." *The 74*, March 1. https://www.the74million.org/article/no-one-would-hire-her-so-she-wrote-title-ix-and-changed-history-for-millions-of-women-meet-education-trailblazer-patsy-mink/.

Stutman, Gabe. 2020. "Rock Thrown through Window of Jewish, Asian-American San Mateo City Council Member's House." *Jewish News of Northern California*, June 8. https://www.jweekly.com/2020/06/08/rock-thrown-through-window-of-jewish-san-mateo-city-council-members-house/.

Swain, Carol. 1993. *Black Faces, Black Interests: The Representation of African Americans in Congress*. Cambridge, MA: Harvard University Press.

Swatt, Steve, and Susie Swatt. 2020. "Will Politics Trump Gender in California This Election Year?" *CalMatters*, September 26. https://calmatters.org/commentary/my-turn/2020/09/will-politics-trump-gender-in-california-this-election-year/.

Swers, Michelle. 2003. *The Difference Women Make: The Policy Impact of Women in Congress*. Chicago: University of Chicago Press.

Takahashi, Jere. 1997. *Nisei/Sansei: Shifting Japanese American Identities and Politics*. Philadelphia: Temple University Press.

Takaki, Ronald. 1989. *Strangers from a Different Shore*. Boston: Little, Brown.

Takeda, Okiyoshi. 2001. "The Representation of Asian Americans in the U.S. Political System." In *Representation of Minority Groups in the US: Implications for the Twenty First Century*, ed. Charles Menifield, 77–109. Boston: Austin and Winfield.

Takemoto, Cindy, and Ann Umemoto. 1971. "Carmen Chow Q & A." In *Asian Women*, 125–126. UC Berkeley: Asian Women's Journal Workshop.

Tate, Katherine. 2003. *Black Faces in the Mirror: African-Americans and Their Representatives in the U.S. Congress*. Princeton, NJ: Princeton University Press.

Thao, Sheng. 2022. Official website. https://www.shengforoakland.com/about (accessed March 14, 2022).

Thomsen, Danielle M., and Michele L. Swers. 2017. "Which Women Can Run? Gender, Partisanship, and Candidate Donor Networks." *Political Research Quarterly* 70(2): 449–463. https://doi.org/10.1177/1065912917698044.

Totenberg, Nina. 2018. "The Quiet Rage of Mazie Hirono." *National Public Radio*, June 7. https://www.npr.org/2018/06/07/617239314/the-quiet-rage-of-mazie-hirono.

Toyota, Tritia. 2010. *Envisioning America: New Chinese Americans and the Politics of Belonging*. Palo Alto, CA: Stanford University Press.

Trump, Donald (@realDonaldTrump). 2020. "It is very important that we totally protect our Asian American community in the United States, and all around the world. They are amazing people, and the spreading of the Virus." Twitter. March 23.

Turhan, Muhammed. 2010. "Social Justice Leadership: Implications for Roles and Responsibilities of School Administrators." *Procedia Social and Behavioral Sciences* 9: 1357–1361.

Turnbull, Lornet. 2014. "Seattle Activist Pramila Jayapal Seeks State Senate Seat." *Seattle Times*, March 10. https://www.seattletimes.com/seattle-news/seattle-activist-pramila-jayapal-seeks-state-senate-seat/.

US House of Representatives. 2018a. "Anh (Joseph) Cao." *Asian and Pacific Islander Americans in Congress, 1900–2017*, prepared under the direction of the Committee on House Administration by the Office of the Historian and the Office of the Clerk. Washington, DC: Government Publishing Office. https://history.house.gov/People/Listing/C/CAO,-Anh-(Joseph)-(C001079)/.

US House of Representatives. 2018b. "Jay C. Kim." *Asian and Pacific Islander Americans in Congress, 1900–2017*, prepared under the direction of the Committee on House Administration by the Office of the Historian and the Office of the Clerk. Washington, DC: Government Publishing Office. https://history.house.gov/People/Detail/16304.

US House of Representatives. 2018c. "Norman Y. Mineta." *Asian and Pacific Islander Americans in Congress, 1900–2017*, prepared under the direction of the Committee on House Administration by the Office of the Historian and the Office of the Clerk. Washington, DC: Government Publishing Office. https://history.house.gov/People/Detail/18323.

Valverde, Kieu-Linh Caroline. 2012. "Whose Community Is It Anyway? Overseas Vietnamese Negotiating Their Cultural and Political Identity: The Case of Vice-Mayor Madison Nguyen." In Valverde, *Transnationalizing Viet Nam: Community, Culture, and Politics in the Diaspora*, 113–144. Philadelphia: Temple University Press.

Van Ingen, Linda. 2017. *Gendered Politics: Campaign Strategies of California Women Candidates, 1912–1970*. Lanham, MD: Rowman & Littlefield.

Vang, Tiffany. 2015. "The Landmark Election of Mee Moua." *MinnPost*, March 10. https://www.minnpost.com/mnopedia/2015/03/landmark-election-mee-moua/.

Vankin, Deborah. 2017. "Bruce Kaji Dies at 91; Japanese American National Museum Founder and Little Tokyo Pioneer." *Los Angeles Times*, November 9. https://www.latimes.com/entertainment/arts/la-et-cm-bruce-teruo-kaji-obit-20171109-story.html.

Vigdor, Neil. 2021. "'Is This Patriot Enough?': Asian-American Veteran Reveals Scars as He Calls Out Bias." *New York Times*, March 28. https://www.nytimes.com/2021/03/28/us/lee-wong-soldier-asian-American.html.

Visalvanich, Neil. 2017. "Asian Candidates in America: The Surprising Effects of Positive Racial Stereotyping." *Political Research Quarterly* 70: 68–81.

Vo, Thy. 2016. "Political Newbies Square Off in Garden Grove's District 3 Council Race." *Voice of OC*, October 5. https://voiceofoc.org/2016/10/two-political-newbies-square-off-in-garden-groves-district-3-council-race/.

Walker, Alice. 1983. *In Search of Our Mothers' Gardens: Womanist Prose*. San Diego, CA: Harcourt Brace Jovanovich.

Wallace, Sophia. 2014. "Representing Latinos: Examining Descriptive and Substantive Representation in Congress." *Political Research Quarterly* 67: 917–929.

Walsh, Joan. 2017. "Pramila Jayapal Wants Democrats to Know That Resistance Is Not Enough." *The Nation*, May 15. https://www.thenation.com/article/resistance-is-not-enough/.

254 REFERENCES

Walters, Dan. 2018. "Walters: Legislature Would Change Election Outcomes with New Rules." *Mercury News*, October 5. https://www.mercurynews.com/2018/10/05/walt ers-legislature-would-change-election-outcomes-with-new-rules/.

Wang, Fei. 2018. "Social Justice Leadership—Theory and Practice: A Case of Ontario." *Educational Administration Quarterly* 54(3): 470–498.

Wang, Ling-chi. 1998. "Race, Class, Citizenship, and Extraterritoriality: Asian Americans and the 1996 Campaign Finance Scandal." *Amerasia Journal* 24(1): 1–21.

Wei, William. 1993. *The Asian American Movement*. Philadelphia: Temple University Press.

Werner, Brian Lloyd. 1993. "Bias in the Electoral Process: Mass and Elite Attitudes and Female State Legislative Candidates: 1982–90." PhD dissertation, Washington University.

Whitby, Kenny J. 1997. *The Color of Representation: Congressional Behavior and Black Interests*. Ann Arbor: University of Michigan Press.

Whitby, Kenny J . 2007. "Dimension of Representation and the Congressional Black Caucus." In *African American Perspectives on Political Science*, ed. Wilbur C. Rich, 195–211. Philadelphia: Temple University Press.

Wilcox, Leslie. 2014. "Ben Cayetano, Part One: Long Story Short with Leslie Wilcox" (video). *PBS Hawaii*, November 21. https://www.pbshawaii.org/long-story-short-with-leslie-wilcox-ben-cayetano/.

Wildermuth, John. 2017. "March Fong Eu, Who Smashed Toilets and Barriers, Dies at 95." *San Francisco Chronicle*, December 22. https://www.sfgate.com/bayarea/article/March-Fong-Eu-who-smashed-toilets-and-barriers-12451437.php.

Winton, Richard. 2001. "Chu Is Known as a Bridge Builder." *Los Angeles Times*, May 18. https://www.latimes.com/archives/la-xpm-2001-may-18-me-65123-story.html.

Women Winning. 2019. "Trailblazers & Changemakers: Nelsie Yang." October 23. https://www.womenwinning.org/trailblazers-changemakers-nelsie-yang/.

Wong, Ashley. 2021. "Sacramento City Councilwoman Mai Vang Announces Resolution Condemning Anti-Asian Hate." *Sacramento Bee*, March 3. https://www.sacbee.com/news/local/article249621663.html.

Wong, Caroline. 2017. *Voting Together: Intergenerational Politics and Civic Engagement among Hmong Americans*. Stanford, CA: Stanford University Press.

Wong, Janelle. 2006. *Democracy's Promise: Immigrants and American Civic Institutions*. Ann Arbor: University of Michigan Press.

Wong, Janelle, S. Karthick Ramakrishnan, Taeku Lee, and Jane Junn. 2011. *Asian American Political Participation: Emerging Constituents and Their Political Identities*. New York: Russell Sage Foundation.

Wu, Ellen D. 2013. *The Color of Success: Asian Americans and the Origins of the Model Minority*. Princeton, NJ: Princeton University Press.

Wu, Judy Tzu-Chun. 2018. "Asian American Feminisms and Women of Color Feminisms: Racialism, Liberalism, and Invisibility." In *Asian American Feminisms and Women of Color Politics*, ed. Lynn Fujiwara and Shireen Roshanravan, 43–65. Seattle: University of Washington Press.

Wu, Judy Tzu-Chun. 2020. "Asian American Feminisms and Legislative Activism: Patsy Takemoto Mink in the US Congress." In *Our Voices, Our Histories: Asian American and Pacific Islander American Women*, ed. Shirley Hune and Gail Nomura, 304–320. New York: New York University Press.

Wu, Nicholas. 2020. "Asian American Lawmakers Sound the Alarm on Coronavirus-Related Discrimination." *USA Today*, March 26. https://www.usatoday.com/story/news/politics/2020/03/26/coronavirus-asian-american-lawmakers-fear-rise-discrimination/2890935001/.

Xiaoqing, Rong. 2017. "The Battle for Chinatown." *Asian American Writers Workshop*, June 2. https://aaww.org/the-battle-for-chinatown/.

Xiong, Yang Sao. 2018. "Insurgent Political Networks and Electoral Mobilization." *Contexts* 17(4): 42–47.

Yam, Kimmy. 2019. "Andrew Yang Says Being Asian American May Explain Lack of Media Coverage." *NBC News*, December 12. https://www.nbcnews.com/news/asian-america/andrew-yang-says-being-asian-american-may-explain-lack-media-n1100921.

Yam, Kimmy. 2021. "Why over 85 Asian American, LGBTQ Groups Opposed the Anti-Asian Hate Crimes Bill." *NBC News*, May 14. https://www.nbcnews.com/news/asian-america/why-over-85-asian-american-lgbtq-groups-opposed-anti-asian-n1267421.

Yamamoto, J. K. 2013. "Helen Kawagoe Council Chambers Dedicated." *Rafu Shimpo*, June 9. http://www.rafu.com/2013/06/helen-kawagoe-council-chambers-dedicated/.

Yamamoto, J. K. 2017. "Councilmember Terauchi Seeking Another Term as Gardena Mayor." *Rafu Shimpo*, March 1. https://www.rafu.com/2017/03/councilmember-terauchi-seeking-another-term-as-gardena-mayor/.

Yamamoto, Mike. 1971. "Male Perspective." *Gidra*, January: 13.

Yang, Andrew. 2020. "Opinion: Andrew Yang: We Asian Americans Are Not the Virus, but We Can Be Part of the Cure." *Washington Post*, April 1. https://www.washingtonpost.com/opinions/2020/04/01/andrew-yang-coronavirus-discrimination/.

Yeung, Bernice. 2011. "Following Her 'True North.'" *Kore Asian Media*, January 31. http://kore.am/jane-kim-following-her-true-north/.

Yoshiko Kandil, Caitlin. 2018. "In 2018, Vietnamese Americans Found New Political Prominence." *NBC News*, December 20. https://www.nbcnews.com/news/asian-america/2018-vietnamese-americans-found-new-political-prominence-n948121.

Yoshimura, Evelyn. 1971. "G.I.s and Asian Women." *Gidra*, January: 4, 15.

Yu, Theodora. 2019. "First Hmong-American Woman to Run for Sacramento City Council in 2020." *Sacramento Bee*, September 2. https://www.sacbee.com/site-services/newsletters/local-news-crime/article234627042.html.

Yuen, Laura. 2018. "New influx of Hmong-American Legislators Appears Likely." *MPRNews*, October 26. https://www.mprnews.org/story/2018/10/26/new-influx-of-hmong-american-legislators-appears-likely

Zhan, Jennifer. 2020. "Andrew Yang Draws Backlash for Op-ed Calling on Asian Americans to Show 'American-ness' amid Coronavirus Pandemic." *Asian American News*, April 3. https://asamnews.com/2020/04/03/former-democratic-presidential-candidate-andrew-yangs-op-ed-about-addressing-asian-american-harassment-discrimination-racism-amid-coronavirus-covid-19-pandemic-draws-online-backlash-from-twitter/.

Zhou, Li. 2021. "This Congress Member Wants Biden to Hire More Asian Americans in Government." *Vox*, February 5. https://vox.com/22262442/judy-chu-asian-american-caucus-biden-administration.

Zia, Helen. 2009. "Lily Chin: The Courage to Speak Out." In *Untold Civil Rights Stories: Asian Americans Speak Out for Justice*, ed. Stewart Kwoh and Russell C. Leong, 35–41. Los Angeles: UCLA Asian American Studies Center and Asian Pacific American Legal Center.

Index

For the benefit of digital users, indexed terms that span two pages (e.g., 52–53) may, on occasion, appear on only one of those pages.

Note: Tables and figures are indicated by *t* and *f* following the page number

Access to Birth Control Act, 175
Aduja, Peter, 38, 47–48, 56, 62, 139
Affordable Care Act (2010), 144
Akaka, Daniel, 118–19, 168–69
American Citizens for Justice, 14
American Community Survey (ACS), 72
American Dream, 1, 38–39
American Indians, 9, 74–75, 112–13, 214–15
Americans of Japanese ancestry (AJAs), 69–70, 117. *See also* Japanese Americans
anti-Asian racism/violence
  activism against, 14
  Covid-19 pandemic anti-Asian racism, 2, 3–4, 28, 115, 150, 155–56, 177–82
  discrimination concerns, 48–49
  examples of, 192–93
  against Hmong Americans, 199–203
  introduction to, 2
  political representation and, 190–92
  responses to, 193–95
  social justice against, 195–98
anti-Black racism, 3–4, 115
APA Institute of Congressional Studies (APAICS), 221
Arai, Clarence, 204–5
Ariyoshi, George, 51
Asera, Larry, 43
Asian, defined, 6
Asian American feminism (AAF)
  bridge feminism, 15–17, 27–28, 156–57
  bridging radical and liberal feminism, 15–17

  "Capitol Hill" feminist, 15–16
  intersectionality, origins and development of, 22–24
  racism and, 11
  rise of, 7–8, 11–13
  womanism and womanist leadership praxis, 7–8, 17–19
Asian American immigration
  first-generation migrants, 59–62, 229n.1
  gendered history of, 26, 29–35
  immigrant rights, 16–17, 173–77, 227
  issue priorities in, 227
  patterns of, 47–64
  political leadership and representation for, 173–77
  racist restrictions against, 49
  Republican Party engagement with, 131–34
Asian American movement (AAM)
  launch of, 7–8, 9–11
  political incorporation of minorities, 20–22
  political transition of, 13–14
  tracing roots of, 11–13
Asian Americans
  defining identity, 8–9
  multiracial Asian America, 219
  in popularly elected offices, 26–28
  population growth, 71–72
  suburban settlements of, 13
  in US politics, 2–4
Asian American Studies Center (UCLA), 25

258 INDEX

Asian American women APAEOs
  experiences of, 37–43, 44, 45, 54–55, 56–59
  growth in numbers of, 67–69
  hate speech against, 192–93
  Hmong Americans, 199–203
  impact of district elections in California, 102–4, 104t
  local political incorporation in California, 90–98
  marginalization of, 74–75
  partisan orientations, 110, 112–14
  political leadership and representation, 154–55
  population growth of, 73–81, 74f, 77t
  progressive-leaning, 4–5
  significance of being foreign-born, 82–85, 82t, 84t
  violence toward, 192–93
Asian American women's movement (AAWM), 11–14
Asian and Pacific Islander American (APIA), 72, 217–18, 228
Asian Indian Americans
  barred from naturalization, 230n.6
  as elected officials, 43–44, 48, 61–62, 83, 88–89, 89f, 105–6, 197
  immigration of, 35
  demography and population growth, 71–72, 87–88
Asian Pacific American (APA) community
  central ideas behind, 7–9
  electoral support building, 23–24
  growth of, 72–73
  introduction to, 1–4
  meaning and boundaries of, 4–6
  political landscape for, 66–67
  population growth in, 73–81, 74f, 76t, 77t, 78t
  quantitative analysis data on, 24–25
  research terminology of, 217–18
  social justice leadership, 214–15
Asian Pacific American elected officials (APAEOs). See also Asian American women APAEOs; California APAEOs; Hawaiian APAEOs
  children of working-class parents, 56–59

community-based infrastructure, 203–12
descendants of Chinese Exclusion, 53–55
ethnic diversification of, 7–8
ethnic identity of mixed ancestry, 222
ethnic parity ratio, 78–80, 79t
evolution of the electoral landscape, 26–27, 31
first-generation migrants seeking education, 59–62
foreign vs. US born, 36–47
gender parity ratios, 81t
geographic representation by state, 86–90, 86f, 89f
growth and transformation of population structure, 71–73
historical and future considerations, 212–15
immigration patterns and political socialization, 47–64
individual partisanship identifiers, 222–23
issue priorities, 226–28
local political incorporation in California, 90–98
in mainland US, 41–47
methods of database construction, 221
nonpartisan ethnic organizations, 204–9
1.5 generation and, 62–64
political refugees, 62–64
political representation and, 8–9, 66–67
political socialization of, 31–35
population growth in, 73–81, 74f, 76t, 77t, 78t
proportional representation, 78–81
representative populations, 218–19
research terminology of, 217
significance of being foreign-born, 82–85, 82t, 84t
social justice concerns among, 27–28
social scientific understanding of, 5
sub-state-office levels, 222
summary of experiences, 64–65
survivors of wartime internment, 51–53
as wartime heroes in Hawaii, 50–51

INDEX

womanist leadership praxis and, 18–19
women-centered nonethnic (partisan)
    organizations, 209–12
Asian Pacific American Institute for
    Congressional Studies (APAICS),
    25, 206–7
Asian Pacific American Leadership
    Institute (APALI), 207–8
Asian Pacific American Women's
    Leadership Institute (APAWLI), 207
"Asian/Pacific Islander, defined, 6
Asian Pacific Planning and Policy
    Council, 206
Asian Women, 12
assimilation, 29–30, 62–63. *See also*
    immigrant incorporation
Awasthi, Richa, 193

Bannai, Paul, 135
Bartlett, Lisa, 146
Bhojwani, Sayu, 209
Biden-Harris administration, 1–3
Black Americans, 30, 45–46, 112–14,
    115, 121–22
Black Democrat, 62–63, 142–43
Black feminism, 17–18
Black Panthers, 52
Blacks in Congress, 152–54, 156
Boat People, 35
Bonta, Rob, 58–59
bridge feminism, 15–17, 27–28, 156–57
Brown, Edmund G. "Pat," 121–22
Brown, Scott, 168–69
Buchholdt, Thelma G., 42–43, 48, 59, 110
Burns, Jack, 70
business and economy issue priorities, 228

California APAEOs
    Democratic Party impact on, 120–23
    demography and ethnic
        representation, 98–104
    descriptive representation, 91–92
    immigration and immigrant
        rights, 173–74
    impact of district elections of women,
        102–4, 104*t*
    Japanese American redress in, 164–68
    legislative term limits, 106–8

local political incorporation of, 90–104,
    92*t*, 94*t*, 96*t*
local to state electoral successes, 104–8
population growth of, 85–86
proportional and substantive
    representation, 100–2
summary of research on, 108–9
sustainable representation, 93–98
tracking of hate crime data, 197
California Asian Pacific Islander
    Legislative Caucus Institute
    (CAPILCI), 208
California Civil Liberties Public Education
    Act (1998), 166
California Common Cause, 102
California Democratic Council (CDC),
    121–22, 189
California Democratic Party, 122–
    23, 137–38
California Evidence Code, 190
California State Assembly, 173–74
California state voting rights act
    (CVRA), 102
California Young Democrats
    (CYD), 121–22
Cambodian Americans, 35, 83
Campos, Nora, 107
campus activism, 10
Cao, Ánh (Joseph), 62–63, 142–43
"Capitol Hill" feminist, 15–16
"career ladder" model of
    officeholding, 104–5
Carter, Jimmy, 14
Cayetano, Ben, 40, 56
Chan, Wilma, 58, 182–84
Chang, David, 119
Chang, Ling-ling, 98, 107–8, 134
Chang, Michael, 61, 137–38, 145–
    46, 207–8
Chang, Stephanie, 196–97, 209
Char, Yew, 37–38, 56
Chen, Lily Lee, 45–46, 48, 59, 95, 110
Chen, Melissa, 194–95
Chicano movement, 52
children of working-class parents, 56–59
Chin, Lily, 14
Chin, Margaret, 58, 184
Chin, Vincent, 14

260 INDEX

Chinese Americans
  descendants of Chinese
    Exclusion, 53–55
  as elected officials, 37–39, 41–42, 45–46,
    57–58, 59–61, 77–78, 197
  immigrants, 32–34, 36, 47, 48–49
  population growth, 71–72
Chinese Exclusion Act (CEA) (1882), 32–
    33, 41, 168–70
Chinese for Affirmative Action, 60
Chinese Newcomers Service Center, 60
Chinese Progressive Association (CPA),
    138, 182–83
Chisholm, Shirley, 15–16, 156, 209–10
Chiu, David, 184–85
Chiu, Kenneth ("Kenny's Law"), 174
Choi, Steven Seokho, 132–33
Chow, Carmen, 12
Chow, Eleanor Kim, 45, 110
Chow, Ruby, 54–55, 137
Chu, Judy, 57, 110–11, 167, 169–70, 173–
    74, 176–77, 180
Chu, Kansen, 107–8
Church of Latter-Day Saints, 88–89
Cisneros, Gil, 133–34
city councilmember, 63–64, 132–33, 143,
    145–46, 185–86, 200, 208, 209
Civil Liberties Act (1988), 164–65,
    166, 205–6
Civil Rights Act (1964), 190, 232n.2
civil rights advocates, 160–61
civil rights issue priorities, 228
civil rights protests, 121–22
civil rights violations, 36, 69–70
classism, 24–25
Clinton, Bill, 114
Clinton, Hillary, 121–22
coalition building and coalition politics,
    15, 18, 20, 21–22, 38–39, 63, 72, 110,
    113–14, 130, 135–36, 147–48, 156–
    57, 213–14
Cohen, David, 141
collective leadership, 18, 156–57
Collins, Patricia Hill, 22–23
"comfort women," 150, 170–73, 182
Comfort Women Justice Alliance, 171
community-based organizations (CBOs),
    18, 203–9

Congressional Black Caucus, 152
Correa, Lou, 107
Covid-19 Hate Crimes Act, 195–96, 213
Covid-19 pandemic anti-Asian racism, 2,
    3–4, 28, 115, 150, 155–56,
    177–82
Cox, T. J., 144–45
Crenshaw, Kimberlé, 22–23

Daily Beast, 119
Dai Thao, 63–64, 185–86, 203
Dai Yen Chang, 37–38
Dandekar, Swati, 44
Del Rosario, Joanne F., 98
Democratic Party
  Asian American nominations, 30
  former Democrats turned
    Republican, 134–36
  former Republicans turned Democrats/
    Independents, 139–41
  ideological fractures within, 163
  impact on partisan orientations, 114–
    20, 123–27, 136–39
  introduction to, 15, 16–17
  party marginalization and
    neglect, 145–47
  rise and dominance of, 111
  winning against Republican
    incumbents, 143–45
  women-centered campaign
    organizations in, 211
Democratic Progressive Caucus, 176–77
Democratic Revolution, 38, 50, 117
descriptive representation, 20–22, 26–
    27, 155–56
Diep, Lan, 141, 209
Diep, Tyler, 107–8, 141
drug abuse, 12–13

EMERGE America, 211
EMILY's List, 210–11
Eng, Mike, 173–74
environment issue priorities, 228
Espero, Will, 140
ethnic parity ratio, 78–80, 79t, 83
ethnic studies in school-based
    education, 10
ethnoburbs, 67–68

ethnoracial power, 206
Eu v. San Francisco County Democratic Central Committee (1989), 122

family, youth, elderly issue priorities, 227
family-based adversity in socialization, 149–50
Fasi, Frank, 118
Feinstein, Dianne, 168–69
feminism. *See also* Asian American feminism
 liberal feminism, 15–17, 156
 movements, 17–18, 56, 64–65, 206, 209–10
 radical feminism, 15–17, 156
Filipino American Political Association (FAPA), 43, 48
Filipino Americans
 as elected officials, 38, 40, 42–43, 77–78, 83
 immigrants, 34, 35, 36
 patterns of immigration, 47–48
 population growth, 71–72
first-generation migrants, 59–62, 229n.1
fiscal and budget issue priorities, 228
Fong, Hiram, 56, 130, 160–61
Fong, Mike, 138
Fong, Paul, 54, 137–38
Fong Eu, March, 41–42, 56, 110, 145, 162–63
Ford, Gerald, 164
foreign born APAEOs, 36–47
Foreign Miner's License Tax (1852), 32–33
Fukawa, June, 95
Fukumoto, Beth, 119
Fukusawa, John, 91–92
Furutani, Warren, 53, 166–67

Gabbard, Tulsi, 118–19
gender discrimination, 15–16, 39, 117, 145. *See also* sexism; sexual discrimination
gendered history of Asian American immigration, 26, 29–35
gender liberation, 15
gender politics, 112–14, 124–27, 125f, 126t, 157–60, 158t
GI Bill, 38, 47–48, 50

Gidra, 11–12
Gil, Dinora, 11–12
Gloria, Todd, 107–8
Gong-Gershowitz, Jennifer, 197
government and public services issue priorities, 228
grassroots activism/organizing, 18, 26, 27–28, 121–22, 176–77, 182–87, 213–14
Great San Francisco Quake (1906), 36–37
Great Society program (19602), 13–14
Green New Deal, 176–77
Green Party, 138, 147
Gym, Helen Hae-liun, 186–87

Harris, Kamala, 1–2, 30, 179
Harris, Shyamala Gopalan, 1
Harvey Milk LGBTQ Democratic Club, 138
Hatch, Orrin, 168–69
hate crimes, 14, 158–59, 174, 179, 195–97, 213, 228
Hate Free Zone, 175–76
hate speech, 192–93
Hawaii
 Asian immigration to, 33–35
 dominance of Japanese Americans in, 68–69
 wartime heroes in, 50–51
Hawaiian APAEOs
 Democratic Party impact, 114–20
 first APAEOs in, 37–41
 immigration and immigrant rights, 174–75
 politics of, 37–41, 68–70
 population growth of, 85–86
 Republican Party impact, 118–20
Hawaiian Organic Act (HOA) (1900), 33–34
Hawaiian sovereignty movement, 10
Hawaii Republican Party, 130
Hayakawa, S. I., 135–36, 167–68
health and safety issue priorities, 227
Heen, William, 69–70
Her, Kaohly, 201–2
Hiram Fong, 38–39
Hirono, Mazie, 56, 174–75
Hmong Americans, 28, 35, 45–46, 83, 185–86, 199–203

262 INDEX

Hmong Innovating Politics, 198
Hoff-Tsuda, Sue, 91
Hom, Tom, 53–54, 134–35, 191
homophobia, 17, 24–25
Honda, Michael "Mike," 52, 118–19, 137–38, 166, 208
House LGBTQ Equality Caucus, 176–77
house representative, 16–17, 118–19
Hu, Grace, 95
Huang, John, 231–32n.1

identity
    defining identity, 8–9
    ethnic identity of mixed ancestry, 222
    fluidity of boundaries, 4–5
    social identity, 5, 22–23, 150
Ige, David, 142
I-Hotel Women's Collective, 12–13
immigrant incorporation, 147–48
Immigration Act (1917), 35
Immigration Act (1952), 34–35
Immigration Act (1965), 34–35
immigration generation, 4–5, 26, 31, 47–64, 192
immigration of Asian Americans. See
    Asian American immigration
Immigration Reform Act (1965), 160–61
Imura, Georgette, 208
Independent Party, 139–41
Ing, Kaniela, 120
Inouye, Daniel K., 50, 118, 164–65
Inspiring South Asian American Women
    (ISAAW), 211
intermarriage patterns, 30
Internal Security Act (1950), 164
International Longshoreman's and
    Warehouseman's Union, 70
intersectionality
    advocating for disadvantaged, 4
    linked fate, 214–15
    of nativity, 48–49, 75, 82–84, 82t, 84t
    oppression and racism, 24–25
    origins and development of, 22–24
    political leadership and
        representation, 155–57
    in political representation, 151–52
Irish Americans, 29–30
issue priorities, 226–28

Italian Americans, 29–30
I Wor Kuen (IWK), 12–13

Jackson, Jesse, 14
Jaffer, Sadaf, 211
Japanese American Citizens League
    (JACL), 164–65, 167–68, 204–6
Japanese Americans
    dominance in Hawaiian politics, 68–70
    as elected officials, 37–38, 39–40,
        42, 56
    immigrants, 33–35
    internment in concentration camps, 36,
        51–53, 159–60
    patterns of immigration, 47, 48–49
    redress in congress and state
        legislature, 164–68
    US incarceration of, 36–37
    as wartime heroes in Hawaii, 50–51
Japanese American women, 12–13
Japanese imperialism, 170–71
Jayapal, Pramila, 16–17, 19, 62, 175–77
Jewish Americans, 29–30
Jindal, Bobby, 131
Johnson, Hiram, 120–21
Justice for Vincent Chin campaign, 14

Kaji, Teruo "Bruce," 42, 47–48
Karla, Ash, 107
Kawagoe, Helen, 42, 110, 205–6
Kawanami, Carol, 91
Kawano, Jack, 117
Kim, Andy, 144
Kim, Jane, 147
Kim, Jay Chang, 130–31
Kim, Young, 133–34, 212
King, Jean Sadako, 39–40, 110
Korean American Coalition of Los
    Angeles, 206
Korean Americans
    as elected officials, 40–41, 44–45, 77–78, 197
    immigrants, 34–35
    patterns of immigration, 47
    population growth, 71–72
    Republican Party engagement
        with, 131–34
Kusumoto, Warren, 146

INDEX   263

labor and jobs issue priorities, 228
labor unions, 39–40, 70, 136, 142, 147, 201–2, 211
Lai, James, 90
Lam, Tony, 46, 62
landownership struggles, 10
Latin Americans, 30, 112–14, 153–54
Leading the Way exhibition, 163
Lee, Alex, 107–8
Lee, Amourence, 193
Lee, Choua, 46, 62
Lee, Clark, 122–23
Lee, Edwin M., 55
Lee, Fue, 200
Lee, Katherine, 98
Lee, Wen Ho, 153
legislative activism, 182–87
liberalization of immigration policy, 67
linked fate, 214–15
Lo, Henry, 57
Laotian Americans, 35, 46, 63–64
Locke, Gary, 55
Los Angeles County Democratic Party, 122–23
Los Angeles Riots, 130–31
Los Angeles Times, 198
Loving v. Virginia (1967), 1
Low, Evan, 197
Low, Polly, 61
Luce-Celler Act (1946), 34

Mah, Theresa, 197
Maharath, Tina, 202
mainland US. *See* United States
Malcolm, Ellen, 210–11
male chauvinism, 12
Mar, Eric, 138, 172
Marxism, 14
Matsui, Bob, 166
Matsumoto, Karyl, 97–98
Matsunaga, "Spark" Masayuki, 50–51, 164–65
mayor, 38–39, 43, 51–52, 55, 107–8, 134, 140, 146
Meng, Grace, 169–70, 179, 180, 192–93, 195–96
Mexican Americans, 29–30
Milk, Harvey, 138

Min, Dave, 107–8
Mineta, Norman, 14, 51–52, 140, 165
Mink, Patsy Takemoto, 15–16, 19, 39, 110, 136, 145, 156, 161–62, 166
Miyake, Norobu, 37–38
model minority label, 2–3, 7, 18–19, 30, 70, 149
Mori, Floyd, 167, 205–6
Moua, Mee, 63, 199–200
multiracial Asian America, 219
Murphy, Stephanie, 143–44
Muslims, 16–17, 115

Nakanishi, Don, 68, 90
Nakano, George, 53, 166
National Asian Pacific American Women's Forum, 175–76
National Directory of Latino Elected Officials, 74–75
National Domestic Workers' Alliance, 175–76
National Organization for Women, 15–16, 209–10
National Origins Act (NOA) (1924), 33–34
National Origins Quota Act, 71
National Women's Political Caucus (NWPC), 209–10
Native Hawaiian and Other Pacific Islander (NHOPI), 72, 217–18, 219
nativism, 2, 24–25, 30, 149, 160, 212–13
nativity. *See also* specific ethnicities
    achievement and challenges, 22, 23–24
    descriptive representation by, 26–27
    gap in Asian population, 89–90
    gender and, 149–50
    geographic impact of, 66–67, 71–72
    intersectionality of, 48–49, 75, 82–84, 82*t*, 84*t*
    length of tenure, 181
    migration impact on, 65
    in political context, 4, 7–8, 30–31, 37, 106, 108–9
    political party participation and, 110–11, 124, 126–27, 128*t*, 147–48
    as tool for institutional change, 10–11
Naturalization Act (1790), 35
Nava, Pedro, 107

264 INDEX

New American Leaders (NAL), 75, 209
New Deal (1930s), 29–30, 135–36
Newsom, Gavin, 55, 197
New York Times, 176–77, 212
Nguyen, Deidre Thu-ha, 107–8, 131–32
Nguyen, Dina, 97–98
Nguyen, Hoa, 192–93
Nguyen, Janet, 107–8, 131–32
Nguyen, Madison, 46–47, 62, 97–98
Nisei people. *See* Japanese Americans
Nixon, Richard M., 130
Nomura-Seidel, Norma, 95
nonpartisan ethnic organizations, 204–9
nonwhite elected officials, 7–8, 23
nonwhite minority community, 1–2

Obama, Barack, 121–22, 144, 183–84
office titles of elected officials
    city councilmember, 63–64, 132–33, 143, 145–46, 185–86, 200, 208, 209
    house representative, 16–17, 118–19
    mayor, 38–39, 43, 51–52, 55, 107–8, 134, 140, 146
    schoolboard member, 75–76, 84–85, 159, 209, 226
    state representative, 38, 44, 197, 198
    state senator, 16–17, 107–8, 141, 196–97, 207, 209
    US senator, 1–2, 38, 50, 56, 69–70, 118, 130, 135–36, 174–75
Olaes, Lorelei S., 97–98
1.5 generation, 62–64
Ong, Wing Foon, 41, 48, 59
oppression, 7, 17–18, 19, 24–25
Organization of Chinese Americans, 206
Organization of Chinese American Women, 206
orientalism, 11

Pacific Citizen, 204–5
Pacific Islanders
    in Democratic Party, 126
    as elected officials, 66, 70, 72–., 73–., 88–89, 217–19
    hate crimes against, 197, 198
    introduction to, 3–4, 6
    population growth, 169–70

social justice concerns, 172
    women in politics, 126–27
Page Act (1875), 32–33
Pakistan and Pakistani Americans, 71–72, 81*t*, 82–83, 218
Pan, Richard, 197
"paper son" method, 32–33, 36–37
parity ratio. *See* ethnic parity ratio
Park Steel, Michelle Eunjoo, 133
perpetual foreigner label, 18–19, 30, 70, 149, 194
Phan, Thai Viet, 198
picture brides, 33–34
pioneers. *See* political pioneers
Pitkin, Hanna, 151
pluralist idea of democracy, 29
political action committees (PACs), 113, 144–45
political firsts, 20–21, 62. *See also* political pioneers; trailblazers
political incorporation
    CBOs and, 204, 214
    challenges to, 64–65
    defining and assessing, 20–22, 26–27, 28
    into Democratic Party, 199
    election success as, 29–31, 59, 84–85, 149
    foreign-born *versus* US-born Asian Americans, 36–37
    introduction to, 3–4, 18–19
    in local California elections, 90–101, 105, 108–9
    patterns of immigration, 47, 48–49
    sustainability of, 66–68
political leadership and representation
    Chinese Exclusion Act redress, 168–70
    civil and voting rights advocates, 160–61
    comfort women justice, 170–73
    Covid-19 pandemic anti-Asian racism, 177–82
    grassroots organizing/organizations, 176–77, 182–87
    for immigration and immigrant rights, 173–77
    intersectionality in, 155–57
    introduction to, 27–28, 149–51
    Japanese American redress, 164–68
    legislative activism, 182–87

of marginalized groups, 151–52
research on, 153–55
statistical outlook on, 157–60, 158*t*
summary of importance, 187–88
in uneven democracy, 151–52
women's rights advocacy, 161–63
political parties and partisanship. *See also*
Democratic Party; Republican Party
accidental or reluctant relationships
with, 142–43
Democratic Party impact in
California, 120–23
Democratic Party impact in
Hawaii, 114–20
Democratic wins against Republican
incumbents, 143–45
statistical patterns of, 124–27, 125*f*,
126*t*, 147–48
former Democrats turned
Republican, 134–36
former Republicans turned Democrats/
Independents, 139–41
gender and race in recruitment and
support, 112–14, 124–27, 125*f*
introduction to, 27, 110–11
party marginalization and
neglect, 145–47
primary political identification, 123–
27, 136–39
Republican Party impact, 114–16, 117,
118–20, 129–31
variation of relationship patterns, 127–
41, 128*t*
volatility of, 114–16
political pioneers
Asian American women, 64–65, 95–98
introduction to, 4, 18–19, 26–27, 31
in mainland US, 41, 43
political socialization of, 47, 56
rise of, 66
women of color, 23–24
political refugees, 35, 62–64
political socialization, 31–35, 47–64, 136–
37, 149, 152, 184, 187, 189–90, 204
political transformation, 18–19,
67, 156–57
Polynesian migration to Utah, 88–89
proportional representation, 20–22

Quan, Jean, 95

race, defined, 229n.2
race politics of partisan orientations, 112–
14, 124–27, 125*f*, 127*f*
racial discrimination, 3–4, 30, 70, 191–92
racism. *See also* anti-Asian racism/
violence; Covid-19 pandemic anti-
Asian racism
anti-Black racism, 3–4, 115
Asian American feminism and, 11
hate crimes, 14, 158–59, 174, 195–97,
213, 228
internalization of stereotypes, 11–12
intersectionality with oppression, 24–25
political experiences of, 15–16
sexual discrimination and, 171
in Trump campaign, 30
radical feminism, 15–17, 156
radical-left movement, 8–9, 12–14, 61–62
radical orientalism, 11
Rainbow Coalition for Asian
Americans, 182–83
Rape of Nanjing Redress
Coalition, 171–72
Reagan, Ronald, 120–21
Reflective Democracy Campaign, 75
representation. *See also* political
leadership and representation
descriptive representation, 20–22, 26–
27, 155–56
delegate style of, 18
proportional representation, 20–22
substantive representation, 20–22, 23,
65, 100–2, 154–57, 181–82
sustainable representation, 21–
22, 93–98
symbolic representation, 152–53, 159–60
underrepresentation of Asian
Americans in politics, 3
Republican National Committee, 115
Republican Party
Democratic wins against Republican
incumbents, 143–45
engagement with Asian
immigrants, 131–34
former Democrats turned
Republican, 134–36

266 INDEX

Republican Party (*cont.*)
 former Republicans turned Democrats/
  Independents, 139–41
 Hawaii Republican Party, 130
 impact on Hawaiian APAEOs, 118–20
 impact on partisan orientations, 114–
  16, 117, 124, 129–31
 party marginalization and neglect, 146
 women-centered campaign
  organizations in, 211–12
Roosevelt, Franklin D., 121–22
Royce, Ed, 133–34, 179

Saiki, Patricia (Pat) Fukuda, 56, 130, 166
Saka, Carolyn, 11–12
same-sex marriage rights, 173–74
Sato, Eunice, 91
Saund, Dalip Singh, 43–44, 48, 59,
  137, 160
Sawant, Kshama, 61–62
schoolboard member, 75–76, 84–85, 159,
  209, 226
separatism, 11
"serve the people" programs, 10–11, 13–14
sexism, 2, 11–12, 24–25, 30
sexual discrimination, 171
Share, Chan, 54
Shirkey, Mike, 196–97
Sikh faith and American Sikhs, 35, 43–44,
  48, 82–83
Sing, Lillian, 59–60, 110, 171, 173
social identity, 5, 22–23, 150
Socialist Alternative, 61–62
social justice leadership (SJL)
 against anti-Asian racism/
  violence, 195–98
 concerns among APAEOs, 27–28
 future studies on, 214–15
 identifying leaders, 225
 introduction to, 4, 5–6, 7
 panethnic forces for, 14
 political representation focus of, 26
 prioritization of, 159
socioeconomic backgrounds, 13
Song, Alfred Hoyun, 44–45, 47–48,
  56, 189–92
Song-Beverly Consumer Warranty
  Act, 190

South Asians, 62, 80–83, 88–89, 126–27,
  175–76, 209, 211. *See also* Asian
  Indian Americans; Pakistan and
  Pakistani Americans; Sikh faith and
  American Sikhs
Southeast Asians, 35, 48, 62, 83, 126, 137–
  38, 198, 211. *See also* Cambodian
  Americans; Hmong Americans;
  Laotian Americans; Vietnamese
  Americans
"Southern Strategy," 115
Stanford, Leland, 120–21
state representative, 38, 44, 197, 198
state senator, 16–17, 107–8, 141, 196–97,
  207, 209
Steele, Andrea Dew, 211
Stefanik, Elise, 212
Stop AAPI Hate, 197
Strickland, Marilyn, 133–34
substantive representation, 20–22, 23, 65,
  100–2, 154–57, 181–82
suburbanization of Asian American
  politics, 67–68
suicide, 12–13
Sumi, Pat, 57, 167
Sung, Betty Lee, 58
sustainable representation, 21–22, 93–98
symbolic representation, 152–53, 159–60

Taiwanese Americans, 45–46, 48, 78–80,
  83, 131–34
Takano, Mark, 140–41
Tam, Lena, 98
Tang, Julie, 60–61, 110, 171–72, 173
Teaching Equitable Asian American
  Community History Act, 197
Teng, Mabel, 97–98
Terauchi, Terrence "Terry," 146
term limits, 26–27, 66–67, 90, 106–8
Thao, Cy, 200
Thao, Sheng, 202–3
Third World Left in Los Angeles, 12
Third World Liberation Front, 10
Tom, Maeley, 208
trailblazers, 4, 26, 31, 56, 59, 110, 134
Tran, Van Thai, 131–32
transformative leadership, 27–28, 149–50,
  156–57, 173, 213–14

triple oppression, 12–13
Trump, Donald, 2, 3–4, 30, 144, 179, 192–93, 195
Tydings-McDuffie Act (1934), 34

Ueberschaer, Wei, 192
underrepresentation of Asian Americans in politics, 3
United Chinese Americans, 195
United Farm Workers (UFW), 58–59
United States (US)
  American Dream, 1, 38–39
  APAEOs born in, 36–47
  APAEOs in mainland US, 41–47
  Asian Americans in US politics, 2–4
  Japanese internment in concentration camps, 36, 51–53
Unruh, Jesse, 121–22
US Capitol riots (2021), 2
US Census Bureau, 6
US Commission on Civil Rights, 232n.2
US senator, 1–2, 38, 50, 56, 69–70, 118, 130, 135–36, 174–75
US Supreme Court, 122

Valesco, Leonard, 48
Vang, Mai, 198
Vang, Samantha, 201
Velasco, Leonard T., 43
Vietnamese Americans
  as elected officials, 46–47, 62–63
  immigrants, 35
  population growth, 71–72, 83
  Republican Party engagement with, 131–34
Vietnam War, 9, 11–12, 62–63
Voting Rights Act (1965), 160–61, 167–68, 190
voting rights advocates, 160–61

Walker, Alice, 17
War Brides Act (1947), 34–35, 57
Warren, Elizabeth, 139

Washington Post, 140
We Belong Together, 175–76
white dominant governing coalition, 21–22
Williams, Das, 107
womanism, 7–8, 17–19
womanist leadership praxis, 7–8, 17–19, 26, 156–57
women-centered nonethnic (partisan) organizations, 209–12
women of color
  comfort women, 150, 170–73, 182
  feminists/feminism, 11, 15–16
  marginalization of, 74–75
  nonwhite elected officials, 7–8, 23
  partisan orientations, 112–14
Women's Campaign Fund, 209–10
Women's Health Protection Act, 176–77
women's liberation, 11
women's rights, 15–16, 161–63, 227
WOMEN VOTE! Project, 210–11
Wong, Judy, 98
Wong, Lee, 193–94
Wright, George F., 130
Wu, David, 153, 169
Wu, Michelle, 139
"Wuhan virus," 3–4, 179. *See also* Covid-19 pandemic anti-Asian racism

xenophobia, 3–4, 192–93, 217–18
Xiong, Jay, 200
Xiong, Tou, 201

Yamauchi, Gary, 143
Yang, Andrew, 194–95
Yang, Jeff, 194–95
Yang, Nelsie, 203
Yellow Peril label, 30
Yih, Mae, 142
Young, Jackie Eurn Hai, 40–41

Zia, Helen, 14

Printed in the USA/Agawam, MA
April 28, 2022

792323.024